WOMEN AND COLONIZATION

Anthropological Perspectives

WOMEN AND COLONIZATION

Anthropological Perspectives

MONA ETIENNE

ELEANOR LEACOCK
Editors

PRAEGER SPECIAL STUDIES • PRAEGER SCIENTIFIC
A J.F. BERGIN PUBLISHERS BOOK

Library of Congress Cataloging in Publication Data
Main entry under title:

Women and colonization.

A J.F. Bergin Publishers Book.
Bibliography: p.
Includes index.
1. Women—History—Addresses, essays, lectures.
2. Colonies—Addresses, essays, lectures. 3. Sex role—Addresses, essays, lectures. 4. Social change—Addresses, essays, lectures. I. Etienne, Mona. II. Leacock, Eleanor Burke, 1922-
GN479.7.W65   301.41'2   79-15318

ISBN 978-0-275-91491-2

Published in 1980 by Praeger Publishers
A division of Holt, Rinehart and Winston/CBS, Inc.
383 Madison Avenue, New York, New York 10017 USA

© 1980 by J.F. Bergin Publishers, Inc.
All rights reserved
J.F. Bergin Publishers, Inc.
65 South Oxford Street, Brooklyn, New York 11217
USA

Preface

This book presents case studies of women's economic, social and political roles in twelve societies, and the changes that followed European colonization. All the studies, with the exception of Chapter 9, were written for this volume. All are by anthropologists who have delved into missionary reports, explorers' and traders' accounts, and other historical records for information about the peoples whom the Europeans encountered in the Americas, Africa, and the Pacific to examine how they dealt with European behavior and intentions. The authors have studied the present day cultures of the peoples about whom they are writing, and most have done fieldwork among them.

The book has been written in response to the growing interest in women cross-culturally and reflects our conviction that the realities of colonization have thus far received inadequate consideration by anthropologists. We focus on colonization and the position of women for two related reasons. The first concerns ideological arguments about the basis for women's inequality. The second concerns practical policies pertaining to women, especially in Third World nations.

Today in the United States there is a resurgence of old arguments that woman's role as housewife follows from her role as mother and is both universal and biologically based. At a time when over half of all women in the United States are in the work force, such arguments may sound hollow; nonetheless they undermine our efforts to combat discriminatory hiring practices and wage levels as well as to achieve adequate child-care facilities and the right to safe abortion when desired. It is important, therefore, to distinguish between the position of women in various societies prior to the emergence of the world capitalist system and their position in the twentieth century as it has been studied by professional anthropologists. This work is a contribution toward that end. We hope it will encourage further ethnohistorical research and make possible a full definition of women's social participation in all its forms.

Such a definition is most important at present when Third World nations are making conscious choices about their futures and are examining their own histories and their past and present values. At this time, when the word "traditional" is being used either invidiously, to suggest "backward," in contrast to "modern," or proudly as an assertion of cultural autonomy, it is necessary to differentiate between traditions that predated colonization and those that took shape in a colonial context. The point is not to derogate the latter; after all, the traditions born of the struggles for independence that followed colonization are most valuable resources. However, it is critical to clarify the fact that egalitarian relations between women and men are not an imported Western value and that, instead, the reverse is true. Egalitarian relations or at least mutually respectful relations were a living reality in much of the world in precolonial times, which was far from the case in Western culture.

We wish to thank our contributors for graciously putting up with our many demands. We especially thank Christine Gailey for her assistance in editing some of the chapters, and Doug Jones for his able and informed copyediting. We are grateful to Elspeth Leacock for the index and to Robert Steven Grumet for the map.

We dedicate this book to the efforts of women wherever they are struggling against colonialism in any of its forms.

Mona Etienne
Ecole des hautes études en sciences sociales

Eleanor Leacock
*The City College
City University of New York*

Contents

Preface   v

Illustrations   ix

Introduction   1
    Mona Etienne and *Eleanor Leacock*

1 Montagnais Women and the Jesuit Program for Colonization   25
    Eleanor Leacock

2 Sunksquaws, Shamans, and Tradeswomen: Middle Atlantic Coastal Algonkian Women During the 17th and 18th Centuries   43
    Robert Steven Grumet

3 The Mothers of the Nation: Seneca Resistance to Quaker Intervention   63
    Diane Rothenberg

4 Contending with Colonization: Tlingit Men and Women in Change   88
    Laura F. Klein

5 Forced Transition from Egalitarianism to Male Dominance: The Bari of Colombia   109
    Elisa Buenaventura-Posso and *Susan E. Brown*

6 Aztec Women: The Transition from Status to Class in Empire and Colony   134
    June Nash

7 "The Universe has turned inside out... There is no justice for us here:" Andean Women Under Spanish Rule   149
   Irene Silverblatt

8 Daughters of the Lakes and Rivers: Colonization and the Land Rights of Luo Women   186
   Achola Pala Okeyo

9 Women and Men, Cloth and Colonization: The Transformation of Production-Distribution Relations among the Baule (Ivory Coast)   214
   Mona Etienne

10 Desert Politics: Choices in the "Marriage Market"   239
    Diane Bell

11 Stability in Banana Leaves: Colonization and Women in Kiriwina, Trobriand Islands   270
    Annette B. Weiner

12 Putting Down Sisters and Wives: Tongan Women and Colonization   294
    Christine Ward Gailey

Index   323

About the Authors   337

References following each chapter

Illustrations

	Lydia Tuspaquin, Eighth Descendant of Massasoit. Courtesy of the Museum of the American Indian, Heye Foundation, New York.	Cover
	Map by Robert Steven Grumet.	xii
1	Marie and Michel Bastien, Northwest River, Labrador, 1951. Photo by Richard Leacock.	25
2	Same as Cover	43
3	Seneca women husking corn for braiding. The Rochester Museum.	63
4	Mrs. Ginny-Jack and Mrs. Minnie Johnson. Photo by Frederica de Laguna.	88
5	Bari woman playing a flute. Photo by Elisa Buenaventura-Posso and Susan E. Brown.	109
6	The seller of maguey capes; the seller of fine chocolate; the salt seller. The Florentine Codex.	134
7	"Priests. Who force indian women to weave clothing, claiming that they are living in sin, they threaten them, beat them, and do not pay them." Guaman Poma.	149
8	Kenya woman weeding cassava. Photo by Esben H. Thorning. Courtesy of UNICEF Regional Office of Eastern Africa.	186
9	Baule women spinning and carding cotton (Kouassi Kouassikro Village, Agba Katienou, 1978). Photo by Susan M. Vogel.	214
10	A "mother-in-law" is painted with dreamings of the initiate's patriline by women of his patriline. Photo by Doug Jervis. Australian National University, Canberra.	239
11	Kiriwina women with their baskets of wealth during a mortuary distribution. Photo by Annette B. Weiner.	270
12	Tongan woman painting bark cloth. Photo by Peter Carmichael. Courtesy of William Collins Publishers, London.	294

WOMEN AND COLONIZATION

Anthropological Perspectives

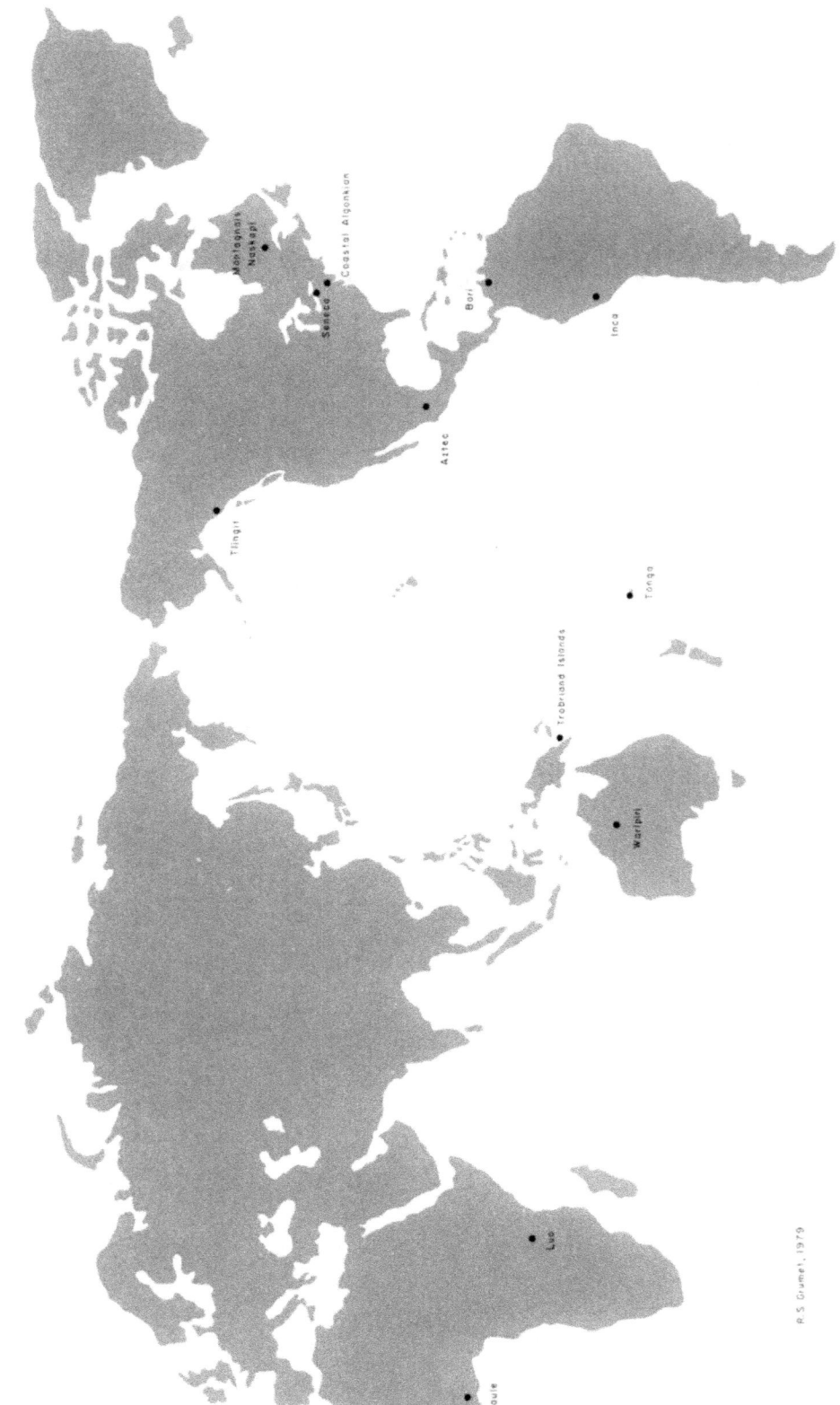

Introduction

WOMEN AND ANTHROPOLOGY: CONCEPTUAL PROBLEMS[1]

In the past ten years, the anthropology of women, inspired and encouraged by the feminist critique of our own society, has made considerable progress. Although many questions remain unanswered and many problems unsolved, they have at least been formulated and are being examined in new and productive ways.[2] The Victorians saw women in non-Western societies as oppressed and servile creatures, beasts of burden, chattels who could be bought and sold, eventually to be liberated by "civilization" or "progress," thus attaining the enviable position of women in Western society. With the development of anthropology as a science in the first half of the twentieth century, the Victorian attitude gradually gave way to what appeared to be a less biased view, exhibiting a new respect for other cultures but, in fact, reflecting a similar bias in a more sophisticated form.

This view, which was to dominate anthropology until recently, is well illustrated by E. E. Evans-Pritchard's 1955 Fawcett lecture to the women students of Bedford College—a memorial lecture in honor of the feminist who had founded the college. In his address, Evans-Pritchard states that "the adult primitive woman is above all a wife, whose life is centred in her home and family (1965:46)...a woman passes at marriage from under the authority of her father to that of her husband....important decisions with regard to the home, the upbringing of children, the betrothing of daughters and sons, and so forth, rest with him and him alone" (:51). Evans-Pritchard has just observed that in many societies women are highly respected and have their own spheres of activity, citing anthropologists (Lowie, Kaberry, Mead, Benedict) who document for various cultures the participation of women in all spheres of social life (:42-43). Yet in generalizing he does not concede that women may participate in decision making even in the "home," but reverts to a view similar to that of the Victorians he has just criticized (:41): women labor only to serve men. Contradictions accumulate as the lecture progresses. Evans-Pritchard informs us that "primitive societies and barbarous societies and the historical societies of Europe and the East exhibit almost every conceivable variety of social institutions, but in all of them, regardless of the form of social structure, men are always in the ascendancy, and this is perhaps the more evident the higher the civilization" (:54). Then, a few moments later, he notes that "in those societies where any sector of the population is in a servile position, the position of women is correspondingly low with regard to the male sex" (:55). He does not, however, associate servility with "high civilization."

2   Introduction

Evans-Pritchard's concern is to persuade women that their subservience to men is part of a natural order of things that they would do well to acknowledge and accept and to persuade potential feminists that their discontent should be subordinated to the broader cause of general inequality. His political message is explicitly formulated: the problems of sexual inequality *and of other forms of inequality* "cannot be solved by an insistence on absolute equality, but rather by recognition of differences, exercise of charity, and acknowledgement of authority. Otherwise antagonism is unavoidable and peaceful and harmonious social life is impossible; and far from the acceptance of authority entailing inferiority, it expresses the only true form of equality obtainable in human relationships, an equality of service" (:56). Evans-Pritchard inverts the message of the Victorians: the assumed acceptance of male authority by primitive women should be taken as a model by his female contemporaries. At the same time he gives wider meaning to this appeal to submission in the interest of "social harmony," suggesting that all subservient people should accept their condition.

The degree of mental confusion that can affect an otherwise perceptive and rigorous scholar when he is defending the status quo is brought out by the flagrant contradiction between Evans-Pritchard's sweeping generalization on the universal ascendancy of men and his modest conclusion. He points out "the entire inadequacy, indeed almost complete lack, of serious scientific research into the questions we have been discussing, both in the primitive field and in our own country" (:57). His references to ethnographic and theoretical works show that Evans-Pritchard has done his homework well but, by his own admission, "with little profit" (:57). The title page carries an interesting footnote stating that the author did not consider the lecture worthy of publication earlier, but now (1965) does, suggesting that timeliness of the political message is more important than scholarly and logical inadequacies.

We have spent time on this short lecture because it touches on the basic issues we will be dealing with here and exemplifies approaches to women, class, and colonization that are still with us. Such approaches characterize the work of the most eminent representatives of an anthropology that takes an essentially static and ahistorical view of the societies it studies, ignoring both the dynamics of precolonial change and the hard realities of colonization. Colonization receives attention from Evans-Pritchard only with reference to his fieldwork difficulties (see, for example, 1940:1-15). Although he defends the value of history, it is rarely integrated in his work. Using Evans-Pritchard's own data, Gough (1971) shows that his ahistorical perspective deforms his view of Nuer society, with regard to both social structure and the position of women.

Overtly stated acceptance of the status quo is less prevalent today among anthropologists than it was several decades ago; but implicit or explicit belief in the universal subordination of women, if not in its inevitability, continues to obstruct efforts to understand both other societies and our own. It finds sustenance in major theoretical works, such as those of Lévi-Strauss, which are especially concerned with the study of kinship and symbolic systems. For Lévi-Strauss, the incest taboo and the exchange of women by men mark the very origins of human society, the transition from the chaotic competitiveness of "nature" to the ordered relations of "culture." Women are perceived as passive participants in a social and cultural universe structured by men. Reified by their sexual and reproductive value, they appear as little more than commodities. This perception of women is associated with a fundamentally Hobbesian view of primitive relations (between men) as a potential state of war. Undomesticated human nature is seen as male and as aggressive and competitive; female passivity is the logical counterpart.

The subordination of women is assumed by Lévi-Strauss. More recent theories seek an explanation of it, and women's reproductive functions have become a major explanatory principle. More Hobbesian than Lévi-Strauss—and compounding this bias with Malthusianism—Harris (1977) and Divale and Harris (1976) speculate that scarce resources and the consequent dangers of overpopulation made women's fertility a constant threat and, together with warfare, led to male "dominance" in the earliest human societies. Meillassoux (1975) takes a diametrically opposite view of the relationship between childbearing and sexual inequality, but builds his argument on similar premises. Acknowledging sexual equality in hunting and gathering societies, he sees the reification and subordination of women as resulting from the value their reproductive capacity takes on in horticultural societies. When a greater productive potential makes population increase desirable, women, as reproducers of producers, become the object of competition between men. Although he explicitly attacks Lévi-Strauss's theory of woman exchange, Meillassoux inadvertently perpetuates its fundamental assumptions by seeing women as valuable objects and men as the sole agents of social organization. However important the contribution of women to production may be, their value as reproducers prevents them from having "status as producers" (:120) and makes them "disappear behind men" (:116). Both Meillassoux and Harris beg the question, explaining the subordination of women by presupposing their reification.

It is not coincidental that the focus on reproduction as an explanatory principle should emerge precisely at a time when the importance of women's role in production has become indisputable. These modernized versions of "biology is destiny" theories do not pretend to revive the idea that gender differences are directly determined by biology, as does sociobiology. They do, however, make assumptions about the differential participation of women and men in reproduction that reflect both the ideology and the realities of maternity in our own society. (For a critique of this approach, see Mathieu 1977; Etienne 1979a, 1979b).

The apparent justification for these theories—the supposedly universal (or, for Meillassoux, quasi-universal) subordination of women—has had an impact on the thinking of both nonacademic feminists and feminist anthropologists. Reflecting the impact of Lévi-Strauss on symbolic anthropology, Ortner (1974) elaborates on his dichotomy associating men with culture and women with nature, and finds the explanation in women's childbearing function.[3] In cross-cultural studies that recognize the productive contribution of women, childbearing and/or childrearing are still seen as decisive in confining women to a supposedly less prestigious sphere of activities than that of men. (e.g., Friedl 1975). Assumptions positing a universal dichotomy between female "private" and male "public" spheres emphasize their differential value and suggest the universal social inferiority, if not the subordination, of women (Rosaldo 1974).

In sum, the entire conceptual framework of anthropology and, as a result, the data on which generalizations are based, suffer from ethnocentric and male-centered bias. The "society" that elaborates belief systems, relations between the sexes, and relations of production is conceived of as a society of men. The view of men as social actors and of women as both peripheral and passive has long determined not only theorizing, but also the perception, the selection, and the organization of data. Either dissenting research has been obscured by the dominant trend or its results have been rationalized into meaninglessness. The resistance of anthropology to recognition of women's productive contribution in hunting and gathering societies, discussed below, demonstrates the strength of sexual stereotypes and the tendency to deny data that contradict them. Malinowski makes no mention of women's wealth in banana leaves, although photos prove that he had the opportunity to observe it (see Weiner, Chapter 7, this volume). Many other examples testify to the "blind spots" that affect our most illustrious precursors and that continue to hamper fieldwork, even for feminist anthropologists. Few return from the field without regrets about faulty observation caused by the persistance of male bias, in spite of their best efforts.

The preconceptions that affect the perception and collection of data also limit the validity of interpretations, even when these are based on accurate and relatively complete information. Our concepts relating to equality and inequality derive from the experience of our own society and this experience is often inappropriately projected onto the institutions and behaviors of others. An example is the generalized tendency to see women's menstrual lodges as signifying their inferiority and their own exclusion from society, while men's houses are taken as evidence of superiority and the exclusion of women from society. Leacock (1978:270) argues that such interpretations make the unproven assumption that women do not participate in decision-making and that separate spheres are unequal spheres. Sacks (1976) develops a similar critique with the concept of "state bias," pointing out that, while the equation of separate with unequal is valid in our own class-based society, it cannot be taken for granted in other types of society. Both authors point to a conceptual flaw in the dichotomy between a male "public" domain and a female "private" (or "domestic") domain, for the two domains can be clearly dissociated only after stratification and the privatization of women's productive and reproductive capacity have occurred.

Another major obstacle to the understanding of societies different from our own is the ahistorical approach. Like other fundamentally racist notions, the idea that societies without written history have no history has lost ground. Yet it continues to function as a concealed assumption, giving a timeless and static view of the past, as Rothenberg (in this volume) specifically notes with reference to Seneca ethnohistory. When historic periods are not clearly defined, it is tempting—but unjustified—to reconstruct a unitary and static "past" in which changing realities are reduced to the lowest common denominator. Worse is the tendency to treat the present, whenever the effects of change subsequent to colonization are not flagrantly visible, as if it were an intact remnant of the unchanged past. It suggests that people live simultaneously in two separate spheres of reality and that precolonial institutions and relations remain basically untouched by colonization until they become "modernized," that is, visibly modeled after those of the colonizer. An ahistorical perspective especially affects the understanding of women's position in colonized societies.

The "traditional/modern" dichotomy also contains an implicit value judgment, not only by suggesting that "traditional" means "static", but by suggesting that "modern" is somehow better. The distinction makes Western society the ideal and is not far removed from nineteenth-century ideas of "progress." The acculturation concept also suggests a static view of colonized societies and a superiority of the behaviors and institutions characteristic of the colonizer. Awareness of the value judgment implicit in this term has led to a tendency to discard it in favor of more neutral terms, such as "culture change" (see, for example, McElroy and Matthiasson 1979), but unfortunately, it is easier to discard the terminology itself than the kind of thinking it reflects. Underlying the superficial neutrality of such terms as "culture change" is the systematic avoidance of the political realities of colonization. Yet colonization and its sequels are the ever present context of survival for the peoples anthropologists study.

WOMEN AND RELATIONS OF PRODUCTION

Women's Position Cross-Culturally

World cultures varied greatly at the time of European exploration, trade, and conquest. In North America alone, myriad peoples each had their own deep cultural and historical roots. North American cultures ranged from those of the Canadian sub-Arctic interior—where people lived close to the land and depended entirely on game, fish, and wild vegetable foods—to Mexico, where great cities dominated the farming villages around them.

Women's social and economic responsibilities and prerogatives also varied considerably from one kind of society to another. In the areas that were to become known as Canada and Australia, hunting and gathering peoples lived in egalitarian bands. The precise tenor of relations between men and women in these areas is still being debated, with some arguing that women owed no special deference to men and others arguing that they did. All students of the subject agree, however, that women's degree of personal autonomy in band societies contrasted sharply with the oppression that characterizes their position in hierarchically organized societies.

In what was to become the eastern United States, and in the lowland forests of South America, horticultural peoples gardened with stones or bone-bladed hoes and digging sticks and supplemented their crops with foods from the forests and streams. Distinct culture patterns accorded with each people's specific history and with the environment in which each lived, but many horticultural societies were organized along egalitarian lines. This was true of the Seneca, an Iroquois tribe of New York State, of the Algonkians in southern New England, and of the Bari on the Colombia-Venezuela border. As described in the chapters that follow, female-male reciprocity and complementarity, rather than female subservience to men, characterized these societies.

In most of the world, differences in wealth and status developed long before European intrusion. Some degree of hereditary rank was recognized and valued among the fishing peoples of the North Pacific coast, as exemplified in this book by the Tlingit of southern Alaska. Differences in rank also obtained in the Trobriand Islands off the coast of New Guinea but were far less marked and formalized than the distinctions between high and low ranking Tonga in the central Pacific. As the chapters on these peoples show, women played socially recognized and valued economic and social roles in these societies. Nonetheless, a marked conflict of interest between women and men and an assertion by men of a need and right to control women are common in New Guinea and in other parts of Oceania. Below, we shall consider why this might be so.

West African farming peoples and East African farmers and cattle herders used iron tools and weapons, regularly held markets for the exchange of food and manufactured goods, and in some areas supported with their labor the growth of urban centers. Long-distance trade in salt, skins, cloth, ivory, gold, and slaves was carried on as caravans moved north and south, connecting the Sudan with Mediterranean countries, and east and west, connecting interior Africa with Arabia and India through bustling port cities where merchant seamen carried on business. Urban centers rose and fell as ambitious chiefs and kings gained wealth and power from controlling and taxing the extensive trade. The wealth of African kingdoms was legendary and in 1067 Al Bekri described the king of Ghana as giving audience to his people in a pavilion surrounded by pages with gold-mounted swords and guarded by dogs with gold and silver collars. In the thirteenth century, Ibn Batuto described the eastern port city of Kilwa as "one of the most beautiful and well-constructed towns in the world." In 1497, when Vasco da Gama sailed around the tip of Africa and up the east coast, he wrote that one emissary to his ship wore a silk-fringed cape and another a satin cap and added, "They were very haughty and valued nothing which we gave them."

Despite the influence of African urban centers on the surrounding countryside, strong egalitarian traditions were maintained in many areas where villagers remained largely self-sufficient. This was apparently true of the agricultural Baule of the Ivory Coast and the cattle-raising Luo of Kenya. The attempt to reconstruct the complexities and variations in women's social participation and female-male relations as they existed in the past is now under way. Two general points have been well documented: first, in non-Moslem African cultures, women's and men's rights and responsibilities were conceived and institutionalized as parallel rather than hierarchical, and the activities and organizations of each sex cross-cut both public and private life; second, women's status in sub-Saharan Africa has for the most part been seriously undermined by colonial policies.

Hierarchical societies based on political organization and economic exploitation are represented in this book by two native American peoples, the Aztecs of Mexico and the Inca of Peru. Both the Aztecs and Inca were late comers who built empires on old, well-established patterns of urban life. In 1325 the Aztecs founded their capital of Tenochtitlan on the site where Mexico City now stands. Cortes was overwhelmed by the wonders of the city, especially the palace—"so marvelous, that it seems...almost impossible to describe its beauty and magnificance"—and the market, where 20,000 to 25,000 people daily bought and sold an enormous variety of foods as well as all manner of tools and utensils, clothes, jewelry, luxuries, wood for building or burning, pipes, paper, and, in short, everything that the townspeople might need or want.

The Inca consolidated their city-state in the central Andes around 1200 AD, and in the 15th century they extended their sway over the entire Andean area—some 2,000 miles from north to south. The Inca empire was extraordinarily well knit. It was cross-cut with highways along which were located hostels for travelers and well-stocked warehouses where supplies were stored to feed Inca armies when needed, to placate subject elites, or support the needy in case of crop failure.

The chapters on the Inca and Aztec indicate ways in which women's status becomes undermined by the growth of state bureaucracies and the consolidation of wealthy and powerful aristocracies. They also show that Aztec and Inca women were nonetheless more respected and had more rights than did women in the Spanish kingdom that conquered them.

Socioeconomic and Sexual Hierarchy

As indicated in the foregoing summary, there is a rough correlation between the position of women vis-à-vis men and the degree of socioeconomic inequality in a society as a whole. This does not mean that female inequality follows from the development of class differences generally; instead, it is our understanding that the origins of both socioeconomic and sexual hierarchy are inextricably bound together.

In order to analyze relationships between socioeconomic and sexual hierarchies, it is necessary to compare different types of societies. The criterion anthropologists commonly use to categorize culture types is the major means of food production. The resulting categories are: gathering-hunting (including fishing); horticultural (gardening with hand tools); agricultural (elaborated cultivation, often with ploughs, on lands prepared by terracing, drainage, or irrigation); pastoral (specializing in herding, and either partly agricultural or involved in trade with a farming society); and industrial.

Comparisons among cultures with different food-producing technologies do show that socioeconomic and sexual hierarchy and efficiency in food production both increase together. However, to assume too close a correlation between technology and social forms leads to problems. Gathering-hunting-fishing peoples are usually organized in egalitarian bands, but the Tlingit are not. Nor are other peoples around the north Pacific coasts and islands. And there are enormous variations among societies classified as horticultural and as pastoral.

Rather than technology as such, therefore, anthropologists have been exploring the Marxist concept, *relations of production*, as basic to socioeconomic differentiation. Technological skills and equipment—the "means of production"—offer potentials for and set broad limits on socioeconomic organization. For example, a gathering and hunting and fishing economy may support either band or village life, but urbanization requires the development of agriculture. However, it is the *relations set up among people* as they produce, distribute, exchange, and consume the goods upon which they live that are crucial for understanding socioeconomic and sexual hierarchies.

A framework for considering relations between socioeconomic and sexual hierarchy in the societies covered in the following chapters is provided by defining four broad types of production relations that have apparently succeeded each other in the course of human history: (1) egalitarian, (2) ranking or transitional, (3) preindustrial hierarchical, and (4) industrial capitalist. (Industrial socialist relations are beyond the purview of this book). Each of these, and especially the third, can be subdivided. Four broadly contrasting configurations, however, serve our purpose here.

It is important to recognize that defining different kinds of production relations is different from describing different particular societies. A great variety of specific cultures has taken shape, each in particular and unique historical and environmental circumstances. Economic relationships only determine social and political forms within broad limits; within these limits, endless choices as to how a culture will be elaborated are made according to a society's particular history. Furthermore, in actual societies, relations of production are virtually never purely of one type. Societies are always changing and new relations are always developing within older ones. In most societies, one type of relations is clearly dominant, but some societies may be in the process of transformation from one type to another. Production relations also become mixed as a result of culture contact; after all, every society studied by anthropologists has to some extent been involved in the worldwide capitalist system.

Egalitarian Relations of Production

Egalitarian relations are based on the direct and more or less equal participation of all adults in the production of basic necessities, as well as in their distribution or exchange and in their consumption. The basic resources—the land itself and the plants, animals, and minerals on it—are available to everybody. The division of labor is by sex only, and relations between the sexes are based on the reciprocal exchange of goods and services.

This basic structure of relations is overlaid in specific cultures by formalities concerning how goods are divided up, how permission to use resources or equipment may be given, and the like. These formalities have sometimes been interpreted as evidence of private ownership in the capitalist sense, especially when people whose freedom is threatened assert their rights to their land and its resources. In egalitarian societies, however, it is impossible to alienate people from their right of access to basic resources.

"Equal" participation should not be taken to mean the same or identical participation. People contribute their work according to their abilities and interests. In sub-Arctic Canada, for example, one woman may by preference devote a lot of time to quill work, another to herbal medicine. Therefore, Fried (1967) characterizes egalitarian society as affording as many statuses in any age-sex category as there are people who wish to fill them. In fact, Fried's principle extends beyond sex categories, for the division of labor is not rigid. An individual may do the work of the other sex not only as a matter of short-term exigency, but also as a matter of long-term interest and commitment.

The full participation of all adults in producing or manufacturing and in distributing and consuming food and other necessities sets egalitarian relations off sharply from those of our society in which a nuclear family is a corporate entity privately responsible for rearing children, and theoretically supported by a wage-earning man who is serviced by a dependent woman. As will become clear in the chapters that follow, in egalitarian society a "private," familial female domain is not defined and made secondary to a public, political male domain. Instead, authority is dispersed and decisions are by and large made by those who will be carrying them out. All manner of social arts are used by both women and men to influence people, resolve problems, and hold groups together. These range from endless talk and discussion through myth making, song, dance, and ritual to merciless teasing, disapproval, and threat of social isolation.

Egalitarian relations characterized most gatherer-hunters as well as many horticultural peoples. Although in horticultural villages decision making was commonly more formalized than among gatherer-hunters, the same principle obtained that people made decisions about activities for which they were responsible. As Grumet points out for the eastern Algonkian, those who did not agree with a decision were not bound by it. People who were put forth to speak for a group could only convey decisions already made; such people held no formal authority.

Contrary to this view of egalitarian relations, the assumption alluded to above—that men are innately more aggressive than women and hence always dominate them—is held by many social scientists, is widely expressed in the media, and is now underwritten by the new field of sociobiology. The older assumption was that universal male dominance followed from greater male strength. Both assumptions gave way to the argument that males began to dominate females as providers of food for them and their children. When this argument was challenged by the knowledge that in warm climates women gatherers produced more food than men hunters, the emphasis shifted to men as providing the more important food.

In addition to female passivity and, indeed, virtual nonentity as a social force, another assumption underlies all such formulations. This is the notion that social relations must be and always have been hierarchically structured. In a sense, all cultures are seen to represent nascent forms of competitive and hierarchical capitalist relations. One purpose of this book is to illustrate the reality of female-male complementarity and to document the clash between this egalitarian principle and the hierarchical organization that European colonization brought about in many parts of the world.

If the "man the hunter and provider" stereotype of male dominance had any reality, female-male complementarity would be less clearly in evidence in Canada, where meat and fish obtained primarily by men were the basic foods, than in Australia, where vegetable foods collected by women were of critical importance. However, as the chapters on the Montagnais-Naskapi of eastern Canada and the Warlpiri of western Australia show, the material on female autonomy is clearer for the hunters than for the gatherer-hunters. We suggest that the reason lies in the nature of the documentation, and not in any basic precolonial difference. The seventeenth-century Jesuits recognized that if they were to achieve their goal of converting the native Canadians, they had to deal directly with women's independence, and they explained the resulting problems in their reports to their superiors. By contrast, the nineteenth-century miners who first related to the Warlpiri of

Western Australia simply took advantage of female autonomy, and were scarcely the kind of people to write about it. In fact, the subsequent history of relations between colonizers and aboriginal Australians meant that women's sexual freedom became transformed into its opposite: prostitution.

Most descriptions of Australian cultures suffer from the male bias epitomized by the paper of Evans-Pritchard discussed earlier. The focus on male initiation ceremonies and on such institutions as the betrothal of female infants to mature men, led anthropologists to point to Aboriginal society as an example of male domination among otherwise egalitarian gatherer-hunters. Recent work has begun to explore female-male complementarity, however (e.g., Berndt 1974), and in her discussions with women, Bell discovered evidence of female autonomy that has persisted despite several generations of profound change. She describes the participation of women in ceremonial decision-making processes; the marriage of older women to younger men; the building of female solidarity among in-laws; and the *jilimi*, the women's section of the camp, which is off limits to men, and where women who wish to can live and carry on affairs with men as they choose, without incurring the obligations of formal marriage.

The position of women among egalitarian horticulturalists is illustrated in the chapters by Buenaventura-Posso and Brown, Grumet, and Rothenberg. Buenaventura-Posso and Brown's description of sexual complementarity and female autonomy in the large collective households of the Bari offers a striking parallel to relations between the sexes in the multifamily lodges of the Montagnais-Naskapi. Furthermore, despite the different circumstances, the process whereby Bari collectives are today being undermined is reminiscent of the goals sought for by the seventeenth-century Jesuits in Canada. Male-headed nuclear family households are being created through a combination of construction projects planned for nuclear family units, economic aid that makes new skills and equipment available to men, trading policies that favor men, an educational program that concentrates on boys, and the virtual bestowal of "chieftainship" upon men by fiat.

Grumet's chapter on the Algonkian peoples of southern New England and eastern New York State reveals female participation in political and economic roles that has been obscured by the male-biased orientation discussed above. As Grumet points out, despite assertions that political leaders among these Algonkians were always men, the ethnohistorical record reveals that women also took on chiefly responsibilities. Far from being "at home" and provisioned by men, Algonkian women were not only farmers, but might also choose to engage in trade or medical practice and do business with the colonists as well as with their own people. Their activities show a continuity with established practices of economic activity that sought to take advantage of the new situation and persisted for some time before being destroyed.

12 Introduction

Rothenberg's chapter on economic reciprocity between the sexes among the Seneca reveals how male bias has led to its misinterpretation. In traditional Iroquois society, women, as the farmers and food processors, made decisions about the allocation of lands and food stores in the large multi-family matrilocal households. Men were responsible for bringing in game and for dealing with the exigencies of warfare. Women's voice in matters of political concern to the Iroquois nation as a whole was expressed through their power to appoint and depose the sachems who made up tribal councils and through the open character of these councils which discussed all affairs with interested parties.

As Rothenberg shows, the importance of the fur trade, the escalation of warfare, and the progressive restriction of lands combined in the early colonial period to dichotomize the female farming sphere as sedentary and the male trading and fighting sphere as mobile and, if anything, to strengthen women's control on the home front. Interpretations of these developments, however, have trivialized men's economic activities, thereby implying that men were idle exploiters of female agricultural labor. Rothenberg indicates, on the contrary, that the early dependence of Seneca society on trade goods, as well as later dependence on cash, made male mobility eminently rational and necessary. In the long run, however, the increasing importance of men's economic and political ties with the colonizers was to undercut the complementarity that men's work originally expressed.

Relations of Production in Ranking or Transitional Society

Ranking society is characterized by inequalities in production, distribution, exchange, and consumption, although these are not as marked as in stratified society. People of high rank contribute to the organization of production and do less of the onerous tasks; they play a critical role in the distribution and exchange of goods; and they consume more than others, although not a great deal more (by contrast with stratified society) and typically in the form of luxuries rather than necessities. The access of low-ranking people to valued resources or prepared lands is somewhat restricted, but, by contrast with stratified society, they have access to land in general. There is a division of labor beyond that by sex. Specialists manufacture desirable items or collect important raw materials to use in trading. Again by contrast with stratified society, however, they also produce some of their own food and other necessities.

The degree of interpersonal differences may be slight or may be considerable in a ranking society, and it is hard to draw sharp lines between egalitarian societies and those that are slightly ranked on the one hand, and stratified societies and those that are strongly ranked on the other. We use the term *transitional* to emphasize this fact, but strictly speaking all social forms are transitional. Societies can be placed on a continuum with respect to the amount of interpersonal social distance they show, but the relations of production that underlie the development of social distance represent a qualitative change from the dominant relations in egalitarian society. This is not mere nitpicking; as will shortly be made clear, it is important to define basic distinctions in economic relationships when it comes to interpreting women's decline in status.

What caused ranking to develop? The existence of egalitarian relations in some societies precludes the pop-science answer that inequalities arise from the competitiveness of human nature. One line of reasoning followed by many anthropologists is that the beginnings of hierarchical organization must have had something to do with population growth. Perhaps population pressure led to competition over resources and enabled the more ambitious to exert control over others. However, the unanswered question concerns whether populations were allowed to grow in the first place, beyond the number that could be readily supported in a given region with the technology available? Women in egalitarian societies apparently controlled population growth by spacing their babies, using various contraceptive and abortive means (some more effective and some less so), sexual abstinence, or, as a last resort, infanticide. In seventeenth-century Canada, the Jesuit missionaries commented on the small families of the Montagnais hunters compared with the large families of the French peasants.

An alternative hypothesis for the development of ranking, and the more likely one in our view, is that the growth of trade was critical. Ethnohistorical research has shown that early trade with Europeans, and the exchange of furs, skins, or other local goods for metal tools, concentrated foods, guns, and clothing undercut the interdependence of cooperatively organized bands and villages. This did not mean the disappearance of egalitarian traditions, but it did mean an unequal access to important resources that undermined the economic structure of egalitarianism. Presumably, something similar happened at many times and in many places in the past, although far more slowly. Both ethnographic and archeological evidence reveal that the link between well-developed trade and social inequalities is a recurrent cross-cultural pattern. Egalitarian gatherer-hunter bands and communal village horticulturalists all engaged in some trade, but critical to the development of ranking would be the point when such trade became important enough to lead to specialization and the consequent reorganization of production relations.

The development of specialization and trade to the point where adults of each sex were producing or procuring significant quantities of different things (rather than virtually the same things) created the possibility for ties of economic dependence that had not previously existed. Therefore, it laid the basis for inequalities both among women and men and between women and men.

With respect to the development of social hierarchy, Fried (1967:182) asks the question: why would people initially give up their full independence? In our view, the answer is that in the earliest stages of such development people would allow special prerogatives to those who had access to specially valued goods or to goods they themselves did not produce. The special respect accorded capable individuals in egalitarian society was based on these individuals' contributions to the group as a whole and simply reaffirmed the structure of egalitarianism. By contrast, prerogatives allowed to individuals on the basis of economic roles that potentially afforded them more or better goods than others led to the eventual establishment of high- and low-ranking statuses. Such individuals might be chiefs or elders responsible for storing and distributing important goods, persons who mobilized production for feasts or organized special projects, priests who received valued goods for their services, war-party leaders who assured access to valued resources or gained desirable booty, and so on. Ethnography and archeology both indicate that people as a whole long resisted the loss of egalitarian principles, but as offices such as these become more important to a society, the restructuring of production relations meant the institutionalization of inequality could not be avoided.

In ranking society a "public" sector of the economy concerned with production for accumulation and trade began to be differentiated from a "private" household or lineage sector concerned with production for subsistence and sharing. The division of labor between men and women then took on new significance. Where women produced for the market and participated directly in trade, they held a recognized status in public life and a high degree of autonomy in family life. Yet the men's spheres of responsibility, hunting and warfare, often led directly into trading and responsibility for external political relations, to the strengthening of patrilineal over matrilineal ties, and the long-range undermining of women's position. As Engels (1972) long ago suggested, this was commonly the case where domesticated animals, typically the province of men, became important forms of wealth.

The chapters on societies with one or another degree of ranking illustrate the kinds of relations between women's economic roles and their sociopolitical positions that call for extensive documentation and analysis. Etienne shows that women's control of cloth production balanced men's control of yam production among the precolonial Baule and gave them an initial advantage in commodity exchange. Women participated in long-distance trade and held public office, and in each village women's and men's societies represented parallel forms of ritual power.

Malinowski had noted women's high status in Trobriand society, but failed to notice its economic base and saw exchange relationships as involving only men. Weiner, however, demonstrates the importance for Trobriand society of women's wealth in banana-leaf skirts, and the importance of sister-brother and wife-husband dyads in the exchange networks.

Among the elaborately ranked Tonga, where stratification was under way at the time of Cook's voyage, the goods produced by women were considered valuables, in contrast to the mundane production of food by men. Wives deferred to husbands, but sisters outranked brothers. As Gailey shows, women were actively involved in the jockeying for position that took place among high-ranking lineages, and they used their *fahu* rights over their brothers and their brothers' children in their political maneuvers.

In Tlingit society individual wealth derived from trade was important before colonization. Klein indicates that women's labor was important to the production of trade goods and that they directly engaged in distribution and exchange, often guiding or even controlling the trading transactions of men. Important ritual and political functions were also accessible to women among the Tlingit.

The Luo have a complex history in an area where urbanization and trade were once important. They were a formerly pastoral people who turned to farming. Pala Okeyo describes the importance of women's usufruct rights to land and to the control of their produce which they sometimes sold in the market. Although the Luo were patrilineal and virilocal, these rights enabled a woman to enjoy considerable autonomy and authority as the head of her household and the potential originator of a new lineage segment.

Production Relations in Preindustrial Stratified Society

The category, preindustrial stratified, covers at least three production modes: Oriental, slave, and feudal. Some authors would include the Aztec and Inca, covered in this book, in the hotly debated Oriental mode. For present purposes, it is not necessary to get into detailed debates, but is sufficient to enumerate broad features that differentiate preindustrial production relations from both the relations of ranking society and the relations of capitalism.

A minimally consuming class of producers supports a maximally consuming class of aristocrats, administrators, priests, army officers, and merchants. Preindustrial stratified society contrasts with capitalist society in that the upper class appropriates labor and produce; these are directly alienated from the producing classes. Some form of factory production and a merchant class that appropriates surplus value commonly exist, but not as the dominant form of production. Similarly, a significant amount of subsistence production continues to take place in the countryside, but rural life is not independent of dominating urban centers that control the distribution and exchange of important raw materials and manufactured goods.

Private ownership is extensive, although not total. It is possible, however, for large numbers of people to be alienated from arable lands and needed resources—that is, to have no access to basic sources of subsistence. The division of labor is carried to the point where urban populations are dependent on market relations for acquiring food and other necessities. By contrast with capitalist production, however, craftsworkers follow through all stages in the manufacture of commodities, produce completed goods rather than repeatedly performing one part of the total operation, and often themselves market some of their produce.

As Engels (1972) suggested, the household in stratified societies is an economically independent unit, within which women's work is privatized. In contrast to the nuclear family of capitalist society, however, the household usually consists of several families; and by contrast with its consuming function in capitalist society, the household is also a productive unit. Relationships within it, however, were patriarchal. In the stratified societies of the ancient east, women were virtual minors in the eyes of the law, relegated to private life and subservient to patriarch-husbands. Yet women had not lost their legal adulthood and social prerogatives quickly or without resistance. Scattered references to legal codes written in different periods of Sumerian history indicate that the process of subjugating women took many centuries (Rorhlich-Leavitt 1977).

The rich ethnohistorical data on the Aztec reveal parallels to the changes that are hinted at in ancient Sumerian materials. Nash uses Aztec historical traditions to show that women's position declined sharply when the Aztecs transformed themselves from a democratically organized and kin-based society into a stratified, military conquest state, especially among the people conquered by the Aztecs.

Silverblatt also refers to a formerly higher status for women in the Inca empire; in some outlying areas they apparently held public office at the time of conquest. She focuses less than Nash, however, on the deterioration of their position in the precolonial period. Both authors demonstrate that women were further oppressed, and often brutally so, by the Spanish conquerers.

Capitalism and Colonization

Capitalism won ascendency in Europe through the process of colonial exploitation (Saffioti 1978). The nature of colonization varied widely, according to the resources of each area and the interests of the colonizers. In Canada, French and English trading companies vied with each other to involve native Canadians in procuring furs for the European market. To the south, Spanish and Portuguese adventurers pursued dreams of gold and sometimes found the precious metal used by native aristocracies in lavish quantities. Soon, however, it was native American lands that the intruders wanted, with native Americans as laborers on plantations and in factories and mines. In all parts of the world, a rising European bourgeoisie sought to make profits from different peoples and their lands, whether through extracting wealth, using native labor, or decimating indigenous populations in order to establish settlements in their territories. As with the origin of exploitation itself, the imposition of capitalist exploitation linked the subjugation of people generally with the special subjugation of women.

WOMEN AND COLONIZATION

Two contradictory views characterize both the study of colonization in general and the study of women in colonized societies in particular: on the one hand, there is a tendency to see colonization as beneficial and, on the other, a tendency to see the colonized as passive victims. In the light of contemporary movements of resistance and revolution, both views have been criticized with respect to colonization in general. Where colonized women are concerned, however, there has been less progress. It is now widely understood, especially by historians (for example, Hopkins 1973), but also by anthropologists (Magubane 1979:258-330) that the recognition of colonial exploitation does not preclude recognition of the colonized as capable of acting to influence their own destiny. The history of slavery in the United States has made notable advances in this awareness (Gutman 1976). With respect to women, however, a "double standard" prevails. Because of assumptions about the passivity of women in general and about their subordination in precolonial societies, the "optimistic" and "pessimistic" views of their condition under colonialism (Dinan 1977) continue to be presented as mutually exclusive alternatives. The case studies in this volume demonstrate the inadequacy of these alternatives. We hope they will contribute to clarifying the contradictions that affect the study of women under colonization.

The Impact of Colonization

The effects of colonization on the position of women in each society studied here cannot be dissociated from its effects on the society as a whole. Changes in relations between the sexes can be expected to reflect changes in other social sectors and especially the transformation of production relations, as outlined above. The causal factors involved are multiple and complex. They involve the particular mode of colonization, itself determined by the political and economic imperatives of the colonizer and by the nature of the colonized society; the precise strategies of exploitation employed by the colonizer; and the strategies of accommodation or resistance adopted by the colonized. The interplay of these variables makes each case unique. The different authors of the present work have focused on those aspects and processes—the precise "moments," so to speak—that have seemed to them most decisive. There are, however, remarkable convergences from one study to another.

While colonization on occasion had a strategic purpose initially (for example, Tonga), its ultimate goal was economic exploitation of both women and men. The necessary transformation of productive relations profoundly affected personal relationships. The impact of colonization on the quality of personal relations between women and men, between parents and children, and among people in general is perhaps most striking in egalitarian societies; this is well illustrated by Leacock for the Montagnais-Naskapi, Buenaventura-Posso and Brown for the Bari, and Bell for the Warlpiri.

The overt use of ideology as a means of instituting compliance is particularly revealing of the connection between colonization and the deterioration of personal relations. It also reveals the connection between the economic exploitation of both sexes and the subordination of women and between sexual inequality and other forms of inequality. In the early centuries of colonial expansion, the Catholic church was a major force in Europe and therefore became instrumental in the colonization of the Americas. Leacock vividly documents the efforts of the Jesuits to impose on the Montagnais-Naskapi the norms of sexual and conjugal behavior that characterized European society, with the patriarchal nuclear family as a model. The Jesuit attack on the autonomy of women was compounded by a systematic attack on individual autonomy specifically and egalitarian relations in general. Control of a husband and father over a wife and offspring, along with control of men over other men, were seen by the Jesuits as the key to restructuring productive relations and attitudes toward colonial domination, bringing the Indians from "savagery" to "civilization." The Jesuit program of conversion had devastating effects on zealots and their victims, fomenting internal conflict and creating the divide-and-rule situation that is the ever present tool of colonization.

The church played a similar role in other societies, introducing the repression and exploitation of women as sexual objects, as reproducers, and as producers and alienating converts from those who resisted indoctrination. In the precolonial stratified societies of the Andes and Mexico, women retained some of the autonomy that had characterized their position prior to conquest by the Inca and the Aztec. Catholicism, however, exacerbated inequalities and undermined those social, political, and economic institutions that still guaranteed those women's rights. The Methodist church played a similar role in Tonga, where it precipitated state formation and encouraged legislation unfavorable to women—outlawing the crucial *fahu* relationship that defined women's rights as sisters and restricting the use of *tapa* (bark cloth), thus weakening women's position as producers of "valuables."

Direct ideological action, the attempt to transform attitudes and beliefs, is only the tip of the iceberg. It was supported by legislation and by force. Its effectiveness was ultimately dependent on structural transformations of indigenous economies. For example, it is because the economic base of the Montagnais-Naskapi near the mission station had already been undermined that they were vulnerable to the Jesuit program for conversion. In the Spanish conquest of the Inca and the Aztec, the church was an arm of the state; Silverblatt and Nash document its participation in economic exploitation. In Tonga, missionary action was often indissociable from economic and political action. In another case, among the Seneca, Quaker intervention was exclusively concerned with economic change.

Whether or not missionizing was important in the societies they study, other authors describe similar changes in the quality of personal relations.

Buenaventura-Posso and Brown show how women's loss of economic autonomy led to the breakdown of harmonious relations between women and men among the Bari. Their description presents similarities with that of Etienne for the Baule, where, in a society practically untouched by missionizing and in many ways very different from Bari society, destruction of the delicate balance of economic rights and obligations has resulted in growing antagonism between the sexes. And, like Leacock, Bell presents a moving account of the deterioration of both conjugal and filial relations among the Warlpiri. Frustrated and humiliated by colonization, Warlpiri men vent their anger on women; unable to rely on kin group protection, women seek economic and emotional security in unrealistic marriages influenced by stereotypes of romantic love. Fundamental to these changes is the alienation of the Warlpiri from their land, the sites of their "dreamings," the vital underpinning of their whole way of life.

The economic thrust of colonization, sometimes masked by ideology, sometimes overt and undisguised, was always present, but the relationship between economic exploitation of colonized peoples and the development of capitalism as a world system emerged most clearly in the late nineteenth and the twentieth centuries. Together and separately, the case studies show how the transformation of production relations worked as a whole. The crucial mechanisms were production for commodity exchange and reliance on commodities. In settlement colonization, expropriation of land limited people's access to strategic resources and forced them into wage labor—on settler farms and ranches or in industry (for example, the Seneca, the Bari, the Luo, the Warlpiri.) Where land was not expropriated, cash crops created pressure on resources and diverted economic activity from subsistence agriculture and craft production (the Baule, Tonga). Whether as wage laborers or as landholding producers, people were drawn into the cash economy by a growing dependence on goods which replaced goods they no longer produced or which had become new necessities. The self-perpetuating process of transforming colonized people into producers and consumers of commodities served the colonial powers' need for both raw materials and markets.

In pursuing this transformation—concurrently with the ideological action described above—the colonizers addressed their demands and their technical innovations to men, thus favoring men's access to cash, the economic dependency of women and, as a result, the emergence of the patriarchal nuclear family. These changes were often compounded by the transition from group rights in land to private property, also accomplished to the advantage of men (Boserup 1970). The effects of individualized land tenure on the position of women are well documented by Pala Okeyo for the Luo. Colonized peoples have often resisted these changes, especially the institutions of the nuclear family and of private property in land, but the process is an ongoing one, encouraged by the legislation of many developing countries, as in the case of the Luo. Among the Baule, where the nuclear family has not emerged and where rights in land are still for the most part collective, pressure on land resources and labor time as a result of cash cropping nevertheless jeopardizes women's use rights and tends to make them economically dependent on men.

The transformations of production relations presented schematically here are richly documented by the case studies. There are, however, two notable exceptions to the proposition that colonization has always been detrimental to women. Klein and Weiner describe the persistence after colonization of precolonial patterns of relations between the sexes. In the case of the Tlingit, Klein suggests that there were contradictions between missionary ideology and the colonizer's attempts to undermine the position of women, on the one hand, and the broader imperatives of colonial practice, on the other. Exploitation of seasonal maritime fishing, a male activity vital to the colonial economy, made women more available and more desirable as wage laborers and salaried employees, first in the canning industry and later in white-collar sectors. This favored their economic autonomy, as well as their education and their access to political office.

The Trobriand case is very different. Weiner documents the limited nature of colonial intervention in the Trobriands and the crucial role of women's wealth in perpetuating basic structures and values of Trobriand society. The combined effect of these two factors is the neutralization of men's cash income by its conversion into women's wealth and its subsequent absorption in ritual exchange. Both authors, however, suggest possible future changes that may affect the position of women unfavorably. As noted above, colonialism is an ongoing process that continues to transform economic structures and relations between the sexes, even where political independence has been attained.[4]

Accommodation and Resistance

Besides the exceptional circumstances described by Klein and Weiner, there were many instances in which some women appeared to maintain or improve their status under colonization. The extent to which colonial powers sought to modify indigenous political structures by direct intervention was variable from one society to another, but differential wealth and power based on commodity exchange and the unequal participation of individuals and groups in colonial political structures generally exacerbated preexisting stratification or promoted its emergence in previously unstratified societies. In the complex interplay between sexual inequality and other forms of inequality, some women could occasionally gain an advantage over other women and over some men. Where they were members of a precolonial or newly created elite, women could especially benefit from the colonial situation. Such cases are analyzed by Nash for the Aztec, Silverblatt for the Inca, and Gailey for Tonga. All three authors also show that the possibilities of exploiting a privileged position in the colonial context brought relative and short-term advantages for a minority, in contrast with long-term loss of status for a majority.

Just as women were not passive in precolonial societies, they were not passive in the face of colonization. Whether women were members of an elite or not, whenever colonial structures offered them the possibility of doing so, they sought—as did men—to conserve or acquire individual advantages, either by pursuing preexisting activities or by adopting new ones. Operating as traders (for example, the Algonkian and the Tlingit), they expanded and adapted their precolonial pursuits. As group land was converted into private property, they became landholders insofar as they had the right and the means to do so (the Inca). In many cases they seized available opportunities to enter into both cash-crop production and wage labor, hoping to conserve or improve their economic status, working to serve men when their common interests of survival made it necessary, but continuing to assert their autonomy when circumstances were favorable.

Often it became apparent, however, that social and economic security for the majority of women in colonized societies could most easily be attained through men. The introduced ideology that perceived women as sexual objects, combined with their relative scarcity under most forms of colonization, made them valuable commodities. This frequently led to widespread prostitution, perhaps facilitated in some cases by precolonial standards of sexual freedom, but primarily determined by women's understanding of their generalized dependency on men and their desire to seek the least disadvantageous adjustment to it—for prostitution was often seen as preferable to marriage. Consorting with the conqueror in more durable relationships was another mode of adjustment, sensitively described by Bell for Warlpiri women. Among the Aztec, women were already familiar with oppression and reification, and the Spanish conquerors' need to reproduce at first an elite and later a labor force offered individual opportunities that women readily accepted, showing considerable discretion in the choice of partners most favorable to their social advancement and using their position to acquire other advantages. Similar behaviors are depicted by Silverblatt for the Inca and Etienne for the Baule.

The recognition that women took advantage of available opportunities, eventually trading on their own sexuality, should not be interpreted as a denial of the brutal exploitation, both sexual and economic, that they were subjected to by the colonizer and which is especially well described by Silverblatt. Nor should the opportunism of women in the pursuit of their individual interest—often at the expense of their compatriots, both women and men—be given more dignity than the opportunism of men. The rejection of the "passive victims" approach to colonized women is, however, necessary in order to recognize what can properly be termed resistance, that is, forms of action that aimed at defending collective interests and represented a struggle against oppression rather than an accommodation to it.

Women's resistance to colonization is best illustrated by Rothenberg for the Seneca and Silverblatt for the Inca. In both cases, women's defense of their collective interests was related to the defense of their society as a whole.

In resisting Quaker attempts to deny them participation in political decision making, to turn over agricultural production to men, and to individualize land tenure, Seneca women were defending themselves and, at the same time, the cultural integrity and the economic interests of all Seneca. Among Andean peoples, the women who actively resisted religious conversion, and their descendants who now live the lonely life of the *puna*, represent resistance both to their own oppression as women and to the destruction of their culture.

These examples point to another way in which the "double standard" referred to above obstructs the understanding of women's resistance to colonization. Psychological explanations suggesting irrational motivations for "resistance to change" are used with respect to men, as Rothenberg specifically points out in the case of the Seneca. But such explanations are far more prevalent and tenacious where women are concerned. "Natural" conservatism, supposed irrationality, and assumed passivity, are all elements of the same stereotype—a stereotype that influences attitudes toward colonized men, but is compounded in the case of colonized women. The chapters in this volume, by suggesting the impact of colonization in all its complexity and the eminently rational responses of women in all their diversity, should contribute to undermining this stereotype.

A divide-and-rule policy characterized colonial domination—as it does class domination. Those groups or individuals who had the opportunity to alleviate their exploitation tended to take advantage of it. Because the overall effects of colonization were detrimental to women, a situation they did not accept passively, it was inevitable that antagonism between the sexes should develop and that, in a short-term perspective, the interests of women and men should not always coincide. In a long-term perspective, however, the forms of resistance adopted by colonized women corresponded with the interests of colonized men, whose advantage over women was only relative to their own oppression. The unified action of women and men in Third World revolutionary movements today demonstrates their common interest and their common understanding. We hope that the present work will encourage support of their struggles by furthering understanding of the relationship between our own cause, as feminists, and theirs.

NOTES

1. The sections entitled "Women and Anthropology: Conceptual Problems" and "Women and Colonization" were written by Mona Etienne. "Women and Relations of Production" was written by Eleanor Leacock.

2. This introduction does not attempt to cover all the important works concerning the anthropology of women. For more complete information, the reader should consult the review articles by Lamphere (1977), Quinn (1977), Rogers (1978), and especially Rapp (1979). For a review of theories on the

origins of sexual inequality, see Reiter (1977). For further theoretical discussion of sexual stratification, see Schlegel (1977). A debate on the issue of relations between the sexes in egalitarian societies is to be found in Leacock (1978).

3. An excellent critique of the dichotomy associating women with nature and men with culture, although not with reference to Ortner's work is to be found in Mathieu (1978) and, in connection with reproduction, in Mathieu (1977).

4. Many works on women in developing countries illustrate this point. See, for example, Wellesley Editorial Committee (1978).

REFERENCES

Bernt, Catherine H. 1974. "Digging Sticks and Spears, or The Two-Sex Model." In Fay Gale, ed., *Woman's Role in Aboriginal Society.* Carlton, New South Wales, Australia: Excelsis Press.

Boserup, Ester. 1970. *Woman's Role in Economic Development.* London: Allen and Unwin.

Dinan, Carmel. 1977. "Pragmatists or Feminists? The Professional Single Women in Accra, Ghana." *Cahiers d'etudes africaines* 17, 1:155-76.

Divale, William T. and Marvin Harris. 1976. "Population, Warfare and the Male Supremacist Complex." *American Anthropologist* 78, 3:521-38.

Engels, Frederick. 1972. *The Origin of the Family, Private Property and the State.* New York: International Publishers.

Etienne, Mona. 1979a. "The Case for Social Maternity: Adoption of Children by Urban Baule Women (Ivory Coast)." *Dialectical Anthropology* 4, 1. In press.

———.1979b. "Maternité sociale, rapports d'adoption et pouvoir des femmes chez les Baoulé (Côte d'Ivoire)." *L'Homme* 19, 3-4. In press.

Evans-Pritchard, E. E. 1940. *The Nuer.* Oxford: Oxford University Press.

———.1965. "The Position of Women in Primitive Societies and in Our Own." In E. E. Evans-Pritchard, *The Position of Women in Primitive Societies and Other Essays in Social Anthropology.* London: Faber and Faber.

Fried, Morton H. 1967. *The Evolution of Political Society.* New York: Random House.

Friedl, Ernestine. 1975. *Women and Men: An Anthropologist's View.* New York: Holt, Rinehart and Winston.

Gough, Kathleen. 1971. "Nuer Kinship: A Re-examination." In T. O. Beidelman, ed., *The Translation of Culture.* London: Tavistock.

Gutman, Herbert G. 1976. *The Black Family in Slavery and Freedom, 1750-1925.* New York: Random House.

Harris, Marvin. 1977. "Why Men Dominate Women." *The New York Times Magazine,* November 13, p. 46.

Hopkins, A. G. 1973. *An Economic History of West Africa.* London: Longman.

Lamphere, Louise. 1977. "Review Essay: Anthropology." *Signs* 2, 3:612-27.

Leacock, Eleanor. 1978. "Women's Status in Egalitarian Society: Implications for Social Evolution." *Current Anthropology* 19, 2:247-75.

McElroy, Ann and Carolyn Mathiasson, eds. 1979. *Sex Roles in Changing Cultures.* Occasional Papers in Anthropology, 1. Buffalo: Department of Anthropology, State University of New York at Buffalo.

Magubane, Bernard Makhosezwe. 1979. *The Political Economy of Race and Class in South Africa.* New York: Monthly Review Press.

Mathieu, Nicole-Claude. 1977. "Paternité biologique, maternité sociale." In Andrée Michel, ed., *Femmes, sexisme et sociétés.* Paris: Presses universitaires de France.

———.1978. "Man-Culture and Woman-Nature?" *Woman's Studies International Quarterly* 1, 1:55-65.

Meillassoux, Claude. 1975. *Femmes, greniers et capitaux.* Paris: Maspéro.

Ortner, Sherry B. 1974. "Is Female to Male as Nature is to Culture?" In Michelle Zimbalist Rosaldo and Louise Lamphere, eds., *Woman, Culture and Society.* Stanford: Stanford University Press.

Quinn, Naomi. 1977. "Anthropological Studies on Women's Status." *Annual Review of Anthropology* 6:181-225.

Rapp, Rayna. 1979. "Review Essay: Anthropology." *Signs* 4, 3:497-513.

Reiter, Rayna Rapp. 1977. "The Search for Origins: Unraveling the Threads of Gender Hierarchy." *Critique of Anthropology* 3, 9-10:5-24.

Rogers, Susan Carol. 1978. "Woman's Place: A Critical Review of Anthropological Theory." *Comparative Studies in Society and History* 20, 1:123-62.

Rohrlich-Leavitt, Ruby. 1977. "Women in Transition: Crete and Sumer." In R. Bridenthal and C. Koonz, eds., *Becoming Visible: Women in European History.* Boston: Houghton-Mifflin.

Rosaldo, M. Z. 1974. "Woman, Culture and Society." In M. Z. Rosaldo and L. Lamphere, eds. *Women, Culture, and Society.* Stanford: Stanford University Press.

Sacks, Karen. 1976. "State Bias and Women's Status." *American Anthropologist* 78, 3:565-69.

Saffioti, Heleith. 1978. *Women in Class Society.* New York: Monthly Review Press.

Schlegel, Alice. 1977. "Toward a Theory of Sexual Stratification." In Alice Schlegel, ed., *Sexual Stratification: A Cross-Cultural View.* New York: Columbia University Press.

Wellesley Editorial Committee, ed. 1978. *Women and National Development: The Complexities of Change.* Chicago: University of Chicago Press. Originally published as a special issue of *Signs* (1977 3, 1).

1   Montagnais Women and the Jesuit Program for Colonization[1]

ELEANOR LEACOCK

During the sixteenth century, the St. Lawrence valley was the scene of French and English competition for furs, especially for beaver which was used in the manufacture of hats. Sporadic trade of furs between native peoples and European fishermen was old, possibly preceding Columbus's first voyage; for when Cartier sailed up the St. Lawrence in 1534, the people he met were familiar with European vessels, products, and interest in furs. By midcentury, ships were coming to the area for the sole purpose of trading, and during the latter part of the century several companies competed unsuccessfully for a monopoly of the trade.

In 1559, a permanent French trading post was established at Tadoussac, downriver from Quebec, chosen by Champlain to be the headquarters of New France and founded in 1608. Three Rivers, further up the St. Lawrence, was established in 1617. Champlain was welcomed by the Algonkins and Montagnais.[2] They saw in him an ally in their warfare with the Iroquois, who, armed with weapons obtained from the Dutch, were raiding north and west for furs. Champlain's main interest was in gaining access to the interior trade through making alliances with Huron and Algonkin middlemen. He agreed to join the Algonkins and Montagnais in a retaliatory expedition against the Iroquois and was led, in the process, to the "discovery" of Lake Champlain. His way west, however, was persistently blocked by friendly noncooperation on the part of both Algonkins and Hurons. They were not eager to relinquish a middleman status that yielded a steady supply of iron tools, utensils (especially copper kettles), clothing, grain, and dried fruit.

Meanwhile, the number of trading vessels sailing up the St. Lawrence increased. Champlain wrote in 1611 that the Indians waited until several arrived before bringing out their furs, so that competition for them would push up their price. An average annual harvest of 15,000 to 20,000 beaver in the first years of the seventeenth century rose to 80,000 by 1670. By that time, the Iroquois had defeated and virtually annihilated the Hurons, the French were about to cede Canada to the English, and the English "company of adventurers" was opening up another route to the west with its post, Rupert's House, on Hudson's Bay. As the interest in furs pushed west, the northern and eastern parts of the Labrador Peninsula remained relatively distant from its influence. Not until the nineteenth century did the Hudson's Bay Company begin setting up posts in the Labrador interior.

Several missionaries accompanied Champlain on his first trips, but missionizing did not begin in earnest until 1632, when Quebec, temporarily occupied by the English, had been regained by the French. The traders were interested in the Indians as a source of furs. By contrast the mission, under the able leadership of the Jesuit Paul Le Jeune was committed to converting them to Christianity, resocializing them, and transforming them into settled farmers, citizens of New France. The Jesuits first worked intensively with the Montagnais-Naskapi, but soon began to pin their hopes on the populous, agricultural Hurons. When the Iroquois decimation of the Hurons dashed these hopes, some Jesuits remained to work with their Montagnais converts, but the main missionizing drive was over.

What was the status of Montagnais-Naskapi women in the early seventeenth century when the French were establishing a foothold in the upper St. Lawrence valley? As is often the case, a look through accounts written at the time yields contrasting judgments. One may read that "women have great power . . . . A man may promise you something and if he does not keep his promise, he thinks he is sufficiently excused when he tells you that his wife did not wish him to do it" (Thwaites 1906:5:179). Or one may read that women were virtual slaves.

> The women...besides the onerous role of bearing and rearing the children, also transport the game from the place where it has fallen; they are the hewers of wood and drawers of water; they make and repair the household utensils; they prepare food; they skin the game and prepare the hides like fullers; they sew garments; they catch fish and gather shellfish for food; often they even hunt; they make the canoes, that is skiffs of marvelous rapidity, out of bark;[3] they set up the tents wherever and whenever they stop for the night—in short, the men concern themselves with nothing but the more laborious hunting and the waging of war....Their wives are regarded and treated as slaves (:2:77).

Fortunately, the ethnohistorical record for the Montagnais-Naskapi is full enough so that contradictions between two statements such as these can be resolved. The view that the hard work of native American women made them slaves was commonly expressed by European observers who did not know personally the people about whom they were writing. The statement about female authority, however, was written by a man who knew the Montagnais-Naskapi well and recognized that women controlled their own work and made decisions accordingly. Paul Le Jeune, superior of the Jesuit mission at Quebec, had spent a winter in a Montagnais lodge in order to learn the language and understand the culture of the people he was supposed to convert and "civilize." He commented on the ease of relations between husbands and wives in Montagnais society, and explained that it followed from "the order which they maintain in their occupations," whereby "the women know what they are to do, and the men also; and one never meddles with the work of the other" (:5:133). "Men leave the arrangement of the household to the women, without interfering with them; they cut and decide and give away as they please without making the husband angry. I have never seen my host ask a giddy young woman that he had with him what became of the provisions, although they were disappearing very fast" (:6:233).

Le Jeune sought to change this state of affairs, and he reported to his superiors in Paris on his progress in "civilizing" the Montagnais-Naskapi through what became a fourfold program. First, he saw permanent settlement and the institution of formally recognized chiefly authority as basic. "Alas!" he wrote, "If someone could stop the wanderings of the Savages, and give authority to one of them to rule the others, we would see them converted and civilized in a short time" (:12:169). Second, Le Jeune stressed the necessity of introducing the principle of punishment into Montagnais social relations. Third, central to Le Jeune's program was education of Montagnais-Naskapi children. "How necessary it is to educate the children of the Savages," he stated. "We shall have them at last if they see that we do not send them to France" (:5:137).

> If we had a good building in Kebec, we would get more children through the very same means by which we despair of getting them. We have always thought that the excessive love the Savages bear their children would prevent our obtaining them. It will be through this very means that they will become our pupils; for, by having a few settled ones, who will attract and retain the others, the parents, who do not know what it is to refuse their children, will let them come without opposition. And, as they will be permitted during the first few years to have a great deal of liberty, they will become so accustomed to our food and our clothes, that they will have a horror of the Savages and their filth (:9:103).

As the quotation suggests, Montagnais-Naskapi culture posed a stumbling block for the Jesuits, in that the Montagnais did not practice corporeal punishment of children. Le Jeune complained, "The Savages prevent their instruction; they will not tolerate the chastisement of their children, whatever they may do, they permit only a simple reprimand" (:5:197). Le Jeune's solution was to propose removing the children from their communities for schooling: "The reason why I would not like to take the children of one locality in that locality itself, but rather in some other place, is because these Barbarians cannot bear to have their children punished, even scolded, not being able to refuse anything to a crying child. They carry this to such an extent that upon the slightest pretext they would take them away from us, before they were educated" (:6:153-55).

Fourth, essential to Le Jeune's entire program was the introduction of European family structure, with male authority, female fidelity, and the elimination of the right to divorce. Lecturing a man on the subject, Le Jeune said the man "was the master and that in France women do not rule their husbands" (:5:179). The independence of Montagnais women posed continual problems for the Jesuits. Le Jeune decided that:

> ...it is absolutely necessary to teach the girls as well as the boys, and that we shall do nothing or very little, unless some good household has the care of this sex; for the boys that we shall have reared in the knowledge of God, when they marry Savage girls or women accustomed to wandering in the woods will, as their husbands, be compelled to follow them and thus fall back into barbarism or to leave them, another evil full of danger (:5:145).

Le Jeune's account of his problems, successes, and failures in introducing hierarchical principles into the ordering of interpersonal relations among the

Montagnais-Naskapi affords a clear record of the personal autonomy that was central to the structure and ethics of their society—an autonomy that applied as fully to women as to men.

MONTAGNAIS-NASKAPI ECONOMY AND DECISION MAKING

The Montagnais-Naskapi lived by hunting and trapping wild game—caribou, moose, beaver, bear, hare, porcupine and water fowl—by fishing, and by gathering wild berries and other vegetable foods. Like foraging peoples everywhere, they followed a regular pattern of seasonal movement according to the provenience of the foods on which they depended. The Montagnais with whom Le Jeune worked summered on the shores of the St. Lawrence River, where groups of several hundred people gathered to fish, socialize, and make and repair canoes, snowshoes, and other equipment. In the fall, groups of some 35 to 75 people separated out to ascend one or another of the rivers that emptied into the St. Lawrence. During the winter hunting season, these bands might split up into smaller groups in order to spread out over a wide area in search of game. However, they kept in touch with each other so that if some were short of food, they could turn to others for help (Leacock, 1969).

The smallest working unit was the group that lived together in a large conical lodge—some ten to twenty people, or, in Western terms, several nuclear families. In early times, as later, residential choices were probably flexible, and people moved about in accord both with personal likes and dislikes and with the need for keeping a reasonable balance in the working group between women and men and young and old. Upon marriage, however, a man ideally moved into his wife's lodge group (Thwaites 1906:31:169). Accordingly, mentions of a Montagnais man's family might include the man's wife's sister, or a son-in-law, or a father-in-law (:6:125,:9:33,:14:143-45). Yet three brothers and their wives shared the lodge in which Le Jeune lived. Le Jeune is silent about the relationships among the wives who, judging from hunting-group compositions in recent times, could easily have been sisters or parallel cousins.[4] In any case, Le Jeune's diary shows that the arrangement was not permanent.

Ethnographic evidence as well as the *Jesuit Relations* indicates that decisions about movements were made by the adult members of whatever group was involved. There is no question about women's importance in making such decisions. In fact, one recorder stated that "the choice of plans, of undertakings, of journeys, of winterings, lies in nearly every instance in the hands of the housewife" (:68:93). Individuals might be chosen as spokespersons to mediate with the French, but such "chiefs" held no formal authority within the group. Le Jeune noted that "the Savages cannot endure in the least those who seem desirous of assuming superiority over the others; they place all virtue in a certain gentleness or apathy" (:16:165).

> They imagine that they ought by right of birth, to enjoy the liberty of wild ass colts, rendering no homage to anyone whomsoever, except when they like. They have reproached me a hundred times because we fear our Captains, while they laugh at and make sport of theirs. All the authority of their chief is in his tongue's end; for he is powerful insofar as he is eloquent; and, even if he kills himself talking and haranguing, he will not be obeyed unless he pleases the Savages (:6:243).

Le Jeune was honest enough to state what he saw as the positive side of Montagnais egalitarianism:

> As they have neither political organization, nor office, nor dignities, nor any authority, for they only obey their Chief through good will toward him, therefore they never kill each other to acquire these honors. Also, as they are contented with a mere living, not one of them gives himself to the Devil to acquire wealth (:6:231).

In his final judgement, however, Le Jeune remained bound by his culture and his missionizing commitment: "I would not dare assert that I have seen one act of real moral virtue in a Savage. They have nothing but their own pleasure and satisfaction in view" (:6:239-41).

THE JESUIT PROGRAM FOR CHANGING MONTAGNAIS MARRIAGE

As indicated above, Le Jeune's original assumption—that he could win the Montagnais to Christianity through converting the men—changed when he learned how far Montagnais family structure was from that of the French. He realized that he would have to give special attention to women as well as men if he was to eliminate the Montagnais' unquestioned acceptance of divorce at the desire of either partner, of polygyny, and of sexual freedom after marriage.

"The young people do not think that they can persevere in the state of matrimony with a bad wife or a bad husband," Le Jeune wrote. "They wish to be free and to be able to divorce the consort if they do not love each other" (:16:41). And several years later: "The inconstancy of marriages and the facility with which they divorce each other, are a great obstacle to the Faith of Jesus Christ. We do not dare baptize the young people because experience teaches us that the custom of abandoning a disagreeable wife or husband has a strong hold on them" (:22:229).

Polygamy was another right that women as well as men took for granted: "Since I have been preaching among them that a man should not have more than one wife, I have not been well received by the women; for, since they are more numerous than the men, if a man can only marry one of them, the others will have to suffer. Therefore this doctrine is not according to their liking" (:12:165). And as for the full acceptance of sexual freedom for both women and men, no citation can be more telling of the gulf between French and Montagnais society than Le Jeune's rendition of a Montagnais rebuff.

> I told him that it was not honorable for a woman to love any one else except her husband, and that this evil being among them, he himself was not sure that his son, who was there present, was his son. He replied, "Thou hast no sense. You French people love only your own children; but we all love all the children of our tribe." I began to laugh, seeing that he philosophized in horse and mule fashion (:6:255).

Converts to Christianity wrestled with the dilemmas posed by the French faith. A recently married young man wished to be faithful to his wife, but felt himself "inclined toward infidelity." Deeply disturbed by his criminal wish, he entreated to be imprisoned or publicly flogged. When his request was refused, "He slips into a room near the Chapel and, with a rope that he finds, he beats himself so hard all over the body that the noise reaches the ears of the Father, who runs in and forbids so severe a penance" (:22:67). The adoption of severe punitiveness both towards the self and others was reported by Le Jeune.

> The most zealous Christians met during the winter, unknown to us, in order to confer together upon the means of keeping themselves in the faith. One of them, in making an address, said that he thought more highly of prayers than of life, and that he would rather die than give them up. Another said that he wished he might be punished and chastised in case he forfeited the word he had given to God. A third claimed that he who should fall into any error must be put into prison and made to fast for four days without eating or drinking. The acts of justice that they see from time to time exercised on delinquents give them these ideas (:20:143).

Upon hearing the news, the fathers informed the converts that "they proceeded with too much severity; that mildness had more power over souls than force." The zealots argued, however, that the first among them who committed a fault, "however inconsiderable, should suffer imprisonment and fasting." This so frightened "the weak," Le Jeune continued, that "the report spread among the unbelievers that the Christian Savages had chains and bonds all ready to bind the refractory." Le Jeune concluded, "Some pagans told us they were risking the ruin of everything and that the Savages would kill one another. All this consoled us much, for we took pleasure in seeing the union of the Christians; it is much easier to temper fervor than it is to kindle it" (:20:143).

Women and children alike suffered punishment at the hands of the converts. "A young Christian, getting into a passion, beat his wife, who had insolently provoked him," Le Jeune wrote. The man then repented of his sin and went to the chapel to pray to God for mercy. Le Jeune had the couple brought to him. "They were properly reprimanded," he reported, "especially the woman, who was more guilty than her husband" (:18:155). As for the children,

> they are all in an incredible state of satisfaction at having embraced the Faith. "We punish the disobedient" said they. A young girl who would not go to the nets, where her father sent her, was two days without food as a punishment for her disobedience. Two boys, who came late to prayers in the morning were punished by having a handful of hot cinders thrown upon their heads with threats of greater chastisement in case the offenses were repeated (:18:171).

Several Christians even had a drunken, young, pagan relative thrown into prison—in Le Jeune's view, "an act fit to astonish all those who know the customs of the Savages, who cannot endure that any one should touch their kinsmen; but God has more power than nature" (:20:153).

In 1640, eight years after Le Jeune's arrival in New France and the setting up of a Jesuit mission, the governor called together a group of influential Montagnais men, and "having recommended to the Christians constance in their marriages—he gave them to understand that it would be well if they should elect some chiefs to govern them" (:18:99). Accordingly, the Montagnais sought advice from the Jesuits, who supervised the election of three captains. The men then "resolved to call together the women, to urge them to be instructed and to receive holy Baptism." The women were used to holding councils of their own to deal with matters of concern to them and reported surprise at being lectured to by the men.

> Yesterday the men summoned us to a council, but the first time that women have ever entered one; but they treated us so rudely that we were greatly astonished. "It is you women," they said to us, "who keep the Demons among us; you do not urge to be baptized....when you pass before the cross you never salute it, you wish to be independent. Now know that you will obey your husbands and you young people know that you will obey your parents, and our captains and if any fail to do so, we will give them nothing to eat. (:18:107).

Women's responses ranged from zealous compliance to rebelliousness. An incident illustrating compliance with a husband's wishes, and suggesting the internalization of guilt, occurred when a Christian woman joined some "games or public recreation" of which her husband did not approve.

> Having returned, her husband said to her, "If I were not a Christian, I would tell you that, if you did not care for me you should seek another husband to whom you would render more obedience; but having promised God not to leave you until death, I cannot speak to you thus, although you have offended me." This poor woman asked his forgiveness, without delay, and on the following morning came to see the Father who had baptized her, and said to him, "My Father, I have offended God, I have not obeyed my husband; my heart is sad; I greatly desire to make my confession of this" (:18:35).

Other women continued to have lovers, to solicit married men to take a second wife, and to defy or leave their husbands. One convert complained, "My wife is always angry; I fear that the Demons she keeps in my cabin are perverting the good that I received in holy Baptism." Le Jeune wrote of this man,

> Another time his wife aimed a knife at his thigh, and he, evading the blow, had only his robe injured, in which this Megera made a great slash. Thereupon he came to us; meeting some Savages on the way, he began to laugh. "See," said he, "the anger of her who considers me her servant; she thought she would be able to irritate me, but I have more power over myself than to fall into passion at the anger of a woman."

Le Jeune added, "It is strange what Enemies the Savages are of anger, and how this sin shocks them," and continued,

> I know not what this simple man has done to win her over to God. "If thou wilt believe," he said to her, "I will love thee above all things; I will wait upon thee in all thy needs, I will even perform the little duties that the women do, I will go for water and wood; I will love thee more than myself." He pinched his arm and said to her, "Dost thou see this flesh? I do not love it; it is God whom I love, and those who believe in him. If thou are not willing to obey him thou must go away from me; for I cannot love those who do not love God."

> His wife derided him: "Dost thou not see that we are all dying since they told us to pray to God? Where are thy relatives? Where

are mine? The most of them are dead. It is no longer a time to believe" (:20:195-97).

Another particularly revealing incident offers an important comment on Montagnais ethics, and indicates the growing distance between the missionized Montagnais, with their acceptance of corporeal punishment, and the unconverted. A Jesuit called some "chief men" together and, after commending them on putting a stop to "the disorderly conduct that occasionally occurred among them," expressed astonishment at their permitting a young baptized woman to live apart from her husband. The captain responsible for her replied that "he had tried all sorts of means to make her return to her duty and that his trouble had been in vain; that he would, nevertheless, make another effort." The Jesuit Father counseled him to consult his people and decide upon what was to be done for such disobedience. "They all decided upon harsh measures." 'Good advice,' they said, 'has not brought her to her senses; a prison will do so.' Two Captains were ordered to take her to Kebec and ... have her put in a dungeon." The woman fled, but they caught her and tied her to take her by canoe to Kebec. At this

> some Pagan young men, observing this violence, of which the Savages have a horror, and which is more remote from their customs than Heaven is from Earth, made use of threats, declaring that they would kill any one who laid a hand on the woman. But the Captain and his people, who were Christians, boldly replied that there was nothing that they would not do or endure, in order to secure obedience to God. Such resolution silenced the infidels.

To avoid being imprisoned, the woman "humbly begged to be taken back to Saint Joseph, promising thence forward she would be more obedient." Le Jeune stated,

> Such acts of justice cause no surprise in France, because it is usual there to proceed in that manner. But, among these peoples.... where everyone considers himself from birth, as free as the wild animals that roam in their great forest ... it is a marvel, or rather a miracle, to see a peremptory command obeyed, or any act of severity or justice performed.

> Some Savages, having heard that in France, malefactors are put to death, have often reproached us, saying that we were cruel—that we killed our own countrymen; that we had no sense. They asked us whether the relatives of those who were condemned to death did not seek vengeance. The Infidels still have the same ideas; but the Christians are learning, more and more, the importance of exercising Justice (:22:81-85).

Shortly afterwards, another act of violence towards a woman again threatened to provoke conflict between Christian and "pagan" Montagnais, and again called for commendation on the part of the recorder (in this instance, not Le Jeune, but Bartholemy Vimont). The Christian relatives of a young woman agreed in family council to beat her for speaking to a suitor against her parents' wishes: "We are taught that God loves obedience. We see the French practicing it; they have such a regard for that virtue that, if any one of them fail in it, he is punished. Parents chastise their own children, and masters their servants.

One of the relatives beat the girl and lectured other girls who had gathered: "This is the first punishment by beating that we have inflicted upon anyone of our Nation. We are resolved to continue it, if any one among us should be disobedient." Vimont commented:

> During the previous year the new Christians had a Savage put in prison. This year they have done more, for this last punishment seems to me very severe to be the first. Those who know the freedom and independence of these peoples, and the horror they have of restraint or bondage, will say that a slight touch of Heaven and a little grace are stronger and more powerful than the cannons and arms of kings and monarchs, which could not subdue them.

The angry suitor appealed to his father, who threatened the Christian Indians. They defended their action, saying that his son had not been affronted and that he should be satisfied with the girl's punishment. At this, Governor Montmagny had the suitor called in and, through an interpreter, warned the young man to be careful, saying he would consider any attack on the Christian Indians to be a personal attack upon him (:22:115-27).

LONG-RANGE IMPACT OF THE JESUIT PROGRAM

One must ask how fairly the *Jesuit Relations* can be used to evaluate the success of the Jesuit program for conversion and resocialization of the Montagnais-Naskapi. After all, the Jesuit fathers were, in effect, soliciting continued support for their work, and they spent many pages describing the piety of their converts. Furthermore, they drew heavily on second-hand reports from adherents to the mission who doubtless presented themselves in a favorable light when repeating conversations and describing incidents. However, as seen by quotations above, both Jesuits and converts reported fully and convincingly on the views and actions of the unconverted. There is no reason to doubt the evidence the *Relations* offer of the conflicting ideologies that caused profound social disruption for the group as a whole and deep psychological turmoil for those individuals, both women and men, who made an often agonizing decision to give up traditional beliefs and practices and adhere to new codes of conduct and commitment. Therefore, although they do not reveal the actual extent of conversion that took place among the Montagnais-Naskapi during the seventeeth century, the *Jesuit Relations* document in detail what is more significant: the nature of responses to the Jesuit program, ranging from zealous dedication, through formal conversion, that might well involve backsliding, to indifference, and finally, to active hostility.

With respect to female-male relations, premarital chastity, male courtship, monogamy, and marital fidelity became accepted as ideal behavioral norms by dedicated converts. In 1639, Le Jeune wrote of the "evil custom" whereby a man who was courting a woman would go to her to make love at night, and he advised the girls to refer their suitors to the Jesuits (:16:61). Several years later Vimont reported that an old woman, "touched by the fear of God," gave the names of young unmarried lovers, who protested that such "suits of marriage" were "customary among them." The young people were lectured by their elders to "declare your affections to your parents; take their advice and that of the Father .... Make your visits by day and not by night; the faith and the prayer forbid this custom (:24:139). Some people, Vimont reported, had already adopted a new form of courtship, whereby a suitor would send a girl a bark painting of a young couple "holding each other by the hand, in the position that they assume in Church when they get married." A girl who was rejecting her suitor would send the drawing back (:22:71).

In keeping with the reciprocity of Montagnais-Naskapi female-male relations, converted men accepted the same standards as were enjoined on women. Le Jeune wrote that he had heard on good authority "that some shameless women, who have approached some men at night and solicited them to do evil in secret, received for answer only these words: "I believe in God, I pray to him every day; he forbids such actions, I cannot commit them" (:16:61). Nor would a "worthy captain" take a second wife, even when solicited by the woman herself, but answered, "You come too late, I have given my word to God I cannot gainsay it. I will obey him; I have said to him, "I will obey thee' and I will do it" (:16:145).

The influence, direct and indirect, of formulating such ideals as these was enhanced by the Jesuit work with children. Le Jeune wrote,

> We have done so much for these poor unbelievers that they have given us some of their daughters, which seems to me an act of God .... These little girls are dressed in the French fashion; they care no more for the Savages than if they did not belong to their Nation. Nevertheless, in order to wean them from their native customs, and to give them an opportunity of learning the French language, virture and manners, that they may afterwards assist their countrywomen, we have decided to send two or three to France, to have them kept and taught in the house of hospital

nuns .... Oh if we could only send a certain one who is to remain in the house of which I have spoken .... The child has nothing savage about her except her appearance and color; her sweetness, her docility, her modesty, her obedience, would cause her to pass for a wellborn French girl, fully susceptible of education.

Le Jeune followed this entry with a reference to his wish for a building in Quebec, where three classes could be lodged, "the first of little French children, of whom there will be perhaps twenty or thirty Pupils; the second, of Hurons; the third, of Montagnes" (:9:103).

For their part, the Montagnais expressed resentment that their presentation of children to the French was not reciprocated. A "captain" complained "One does not see anything else but little Savages in the houses of the French; there are little boys there and little girls,—what more do you want? ... You are continually asking for our children, and you do not give yours; I do not know any family among us which keeps a Frenchman with it" (:9:233).

The contrast between the Montagnais attitude towards sharing children and that of the French was expressed by Le Jeune's statement that "they think they are doing you some great favor in giving you their children to instruct, feed and dress" (:5:197). Perhaps no incident in the *Relations* more poignantly reveals the cultural distance to be spanned by Montagnais converts than that in which a French drummer boy hit a Montagnais with his drumstick, drawing blood. The Montagnais onlookers took offense, saying, "Behold, one of thy people has wounded one of ours; thou knowest our custom well; give us presents for this wound." The French interpreter countered, "Thou knowest our custom; when any of our number does wrong, we punish him. This child has wounded one of your people; he shall be whipped at once in thy presence." When the Montagnais saw the French were in earnest about whipping the boy,

> they began to pray for his pardon, alleging he was only a child, that he had no mind, that he did not know what he was doing; but as our people were nevertheless going to punish him, one of the Savages stripped himself entirely, threw his blanket over the child and cried out to him who was going to do the whipping; "Strike me if thou wilt, but thou shalt not strike him," And thus the little one escaped (:5:219).

This incident took place in 1633. How was it possible that scarcely ten years later, adults could be beating, withholding food from, and even, if the report is accurate, doing such things as throwing hot ashes on children and youths? Above, I have referred to the punitiveness toward the self and others that accompanied the often tormented attempt on the part of converts to reject a familiar set of values and replace it with another. This psychological response is familiar. To say this, however, merely presses the next question: Why did some Montagnais feel so strongly impelled to make this attempt? The answer is that the Jesuits and their teachings arrived in New France a full century after the economic basis for unquestioned cooperation, reciprocity, and respect for individual autonomy began to be undercut by the trading of furs for European goods. On the basis of new economic ties, some Montagnais-Naskapi were interested in attaching themselves to the mission station and the new European settlement, thereby availing themselves of the resources these offered. By the same token, some were prepared to accept the beliefs and ritual practices of the newcomers, and to adopt—or attempt to adopt—new standards of conduct.

Elsewhere, I have documented the process whereby the stockpiling of furs for future return, to be acquired when the trading ships arrived, contradicted the principle of total sharing based on subsistence hunting, fishing, and gathering (Leacock 1954). The process has subsequently been well described for the Canadian sub-Arctic generally, and it has been pointed out that parallel processes are involved when a horticultural people becomes involved in exchange relations with a market economy (Murphy and Steward 1955).

At the same time that the fur trade was undercutting the foundation for Montagnais-Naskapi values and interpersonal ethics, the terrible scourge of epidemic disease, the escalation (or introduction) of warfare, and the delusion of relief from anxiety offered by alcohol were also undermining Montagnais-Naskapi self-assurance. Alfred Goldsworthy Bailey (1969) has described the effects of these developments in a review of the conflict between European and eastern Algonkian cultures during the sixteenth and seventeenth centuries. Fear of disease, particularly smallpox which raged in the decade after the priests' arrival, was only equaled by fear of the Iroquois. The prolonged and intricate torture of Iroquois prisoners, into which women entered with even more zeal than men, was a grim expression of profound fearfulness and anger. Alcohol, which temporarily elated the spirits, led to fights around the European settlement; in 1664 there is reference to a case of rape committed under its influence (:48:227).

This is not to say, however, that Montagnais-Naskapi society as a whole was thoroughly disrupted. The violence that occurred around the European settlement contrasts not only with the friendliness, gaiety, and lack of quarreling that Le Jeune described during the winter he spent in the interior in 1633-34, but also with the general cooperativeness and good will—albeit laced with raucous banter and teasing—that characterized Montagnais-Naskapi life in later centuries in the rest of the Labrador Peninsula. Quebec was, after all, a gateway to the North American interior, and fur-trading posts and mission stations pushed ever westward. The nonracist policy of building a French colony in part with resocialized Indians was abandoned and replaced by a hardening color line. In time, all Montagnais-Naskapi became Catholic, but without the close supervision of the Jesuits, they retained established religious practices and added Catholic sacraments and prayer. During the summer of 1951, the "shaking-tent rite," in which a religious practitioner converses with the gods, both gaining useful information and entertaining an audience in the process, was still being practiced in eastern Labrador.

The pace of change in most of the Labrador Peninsula was slow, as Indians living far from centers of early settlement and trade gradually became drawn into a fur-trapping economy. In the summer of 1950, I was able to document the final stages of transition in southeastern Labrador, at a time when the next major change was about to transform life for French and English fishermen and fur-trappers as well as Montagnais-Naskapi hunter-trappers; a railroad was being built into a huge iron mine deep in the north-central part of the peninsula. When I was there, conditions in the north woods were still such that the traditional Montagnais-Naskapi ethic of cooperativeness, tolerance, and nonpunitiveness remained strong.

What about the relations between women and men? As in seventeeth century accounts, one can still find contrasting judgements. Burgesse (1944) has written that:

> labour is fairly equitably divided between the sexes under the economic system of the Montagnais. Each sex has its own particular duties but, within certain limits, the divisions between the types of work performed are not rigid. A man would not consider it beneath his dignity to assist his wife in what are ordinarily considered duties peculiar to the woman. Also, women are often enough to be seen performing tasks which are usually done by men. On being questioned in regard to this aspect of their economics, the Montagnais invariably reply that, since marriage is an union of co-equal partners for mutual benefit, it is the duty of the husband to assist his wife in the performance of her labors. Similarly, it is the duty of the wife to aid the husband....
>
> The Montagnais woman is far from being a drudge. Instead she is a respected member of the tribe whose worth is well appreciated and whose advice and counsel is listened to and, more often than not, accepted and acted upon by her husband (4-7).

Earlier, and by contrast, Turner had written:

> The sexes have their special labors. Women perform the drudgery and bring home the food slain by their husbands, fetching wood and water, tanning the skins, and making them into clothing. The labor of erecting the tents and hauling the sleds when on their journey during the winter falls upon them, and, in fact, they perform the greater part of the manual labor. They are considered inferior to men, and in their social life they soon show the effects of the hardships they undergo (1894:271).

One could take these statements at face value as reflecting differences between two Montagnais-Naskapi bands, for the first statement refers to the southerly Lake St. John people and the second to the Ungava people of the north. However, the continuation of Turner's account reveals realities of Ungava life that contradict his formal statement.

> An amusing incident occurred within a stone's throw of Fort Chimo. An Indian had his clothes stripped from him by his enraged wife. She then took the tent from the poles, leaving him naked. She took their property to the canoe, which she paddled several miles upstream. He followed along the bank until she relented, whereupon their former relations were resumed, as though nothing had disturbed the harmony of their life. The man was so severely plagued by his comrades that for many days he scarcely showed his head out of the tent (Ibid.).

Translating the incident into the terms of political economy, women retained control over the products of their labor. These were not alienated, and women's production of clothing, shelter, and canoe covering gave them concomitant practical power and influence; despite formal statements of male dominance that might be elicited by outsiders. In northern Labrador in the late nineteenth century, dependence on trading furs for food, clothing, and equipment was only beginning. Band cohesion was still strong, based on the sharing of meat, fish, and other necessities and on the reciprocal exchange of goods and services between women and men.

By the middle of this century, the economic balance had tipped in favor of ultimate dependence upon the fur trade (and, in many cases, wage labor) throughout the entire Labrador Peninsula. The Montagnais-Naskapi lived in nuclear family units largely supported by the husband and father's wages or take from the trap line. Nonetheless, the resources of the land were still directly used, were still available to anyone, were acquired cooperatively insofar as it was most practical, and were shared. Furthermore, partly through their own desire and partly in accord with the racist structure of Western society, the Montagnais-Naskapi maintained their status as a semi-autonomous people and were not separated into an elite minority versus a majority of marginal workers. Thus, a strong respect for individual autonomy and an extreme sensitivity to the feelings of others when decisions were to be made went with a continuing emphasis on generosity and cooperativeness, which applied to relations between as well as within the sexes.

In my own experience living in a Montagnais-Naskapi camp, I noted a quality of respectfulness between women and men that fits Burgesse's characterization. I also observed such behavior as an ease of men with children, who would take over responsibility even for infants when it was called for, with a spontaneity and casual competence that in our culture would be described as "maternal". Nonetheless, men were "superior" in ways commonly alluded to in anthropological literature. The few shamans who still practiced their art (or admitted practicing it to an outsider) were men; band chiefs were men; and patrilocality was both an ideal and statistically more common among newlyweds than matrilocality. In short, Montagnais-Naskapi practice at this time fitted what is considered in the anthropological literature to be usual for people who live (or have recently lived) by direct acquisition and use of wild products: strongly egalitarian, but with an edge in favor of male authority and influence.

Seventeenth century accounts, however, referred to female shamans who might become powerful (Thwaites 1906:6:61;14:183). So-called "outside chiefs," formally elected according to government protocol to mediate with white society, had no more influence within the group than their individual attributes would call for (Leacock 1958); and matrilocality had only recently given way to patrilocal postmarital residence (Leacock 1955). As markedly different as Montagnais-Naskapi culture continued to be from Western culture, the ethnohistorical record makes clear that it had been constantly restructuring itself to fit new situations and that the status of women, although still relatively high, had clearly changed.

NOTES

1. This article is based in large part on a paper written in collaboration with Jacqueline Goodman (Leacock and Goodman 1976). An ethnohistorical summary of Montagnais-Naskapi culture in the seventeenth century can be found in Leacock (forthcoming).

2. The anthropological term for the native population of the Labrador Peninsula, exclusive of the Eskimo, is "Montagnais-Naskapi." At times I shall use the simpler "Montagnais," a name applied by the French to the various groups that summered on the north shore of the St. Lawrence river. Like the Algonkins, the Montagnais are an Algonkian-speaking people.

3. Actually, men usually made canoe frames, and women covered them, though either sex could do both if necessary.

4. Parallel cousins are the children of two sisters or two brothers (and their spouses). Children of a brother and a sister (and their spouses) are called "cross-cousins." As is common in many kin-based societies, the Montagnais-Naskapi terms for parallel cousins were the same as for siblings, while the terms for cross-cousins, who were desirable marriage partners, connoted something like "sweetheart" (Strong 1929).

REFERENCES

Bailey, Alfred Goldsworthy. 1969. *The Conflict of European and Eastern Algonkian Cultures, 1504-1700.* Toronto: University of Toronto Press.

Burgesse, J. Allan. 1944. "The Woman and the Child among the Lac-St-Jean Montagnais." *Primitive Man* 17:102:1-19.

Leacock, Eleanor. 1954. "The Montagnais 'Hunting Territory' and the Fur Trade." *American Anthropological Association Memoirs* 78.

———. 1955. "Matrilocality in a Simple Hunting Economy (Montagnais-Naskapi)." *Southwestern Journal of Anthropology* 11:31-47.

———. 1958. "Status Among the Montagnais-Naskapi of Labrador." *Ethnohistory* 5:200-9.

———. 1969. "The Montagnais-Naskapi Band." In David Damas, ed., *Contributions to Anthropology: Band Societies*. National Museums of Canada Bulletin 228. Ottawa: Queens Printer for Canada.

———. Forthcoming "The Montagnais-Naskapi of the Seventeenth Century: Social Relations and Attitudes, from the Relations of Paul Le Jeune." In June Helm, ed., *Subarctic*. Handbook of North American Indians, vol. 6. Washington: Smithsonian Institution.

Leacock, Eleanor and Jacqueline Goodman. 1976. "Montagnais Marriage and the Jesuits in the Seventeenth Century: Incidents from the Relations of Paul Le Jeune." *Western Canadian Journal of Anthropology* 6, 3:77-91.

Murphy, Robert F. and Julian H. Steward. 1955. "Tappers and Trappers: Parallel Processes in Acculturation." *Economic Development and Cultural Change* 4:335-55.

Strong, William Duncan. 1929. "Cross-cousin Marriage and the Culture of the Northeastern Algonkian." *American Anthropologist* 31:277-88.

Thwaites, R. G., ed. 1906. *The Jesuit Relations and Allied Documents*, 71 vols. Cleveland: Burrows Brothers Co.

Turner, Lucien. 1894. *Ethnology of the Ungava District, Hudson Bay Territory*. 11th Annual Report, Bureau of American Ethnology.

2 Sunksquaws, Shamans, and Tradeswomen:
Middle Atlantic Coastal Algonkian Women During the 17th and 18th Centuries

ROBERT STEVEN GRUMET

The consolidation and expansion of the modern nation-states of Western Europe occurred simultaneously toward the end of the fifteenth century. Revolutionary technological advances in guns, ships, and sails coupled with increased production, population, and increasingly efficient bureaucracies enabled the burgeoning Portuguese and Spanish monarchies to expand into Africa, Asia, and Oceania. The bureaucratically recognized discovery of America accomplished under Spanish auspices in 1492, quickly drew both powers into extensive colonial enterprises throughout the New World.

Iberian navigators swiftly charted much of the American coastline from Patagonia to Newfoundland. Rapacious military columns searching for precious metals and slaves probed deeply into both continents by 1550. The Portuguese confined most of their colonial activities to South America, while Spain concentrated on developing and holding its South and Central American and Caribbean empire. Overextended and concerned with the protection of the all-important lifeline between the American colonies and the homeland, the Spanish restricted further expansion into North America to the occupation and fortification of the strategic Florida coastline astride her main convoy route.

Both France and England fitfully contested the sixteenth-century Iberian colonial monopoly. The English crown supported the voyages of the Cabot brothers to the mouth of the St. Lawrence River in 1497 and 1498. British joint-stock companies chartered during the latter 1500s sponsored voyages of discovery and colonies in Newfoundland and Virginia. Preoccupied, however, with civil war, the Reformation, and massive population losses caused by the Black Death and other epidemics, neither France nor England was able to threaten substantially the Spanish hold over its northern frontier during the sixteenth century.

Spanish control over North America noticeably weakened during the first decades of the seventeenth century. Largely freed from the struggles of the preceding century, the floodtide of English, French, and Dutch imperialism washed Middle Atlantic shores. Champlain's voyages between 1604 and 1618 established French hegemony in lower Canada and the maritime provinces. The Dutch, winning independence from Spain in 1609, struck at Spanish, Portuguese, and Arabian shipping lanes and seized an extensive overseas empire in the space of a very few years. English freebooters and slavers scoured the Atlantic shoreline from Maine to the Carolinas, trading and raiding for furs and slaves. Dutch claims to the Delaware and Hudson River valleys were secured by the autumn 1609 voyage of Henry Hudson. To the south the third English attempt to plant a colony in Virginia finally succeeded when Jamestown was founded in 1607, and Massachusetts Bay was settled in 1620 at Plymouth.

The English and Dutch soon consolidated their positions along the coast. Reconnoitering expeditions fanned out from New England, New Netherland, and Virginia. Native groups were contacted along the coast and in the immediate interior, and a complex system of alliances with native groups was swiftly grafted upon the ready baroque complexities of European international diplomacy.

Fiercely competitive and mutually hostile, the European colonists immediately vied for native furs, foodstuffs, and military support. Intercolonial rivalry in the Middle Atlantic region matched the tempo of the international struggle for imperial supremacy that gripped the Western European nations during the seventeenth century. Colonial policies concerning the Coastal

Algonkians were governed by the requirements of empire throughout the historic contact period. Often ignored by scholars, the imperial context of native-European contact in the Middle Atlantic region is essential to the analysis of Coastal Algonkian culture.

The coastal Algonkian peoples of the Middle Atlantic coast were among the first Native Americans to experience extensive direct contact with European colonies. This contact was punctuated by wasting epidemics, warfare, and increasing demands for native lands. Noting the punishing circumstances that accompanied European intrusion into the region, scholars have traditionally held that Coastal Algonkian society quickly buckled and broke under the strain of contact. The case for this opinion has indeed been convincing; the majority of the Coastal Algonkian population was in westward exile by the end of the eighteenth century.

This study differs from its predecessors in that it stresses the adaptive dimensions of the native response to European intrusion. This viewpoint is supported by the fact that the Coastal Algonkians managed to maintain an independent existence in the midst of a pervasive and often hostile European presence. A review of the ethnohistoric documentation further shows the persistence of native cultural forms throughout the Middle Atlantic region. Nowhere is this more convincingly demonstrated than in the continuing importance of women in Coastal Algonkian society during the seventeenth and eighteenth centuries. It is the purpose of this chapter to examine the impact of European colonialism upon the position of Coastal Algonkian women during the historic contact period.[2] Their continuing authority will be examined in its political, religious, and economic contexts. It will be shown that changes in these variables did not disrupt or distort native life in the Middle Atlantic region.

The Coastal Algonkians were a farming, fishing, hunting, and gathering people who closely followed the seasons and watercourses of their Middle Atlantic homeland.[3] They lived in villages and camps of bark-, grass-, or mat-walled longhouses and round houses that sheltered anywhere from a few families to several hundred individuals. Certain communities occasionally swelled to contain several thousand people during festivals, trade fairs, and wartime. Groups that lived close to the seashore primarily depended upon the products of the sea. They netted, speared, and trapped fish, caught and gathered shellfish—grinding the shells of periwinkles and quahogs into a medium of exchange commonly known as wampum—gathered grasses and berries from the dunes, and rendered whales stranded on the beaches into oil. These they traded for the agricultural and hunting produce of their interior neighbors, who further supplied stone tools, wood, and other forest and fresh-water resources to the outer coastal groups.

46   Women and Colonization

The Coastal Algonkian peoples centered their habitations in the sheltered bays and harbors of the coast and along the banks of the great rivers that reached into the interior toward the Appalachian Mountains. Their major groups included the Wampanoag and Massachusett of Massachusetts Bay, the Narragansett and Niantic of Rhode Island, the Mohegan and Pequot of eastern Connecticut, their Montauk neighbors on eastern Long Island, the Delawaran-speaking groups from western Long Island and southeastern New York south to eastern Pennsylvania and upper Delaware, the Nanticoke, Conoy, and Accomack of the Delmarva Peninsula, and the Powhatan of the western shore of the lower portion of Chesapeake Bay. It is important to note that each of these names generally referred to a linguistic group and not to a political entity. Coastal Algonkian society was exceedingly localized, and groups joined with or fought each other without regard to a larger "Algonkian" identity.

SUNKSQUAWS

A reexamination of the upper Delawaran data from northern New Jersey (Grumet 1979) has revealed the existence of five levels of sociopolitical integration in Coastal Algonkian society.[4]

The clan: Matrilineal-matrilocal corporate kinship groups were the primary locally important form of Coastal Algonkian sociopolitical organization. All domestic affairs were regulated by the matriclan. Decisions concerning subsistence, social life, and family religious obligations were made by the corporate kingroup. The clan was also the least visible societal form in the ethnohistoric documentation. This was due to the fact that European chroniclers were primarily concerned with their relations with the native groups. Clans were almost wholly concerned with domestic issues that rarely found a place in the international arena. Their activities were thus rarely included in the European records.

The village: The Coastal Algonkian village usually consisted of several long- or roundhouses, each containing a matrilineal-matrilocal kinship group. Settlements contained from one or two small familial segments to upwards of several hundred individuals. The village was the primary international agent of Coastal Algonkian society. Concerned with adjudicating intravillage affairs and mobilizing for extra-village issues, the village level of organization was a conspicuous ethnohistoric sociocultural entity in the Middle Atlantic region.

The district: The district consisted of a fluid combination of villages and matrisib segments located in a limited area. Not to be confused with a family hunting territory which did not exist among the coastal groups during the contact period, the district was a cooperatively exploited economic zone that permitted members of different social groups to use a wide range of planting areas, gathering zones, hunting and fishing locales, and other resource extraction activity sites. Districts were a flexible intergroup sociopolitical entity that permitted cooperation without co-optation.

The tribe:[5] Tribes consisted of a set of villages from a limited portion of a river's drainage system. More formal and territorially larger than the district organization, the tribe was a high-level response to international stress. The tribal structure was invoked when issues regarding major economic relationships, international diplomacy, and warfare were raised. Tribal constituency was not fixed and varied in direct proportion to the types of problems presented. Locality and autonomy were cardinal principles of Coastal Algonkian life, and individuals and groups not in accord with group policies could not be forced into conformity. The ever changing nature of international relations insured constant changes in tribal group membership.

The Confederacy: Not present for appreciable periods of time in the upper Delawaran data, the confederacy did occur in Massachusetts Bay, the mid-Hudson region, and the Chesapeake Bay. Relatively inflexible and riddled with problems of succession and jurisdiction, this level of sociopolitical integration functioned most coherently during times of unusual international stress. Many Coastal Algonkian confederacies were, however, successfully maintained during less stressful times throughout the early historic contact period. These confederacies were located at or nearby centers of European intrusion, sources of nearly continual stress. Colonial authorities carefully identified and cultivated native leaders and polities favorably disposed towards them. These international relationships frequently determined the continued existence of many confederacies. Far more stratified than other forms of Coastal Algonkian sociopolitical organization, confederacies also contained larger populations and encompassed considerable territories.

Each level of Coastal Algonkian sociopolitical integration was governed by a civil leader and council during peacetime; civil leaders were known as *sachems, sagamores,* or *cockarouse.* Each level further had a war captain and staff which took over the governmental reins during periods of hostility. Neither form of government unilaterally assumed authority. Civil polities were required to declare war and install the military regime, and the war leadership, in its turn, was obliged to reinstate the civil government in order to conclude a peace. Control thus continually lay with the civil leadership in Coastal Algonkian society.

Civil decisions were made by consensus throughout the Middle Atlantic region. Consensus was not unanimity of opinion or decision. It was arrived at when people consented to judgment and decision (Silberbauer n.d.: 11) Those not in accord with a specific policy were free to remove themselves from those who invoked it. This lack of formal constraints led many observers to discount the efficacy of Coastal Algonkian leaders and polities.[6]

Accounts by a wide variety of European observers delineated the considerable authority of Coastal Algonkian civil leadership. Succession was matrilineally determined with a rule of primogeniture (see Wallace, 1947; Barnes, 1968; and Simmons and Aubin, 1975). Ability was a paramount consideration, and incompetent leaders could be superseded by their younger siblings. Unable to arbitrarily order any action, those in leadership positions were provided an opportunity, rather than a mandate, to authority; power depended upon the power of persuasion rather than the persuasion of power. Subtle diplomatic skills and an abundant amount of time for what Silberbauer termed "the attrition of alternatives" (: 12) were required for effective leadership. The elaborate rituals and time-consuming deliberations irritatingly noted by Europeans were thus an intimate part of the traditional Coastal Algonkian governmental process. All viewpoints were entitled to a hearing, and the input of participants often substantially altered the shape of the final decision.

Civil leaders were permitted multiple spouses. They were thus able to establish strong, reciprocal, kinship relationships with other lineages. The first wife of a chief was considered the most important and had to come from a highly ranked matrilineage. A rule of exogamy insured that first wives came from other groups, thus forming a basis for intergroup relationships. Other wives could come from within the group, thus cementing internal relations. Particularly successful upper-level chiefs often had spouses from many of the lineages of their constituencies. These connections thus facilitated relations with constituent groups, and enabled the children of these unions to succeed to leadership positions in their respective groups. This insured a continual line of succession in these polities.

Civil leaders further had the right to gather and redistribute internally produced and externally obtained resources, exact fines and blood money, determine the timing of food getting and other resource extraction activities, and mediate civil disputes. Their power over domestic production and trade formalized reciprocal relationships both within and without their groups. Their prerogative to mediate internal civil disputes further allowed them to have a say in determining the continued structure of their constituencies. Superior civil chiefs were thus able to attract desirable followers and drive away malcontents. It is clear that astute, subtle, and facilitative civil leaders possessed considerable authority so long as they were not authoritarian.

War leaders achieved their positions through appropriate vision experiences, and their vocations were confirmed by demonstrated proficiency. These war captains were given total control over their group during time of war. More authoritarian than civil leaders, war captains were nevertheless constrained by the will of their followers. War leaders needed followers and their material support, and unsuccessful or immoderately overbearing war captains invariably found themselves without either.

Both civil and war leaders depended upon a council for advice and consent. Civil councils consisted of aged and respected leaders, while military staffs were made up of older, successful warriors. These councils were convened at every level of Coastal Algonkian society. Thus, members of a confederacy council included the siblings of the confederacy chief who often served as the sachems of the constituent tribes, other tribal chiefs, and a selection of outstanding council members from the tribes. Tribal councils consisted of district chiefs, often close relatives of the tribal sachem, and a representative sample of aged district leaders. And so it went down to the clan level, for which no formal documentary information has survived.

The position of Coastal Algonkian women in this leadership structure has not received attention in the secondary literature. Both Heckewelder (1876) and Zeisberger (1910) failed to mention women in their lengthy descriptions of Delawaran leadership during the westward exile. Eight out of eleven sources listed in Kinietz (1946: 29) noted that women could not be chiefs. The remaining three citations made no mention of women leaders. These same sources stated that "women had no voice in council and were only admitted at certain times" (: 56). Roger Williams translated the Narragansett term *saunks* as "the Queen, or Sachims Wife," with the plural "Queenes" translating out as *sauncksquuaog* (Williams 1866:163). He nowhere indicated that these *sauncksquuaog* were anything more than wives.

The ethnographic record has indicated otherwise. Even a cursory scanning of the widely available primary documentation clearly shows the considerable role played by Coastal Algonkian women throughout the historic contact period. Many sources state that women were able to inherit chiefly office.[7] Others note that women sachems were often the sisters or wives of male leaders who succeeded them upon their decease. This does not mean that every "sunksquaw's" husband or brother was a leader. Many women sachems were married to men who made no pretension to leadership.

The first mention of a women leader occurred simultaneously with the first records of the first successful English colony in the Middle Atlantic region. The English colony of Jamestown was established in Virginia in 1607, and the colonists immediately became embroiled in the tortuous politics of the Powhatan confederacy and its neighbors. John Smith mentioned the "Queene of Appamatuck" in his first reports (1907: 101). Noting that she was the elder sister of Wahunsunacock, the paramount sachem of the Powhatan confederacy, Smith further recorded her presence in several confederacy councils, including the one that meditated his death. Rescued from execution by Wahunsunacock's daughter Mataoka, or Pocahontas, Smith later burned the Appamatuck queen's village in 1610. This attack was one event in a bewilderingly complex and poorly understood series of English raids upon the Powhatan and their neighbors during the 1610's. Infuriated by English belligerence, the Powhatan attacked the English in 1622 and again in 1644. Both wars caused extensive losses to both sides, the latter conflict bringing an end to the independent existence of the Powhatan confederacy in 1646. This did not, however, put an end to the ability of women to lead groups in the Chesapeake Bay region. George Fox, the founder of the Quaker religion, wrote that "the old Empress [of Accomack]...sat in council" during his visit to their town in Maryland on March 24, 1673 (1952: 653). Writing in 1705 about the natives of Virginia, Robert Beverley listed "Pungoteque, Govern'd by a Queen, but a small nation" and "Nanduye. A seat of the Empress. Not above 20 Families, but she hath all the Nations of this shore under Tribute" (Beverley 1947: 232). These sources clearly indicate that women led groups at both the village and tribe level long after the earlier Powhatan confederation was dispersed.

The English established colonies in Massachusetts Bay at Plymouth in 1620 and near modern Boston nine years later. These settlements were preceded by an outbreak of bubonic plague that swept away much of the native population of southern New England between 1617 and 1619. The effects of this epidemic, coupled with continual warfare with the Abenaki to the north in Maine, severely weakened the Massachusett and Wampanoag confederacies of the area and led the Wampanoag to ally themselves with the English when they established their first colony at Plymouth in 1620. The Massachusett chose to remain aloof and were subsequently attacked by the English the following year. It was at that time that Squa-Sachim, or the "Massachusetts Queen" was noted as the leader of the Massachusett confederacy (Mourt 1841: 225). She was the widow of the paramount sachem Nanepashemet, who was killed by an Abenaki war party in 1619.

The disasters that befell the Massachusett markedly reduced the ability of the "squa-sachim of Puckanokick" to maintain control over the constituent groups of the confederacy (Winslow 1841: 317). She was forced to align herself with the English, and their records show that she continually sold land to them and represented their interests in native diplomacy up to her death in 1667.

The increasing number of English settlers in Massachusetts Bay during the first three quarters of the seventeenth century led to a corresponding increase in the desire for native land. The native population, continually decreasing and increasingly demoralized, sought to accomodate their English allies. A devastating smallpox epidemic struck the Wampanoag and their neighbors in 1633. In 1637 the English allied with the Mohegan and Narragansett to disperse the populous and powerful Pequot group in western Connecticut. English attempts to convert the southern New England groups to Christianity in mission stations seriously competed with the authority of the traditional confederacies. England had further consolidated her hold over the Middle Atlantic region by expelling the Dutch from New Netherland in 1664. Events were quickly building to a major war between the English and the native confederacies.

The influential Narragansett sunksquaw Quaiapan, also known as Magnus and Matantuck, was first mentioned in 1667, the year of Squa-Sachim's death. Sister to the Niantic sachem Ninigret, she was married to Mexanno, son of the Narragansett leader Canonicus. She achieved her first documentary notices after she had dispatched a force of 300 warriors against the interior Nipmuck for defying her authority. This force terrorized and plundered their villages. Asked for the reasons for the attack by the Massachusetts Bay Colony Commissioners, she proved herself an accomplished Coastal Algonkian diplomat in stating that her warriors "did in moderacion deal with those Nipnape Indyans...in lov...[and] in a mild and gentell manner" (Eva Butler, quoted in Speck 1947: 50).

The Narragansett continually counseled the Wampanoag against going to war with the English. When the conflict, known as the King Philip's War finally broke out in 1675, the Narragansett chose neutrality. Quaiapan was a village leader in 1675 and commanded the Queen's Fort to the north of the main Narragansett fortress in the swamps of Rhode Island. The Narragansett were forced into the widening conflict when the English attacked the main Narragansett fortress during the winter of 1675–76. The English records note that Quaiapan commanded her warriors from her bastion near the Great Swamp until she was killed by English forces in the spring of 1676 (see Leach 1958).

The Pocasset sunksquaw Weetamoo was first noted as the widow of the Wampanoag sachem Alexander, the brother of King Philip who died in 1662 (N.S., 1913a: 25). Later, she married Ninigret's son Quinnapin, and her sister became the spouse of King Philip after he succeeded his brother (N.S., 1913b: 55). Weetamoo became his ally soon after the conflict began and served as a war chief commanding over 300 warriors. The English captive Mary Rowlandson was given to Weetamoo following her capture in autumn 1675. Rowlandson described Weetamoo's appearance and behavior in her captivity journal published after the war (Rowlandson 1913). Weetamoo's forces dwindled as the tempo of English attacks increased during the spring of 1676. Reduced to less than 30 warriors, her followers were finally dispersed during the summer of 1676. Weetamoo herself drowned in early August during an attempt to escape into the interior (N.S., 1913c: 96).

Awashonks was another of Ninigret's sisters. She became the squaw sachem of the Sakonnet tribe of the Wampanoag confederation sometime before she first appeared in the documentary record in the July 24, 1671 submission to English jurisdiction. Her brother Tokamona, a Sakonnet under-sachem, opposed her moves, especially objecting to the clause stipulating that they surrender their firearms to the Plymouth colony. Awashonks managed to collect over 53 guns despite this opposition, but she was unable to get the English to come for them. They remained in her house until Tokamona signed the treaty on November 3. A number of old weapons were then sent to Plymouth as a token of submission while the more serviceable pieces were kept by the Sakonnets.

Awashonks sold a portion of Sakonnet territory to the English on July 31, 1673 (Church 1975: 25). Her brother was killed by a Narragansett war party the following year. She received a Wampanoag war embassy in early 1675,

52 Women and Colonization

but chose to remain neutral in the impending conflict. English aggressions and her people's desire for revenge finally forced her entry into the conflict in late 1675. Awashonks led her people against the English until forced to surrender in May 1676. Instrumental in convincing many of her warriors to then side with the English, Awashonks thus saved her followers from deportation into slavery to the West Indies, a fate met by many of the native belligerents at the close of the King Philip's War in 1676.

Further examples of woman's leadership come from the Esopus, a Delawaran group that inhabited the western portion of the mid-Hudson valley in New York state. This region became the heartland of the Dutch colony of New Netherland when it was established during the 1620s. The Esopus were first contacted by Europeans during the early Dutch trading expeditions of the 1610s. Bypassed by the Dutch traders in favor of the more lucrative commerce upriver controlled by the Mahican and Mohawk groups, the Esopus were also able to avoid participation in the Dutch wars of extermination against the lower Hudson River Delawarans in 1640–45 and 1655–57. Dutch expansion into their fertile lands in the Walkill valley during the late 1650s finally led to the Esopus wars of 1659–64. This conflict caused heavy losses among the Esopus and their allies. A combination of women and the young men (called "barebacks"), finally forced the war captains to sue for peace with the Dutch in 1664.

This alliance between the Esopus women and young men persisted long after the end of the Esopus wars. The English took control of New Netherland on September 6, 1664, and the "Esopes young men" signed as a political entity in the October 7, 1665 renewal of peace with the English government of New York (O'Callaghan and Fernow 1856–87: 13: 401). Heckewelder provided further evidence of the power of Delawaran women over young men over 100 years after the Esopus conflict (1876: 161). He reported that the mothers of persons interested in marriage served as negociatrixes for them. While final veto power often lay with the couple, the mothers arbitrated all other aspects of the arrangement.

The Esopus conflict did not destroy the Esopus confederation. The woman sachem Mamanuchqua was named as one of the five Esopus sachems in documents dated between 1675 and 1682. Listed in the company of two major Esopus sachems as Mamareoktwe on April 24, 1675 (Anon. 1906: 218), she next signed as Mamaroch with a notation of "her mark" next to her name in a document dated September 15, 1677 (O'Callaghan and Fernow 1856–87: 13: 507). Signing without reference to her gender as Mamaprocht in the January 19, 1681 reaffirmation of friendship with New York (Philhower n.d.), she made her last documentary appearance as the Esopus "squae" who participated in land sales near Catskil finalized on July 19–20, 1682 (O'Callaghan and Fernow 1856–87: 13: 572; Leder 1956: 65–68).

Ethnohistorians have traditionally assigned male gender to native figures in the documentary record unless otherwise identified. They have also tended to not identify native individuals as leaders unless so identified in the specific source. This policy, while properly cautious, has fostered the notion that all native persons mentioned in the documentation were both male and commoners unless otherwise identified. This practice has successfully masked the identities of a substantial number of Coastal Algonkian leaders of both sexes.

SHAMANS

Numerous sources have emphatically denied women's participation in spiritual and healing activities. Robert Beverley noted that native Virginian women never "intermeddled with any offices, that relate to the Priesthood, or Conjuration" (1947: 214). He further excluded women from the healing arts by observing that "their priests [were] always physicians, and by the method of their education in the priesthood, are made very knowing in the hidden qualities of plants" (1947: 217). William Simmons noted the existence of a single woman *powwow* in his survey of Southern New England shamanism and cosmology (1976: 223), citing the example of a woman religious practitioner from a statement by the English missionary John Eliot. Eliot wrote in 1647 that the minor Wampanoag sachem Waban "hath six sonnes, one of his sons was a Pawwaw, and his wife a great Pawwaw" (Eliot 1834: 19). Moreover, Daniel Gookin reported in 1674 that "there are among them certain men and women, whom they call powwows. These are partly wizards and witches...and partly are physicians" (Gookin 1792: 154). A further six or eight woman practitioners were observed working over the ill Wampanoag sachem Massasoit in March, 1623 (Winslow 1841: 317). The Quaker Roger Williams reported that the Narragansett had a woman's god called Squaunit (1866: 149).

More complete accounts of Coastal Algonkian medicine women appear in the reports of Tantaquidgeon (1972) and Heckewelder (1876). Writing about Delawaran culture, Tantaquidgeon stated that their herbalists were "generally women [though] occasionally a man [is] blessed with a vision (: 11). She further noted the existence of "certain men and women whose supernatural power enabled them to communicate with the dead, to locate lost persons and objects, and to foretell coming events" (: 18). Tantaquidgeon also recognized "the love doctor, usually a woman, [who employed] two varieties of roots for the magical rite" (: 15). A love doctor was reputed to be able to make a medicine sufficient to either bring couples together, keep them together, or break them apart.

The social significance of the love doctor has not been examined in the secondary literature. The ability to "match-make" couples and separate them determined the fate of many nuptial unions. Such an ability had enormous ramifications in the ongoing structure of native society. Women love doctors thus complemented mothers in controlling the majority of Coastal Algonkian marriage choices, a formidable and normally discreetly exercised source of power in native Middle Atlantic society.

Heckewelder wrote that "there are physicians of both sexes, who take considerable pains to acquire a correct knowledge of the properties and medical virtues of plants, roots, and barks" (1876: 228). He further wrote that woman physicians were particularly effective in the treatment "of complaints peculiar to their sex" (: 229). Both Heckewelder and Zeisberger noted that elder women and men specialized in the preparation of magic charms and potions. Heckewelder wrote that these included rain makers, producers of good luck charms for bad hunters, and brewers of love potions (: 236). Zeisberger stated that "older men and women, have another *beson* [medicine], supposed to have the magic power of bringing many presents to them" (1910: 83). He further reported that these were usually sold "by old women, who thus support themselves and promote superstition among the young" (: 83). In addition, "the graves are generally dug by old women as the young people abhor this kind of work" (: 89). Zeisberger also wrote that many old women were also considered witches who were alternately feared, propitiated, or burned (: 128).

The ethnohistoric evidence thus demonstrates that women participated in all Coastal Algonkian societies that did not have full-time organized priesthoods, which were found only in the Chesapeake Bay region. The southern New England and Delawaran practitioners discussed here were usually generalists who participated in many other institutions in their societies. Those who were both shamans and leaders, or shaman-warriors, possessed potent combinations that were especially influential. It must also be emphasized that spiritual sanctions were necessary concomitants to sociopolitical authority. People have always tended to follow leaders blessed by the support of heaven. Thus, group leaders always needed and rewarded the sponsorship of medicine persons.

It has been noted in neighboring societies that woman shamans were regarded as particularly powerful by virtue of their sex (Snow 1976: 283). These shamans were seen as possessing both male and female spirit power; thus the possible reason for Waban's son's wife being a "Great Pawwaw." It therefore followed that a woman shaman's support of a leader was highly desirable in societies where men had not yet seized control over the sacred. Such a monopoly could only occur in a stratified society like that present in the Chesapeake Bay region. Other Coastal Algonkian societies were not so stratified and did not have full-time priesthoods. Women in these latter societies thus persisted in possessing religious authority and controlled the rights to their abilities.

TRADESWOMEN

No single ethnographic fact of Coastal Algonkian life has been more firmly entrenched in the ethnohistoric documentation than the universal existence of the sexual division of labor throughout the Middle Atlantic region. John Smith phrased this ideology in 1607 thus:

> The men bestow their times in fishing, hunting, warres, and such man-like exercises, scorning to be seen in any woman-like exercise, which is the cause that the women be very painefull, and the men often idle. The women and children doe the rest of the worke. They make mats, baskets, pots, mortars, pound their corne, make their bread, prepare their victuals, plant their corne, gather their corne, beare all kinds of burdens, and such like (1907:64).

De Rasieres reported in 1628 that "the men would not once look to [cultivation], for it would compromise their dignity too much, unless they are very old and cannot follow the chase," (1909: 107). And Van der Donck noted of men in the New Netherland groups that

> when abroad they spend their time in hunting, fishing, or war; at home they smoke tobacco and play a game with pieces of reeds, resembling our card playing. The old men knit nets, and make wooden bowls and ladles. Labour among the young men is uncommon, and nearly all the necessary labour is done by the females (1968:94).

The modern scholar Ruth Carol Barnes found this division of labor so striking that she suggested a structural view of Delawaran society that divided it between a patrilineal, male-dominated hunting winter and a matrilineal, woman-dominated planting summer (1968: 15–16).

The actual division of labor in Coastal Algonkian society was in fact far less clear-cut. Van der Donck amended the above statement: "All their agriculture is performed by their women. The men give themselves very little about the same, except those who were old. They, with the young children, will do some labor under the direction of the women" (1968: 96). And Roger Williams noted that

> the Women set or plant, weede, and hill, and gather and barne all the corne, and Fruites of the field: Yet sometimes the man himselfe (either out of love to his wife, or care for his Children, or being an old man) will help the Woman which (by the custome of the Countrey) they are not bound to.
>
> When a field is to be broken up, they have a very loving sociable speedy way to dispatch it: All the neighbours men and Women forty, fifty, a hundred, &c., joyne, and come in to help freely.
>
> With friendly joyning they break up their fields, build their Forts, hunt the Woods, stop and kill fish in the Rivers (1866: 123).

This last statement presents a significant departure from the classic view of the

Coastal Algonkian division of labor. Even the more extreme passages mention the participation of certain old men and children in agriculture. The Williams account expands this by contrasting an ideology, "by the custome of the Countrey," with actual, observed behavior.

Production specializations certainly existed. Individual hunting of large game was generally the business of adult men. Tending gardens was generally performed by women. An exception to this was the cultivation of tobacco, small plots of which were planted by men (Williams 1866: 43). Many individual tasks were also the provinces of specific sexes. Gookin (1792: 151) noted that "the baskets and mats are always made by their women; their dishes, pots, and spoons are the manufactures of the men." Zeisberger reported that wampum belts were made by women (1910: 95). It is important to note, however, that such sexual labor preferences blurred as one aged. Older individuals of both sexes frequently performed tasks associated with a particular gender. It should be further noted that people of both sexes were capable of filling in when suitable specialists were absent.

The Coastal Algonkian data clearly indicate that all major tasks were cooperatively performed. Williams (1866: 188–89) noted that deer drives and the setting of deer traps were performed in groups of men and women. He further reported that both sexes participated in house building, the men getting the poles, and the women making and placing the mats that were the walls (: 60). Fishing was also a cooperative venture. Both sexes produced the weirs and nets that collected a portion of the enormous anadramous fish runs every spring. Men and women further speared, netted, and hooked fish from the shore and from canoes. Shellfishing, wild-plant gathering, and small-game hunting were also performed with equal competence by members of both genders. Thus, the major part of domestic production was achieved cooperatively in Coastal Algonkian society.

Trade was a significant component of the traditional Coastal Algonkian economy. Roger Williams again provided an excellent ethnographic description.

> Among themselves they trade their Corne, skins, Coates, Venison, Fish, &c. and sometimes come ten or twenty in a Company to trade amongst the English. They have some who follow onely making of Bowes, some Arrowes, some Dishes and (the Women make all of their earthen Vessells) some follow Fishing, some hunting: most on the sea-side make Money, and store up shells in Summer against Winter whereof to make their money (1866: 179-80).

Coastal Algonkian women played a major role in trade activities throughout the region. An English visit to the village of the Massachusetts Squaw sachem, on September 21, 1621, revealed that "almost all the women...sold their coats from their backs...[the English] promised them to come again to them, and they us to keep their skins" (Mourt 1841: 228). And Heckewelder noted that "the husband generally leaves the skins and peltry which he has procured by hunting to the care of his wife, who sells or bargains them away to the best advantage for such necessaries as are wanted in the family; not forgetting to supply her husband with what he stands in need of" (1876: 158).

This was the continuation of a venerable tradition. Women were first mentioned as traders in the following reference by Henry Hudson's first mate John Juet made during their visit to New York Harbor on September 12, 1609: "there came eight and twentie Canoes full of men, women and children to betray us: but we saw their intent, and suffered none of them to come aboord us...They brought with them Oysters and Beanes, whereof we bought some" (Juet 1909: 20). Much later on one trader at Albany, New York recorded that fully 20 percent of his transactions between 1695 and 1726 were made with women (Norton 1974: 28). Goods of specific interest to women, such as needles, awls, cloths and woolens of various types, kettles, flour, molasses, and tea, made up an even larger percentage of all goods traded in the Upper Delawaran area between 1630 and 1758 (see Grumet 1979).

Zeisberger particularly noted that "Many engage in rum traffic, especially women, who fetch it from the white people and sell at a considerable profit to the Indians, often taking from the latter everything they have, sometimes even their rifles on which they depend for subsistence" (1910: 90). He further identified these liquor peddlers as old women (: 118–19). The aged further made their living through the manipulation of the supernatural realm: "There are jugglers of another kind, in general old men and women, who although not classed among doctors and physicians, yet get their living by pretending to supernatural knowledge" (Heckewelder 1876: 236). Zeisberger provided further detail, reporting that

> older men and women have another Beson, supposed to have the magic power of bringing many presents to them. This charm they guard jealously among their most precious belongings, and it is said to have the effect of bringing them food, clothing, and whatever else they may need....A little of this preparation....is sold with a white and black wampum shell for a considerable price, often for a belt of wampum with several pounds in money....Usually, this is done by old women, who thus support themselves and promote superstition among the young (1910:83).

This institution combined the support of the aged with a reverence for their accumulated spiritual power and the perpetuation of the religious beliefs of the people. This security was also extended to aged men.

> When a whole party goes out to hunt, they govern themselves according to the wishes of the oldest or most expert, particularly if

he be a member of the council....If several take aim at once and they cannot determine which of them made the best shot, the skin is given to the oldest of the party, or, if he happened to be one of those taking aim, he is said to have killed the animal.... Such old men, accompanying a hunting party, get both meat and skins, for the good hunters will not let them return empty-handed (:91).

These data have established that women had prominent roles in both the domestic modes of production and in foreign trade. The disposition of goods within Coastal Algonkian society presents a further interesting feature. Zeisberger wrote that the production of each spouse is the property of the other (1910: 16), and Heckewelder noted that "the husband generally leaves the skins and peltry which he has procured by hunting to the care of his wife.... When a woman has got in her harvest of corn, it is considered as belonging to her husband....The sugar which she makes out of the maple tree is also considered as belonging to her husband" (1876: 158).

It is important to note that this internal exchange did not extend to either sex's tools of the trade or other means of production. Furthermore, the exchange continued after death.

> of inheritances they know nothing. Every Indian knows that what ever he leaves at his death is divided among his friends.... The friends do not keep a single article....They give what the deceased has left to their friends....If a dying Indian leaves his gun or any other trifle to a particular friend the legatee is immediately put in possession and no one disputes his right. The widow gets nothing, yet whatever the husband has given to his wife during his life-time remains her property. Therefore we need not wonder that a married Indian pair should not have their goods in common, for otherwise the wife would be left wholly destitute after her husband's death. In like manner the husband inherits nothing when his wife dies (Zeisberger 1910:87).

Goods and wealth flowed through many channels in Coastal Algonkian society. The civil sachems were required to entertain strangers (Beverley 1947; 188; Winslow 1841: 361), to "care for the widow and fatherless, also for such as are aged and any way maimed, if their friends be dead, or not able to provide for them" (: 360), and to cater all public events under their sponsorship. They were accordingly permitted a share of all major game taken, all whales and wrecks stranded on the beaches, and the first fruits gathered in their territories (Mayhew, in Speck 1928: 26–27). The alliance between sachems and shamans was further sealed by way of the following practice, described by Winslow:

> once a year the *pnieses* [shamans with war visions] use to provoke the people to bestow much corn on the sachim. To that end,

they appoint a certain time and place, near the sachim's dwelling, where the people bring many baskets of corn, and make a great stack thereof. These the *pnieses* stand ready to give thanks to the people, on the sachim's behalf; and after acquaint the sachim therewith, who fetcheth the same, and is no less thankful, bestowing many gifts on them (1841:362).

This source of income was certainly available to sunksquaws and the gifts from the activity to *pnieses* were likewise made to woman shamans.

This review has demonstrated that women played a key role in all phases of traditional Coastal Algonkian economic life. Like men, they were required to give a portion of what they produced to others, but both in return received goods others had produced. Both were also required to make gifts to political leaders, as indicative of their support, without which leadership ceased to be leadership. This egalitarian mode of production, and a corresponding, egalitarian sociopolitical organization characterized the middle Atlantic region except for the Chesapeake Bay area, and it persisted through the entire colonial period.

NOTES

1. Funding for this article was provided by a Phillips Fund Grant from the American Philosophical Society. I am indebted to the editors of this volume for valuable criticisms, and also acknowledge the assistance of Prof. Leigh Marlowe.

2. The sociocultural position of women in northeastern woodland society, of which the Coastal Algonkian were a part, has been the subject of a volume of inquiry unique in native North American ethnology. A significant portion of this literature has assessed the importance of women in several Iroquoian-speaking societies (Powell 1880; Randle 1951; Richards 1957; Brown 1970; Rothenberg, this volume). Far less scholarly attention has been focused upon the women of the neighboring Middle Atlantic Coastal Algonkians.

3. An excellent review of Coastal Algonkian culture and history may be found in Brasser (1971).

4. The most extensive accounts of Coastal Algonkian leadership are contained in Smith (1907), van Wassenaer (1909), Winslow (1841), de Rasieres (1909), van der Donck (1968), Gookin (1792), Penn (in Myers, 1937), Heckewelder (1876), and Zeisberger (1910).

5. I use the term tribe for want of a better word, but it is important to understand that it does not denote a fixed population living in a clearly defined territory under an established leadership.

6. Newcomb (1956:52) wrote that Delawaran leaders "had limited power and authority...owed allegience to no higher authority...and had little real authority." Van Wassenaer (1909:69), writing about the Natives of New Ne-

therland in 1624, stated that "there is little authority known among these nations."

7. Flannery (1939:145) listed women's inheritance of chiefly rank among the Massachusett, Natick, Saconnet, Martha's Vineyard (Wampanoag), Narragansett, Western Niantic, Scaticook, Piscataway, and Powhatan groups.

REFERENCES

Anonymous. 1906. *Olde Ulster* 2, 7:218.

Barnes, Ruth Carol. 1968. "Subsistence and Social Organization of the Delaware Indians: 1600 A.D." *Bulletin of the Philadelphia Anthropological Society* 20, 1:15-29.

Beverley, Robert. 1947. (orig. 1705) *The History and Present State of Virginia*, Louis Wright, ed. Chapel Hill: University of North Carolina Press.

Brasser, Theodore J.C. 1971. "The Coastal Algonkians: People of the First Frontiers." In Eleanor Burke Leacock and Nancy Oestreich Lurie, eds., *North American Indians in Historical Perspective*. New York: Random House.

Brown, Judith K. 1970. "Economic Organization and the Position of Women Among the Iroquois." *Ethnohistory* 17, 3-4:151-68.

Church, Benjamin. 1975. *Diary of King Philip's War, 1675-76*, Alan Simpson and Mary Simpson, eds. Chester, Connecticut: The Pequot Press.

van der Donck, Adriaen. 1968. *A Description of the New Netherlands*, Thomas O'Donnell, ed. Syracuse: Syracuse University Press.

Eliot, John. 1834. (orig. 1647) "The Day-Breaking, if not the Sun-Rising of the Gospel with the Indians of New England." *Collections of the Massachusetts Historical Society*, 3d series, Vol. 4, pp. 1-23.

Flannery, Regina. 1939. "An Analysis of Coastal Algonquian Culture." *Catholic University Anthropological Series*, no. 7.

Fox, George. 1952. *Journal of George Fox*, John L. Nickalls, ed. London: Cambridge University Press.

Gookin, Daniel. 1792. (orig. 1674) "Historical Collections of the Indians of New England." *Collections of the Massachusetts Historical Society*, 1st series, Vol. 1, pp. 141-229.

Grumet, Robert Steven. 1979. " 'We Are Not So Great Fools': Changes in Upper Delawaran Socio-Political Life, 1630-1758. Ph.D. diss., Rutgers University, New Brunswick, N.J.

Heckewelder, John. 1876. "History, Manners, and Customs of the Indian Nations Who Once Inhabited Pennsylvania and the Neighbouring States." *Memoirs of the Historical Society of Pennsylvania*, Vol. 12.

Juet, Robert. 1909. (orig. 1610) "Extract from *The Third Voyage of Master Henry Hudson*." In J. Franklin Jameson, ed., *Narratives of New Netherland, 1609-1664*. New York: Charles Scribner's Sons.

Kinietz, W. Vernon. 1946. "Delaware Culture Chronology." *Prehistory Research Series, Indiana Historical Society*, Vol. 3, no. 1.

Leach, Douglas Edward. 1958. *Flintlock and Tomahawk: New England in King Philip's War.* New York: Macmillan.

Leacock, Eleanor Burke. 1978. "Woman's Status in Egalitarian Society: Implications for Social Evolution." *Current Anthropology* 19, 2:247-75.

Leder, Lawrence H., ed. 1956. *The Livingston Indian Records, 1666-1723.* Gettysburg: Pennsylvania Historical Association.

Lindestrom, Peter. 1925. *Geographia Americae, with an Account of the Delaware Indians...1654-1656,* Amandus Johnson, ed. Philadelphia: Swedish Colonial Society.

Mourt, George. 1841. (orig. 1622) "Mourt's Relation." In Alexander Young, ed., *Chronicles of the Pilgrim Fathers of the Colony of Plymouth, from 1602 to 1625.* Boston.

Myers, Albert Cook, ed. 1937. *William Penn: His Account of the Lenni Lenape or Delaware Indians, 1683.* Moylan, Pa.: Albert Cook Myers.

Newcomb, William W., Jr. 1956. *The Culture and Acculturation of the Delaware Indians.* Anthropological Paper No. 10, Museum of Anthropology, University of Michigan, Ann Arbor.

Norton, Thomas Elliot. 1974. *The Fur Trade in Colonial New York, 1686-1776.* Madison: University of Wisconsin Press.

N.S. 1913a. (orig. 1675) "The Present State of New-England with Respect to the Indian War." In Charles H. Lincoln, ed., *Narratives of the Indian Wars: 1675-1699.* New York: Charles Scribner's Sons.

―――. 1913b. (orig. 1676) "A Continuation of the State of New England." In Charles H. Lincoln, ed., *Narratives of the Indian Wars: 1675-1699.* New York: Charles Scribner's Sons.

―――. 1913c. (orig. 1676) "A New and Further Narrative of the State of New-England." In Charles H. Lincoln, ed., *Narratives of the Indian Wars: 1675-1699.* New York: Charles Scribner's Sons.

O'Callaghan, Edmund Bailey and Berthold Fernow, Eds. 1856-87. *Documents Relative to the Colonial History of the State of New York,* 15 Vols. Albany.

Philhower, Charles A. n.d. *The Charles A. Philhower Collection. AC 1810,* Alexander Library, Rutgers University, New Brunswick, N.J.

Powell, John Wesley. 1880. "Wyandot Government: A Short Study of Tribal Society." *Annual Report of the Bureau of American Ethnology* 1:59-69.

Randle, Martha C. 1951. "Iroquois Women, Then and Now." In William Fenton, ed., *Symposium on Local Diversity in Iroquois Culture,* Bureau of American Ethnology, Bulletin No. 149.

de Rasieres, Isaack. 1909. (orig. 1628?) "Letter of Isaack de Rasieres to Samuel Blommaert." In J. Franklin Jameson, ed., *Narratives of New Netherland, 1609-1664.* New York: Charles Scribner's Sons.

Richards, Cara B. 1957. "Matriarchy or Mistake: The Role of Iroquois Women Through Time." In Verne F. Ray, ed., *Cultural Stability and Culture Change*, Proceedings of the 1957 Annual Spring Meeting of the American Ethnological Society. Seattle: University of Washington Press.

Rowlandson, Mary. 1913. "Narrative of the Captivity of Mrs. Mary Rowlandson, 1682." In Charles H. Lincoln, ed., *Narratives of the Indian Wars: 1675-1699*. New York: Charles Scribner's Sons.

Silberbauer, George. n.d. "Political Process in G/Wi Bands." Unpublished Manuscript.

Simmons, William S. 1976. "Southern New England Shamanism: An Ethnographic Reconstruction." In William Cowan, ed., *Papers of the Seventh Algonquian Conference*. Ottawa: Carleton University Press.

Simmons, William S. and George F. Aubin. 1975. "Narragansett Kinship." *Man in the Northeast*, No. 9, pp. 21-32.

Smith, John. 1907. *The Generall Historie of Virginia, New England, and the Summer Isles*, 2 Vols. Glasgow: James MacLehose & Sons.

Snow, Dean R. 1976. "The Solon Petroglyphs and Eastern Abnaki Shamanism." In William Cowan, ed., *Papers of the Seventh Algonquian Conference*. Ottawa: Carleton University Press.

Speck, Frank Gouldsmith. 1928. *Territorial Subdivisions and Boundaries of the Wampanoag, Massachusett, and Nauset Indians*. Indian Notes and Monographs, Number 44, Museum of the American Indian. New York: Heye Foundation.

———. 1947. *Eastern Algonkian Block-Stamp Decoration: A New World Original or an Acculturated Art*. Trenton: Archaeological Society of New Jersey and the State Museum.

Tantaquidgeon, Gladys. 1972. *Folk Medicine of the Delaware and Related Algonkian Indians*. Harrisburg: Pennsylvania Historical and Museum Commission.

van Wassenaer, Nicolaes. 1909. (orig. 1630) "Historische Verhael." In J. Franklin Jameson, ed, *Narratives of New Netherland, 1608-1664*. New York: Charles Scribner's Sons.

Wallace, Anthony F. C. 1947. "Woman, Land, and Society: Three Aspects of Aboriginal Delaware Life." *Pennsylvania Archaeologist* 17, 1-4:1-35.

Weslager, Clinton Alfred. 1972. *The Delaware Indians: A History*. New Brunswick: Rutgers University Press.

Williams, Roger. 1866. "Key Into the Language of America," James H. Trumbull, ed. *Publications of the Narragansett Club*, 1st series, Vol. 1 (Providence).

Winslow, Edward. 1841. (orig. 1624) "Good Newes from New England." In Alexander Young, ed., *Chronicles of the Pilgrim Fathers of the Colony of Plymouth, from 1602 to 1625*. Boston.

Zeisberger, David. 1910. "History of the North American Indians," A.B. Hulbert and W.N. Schwarze, eds. *Ohio Archaeological and Historical Publications*, Vol. 19, pp. 1-189.

3 The Mothers of the Nation:
Seneca Resistance
to Quaker Intervention

DIANE ROTHENBERG

Seneca Indian economic and social survival strategies in the late eighteenth and early nineteenth centuries were differentially affected by the colonizing powers with which they had to deal. The end of the American Revolution marked a sharp change in administrative policy vis-a-vis the Indians. The British had attempted to control inland colonial settlement, partly to placate Indian allies and partly because the administration of widely dispersed settlements would have been almost impossible for them. Pressures for territorial expansion by the colonists erupted at the end of the revolution and land hunger and land speculation were rife. The federal government was intensely involved in land deals both to satisfy colonists' demands and to raise money, and it was extremely eager to acquire public lands for rapid resale and quick settlement. This aim was continually frustrated by active Indian resistance. The initial efforts to grab land through military conquest proved both expensive and time-consuming, and the United States could afford neither money nor time in their efforts to acquire the Ohio lands which they were counting on to pay off the huge national debt. The application of the "conquest theory" was a dismal failure and merely aggravated Indian hostility, which vented itself in frontier raids that virtually made the area under consideration uninhabitable and thus unsellable.

The alternative to the conquest theory was provided by Secretary of War Henry Knox who took office in 1789. He proposed "civilizing" the Indians and offered a number of reasons to endorse such a policy. First, and above all, conciliation was far less expensive than conquest: Knox estimated that $200,000 would be necessary to wage a war against the Indians. Furthermore, the international reputation of the United States would be enhanced by a humanitarian policy. Providing funds for missionary teachers was economical and humanitarian but would attain the same end: acquisition of Indian land. He reasoned that, as the Indians were converted to an agricultural way of life, which required far less land than did a hunting economy, they would be willing to transfer their surplus lands to the United States (American State Papers 1832: June 15, 1789; July 7, 1789). The offer by the Quakers to expedite this policy at their own expense was gratefully received.

Benevolence is an inadequate explanation of why the Quakers chose to offer themselves as a privately funded group to carry out federal policy unless we understand that benevolence itself had become highly institutionalized and instrumental within the Quaker movement. The province of Pennsylvania, as William Penn had envisioned it, was to be the site of a "holy experiment" in the reconciliation of spiritual and material development. By the middle of the eighteenth century, when material concerns had apparently come to far outweigh spiritual ones, the Quakers instituted reforms and became an inwardly directed, exclusive society, advocating a separation from worldly interests and ostentation. But they remained a Philadelphia society of rich merchants whose fortunes were built on international colonial commerce rooted in the Indian fur trade. With their withdrawal from formal political participation in 1756, benevolence offered a new channel through which to influence and direct public policy. Benevolent contribution became an acceptable and institutionalized substitute for luxury as a way in which to display wealth, acquire prestige, and remain influential both within the community and in the outside world. In effect, the Quakers were trying another "holy experiment," but this time with benevolence as a mediating device between spiritual and material success, and as a symbol of successful mediation.

The period of the American Revolution created enormous problems for the Quakers. Most chose pacifism and thus incurred the animosity of the colonists. The repercussions of their choice required deliberate remedial steps after the war, and benevolence provided the means. By assuming the task of civilizing the Indians as a private philanthropic enterprise, they released the impoverished United States from financing a program that it wished implemented. Without compromising themselves on the issue of political participation, the Quakers were able to achieve not only public recognition and praise, but a certain degree of control of policy and a direct line of communication with government.

The fact that the benevolent intentions of the Quakers corresponded perfectly with the pragmatic policy of the United States meant that in their dealings with the Indians they would serve as guides to lead the Indians from "barbarism" to "civilization," from tribal society to incorporation into the American polity. Had the Quaker mission succeeded in its long-range goals, the result would have been the social and cultural genocide which was the goal of white well-wishers until recent years (see Hertzberg 1971).

The contemporary Allegany Seneca, whose reservation is located on the New York-Pennsylvania border in Cattaraugus County, are one of three remaining Seneca groups in New York State.[1] Together with the nearby Cattaraugus they made radical changes in their political organization and, in 1848, established the Seneca Nation; they have been governed by democratically elected officials since that time. The third group, the Tonawanda Seneca, declined to participate in the "revolution" towards electoral government and retained the older political system of appointed chiefs. Today, the combined population of the Seneca Nation is approximately 2,500 people; the Tonawanda number about 400. Economically the Seneca are integrated into the life of the surrounding semirural and economically depressed environment of western New York and are overwhelmingly wage laborers. They have retained some measure of social exclusivity, which is steadily diminishing as a result of modern technological pressures and integrated education. The site of the Allegany Reservation, which flanks the Allegheny River for approximately 40 miles, encouraged constant contact with settlers, who used the river for transportation. Superficially the Indian population is virtually indistinguishable from its white neighbors, but a considerable effort is being made to retain and transmit distinctive cultural features, including ceremonies and dances, language, and techniques of food preparation and crafts, all of which are seen to be endangered by the white "monoculture." One of the male leaders of the traditionalist longhouse religion remarked to me that, if the religion is to survive, it will be through the efforts of Seneca women.

THE SENECA NATION: PRE-NINETEENTH CENTURY CONTACT AND COLONIZATION

The Seneca constituted one of the five nations of the League of the Iroquois, which was expanded to include the Tuscarora in the late eighteenth century. Whether the league, a loose confederation of Mohawks, Oneida, Onondaga, Cayuga, and Senecas, was formed before European influence was felt in the New World or in response to some of the new pressures created by the European intrusion is still conjectural. It appears from traditional accounts to have been created to reduce belligerency among the participating tribes, rather than as the offensive alliance it later became, and to have been in existence since at least 1450 A.D. Metaphorically, its structure was the longhouse, the matrilocal, multiple-family Iroquois residential structure which housed a matrilineally related group of women with their husbands and children. The Mohawks were guardians of the eastern "door"; the Seneca, located in the Genesee region, protected the western; and each tribe constituted one of the "fires," as each family unit did in the longhouse.

The principle guiding decision making in the league, as well as at the local level, was unanimity; majorities did not rule. The representatives of each group, sachems chosen by clan mothers, arrived at unanimous decisions in separate enclaves and then spoke as the single voice of their group. Whatever unanimity indicated, however, the machinery to enforce decisons was lacking. Only the coercive power of public opinion could control behavior, and the more distant communities were from the central "fire" of the Onondaga the more the influence of the league dissipated. Real action was determined and controlled by the local group. In the antagonism between the French and the English for hegemony in North America the Mohawks in the east had strong ties to the English, whereas the western Seneca's trade connections allied them more often to the French. Enforcement of league decisions on those Senecas in the Allegheny region and further west into the Ohio area—for all practical purposes quite out of reach of the western "door" from which they had exited—was especially difficult both because of the distances involved and because these Seneca colonies had interests frequently more coincidental with their western Indian neighbors than with their eastern confederates. Because of the strategic power of the league in relation to the colonial powers, concurrence of its members in most decisions was common, not only because it was expected, but because it was advantageous. When it was not advantageous, separate and contrary action would be taken in spite of the principle of unanimity.

The Effects of Trade and Warfare.
Sedentary Women and Mobile Men

Both the strength of the league and the development of Seneca colonies west of their Genesee homeland are directly related to the economic activities and rivalries of Europeans and to the changes in natural resources which these activities effected. The thirty years following 1603 were a period of extensive Atlantic-seaboard settlement by Europeans who wanted furs, particularly beaver skins, for export. As George Hunt remarks, "Competition for trade was, or soon became, a struggle for survival" (1940: 19) as Indians quickly became dependent on metal tools and firearms and lost skill in the manufacture and use of the older technology. It is apparent, too, that the group with metal weapons and firearms had a military advantage that had to be matched by any other group which hoped to survive.

Trade goods had an early and profound effect on Indian groups. European trade goods appear in Iroquois archeological sites as early as 1570 in the Niagara frontier area (White 1961). James A. Tuck, discussing archeological remains dating before 1654, the date of the initial contact between the Onondaga and Europeans, notes that

> steady decay in native arts and crafts provides a measure of the growing importance of European trade goods. Stone axes, knives and arrow points disappear and metal ones take their place. By the time of the first recorded contact between Onondagas and Europeans the native manufacture of pottery had become virtually a lost art (1971:40).

By the 1670s European trade goods totally dominate the archeological record and "virtually the only items of native manufacture found there are tobacco pipes" (: 41). It is precisely this kind of involvement in the dynamics of trade that would influence the Seneca not only through the period of their expansion during the seventeenth and eighteenth centuries, but into the early reservation period as well.

Initially the requirements of the fur trade could be supplied from local resources, but beaver was never abundant in New York, and by 1640 the local beaver supply was exhausted. The need to find new sources of supply led to a period of warfare and expansion—which removed men for longer periods of time and for further distances than had previously been the case—led to an intensification of the practice of adopting captives to substitute for men (or women) lost in battle, and probably resulted in an acquisition of more power and social control by women than had previously been the case (see Richards 1957).

Anthony F. C. Wallace provides a general description of the sedentary women and the mobile men of Iroquois society.

> It is not an exaggeration to say that the full time business of an Iroquois man was travel, in order to hunt, trade, fight and talk in

council. But the women stayed at home. Thus, an Iroquois village might be regarded as a collection of strings, hundreds of years old, of successive generations of women, always domiciled in their longhouses near their cornfields in a clearing, while their sons and husbands travelled in the forest on supportive errands of hunting and trapping, of trade, of war, and of diplomacy (1970: 28).

This is a fair, normative description, but it shares the problem of all attempts to give an "ideal" cultural description in that it ignores the changes through time. Judith Brown (1970), who has properly related the powerful position of Iroquois women to their control of economic organization, consciously chooses to leave the time unspecified, although her data come from the seventeenth and eighteenth centuries. Richards, specifically concerned with the temporal problem, demonstrates the acquisition of more power and more local control by women during these two centuries (1957). What is obviously suggested is an increasing female control over local resources and local affairs as male activities associated with long-distance warfare and trade took men further away for longer periods of time (see Ember and Ember 1971; Ember 1974).

The Mothers of the Nation: Women and the Land

Students of the Iroquois have evaluated the status of Iroquois women as high on various counts (Brown 1970; Carr 1883; Stites 1905), and the basis of their judgments directly or indirectly refers back to female control of the means, processes, and distribution of local subsistence production. The land "belonged" to the women: the concept of ownership, however, was not an Indian one, and the issue became relevant only when sale of land to whites was a possibility (Brown 1970: 159–60; Carr 1883: 216–19; Washburn 1971; Wallace 1957; Snyderman 1961). In council in 1791, Red Jacket, who was the sachem designated as the official speaker for the women, announced for them that "you ought to hear and listen to what we women shall speak...for we are the owners of the land and it is ours" (Snyderman 1961: 20). This fundamental ownership was recognized by the revised Constitution of the Seneca Nation of 1868. Although women were disenfranchised and the former, clan-based political structure, through which women exercised control by the appointing and removal of sachems, was abolished (Noon 1949: 36), it was still required that three-fourths of the clan mothers consent to any decision to sell tribal land (Whipple 1889: 399). In no instance does any authority suggest that land was legitimately under male control; but whites, of course, always assumed male control to be operative, and negotiations with Indian males for land sales was the rule.

In addition to the land itself, women owned the tools of agricultural production and food preparation, even when these tools were manufactured by men. Men's equipment was owned by men, but the distribution of the food products acquired with them (i.e., meat, fish, etc.) seems usually to have been at the discretion of the women. Certainly, women controlled the distribution of cooked food. Women also determined the distribution of surpluses, which would have come largely from their cornfields and were stored in pits against times of shortages. This control has special significance since it is likely that surpluses were exchanged intertribally (Parker 1912: 34—36) and thus has implications for female participation and decisions in intertribal trade and politics. Furthermore, to the extent that war parties were dependent on provisions supplied by women, they could make significant determinations for or against military action by refusing provisions. Productive activities were carried on by work groups under the direction of a head woman who was chosen for her ability by other women. This system provided frequent opportunity for female competence and experience to be exercised and rewarded by social recognition. The communal and cooperative work structure persisted long after the matrilocal residence pattern was abandoned. Writing in 1912, Arthur Parker described contemporary agricultural work groups under the direction of a head woman. Moreover, men who participated were under her direct supervision.

The presence of matrilocal, multifamily dwellings both facilitated such work groups and supported the independent position of women. These domiciles, which were built by the men but owned by the women and transmitted through the matrilineal clan, offered a maximum degree of protection to the women, whose husbands were frequently away, and provided the basis for the easy rejection of a husband who did not perform up to standards.[2]

While matrilocality provides a convenient residential arrangement to enhance female independence and to facilitate work groups composed of related women, any residential arrangement along with village endogamy (marrying within a village), would accomplish the same end. Men and women from the same clan were prohibited from marrying, but Seneca villages invariably contained two or more clans and village endogamy was a frequent practice. William Allinson, a Quaker who visited the Allegany Seneca settlement in 1809, presents a description of the marriage and residential patterns of the time. His visit occurred eleven years after both the establishment of the reservation boundaries and the introduction of the Quaker missionaries, and by this time there appeared to be a preferred pattern of virilocality (in which the wife goes to live at the residence of her husband) but within an apparently endogamous community. Allinson reports that marriages were arranged by the mothers or eldest sisters of young people on the basis of the young man's stated choice. A gift of trinkets worth approximately six to ten dollars was presented by the man and returned if his proposal was not accepted. If it was accepted, the mother of the girl then accompanied her to the house of the man, who was probably living with his mother, and left her there; but "as the Seasons for planting, hoeing, gathering corn, procuring Fire wood and other business came on, the female connections of the young woman assist her in the different operations during the first year at the end of which without any ceremony the marriage is considered valid & honorable" (Allinson 1809: 55–56). These activities occupied much of the year and indicate the close presence of the girl's family. With endogamy as the general rule within a village with a clustered type of settlement, specific residence rules have little significance for work-group organization; related women could as well work together in one field even if they didn't share one roof.

Men's Activities and Economic Viability

While women were rooted to the locality and the annual agricultural cycle, men had a more flexible annual pattern in which to "hunt, trade, fight and talk in council" (Wallace 1970: 28), but it is certainly a European bias that minimized Indian males' contributions to subsistence. The distortion is exemplified by Martha Randle's contention that "men's hunting added an important relish to the diet. A good meat provider was considered the best husband. But hunting was more a prestige and recreation point than a necessity" (1951: 172). If this were true before the coming of Europeans, we cannot verify it, but it is a totally inaccurate evaluation of the importance of men's hunting during the period of European colonization. I would insist, on the contrary, that it is important to realize that the postconquest hunting activities of men contributed a crucial element to overall subsistence, not in terms of protein, which women and children could and did provide for themselves at least by fishing (Quain 1937: 251), but in terms of trade goods and cash to purchase those trade goods which women's activities, on the whole, could not generate. Furthermore, the women recognized the essential contribution the men were making and encouraged them to continue it. The trivializing of this aspect of the economic organization reduces the insistence of women on maintaining their control over local agricultural production to a kind of senseless conservativism, if not virtual martyrdom, perpetuating a system in which women performed as slaves to self-indulgent men. It seems likely that the prejudiced statements made by white observers about a division of labor which was foreign, and hence pernicious, to them worked to devalue the importance of hunting as a real economic activity; these evaluations have been too easily accepted by social historians as a reflection of Indian reality. It is on these very judgments, in fact, that white rationales for restructuring Indian societies frequently were based.

Although domestic manufacture (particularly of artifacts made of wood and corn husks) did not disappear, and some of this technology has continued until the present, it would be difficult to exaggerate the Indian dependency on trade goods which was created by the fur trade, by European gift-giving diplomacy (see Jacobs 1950), and by a deliberate policy of generating colonial markets for the products of England's industrial revolution, particularly hardware and textiles. The Iroquois, in their strategic position of power balancing between the French and English until the defeat of the French in the 1760s, were the recipients of vast quantities and varieties of goods. These included not merely the finery, trinkets, and liquor often cited and regarded by whites as easily expendable to the Indians when their access to these goods was reduced, but the firearms, ammunition, metal tools, and metal kettles that became essentials in the Indian communities from which the old technology rapidly disappeared. The ceremonial dress of contemporary Seneca women is not a skin garment from some long-forgotten past, but a calico dress derived from the textiles brought in through the fur trade.

For the Seneca of the late 1790s and early 1800s, whose political importance had disappeared and who were no longer the recipients of gifts, cash or cash substitutes were their only access to essential trade goods, and it was men's activities that provided these resources. A Pittsburgh merchant describes what the Seneca brought for trade in 1803: "They generally came down twice a year, with their canoes heavy loaded, with furrs, peltry, mogasons, deer hams, tallow, bear skins" (Wrenshall 1816: 125–26). For the period around 1816 these products were supplemented by additional ones produced by men, and Wrenshall remarks that

> They have besides a sawmill, and being surrounded with lofty pine trees, they cut them into boards or scantling and float them down to Pittsburg at the time of high water. And on these rafts they bring their peltry, furrs, and good canoes, to push up their return cargoes...and sometimes shingls, the latter of which I have bought for one dollar and fifty cents per thousand and paid for them in merchandize (:131).

These trade goods were the products of male activity, necessary to the economic viability of the community and made possible because women were engaged in subsistence and agriculture.

While the physical labor that women were observed to perform and their deference to men in such matters as eating order inclined some white observers to regard their position as subservient to men (e.g., Morgan 1851), refutations of this evaluation by other observers (see Heckewelder 1817) are numerous. The most famous assessment of the life of a Seneca woman was supplied by a female participant in that life of the prereservation period who compares the burdens of Seneca women favorably with those of white women. Mary Jemison, the white captive, recalls:

> Our labor was not severe, and that of one year was exactly similar in almost every respect to that of others, without that endless variety, that is to be observed in the common labor of white people. Notwithstanding the Indian women have all the fuel and bread to procure, and the cooking to perform, their task is probably not

harder than that of white women who have those articles provided for them; and their cares certainly not half as numerous, nor as great. In the summer season we planted, tended and harvested our corn, and generally had our children with us, but we had no master to oversee or drive us, so that we could work as leisurely as we pleased (quoted in Seaver 1961:55).

THE SENECA AND THE QUAKERS

The life of the Indians entered a new period of adjustment with the defeat of their English allies in the Revolutionary War and with the introduction of new policies and new goals by the United States. Systematic losses through treaties and sales constricted their land base and in 1798 the remaining land was being surveyed to establish reservation boundaries. In this same year a group of Philadelphia Quakers established a mission among the Allegany Seneca.

Seneca Strategy and Quaker Motivation

The Quakers came to the Seneca community by invitation. Indeed, throughout the 1790s the Allegany Seneca leader Cornplanter had sent repeated appeals for white assistance to the government of Pennsylvania (e.g., McAllister: March 2, 1790), and the arrival of the Quakers was well received; the Seneca made every effort to encourage them to remain. The reason for Seneca receptivity that is commonly given is that the Indians were eager to receive instruction in white technology, but, in fact, only variable interest was shown in what the Quakers wanted to teach. It seems apparent that the Seneca envisioned the Quakers serving other important functions. The Quakers were a potential source of necessary services (such as blacksmithing) and of trade goods, not only through gifts but, it was hoped, through the establishment of a local trading post. The isolation of the Allegany Seneca was a mixed blessing, and the leaders of the community saw a great advantage in having local trading facilities which would reduce the need for men to travel to distant markets, where they frequently had trouble with white men and almost always procured liquor. Although some Quakers understood the benefits of establishing a local trading post,[3] the proposal was rejected by the administrators of the mission (Indian Committee Collection Report: Box 2. Dec. 14, 1803). They were willing to give necessary tools and equipment as gifts at first, and newly introduced activities (such as spinning) were initiated with Quaker-supplied materials as inducements; they were reluctant, however, to continue supplying material goods, which they claimed produced a state of dependency among the Indians, and they refused to maintain a store. Their decision committed the Indians, necessarily, to distant markets and male mobility.

Even if the Quakers were not a source of supply, their presence was still essential to the Seneca. Indian lands were under continual pressure from white

The Mothers of the Nation   73

interests, and the Quakers—as the trusted, locally established, and respected representatives of the dominant society—offered the Seneca the most immediate protection from white chicanery. White settlement of the area was late in coming and not really underway until after 1816, but by 1809 the Ogden Land Company was actively engaged in attempts to acquire Seneca lands to which the company had bought the pre-emption rights.[4] Although the Seneca did not absolutely trust the motives of the Quakers and repeatedly asked for assurances that they would make no claims on Seneca lands as payment for services rendered, the Senecas had little choice but to encourage the continued presence of the Quakers to intercede for them on all levels of white society. The strategies adopted by the Senecas represent a response to a number of interconnected problems: the protection of their lands, which required that they encourage the Quakers; the demands of economic viability, which frequently forced them to act contrary to Quaker advice and threatened to alienate the Quakers from them; and a changing environment, particularly with reference to white settlement and white markets which required a flexibility on the part of the Indians in order to make rapid and appropriate adjustments.

The Quakers came to their missionary task with a clear and evolutionary notion of what constituted cultural and social progress and with a commitment to lead the Indians through those necessary steps—including a conversion to male agriculture from which would follow a love of private property—which they understood to be definitionally intrinsic to the state of "civilization." Fundamental to this goal was the restructuring of the village-oriented, matrilineal, extended kinship unit with a philosophy of economic reciprocity in favor of nuclear families living on isolated homesteads, conserving their resources within the nuclear family, and with men farming lands that their sons would inherit. Women were "to turn their attention to the business of the house, and the concerns more properly allotted to females in all civilized societies" (Jackson 1830: 50).

Unlike other missionaries, the Quakers did not come to convert the Indians to Christianity; perhaps this is why we tend to assume that their judgments and observations were more reliable than those of other missionaries. Although they assumed that such a religious commitment would come with the accomplishment of civilization, the Quakers were by then an exclusive religious and social sect, with birthright and not conversion the basis of membership (Sydney 1963: 327). Their efforts, as a result, were directed towards the socioeconomic life of the Indians and not toward their spiritual life. Any resistance to Quaker proposals for such restructuring was interpreted by them as the result of "habits of mind" (i.e. culture), laziness, or maliciousness on the part of Indians (or sinister whites). Although the Indians were prepared to entertain the possibility of alternative strategies in their attempt to achieve social and cultural survival, the Quakers understood no alternatives to their concepts of progress and civilization.

"A Nation of Farmers:" The Quaker Program and the Seneca Response

The crux of the Quaker program was the removal of women from agricultural activities and the establishment of men in their place. To justify the continuation of the mission and to insure its continued support, it was necessary to see evidence that this goal was being achieved. Frequently, students of the Seneca have uncritically accepted Quaker claims of success at face value, and Anthony F. C. Wallace tells us, for instance, "Now, and suddenly, they embraced the rural technology of the white man and became a nation of farmers" (1970: 310). The same series of Quaker letters and reports which give indications of success, however, give many instances of discouragement and failure. What the Quakers took to be signs of initial success, such as male activity in land clearing, somehow did not result in the desired end. For instance, the visiting Quaker committee in 1817 remonstrated the Indians, saying,

> You are very capable to calculate what is for your advantage and what is not. We therefore desire you would take into consideration whether you would not have been in a better situation generally if you had employed the same time which you have spent in cutting and rafting timber in cultivating your good land.... Yet it is evident their attention to cutting and rafting pine timber has much retarded their progress in agriculture (I.C.C.: Box 3. October 16, 1817).

If the Quakers converted the Seneca into a nation of male farmers, it was a most temporary conversion. Evidence indicates that although subsistence farming (by women) continued, and some few men became successful farmers, the vast majority of men did not farm as a primary economic activity. In 1893 the Indian agent wrote that "the people on this reservation are not as a rule engaged extensively in agriculture....[They] have recently begun to develop their lands, having for many years supplied their actual necessities by selling timber, bark and ties. They have been making fair progress in farming for two or three years past" (Adams 1893: 38). Whatever future prospects may have seemed likely in 1893, Dorothy Skinner wrote in 1929 that "the Indians of the Allegheny Reservation do very little farming at the present time. They do laboring work at the various small towns near the reservation" (1929: 1). And, if we did not know that the following testimony was dated August 23, 1920, we might suppose it was at least 120 years earlier, for Mr. John Van Arnum appealed to the Everett Commission, which was investigating the condition of the New York Indians, in the following terms: "We can hunt nor fish no longer, give us education to help us live. We need knowledge in agriculture work to develop our lands.... It is education we need in agriculture so that when the young arise to become citizens, we can compete with any man" (quoted in Everett 1922: 191).

When Cornplanter appealed for white aid in the 1790s, he did so in the same terms as Mr. Van Arnum, referring to the disappearance of the game; but year after year the Quakers reported the men away hunting in the wintertime, which invariably interfered with what the Quakers wanted them to be doing. In 1805, Seneca men were unavailable for employment by the Quakers, who had to find non-Indians to assist them; in 1807, cattle died because of lack of attention while the men hunted. The ability of Seneca males to prosper by hunting through this period is attested to by the report of John Norton, who visited the settlement in 1809. Because his assertions are so different from those usually advanced in support of Quaker claims, I will quote him at length:

> These people have an advantageous situation; although their Reserve is only half a mile on each side of the river, for forty miles in length, yet it takes in the most valuable kind of land, and that purchased by the people of the United States adjoining to it, being rough and broken, and not likely soon to receive inhabitants, forms the most valuable hunting ground of any possessed by the Five Nations. They can conveniently take skins, meat and timber, to Pittsburgh, where they generally get a good price for these articles; the distance is only about 150 miles, and when the water is high, they can descend with Canoes or boats in two or three days ....Our Host told me that Friends had taught several of their people to plow, and to do Blacksmith work, and some of their women to spin....but that many found it more to their interest to hunt than to work; that for his part he had acquired all his property by hunting, and that with the produce of the Chase, he had hired people to build and work for him (1970:9).

Norton noted that his host was the wealthiest man in the community.

It was not the disappearance of local fur resources but rather the embargo of 1808—when the United States closed North American ports to English ships and, by so doing, eliminated markets for furs—that forced Seneca men to find new cash-producing activities. Markets for agricultural products were not locally available and the means of transporting these products to distant markets did not exist; agriculture would not answer. Not surprisingly, the new resource that was exploited was lumber, which stimulated the initial white settlement of the area. At first the Indians cut and rafted lumber for themselves; by the 1830s they constituted a labor force for white entrepreneurs and gained a reputation as excellent raftsmen (Kussart 1938). These cutting and rafting activities were more intensely deplored by the Quakers than the reliance on hunting had been. It represented a new way of continuing the pattern of sedentary, agricultural women and mobile, cash-producing men, which the Quakers had hoped would become obsolete with the hypothetical vanishing of game.

Because I am proposing an explanation of Seneca behavior which favors regarding them as rational actors, it is appropriate to consider briefly an alternative explanation of this same behavior which has been much favored. The Quakers called it their "habits of mind," and anthropologists call it "cultural persistence." The argument is advanced that resistance to Quaker teachings and advice stemmed from the hold that previous behavioral patterns exercised on the Seneca population, a resistance to change and a selective preference for new activities which would conform in structure to traditional activities. Morris Freilich (1958:473–83) has argued that contemporary Mohawk males engage in high-rise steel construction work because such an activity, with its excitements, dangers, and geographical mobility, structurally resembles the older warrior patterns through which men acquired prestige—that in effect, the older activity is replaced by a structurally comparable new one because it offers similar psychological compensations.

Although it would be foolish to suggest that culture does not influence behavior, the Seneca evidence demonstrates time and time again a flexibility and receptivity to new ideas, techniques, and behaviors which would belie the assertion that the Senecas were bound within the tight constraints of a previous culture. It was almost axiomatic among whites that Indians would not work for wages, but in 1810 many young men became wage laborers and wage-labor activity became the primary source of employment in the nineteenth century, not in the spectacular short-term contract employment of steel work but in the steady employment offered by the railroad and growing local industries. Although women mocked men who took up the hoe, they themselves took with enthusiasm to the new skills, which involved novel motor habits, such as spinning, knitting, and weaving taught by the Quakers. Insofar as culture conditioned their cognitive context, the Seneca must have preferred activities which were familiar in that context, but the culture model's inability to account for change and for novel choices forces us to reject it as sufficient explanation and to consider the influence of culture as one of many variables that explain behavior.

The Quakers, as we have said, were initially received by the Seneca "with an apparently hearty welcome, and treated with kindness" (I.C.C.:Box I. May 11, 1798). Acting as spokesman for the group, Cornplanter extended total freedom of land utilization to the Quakers. When the latter indicated that they had sent a boatload of goods which had not yet arrived, they were loaned Indian tools and presented by the women with the seeds of "corn, potatoes, beans, squashes, and a variety of other garden seeds which they presented as a present to Friends, observing 'that it was very hard to come so far and have nothing to begin with' " (Jackson 1830:32). The Quakers purchased a small house from the woman who owned it along with her daughter.

A reciprocal exchange was maintained throughout the summer. Halliday Jackson noted that "a great number of them came flocking about Friends, especially the women, who appeared kind and respectful, frequently supplying them with venison, fish, strawberries, and such other delicacies, as their country afforded" (ibid.). We should note that the inclusion of venison in the list suggests the control that women had over the meat procured by the men, as well as over their own products. In exchange, the Quakers distributed "useful articles, such as needles, thread, scissors, combs, spectacles, etc., which were sent for that purpose, and were received by the natives with lively marks of gratitude" (:32–33).

Although the women were very eager to observe the Quakers' agricultural practices, they wanted this information for their own use. As Wallace tells us, "Agriculture by men had been resisted as an effeminate occupation with the women themselves taking the lead in ridiculing male farmers as transvestites" (Wallace 1970:310). Allinson illustrates: "If a Man took hold of a Hoe to use it the Women would get down his gun by way of derision & would laugh & say such a warrior is a timid woman" (Allinson 1809:42). It is women who mock men; men seemed not to have any stake in other men's experimenting with farming. The women seemed to have no objection to men learning to plow fields that the women would then work, and men had always assisted women in the preparation of fields by clearing land and burning the timber and brush (Parker 1912:21). In the spring of 1801 an experiment was conducted whereby every other row in a cornfield was prepared with the plow; the alternating rows were prepared in the traditional manner. The advantages of the plowed rows in terms of increased yields were apparent, and thereafter the plow was increasingly used for field preparation.

In general, aspects of the novel agricultural activities that were introduced were selectively adopted by the men. In spite of the fact that there is no physical reason why women cannot plow, Quaker instruction in its use was exclusively directed toward Seneca men. But plows and oxen to pull them were scarce and expensive commodities. By 1811 there were only six yoke of oxen and four plows, owned as collective property (I.C.C.:Box 2. February 12, 1811), and wages were earned by those men who were able to plow for others. In 1819, for instance, it was reported that a young man had plowed 22 acres for other Indians at the rate of two dollars per acre (Society of Friends 1840: 138), and plowing thus became not an early step in a total male agricultural cycle, but a specific cash-producing activity.

Animal husbandry was another activity in which men were actively engaged, which initially the Quakers applauded as leading to their social-conversion goals, but later deplored as being diverting. By 1817 the Quakers were saying that "they have more horses than is of any advantage to them" (I.C.C.: Box 3. October 16, 1817), although it seems likely that the Indians needed the horses for hauling lumber, a pursuit the Quakers found objectionable. Animals were raised for sale—"they have a number of fat cattle to sell this fall and hogs in abundance" (I.C.C.:Box 2. November 2, 1805)—and in 1814, when Halliday Jackson noted that little agricultural progress was being made, he observed that there had been a rapid increase in the number of swine which were not only salted for family consumption, but also raised and sold for the rapid income they would produce.

A distinct association of crops with one or the other sex developed among the Senecas; corn, beans, squash, potatoes, and vegetables in general, were raised by women, and animal fodder crops, particularly oats, and some wheat and hay were raised by the men. This is the same general pattern described by Shimony with reference to the Six Nations Reserve in Canada (1961:154–55). That corn remained a woman's crop is indirectly confirmed by a typical statement made in 1810 which reports that "several of their men have sowed spring wheat this season, and we believe an increasing disposition prevails amongst them to render assistance to their women in the planting of corn" (I.C.C.:Box 2. June 16, 1810). Corn remained the main food crop and was the crop most often mentioned as being sold to whites.

The Selective Conservatism of Seneca Women

While women conservatively retained their former agricultural control, they eagerly made themselves available to the Quakers to be taught a whole new range of additional skills—soap making, knitting, household management skills, and others—and they added the new tasks to the old ones. That the Quakers, in their professed desire to relieve the women of onerous tasks, probably merely added a whole new set to the old ones is an interesting possibility. (Recall Mary Jemison's description of the life of a Seneca woman as pleasant, productive, and not excessively burdened when compared with that of white women of the same period.) Under the Quakers' direction, those household chores that had been casual were encouraged to become a focus of compulsive attention, but we may assume that the continuing criticisms of an overall "negligent" attitude toward housekeeping reflected the firm grip that Seneca women kept on the reality of important versus trivial activity.

When spinning and weaving were introduced in 1805 the women were receptive, but the activity was relegated to the leisure-filled winter season. The new activities were organized along the lines of traditional women's work groups, and in this context the women responded positively to the new activity. The public support by head women under whom the others worked proved invaluable to the Quakers when opposition arose to the teaching of spinning; because of this intervention, the activity was continued. Only one woman became a proficient weaver, and she quickly turned this skill to a cash advantage by selling her products to white neighbors; her elderly husband assisted her in this activity, but in a minor role (I.C.C.:Box 2. September 20, 1811). By 1820 the interest in spinning and weaving had disappeared (I.C.C.:Box 2. April 15, 1820) because, I believe, not only of the relocation of the activity to the private and unsocial domestic environment of the home (once there were enough spinning wheels to go around) and away from the social environment from which women derived much pleasure and prestige while working, but even more as a result of the Quaker refusal to continue to supply the raw materials, the acute problem of the procurement of raw materials in other ways, and the easy availability of more attractive commercially produced textiles which cash could purchase (Hedrick 1933:164).

The second area of female "conservativism" in relation to Quaker social restructuring emerged over the issue of private property. The division of the reserved land held communally by the Senecas into privately owned property was a fundamental goal of the Quaker program from its inception, but initially the Quakers demonstrated a sensible, gradualistic approach, believing that a commitment to private property would develop out of economic restructuring. But the failure to induce men to farm, apparent by 1816, persuaded the Quakers that a concerted campaign to divide the land into private lots and transfer control to the men was absolutely necessary. This action, taken at that time, was triggered by the aggressive moves of the land company to acquire Indian lands, and the Quakers insisted that the land could only be protected by individual ownership. In 1819 one of the missionaries reported to the committee the substance of conversations he had been having with the Indians concerning the land divisions. His letter reveals that early Seneca objections were concerned with the effect the divisions would have on the subsistence economy and access to resources and on the division of labor and the rights of women. We should especially note that the women emerge here, as they rarely do in Quaker reports, as directly and specifically opposed to the proposed changes.

> Many questions arose such as how will we do where our fields lay promiscuously or in confused division and all shapes & lines splitting & separating them & perhaps occupied by others, without a consideration for them. The women seemed to claim such parcels of land for planting corn, & potatoes, etc, on and the idea of a division into lots became very unpopular with them because they were sensible that clearing land was a hard task to perform by them & much difficulty to get their men to do it on account their favorite scheme cuting pine logs to run to market instead of the labour of the field for subsistence...many cut where most convient without control. Many think that if divided into lots they cannot do this & that lots that may fall to them will not have within its lines bottom lands for planting, and pine for rafting & say [the lands are] better owned in common (I.C.C.:Box 3. March 17, 1819).

In spite of these objections, the Quakers were encouraged to believe they had widespread Indian support for the divisions; but an active opposition arose in which the women figured prominently, and the surveyor sent in by the Quakers was ordered off Indian land. The tensions which arose over this issue were central to the brief but violent opposition which arose in general against the Quakers, and it is apparent that Quaker mediation was considered less essential than was Indian judgment about how best to protect their lands. In spite of repeated calls by white men over the years for such land divisions to take place, Seneca lands are still tribally owned.

EROSION OF POWER: THE EFFECTS OF COLONIZATION

As Seneca life changed under the influence of white society, the power and position of Seneca women changed as well, although they continued to control a large measure of the subsistence production. Repeated accounts by travelers of their buying corn from Indian women would indicate that they probably derived some small cash return through the sale of surplus produce. Women continued to participate equally with men in overseeing the general conduct of ritual life, and the celebration of the three sisters of corn, beans, and squash—which is the special domain of women (Randle 1951)—further reinforced female control of these basic subsistence items. Male crops are excluded from ritual consideration.

Evidence that the important position of women was being challenged appears sporadically in the record. John Adlum, traveling among the Senecas in 1794, observed that "if the Indians go to war without the consent of the great woemen the mothers of the Sachems and Nation, The Great Spirit will not prosper them in War, but will cause them and their efforts to end in disgrace" (quoted in Kent and Deardorff 1960:465). The debate about going to war was heated and the women were adamantly opposed. Cornplanter, who was advocating the action,

> eventually got tired of the obstinacy of the Woemen and to do way (with) the superstition of the men respecting it, rose and made a speech against superstition, he called it folly and nonsense, and was surprised that men of understanding had so long submitted to this ancient custom handed down to them by their ancestors, and now was the time, for men to decide for themselves and take this power from the women (:466).

Handsome Lake, the Seneca prophet who rose to power after 1799 and around whose teachings the current Seneca longhouse religion is structured, endorsed a modification in the structure of Seneca society away from matrilineal unity and towards the primacy of the nuclear family. As Wallace writes,

> It is plain that he was concerned to stabilize the nuclear family by protecting the husband-wife relationship against abrasive events. A principal abrasive, in his view, was the hierarchical relationship between a mother and her daughter. Mothers, he believed, were all too prone to urge their daughters toward sin by administering ab-

ortifacients and sterilizing medicines, by drunkenness, by practicing witchcraft, and by providing love magic....Thus, in order to stabilize the nuclear family it was necessary to loosen the tie between mother and daughter....Although he did not directly challenge the matrilineal principle in regard to sib membership or the customs of nominating sachems, he made it plain that the nuclear family, rather than the maternal lineage, was henceforward to be both the moral and economic center of the behavioral universe (1970:284).

The final challenge to women's control came with the replacement in 1848 of the traditional political structure, in which sachems were appointed by the women and administered power under their watchful eye, by a system of elected representatives. Women were disenfranchised and did not regain voting privileges in the Seneca Nation until 1964 (Abler 1969). This radical change in political structure which had been advocated and supported by whites (the Quakers prominently among them; Abler 1967) was the culmination of the loss of female power. As whites dealt with "chiefs"—self-appointed or white-appointed spokesmen over whom women at best had tenuous control— rather than with Sachems—over whom women had direct control—the action of these chiefs was frequently independent of review by either women specifically or the community at large. In negotiations between Indian men and white men, the intervening presence of female mediators was unexpected and unwelcomed by the whites and inhibited the exercise of full control by Indian men, who were observing the independent action of white men in male-oriented American society.

In spite of the urging of both the Quakers and Handsome Lake for domestic reform, the pattern of brittle marriages and serial monogamy persisted. These continued to be associated with mobile males who engaged in a series of cash-productive occupational specialties: hunting, lumbering and rafting, railroad work, and the construction industries. Women continued to form a stable, sedentary base for the society and, as long as they had primary access to resources through their persistent activity in subsistence production, the comings and goings of men in cash pursuits contributed to, rather than diminished, the viability of the social unit. Women's enterprise in developing small-scale, cash-productive activities of their own, such as trading, craft production, and, eventually, domestic service in white homes, rendered them even more independent. But those conditions which had so enhanced the power and position of Seneca women in the late seventeenth and eighteenth centuries (e.g., warfare and long-distance trade in particular), coupled with the legitimate claims women had to political and economic control, were gone. The economic options open to both men and women became more varied, encouraging some men to become sedentary and some women more mobile. The activities of non-Quaker missionaries intensified, but with a primary stress on conversion and behavior appropriate to Christians. Permanent settlements by whites were made in communities surrounding the reservation and on reservation land itself. This growing white population not only provided behavioral models, but also furnished local markets for the sale of Indian goods and services. Thus, activities close to home increasingly became economically feasible. The structure of Seneca society came more and more to resemble that of white society, and the position of Seneca women came more and more to resemble the position of the women of the white man.

CONCLUSION

The preceding discussion, while considering the precapitalist condition of Seneca society, has focused on the period during which white capitalism was effecting significant changes in Indian society. Through Quaker missionary intervention, the Allegany Senecas were exposed to a total program of socioeconomic development rooted in capitalist ideology, aspects of which they differentially accepted or rejected. Because the wisdom of the Quakers' program has not been questioned, and because the Quakers' behavior has not been critically examined (see, however, Berkhofer 1965), Indian responses that were contrary to Quaker proposals have been superficially interpreted as examples of counterproductive cultural conservativism. Seneca women, because they opposed modification of the traditional division of land and labor, have appeared in the literature as a particularly conservative force, and their motivation has been explained by platitudes concerning the psychological and cultural imperatives of women in traditional societies.

On the contrary, I would contend that the apparent conservativism of Seneca women was selective and was part of a rational strategy to maintain their control of the local production which provided the subsistence base for a society dependent on a complementarity of economic sex roles. The Seneca needed more than food, and the traditional division of labor provided the means whereby they could meet the entire range of their needs. The resistance to the transferrence of agricultural production to males insured both a continued access to cash, which agricultural production in the absence of markets and transportation could not provide, and a continued female economic control upon which the influential position of women rested. That this conservativism was selective and economically rational is supported by the apparent willingness of Seneca women to accept technological innovation for both sexes. The pattern emerging from a detailed examination of the relevant documents (Rothenberg 1976a) indicates that the Seneca were attempting to keep their economic options open by maximizing the flexibility of their social structure, which stemmed from its dual and complementary economic sex roles, within an environmental context of rapid and unpredictable socioeconomic change. That they did so even to the extent of jeopardizing the good will of the Quakers, whose attention was important to them, testifies to the importance that they attributed to this flexibility for the security of the community. That the Seneca are still a viable social unit with a secured land base testifies to the wisdom of their choices.

NOTES

1. Some of the material contained in this chapter appeared first in 1976 in *The Western Canadian Journal of Anthropology* (Rothenberg 1976b).

2. There has always been some problem with identifying the Seneca as strictly matrilocal. Randle remarks that "Matrilocality was the basis of the theory of the League, though habits of patrilocality and matrilocality were not well defined" (1951:170n.), although Gough reminds us that "it would be very unlikely, if not impossible, for matrilineal descent groups to develop except out of prior matrilocal residence" (1962:552). Again, the problem of structural definition may be a function of temporal variation. For the early part of the seventeenth century, the cases that Cara Richards (1957) finds documented in the *Jesuit Relations* (Thwaites 1896-1901) suggest to her a variable pattern of residence tending towards patri-virilocality, and she challenges the validity of classifying the Iroquois as matrilocal—as is done, for instance, by Murdock in the Ethnographic Atlas (1967) for the period around 1750. Both inferential and archeological evidence suggests that matrilocality was a common residential pattern before the coming of the whites; Richards' evidence suggests that it was not during the early seventeenth century; and Morgan's sources for his evaluation of matrilocality (upon which the Murdock ratings are based) are mid-eighteenth century accounts (Morgan 1965:129–30).

Rather than reject any of these ratings, we should consider that external influences are being reflected in changing patterns of residence in accordance with Murdock's suggestions that "it is in respect to residence that changes in economy, technology, property, government, or religion first alter the structural relationships of related individuals to one another" (1949:202). The exploitation of local fur resources in the early seventeenth century ceased with the extinction of the beaver in New York in 1640 (Hunt 1940:33–34). The quest, after 1640, for new sources of fur led men into ever widening spatial explorations and produced the intensification of the condition of sedentary women and mobile men to which matrilocality is a likely residential response and of which increasing female responsibility for local affairs is a likely consequence.

3. Halliday Jackson discussed the fact that in 1799 the Indians had brought back kegs of beer from Pittsburgh when they went to sell their furs. He suggested in a footnote to this information that "a trade upon benevolent principles would be advantageously opened by friends with the Natives giving them more for their peltries than others and thus superseding the necessity of their going to a distant market. It should be a barter with useful *supplies*" (1810:122n.; emphasis in original).

4. What the Ogden Company purchased when they bought the pre-emption rights to the Seneca reservations was not land, but merely rights to purchase land which were contingent upon the Indians' willingness to sell. Unless the company could acquire the land, its investment of approximately $90,000 for these rights would have been a total loss. Thereafter, every means that the politically influential Ogden's who owned the company could use to bring pressure on the Indians to sell was used. They manipulated federal and state politics to remove the Indians to western lands, particularly to Wisconsin, Arkansas, and Kansas; they bribed individual Indians and advisers of Indians; and they offered a series of alternative suggestions by which they could acquire the more valuable reservation lands in the northern part of New York State, particularly those around Buffalo and Rochester, and remove all of the Seneca to the comparatively worthless land of the Allegheny reservation. It was not until 1842 that the company acquired the valuable lands it sought, and this process of acquisition is amply documented in various accounts (e.g., Society of Friends 1840).

REFERENCES

Abler, Thomas S. 1967. "Seneca National Factionalism: The First Twenty Years." In E. Tooker, *Iroquois Culture, History and Prehistory*, Proceedings of the 1965 Conference on Iroquois Research. Albany: New York State Museum.

———. 1969. *Factional Dispute and Party Conflict in the Political System of the Seneca Nation (1845-1895): An Ethnohistorical Analysis.* Toronto: National Library of Canada (microfilm).

Adams, W., ed. 1893. *Historical Gazeteer and Biographical Memorial of Cattaraugus County, New York.* Syracuse: Lyman, Horton & Co. Ltd.

American State Papers. 1832. Class I, Indian Affairs, Vol. I. Washington, D.C.: National Archives.

Allinson, William. 1809. "Journal of William Allinson of Burlington" (ms.). Haverford, Pa.: Haverford College.

Berkhofer, Robert F. 1965. *Salvation and the Savage: An Analysis of Protestant Missions and American Indian Response 1778-1862.* Lexington: University of Kentucky Press.

Brown, Judith. 1970. "Economic Organization and the Position of Women among the Iroquois." *Ethnohistory* 17, 3-4:151-67.

Carr, Lucien. 1883. "On the Social and Political Position of Women among the Huron-Iroquois Tribes." *Harvard University Peabody Museum of Archaeology and Ethnology Report,* no. 16, pp. 207-32.

Ember, Carol. 1974. "An Evaluation of Alternative Theories of Matrilocal versus Patrilocal Residence." *Behavior Science Research* 9, 2.

——— and Melvin Ember. 1971. "The Conditions Favoring Matrilocal vs. Patrilocal Residence." *American Anthropologist* 73:3:571-594.

Everett, Edward A., Chairman. 1922. *Report of the New York State Indian Commission to Investigate the Status of the American Indian Residing in the State of New York.* Albany: New York State Legislature, March 17, 1922. Privately printed in 1972.

Freilich, Morris. 1958. "Cultural Persistence among the Modern Iroquois." *Anthropos* 53:473-83.

Gough, Kathleen. 1962. "Variations in Residence." In D. M. Schneider and K. Gough, eds., *Matrilineal Kinship.* Berkeley and Los Angeles: University of California Press.

Harder, John F. 1963. "The Indian Policy of Henry Knox 1785-1794." M.A. thesis, University of Wisconsin-Milwaukee.

Heckewelder, John. 1817. *History, Manners, and Customs of the Indian Nations.* Philadelphia: Historical Society of Pennsylvania.

Hedrick, Ulysses P. 1933. *A History of Agriculture in the State of New York.* New York: State Agricultural Society.

Hertzberg, Hazel. 1971. *The Search for An American Indian Identity: Modern Pan-Indian Movements.* Syracuse: Syracuse University Press.

Hunt, George. 1940. *The Wars of the Iroquois: A Study of Intertribal Trade Relations.* Madison: University of Wisconsin Press.

Indian Committee Collection (I.C.C.). Philadelphia Yearly Meeting Archives. Philadelphia, Pa.: Friends' Book Store.

Jackson, Halliday. 1806-1818. "Journals" (mss.) West Chester, Pa.: Chester County Historical Society.

———. 1830. *Civilization of the Indian Natives.* Philadelphia: Marcus T. C. Gould.

Jacobs, Wilbur. 1950. *Wilderness Politics and Indian Gifts: The Northern Colonial Frontier 1748-1763.* Lincoln: University of Nebraska Press.

Kent, Donald H. and Merle H. Deardorff. 1960. "John Adlum on the Allegheny: Memoirs for the Year 1794." *Pennsylvania Magazine of History and Biography* 84, 3-4.

Kussart, Serepta. 1938. *The Allegheny River.* Pittsburgh, Pa.: Burgum Printing Co.

"McAllister Collection" (mss.). Philadelphia: Historical Society of Pennsylvania.

Morgan, Lewis H. 1851. *League of the Ho-De-No-Sau-Nee, or, Iroquois.* New York: Dodd, Mead & Co.

———. 1965. (orig. 1881). *Houses and House-Life of the American Aborigines.* Chicago: University of Chicago Press.

Murdock, George P. 1949. *Social Structure.* New York: Macmillan Co.

———. 1967. *Ethnographic Atlas.* Pittsburgh: University of Pittsburgh Press.

Noon, James A. 1949. "Law and Government of the Grand River Iroquois." The Viking Funds, Inc. No. 12.

Norton, Major John. 1970. *The Journal of Major John Norton (1809-1816),*

Carl F. Klinck and James J. Tolman, eds. The Publications of the Champlain Society, vol. 46. Toronto: Champlain Society.

Parker, Arthur C. 1912. "Iroquois Uses of Maize and Other Food Plants." *New York State Museum Bulletin*, no. 144. Albany: University of the State of New York.

Quain, Buell. 1937. "The Iroquois." In M. Mead, ed., *Cooperation and Competition Among Primitive People*. New York: McGraw-Hill.

Randle, Martha. 1951. "Iroquois Women Then and Now." In W. Fenton, ed., Symposium on Local Diversity in Iroquois Culture. Washington: Bureau of American Ethnology, Bulletin No. 149.

Richards, Cara. 1957. "Matriarchy or Mistake: The Role of Iroquois Women Through Time." In V. Ray, ed., *Cultural Stability and Culture Change*. Proceedings of the Annual Meeting of the American Ethnological Society, Seattle, Washington.

———. 1967. "Huron and Iroquois Residence Patterns 1600–1650." In E. Tooker, ed., *Iroquois Culture, History and Prehistory*, Proceedings of the 1965 Conference on Iroquois Research. Albany: New York State Museum.

Rothenberg, Diane B. 1976a. *Friends Like These: An Ethnohistorical Analysis of the Interaction Between Allegany Senecas and Quakers, 1798-1823.* Ann Arbor, Mich.: University Microfilms.

———. 1976b. "Erosion of Power: An Economic Basis for the Selective Conservatism of Seneca Women in the Nineteenth Century." *Western Canadian Journal of Anthropology* 6, 3.

Seaver, James E. 1961. (orig. 1824) *A Narrative of the Life of Mrs. Mary Jemison, The White Woman of the Genesee*. New York: Corinth Books.

Shimony, Annemarie. 1961. "Conservativism Among the Iroquois at the Six Nations Reserve." *Yale University Publications in Anthropology*, no. 65.

Skinner, Dorothy P. 1929. "Seneca Notes Collected on the Allegheny Reservation, New York, 1928 and Cornplanter Reservation, Pennsylvania 1929" (ms.). James Prendergast Library, Jamestown, N.Y.

Snyderman, George S. 1961. "Concepts of Land Ownership Among the Iroquois and Their Neighbors." In W. Fenton, ed., Symposium on Local Diversity in Iroquois Culture. Washington: Bureau of American Ethnology, Bulletin No. 149.

Society of Friends. 1840. *Statement of Facts for the Information of Our Own Members, in Relation to the Circumstances of the Seneca Indians in the State of New York*. Philadelphia.

Stites, Sara H. 1905. *Economics of the Iroquois.* Bryn Mawr College Monograph Series, Vol. I, No. 3. Lancaster, Pa.: New Era Printing Co.

Sydney, James V. 1963. *A People Among People: Quaker Benevolence in Eighteenth Century America*. Cambridge, Mass.: Harvard University Press.

Thwaites, Reuben G., ed. 1896-1901. *The Jesuit Relations and Allied Documents.* Cleveland, Ohio: Burrows.

Tuck, James A. 1971. "The Iroquois Confederacy." *Scientific American* 224, 3:32-42.

Wallace, Anthony F. C. 1957. "Political Organization and Land Tenure Among the Northeastern Indians 1600-1830." *Southwestern Journal of Anthropology* 13:301-21.

———. 1970. *The Death and Rebirth of the Seneca: The History and Culture of the Great Iroquois Nation, Their Destruction and Demoralization, and Their Cultural Revival at the Hands of the Indian Visionary, Handsome Lake.* New York: Alfred A. Knopf.

Washburn, Wilcomb E. 1971. *Red Man's Land—White Man's Law: A Study of the Past and Present Status of the American Indian.* New York: Charles Scribner's Sons.

Whipple, J.S., Chairman. 1889. *Report of the Special Committee to Investigate the Indian Problem of the State of New York Appointed by the Assembly of 1888.* Albany: Troy Press Co.

White, Marian. 1961. "Iroquois Culture History in the Niagara Frontier Area." Museum of Anthropology, Anthropological Paper no. 24. Ann Arbor: University of Michigan.

Wrenshall, John. 1816. "The John Wrenshall Journal" (ms.) Pittsburgh: Historical Society of Western Pennsylvania.

4 Contending with Colonization:
Tlingit Men and Women in Change

LAURA F. KLEIN

European competition over Alaska began with its "discovery" by the Russians in 1741 and continued until the purchase by the United States in 1867. The settlement and influence by Europeans and Euro-Americans continues today, but change for the native peoples was most intensive during the mid-nineteenth century and the very early years of the twentieth under U.S. dominion.

These two centuries of Russian and U.S. control were times of intense change throughout the world. Industrialization in the wake of the industrial revolution caused rapid and major changes in the daily lives of Europeans and Euro-Americans. Further, political structures in Europe and the United States were rocked by revolutions and turmoil. France, Italy, and Germany underwent total reorganizations during these years, and many of their policies abroad revolved about their internal problems. The American revolution and the civil war in the late eighteenth and mid-nineteenth centuries reflected the same type of disorder.

New colonial interests appeared in Asia as well as in the unclaimed areas of the Americas. The lure of the opportunities and riches of the new lands vitally interested the leaders and entrepreneurs of the European and Euro-American nations. The external political course of European history is best seen as a combination of commercial ventures, alliances, and wars. Interest in the territory of Alaska involved most directly the Russians, English, Chinese, and Euro-Americans.

One of the early attractions of Alaska for the Europeans and Euro-Americans were the sea otters found along the coast, whose luxurious fur pelts brought high prices in the international market. The best customers for these furs were the Chinese whose towns were "opened" to external trade in 1775. Alaska also was valued as a base for strategic ports. It was the nearest unoccupied territory to China and Japan and, hence, a convenient supply area.

Before its revolution, Russia was becoming interested in expanding its trade networks throughout the world; commercial interests, and Asian trade in particular, were the major concerns. Often these areas of interest coincided, and therefore conflicted, with those of the English, and during the early nineteenth century the Near East and central Asia saw such antagonisms grow. The building conflict reached a head in Crimean War (1854–56), in which Russia fought against the combined strength of Turkey, England, Sardinia, and France. After Russia's defeat, the Treaty of Paris left the country in severe trouble. Russia survived with little international respect, with vulnerable borders, and with extreme financial difficulties. They did not lose their colony in Alaska, however; early in the war England had declared it out of the boundaries of the conflict and, hence, not part of the conclusion. Russia was overextended, however, and concentrated its remaining ambitions on the Amur Basin in northeastern Asia.

Russia and the United States were allies of a sort throughout this time. The United States remained neutral during the Crimean War. During the American Civil War, Russia returned the favor and publically announced support for the Union. England and France remained officially neutral and this was interpreted in the United States as support for the Confederacy. The only real area of dispute between Russia and the United States involved the closure of Alaskan waters to non-Russian vessels. Incidents involving the seizure of American traders and fisherman in Alaskan waters were of concern to both nations, each of which needed allies.

With the sale of the territory to the United States in 1867, Alaska's fate, in terms of European and Euro-American competition, was sealed. England thereafter settled for its lands in Canada and Russia left North America completely. Soon the imperial lure of Africa and Asia set the Europeans on a different track and Alaska settled back into international obscurity.

Alaska today is one of the most misunderstood areas in the United States. Most Americans picture ice, snow, igloos, and fur-clad Eskimos when the state is mentioned. In Washington, D.C., people make laws on the premise that Eskimos with guns are not real Eskimos and that Alaskan natives with landclaims money are rich Euro-Americans. To anyone familiar with Alaska these images are ludicrous; they are, however, quite real in the forming of policy for the state. This phenomenon is not new to Alaska; misunderstanding, lack of interest, and special rules are themes running throughout the Euro-American history of the area. The object of this chapter is to recount how Alaska's unique colonial history has affected one group of native Alaskans—the Tlingit.[1] The Tlingit today are a thriving people who follow a way of life midway between traditional Tlingit culture and Euro-American culture. The fit between colonial interests and practices on the Alaskan coast and the traditional culture was such that neither clearly prevailed.

The relatively late time of contact, the countries involved, and the primary purposes for contact in southeastern Alaska are notably different from those in other areas of the United States. Certainly, the coming of whites into a native territory produces enormous changes in the native ways of life. More directly, the way in which this contact takes place has very important influence on the direction of these changes. The purpose of contact, the compatability of the subsections of these cultures that actually come into contact are key elements (Spicer 1961; Linton 1940; Barnett et al. 1954).

The specific area of change to be investigated in this chapter is that of sex roles. Ideal sex roles, as they appear in contemporary Tlingit situations, are more similar in theme to the traditional ones than they are to those preached by the Europeans who first came to the coast. These Westerners wanted to create an atmosphere in which they could most efficiently, profitably, and pleasantly accomplish their own purposes. Missionaries, for example, believed that a specific family structure, dress, hygiene, and type of education went hand in hand with the belief in Christ; male traders seemed to expect to deal with male traders. The European colonizers, then, expected the people with whom they dealt to have the same, rather strict and limited sex-role pattern as they. Among the Tlingit this expectation was not valid. Many factors intervened to make the transformation of sex roles to a Western pattern inefficient and quite impractical. After reviewing the history of colonization in southeastern Alaska and the nature of the Tlingit themselves, the key elements of change will be traced and their implications in the present and for the future discussed.

THE COLONIZER'S PERSPECTIVE

The earliest European history of Alaska falls within the typical pattern of eighteenth-century colonial expansion. The first recorded European discovery came in 1741 with the voyage of Vitus Bering, a Dane sailing under a Russian flag. Russian traders, called *promyshlenniki*, entered the waters to initiate fur trade within two years. An equally important journey, which publicized to the entire world the value of furs in Alaska and the eagerness of Asian dealers to buy them, was that of Captain Cook in 1778 for England. Soon after, boats from all the major European powers came to Alaskan waters. While French and "Boston men" appeared intermittently, the west coast of North America was most ardently sought by Russia, Britain, and Spain, with its division ultimately falling in that order from north to south. All made early claims on the area that became southeastern Alaska, but it was the Russian fur traders who first took control of the area, and they continued to be the major force for the first century of contact. The *promyshlenniki* are remembered as being consistently disreputable and engaged in generally antagonistic relations with the native peoples. In 1799 the Russian trade companies were consolidated into the Russian-American Company, which represented the colonial government of Alaska throughout the Russian period. Russian Orthodox missions and missionaries were supported by the crown but were often discouraged and discredited in reports sent to Russia by the company (Okun 1951:211).

The bulk of the Russian oppression fell on the Aleuts to the north and west of the Tlingit. When the profits in the sea-otter fur trade moved to Tlingit waters, the Russians impressed the Aleuts into doing this hunting since the Tlingit were feared by the Aleuts and Russians alike (Andrews 1967:49—50). Individual Russians entered the area, but not eagerly. Alekandr Baranov, Russian governor of Alaska, managed to establish the new Russian capital of Fort Archangel (Sitka) within Tlingit territory. In 1802, however, the Tlingit burned the fort and killed or drove out its occupants. After it was reestablished it remained an armed camp. In Russian dispatches of the day, the Tlingit were termed "not completely independent" in a tripartite classification of "actually dependent," "semi-dependent," and "completely independent" (Okun 1951: 193). But, as State Councillor Kostlivtsov reported in 1860,

> The Kolosh [Tlingit] cannot in any respect by regarded as dependent on the Company, rather it may be said that, in turn, the Company's colonies on the American coast depend on them; for the Kolosh have only, so to speak, to begin to make a little noise to deprive the port of Arkhangelsk and its entire population of all fresh food and even of the opportunity to show their faces a few yards outside of the fortifications (quoted in Okun 1951:207).

At mid-century, the profits from sea otter hunting dropped dramatically, because of overhunting and loss of markets, and monetary problems affected

Russia. At first much of southeastern Alaska was leased to the Hudson's Bay Company and then, in 1867, the territory was sold to the United States. There continues to be disagreement in the literature concerning the reasons why Russia sold Alaska at this time and why the United States decided to buy it. Clearly, Russia was having economic problems at home and was geographically overextended. Russian America, which had reliably brought in profits, now was becoming an expense. The lease of land to their Crimean enemy, Britain, was an embarrassment and politically unsound. Russia seemed to have three choices: it could pour money into the colony to build it up and defend it; it could let it decline under the control of the Company and risk its seizure by Britain or the United States; finally, it could be sold (Jensen 1975:49). By selling it to the United States, an informal ally, Russia would obtain needed money and guarantee that it did not fall into British hands. Alaska was never a Russian priority and in 1862 there were only 577 Russians in the entire colony (Gibson 1976:26).

To indicate that the 1867 sale was unpopular in the United States is an understatement. For sixteen months after the sale had been finalized the United States Congress refused to allocate the money; only intense lobbying and the pressure of international embarrassment forced the payment. Why was this enormous addition to the United States so unpopular? Clearly, few saw Alaska's potential; the press reviled the purchase as Secretary of State Seward's "folly" or "ice box" and ran editorials against "Walrussia." Alaska was presented as far away, very cold, inhabited by hostile and peculiar peoples, and of little apparent use. The fur days were gone and the gold and oil days in the foggy future. Why then, with such opposition, did the sale take place at all? Traditionally cited reasons include manifest destiny, friendship with the faltering Russia—which had offered moral support to the Union during the Civil War—and the availability of ports to encourage Asian trade. Also, it has been noted that possession of Alaska by the United States bounded British Columbia by the United States both north and south at a time when the ownership of this territory had not been completely conceded to England. The purchase would also provide safe waters for U.S. Fishing boats in the North Pacific. Finally even though grossly underestimated, the apparent resources of the territory exceeded the asking price of $7,200,000 (Jensen 1975; Kushner 1975; Hinkley 1972).

None of the causes for sale involved clear plans for the financial exploitation of the region. It was the possession of the geographic area rather than control of specific land or people that was important. The United States owned Alaska but it hardly understood what it owned, and even the initial physical exploration of many major areas was not completed until the turn of the century (Sherwood 1965:9). Rich as it turned out to be, this was a largely hidden asset to the world during most of the nineteenth century.

Having bought Alaska, the U.S. government apparently decided to have as little to do with it as possible. Alaska was organized as a customs district and largely ignored; Ernest Gruening (1954:33) characterized the period up until 1884 as the "era of total neglect." When the Euro-American residents of Sitka feared a Tlingit attack in 1877 their pleas for aid from the United States military went unanswered. Only in 1879, after Britain had sent a gunboat from Vancouver Island to protect them, did the United States send troops. Officially, then, Alaska was left alone. It was a possession set aside and not an integral part of the American scene.

THE TLINGIT: PRECONTACT

The life of the Tlingit up to the time of purchase was one of relative plenty. Yearly salmon runs, as well as abundant quantities of other fish, sea mammals, land mammals, and a variety of wild plants were the bases of a subsistence economy which demanded constant labor during summer months, but little at other times. Fishing and hunting were largely male pursuits. Informants report grandmothers and other female ancestors who were skillful in these activities, but the scope of women's participation is unclear. Seemingly, the more important work for women was the preparing and storing of foods. Fish and some meats were dried and smoked, transforming perishable resources into year-round food. The collection of berries, seaweeds, and other vegetation and much of the hunting was scheduled for the slack periods between the fish runs. All food, once collected, was placed in the women's hands for preservation and rationing. In this way, foods collected in August could feed the families or diligent women in February. Surplus foods and furs were collected and set aside for trade, luxury use, and feasting.

Trade for prestige was carried on between neighboring coastal peoples and with the inland sub-Arctic peoples. The luxury and unique items of each people spread along the coast in this way from the Inuit (Eskimo) territory to California. In the fall men would pack their trade goods into seagoing canoes or onto their backs and proceed on the trade routes. One addition noted by early European explorers was a single woman who frequently went along. The job of this woman was to assure that the male traders got a good return for their goods. She, in other words, set the prices (Marchand 1801:242; Wood 1882:333; Krause 1956:136). There are a number of stories in this literature that tell of deals vetoed by wives and of men who refused to go to a certain trading post because the trader's native wife would not allow them to cheat him; today, this is explained with the phrase, "Men are foolish with money." The manipulation and saving of wealth was, and remains, in the hands of the women; this is considered their duty and responsibility. If a man had a good fishing season but was left with little material wealth at its end with which to potlatch or trade, it was his wife who was to blame. It is in a man's very nature, it is said, to be friendly and to share good fortune with friends while it is a woman's responsibility to keep this tendency in check.

Trade and the conservation of wealth is important in Tlingit society, and it goes to the very heart of the ethos of the Northwest Coast where wealth is necessary to elevate status and to confirm already high status. The symbol of this wealth is the feast known as the "potlatch." The Tlingit ranking system and potlatching are well known, but it is worth repeating the often used Northwest Coast formula, wealth plus birth equal status. All Tlingit are entitled to particular names, privileges, and the use of particular emblems by their position in the kinship units. Their position in their lineages and the attending privileges are only valid for adults if they show themselves worthy. This is done through the giving of potlatches. A person taking a chiefly name, for example, must give a worthy potlatch for an opposite clan which is invited to witness the acquisition. Women as well as men take important names and occasionally there is mention of a woman taking a name associated with a chief's position (de Laguna 1972:463); it is not clear, however, how often the position itself went to women taking the associated names. Less high ranking names can also be taken by other clan members at the same time and in the same potlatch. Potlatches are given using the combined wealth of clan members and not just that of the person taking the highest name and honors. Potlatching involves both feasting, in which clan members and members of another clan are required to eat heartily of extravagant amounts of food, and gift giving. The accumulation of the gifts is also managed by women. In 1896 Knapp and Childe reported that "since very ancient times the women have been the keepers of the family treasures, they are generally in a position to dictate terms" (1896: 61).

The part of Tlingit life least apparent to the early Europeans was that daily life that went on in the villages. Europeans tended to build their own towns (for example, Juneau and Sitka), and it was only the especially ambitious and courageous trader or missionary who attempted to live in the native villages. The winter villages were to be found along the shores on the many islands of the Alexander Archipelago and the nearby mainland; most were placed on the shores of rivers or on the quieter bays. Houses formed rows of up to three-fourths of a mile long (Emmons 1916: 13) along the beaches just beyond the high-tide lines. The beaches were used to secure canoes and for the location of drying racks. Other structures in an established town would include death houses, women's huts (for birth, puberty, seclusion, and menstruation), storage houses, and the famous totem poles. Winter towns were permanent and some were the homes of up to 1000 people. During summer seasons some of the inhabitants would move out to temporary camps near fishing streams. It was the appearance of such camps that often lead Europeans to remark mistakenly on rather squalid living conditions.

The winter houses were large rectangular wooden structures which housed a number of related nuclear families in individual compartments. Based on an avunculocal residence pattern,[2] one could expect to find a man and his nuclear family along with his sisters' sons and their families living in this house; many houses also had slaves. Kinship was reckoned matrilineally with moieties and clans.[3] House groups represented the smallest functional unit within the system. The highest ranking member of the clan in a house would be the house chief (*hitsati*). The highest ranking *hitsati* within a local clan would be the clan chief, and the highest ranking clan chief in town, the town chief. The latter two were referred to as *aankaawoo* ("wealthy person"), and that title was extended to many other wealthy men and women. None of the so-called chiefs had real power. Disputes within kinship units were settled in family meetings and those between kinship units were settled either through peaceful discussion or more violently through war and feuds. A woman was expected to back her own clansmen rather than those with whom she resided (her husband's clansmen) if the dispute were to involve these two groups.

Marriages were between individuals of opposite moieties, and a wife and husband were to be as closely equal in rank as possible. Divorce was common and polygamy relatively unusual. A woman moved to her husband's house at marriage but never was incorporated into his clan, remaining a vital part of her own clan and individually determining her own ranking. An exception to this that applied to both sexes is that any great shame befalling a member of a clan—such as being exposed as a witch, thief, or slave—would reflect badly on the rank of all of that clan.

Traditional religion is rather poorly recorded but there were a number of mythological beings as well as individual guardian spirits. Shamans or "Indian doctors" employed their spirits to cure illness and expose witchcraft; both men and women were doctors and witches. Doctors could become quite wealthy by curing high ranking patients. Because of the emphasis on ranking the patrons were compelled by the unstated threat of public dishonor to pay the doctor according to what they felt their lives were worth. In other words, only by paying dearly could a rich person reinforce public recognition of his or her ranking. Hence the doctors role could be an economically lucrative one as well as a spiritual calling.

FUR TRADERS, MISSIONARIES, AND INDUSTRIALISTS

Ordinary, day-to-day Tlingit life formed the base from which the Tlingit reacted to European demands. It was just these daily routines and expectations, however, that were hidden from European eyes and which were the most misunderstood and troublesome to Europeans and Euro-Americans when they first became involved with the Tlingit on the local level. While the governmental interest in Alaska was rather superficial, many individual Europeans and Euro-Americans came to the area to pursue their own goals. Some came to fill their pockets and others to save souls; and for either task direct contact with the native peoples was a necessity. The early part of the nineteenth century saw the appearance of the bulk of the fur traders and the latter part missionaries and industrialists.

Fur Traders

The traders came into a system that understood and appreciated trade. The Tlingit had operated as middlemen in the precontact trade routes, and they controlled the routes to the north and into the interior. They had no unique trade goods of their own and it was through monopolizing the trade north and east that the Tlingit became an important trading power. The Tlingit jealously guarded this monopoly and continued to act as middlemen between the interior peoples and the Europeans. When the Hudson's Bay Company threatened this monopoly by building trading posts at the heads of strategic rivers, a contingent of Tlingit went to the European manager and stressed the lack of wisdom in this "in terms he was not used to hearing." In 1852, to emphasize the point, Tlingit destroyed the Hudson's Bay Company's post at Fort Selkirk, allowing the employees to escape to the safety of the coast to spread the warning (Drucker 1963: 32-33).

From the earliest contact the Europeans learned to respect the Tlingit as traders. In 1789 Captain Dixon described a "considerable degree of cunning" (: 220). The French explorer La Perouse explained, "They showed to our great astonishment, great familarity with trading and they made bargains as astutely as European merchants" (quoted in Krause 1956: 130).

The immediate importance of trade to the Tlingit was, again, to accumulate wealth to support potlatches which would increase or define rank. The long-range importance of traditional trade to the Tlingit would be an historic one. The Tlingit were well adapted to compete with Europeans at their level of interest. Europeans wanted furs and the Tlingit wanted prestige items, and both wanted to increase their own wealth and social standing. From historical sources it seems that they were able adversaries. Bargaining and "getting the better" of a trade partner were concepts well entrenched in the Tlingit system. In native trade with the interior Athapascans, for example, Tlingits prided themselves on giving nothing of worth for a return of items of great value (copper and interior furs). The European traders, then, to their great disappointment, did not meet a group of innocents. It might be only a minor exaggeration to state that the European traders were welcome and Tlingit culture ready to cope with them. [Codere (1950: 8) notes a similar situation among the Kwakiutl to the south.] From the first, they were not afraid of the Europeans. As early as 1775 Juan Francisco de la Bodega y Quadra remarked with some surprise that the natives near Sitka charged the Spanish for fish and water and tore down the Spanish claim markers as their ships sailed off (Krause 1956: 16).

As mentioned above, the traditional attitude among the Tlingit was that women should be trained to handle wealth and manage trade. Traders' accounts usually discussed women's managerial skills in terms of a woman's power in an European trade arrangement. This is often in the form of a complaint; either a woman had concluded a hard bargain or had vetoed a trade her man had foolishly made. Wood complained in detail:

> The Alaskan women are childish and pleasant, yet quick-witted and capable of heartless vindictiveness. Their authority in all matters is unquestioned. No bargain is made, no expedition set on foot, without first consulting the women. Their veto is never disregarded. I bought a silver-fox skin from Tsatate, but his wife made him return the articles of trade and recover the skin, in the same way I was perpetually being annoyed by having to undo bargains because "his wife said *clekh*," that is, "no." I hired a fellow to take me about thirty miles in his canoe, when my own crew was tired. He agreed, I paid him the tobacco, and we were about to start when his wife came to the beach and stopped him. He quietly unloaded the canoe and handed me back the tobacco (1882: 333).

Wood had earlier attempted to rent a canoe from a "person of great consequence" whose "influence surpassed even the usual wonderful authority of the Alaskan woman" (:325). Others complained in a similar fashion: "The women are far keener at a 'dicker' than the men, and much more difficult to cheat" (Knapp and Childe 1896:61–62); "No person is more stubborn than the average Thlinget woman" (Jones 1914:51). When the women are trading, "They are even more inclined to be stubborn than the men" (Krause 1956:136). This was clearly an annoyance but the fact of the general skill of the Tlingit as a people was also an annoyance. The fact was clear to the traders, however, that if they wished to trade with the Tlingit they had no choice but to follow the rules. The Europeans and Euro-Americans disliked dealing with the women because they were unaccustomed to finding women in this position, but also because the women were too skillful. In a world of shrewd traders it must have added insult to injury to have the shrewdest be women. While the Europeans may have preferred to deal with men, the Tlingit were aware that this was often not in their economic interest, and they therefore had no reason to go along with it. The Europeans had no way to enforce their preference nor did they have any missionary zeal to do so. They did not need to permanently transform the Tlingit world since they expected to be in it for only a short time. They left us records of women in trade positions but they did little to change the situation.

In her recent study of early European contact on the coast, Erna Gunther sums it up most succinctly.

> The Tlingit were a large enough group to maintain their way of life, and in spite of their local quarreling they maintained a united

front against the Russians. They were the first Northwest Coast people to live with foreign settlers. The fur traders, explorers, and later the whalers came and went. They were interested in their own business, but not in changing the culture of the Indians or offering them new philosophies, like the teachers and missionaries who came later in the nineteenth century. The canneries, logging camps, and miners also were also not concerned with the social problems of acculturation; so the Indians were free to use the trade goods in their own ways and come into town when necessary, but to carry on much of their old life, at least during the first half of the nineteenth century (1972:181).

Missionaries

The newcomers who cared the most about the personal lives of the Tlingit people were, of course, the missionaries. Surprisingly, they were welcomed like the traders and for much the same reason. The Reverend William Duncan, an Anglican missionary among the Tsimshians in northern British Columbia and later Alaska, provided jobs and new wealth along with religion for the members of his Christian community of Metlakatla. The Tlingit's prosperity under Duncan was a model to others of the rewards of Christianity; it was this economic message that came through to the Tlingit and they requested a similar mission from the Anglicans (Drucker 1965:203). The Anglicans limited their mission to the Tsimshians but the Presbyterians came. They did not always come up to the promise of Duncan's community, and there was a definite difference in goals between the natives and the missionaries. In 1885 the German geographer Aurel Krause reported after a year of study in the region:

> According to the current reports of the missionaries themselves regarding their efforts, the possibility of further civilizing the Tlingit holds a great future, but these statements are all too optimistic and highly colored. It is true that the Tlingit Indians in almost every place are favorably inclined to the building of schools, but to every outsider it is obvious that selfish motives, above all, ambition to imitate the white man, are the driving forces behind this amiability....But, just as for every other service, he expects a reward for it....the Chilkat, after they had gone to church for half a year and sent their children to school, went to the missionary and complained that they had not been rewarded for their virtue and had not received boards to build their houses as the Tsimshian had (1956:230).

In the late 1870s Sheldon Jackson and Amanda McFarland reached the Tlingit town of Wrangell, which had had no formal mission for a decade, where they found two Tsimshians running a small school and religious congregation. One, Mrs. Dickinson, was caught off guard and rushed to meet Sheldon Jackson on his arrival: "When we reached Wrangel this woman was a hundred miles up the Stickeen River gathering her winter supply of berries. Learning from a passing steamer that the missionaries had come, she placed her children, bedding, and provisions in her canoe, and paddled home, against heavy head winds, to give us welcome" (Jackson 1880:147). Unlike his European predecessors, Sheldon Jackson was not impressed with the station of Tlingit women. He found "degradation" in their hard work, imprisonment, tattooing, use in slavery, and sale to men (:115—18). Of course, hard work can also imply involvement in the economy; tattooing, high status within the ranking system; "imprisonment," the seclusion and training of puberty; "sale" to men, bridewealth in marriage; and use in slavery, an advantage over immediate death for captives. Jackson saw Tlingit women as being in a sorry state, indeed: "Despised by their fathers, sold by their mothers, imposed upon by their brothers, ill-treated by their husbands, cast out in their widowhood, living lives of toil and low sensual pleasure, untaught and uncared for, with no true enjoyment in this world and no hope for the world to come, crushed by a cruel heathenism" (:123). It should be little wonder that an immediate priority for the new missions was the freeing of women from this perceived wretchedness: "Mrs. McFarland felt from the very commencement of the mission, the need of a "Home" into which she could gather such promising girls as were in danger of being sold, and train them up to be the future Christian teachers, wives, and mothers of their people" (:217).

Schools were set up at all missions. Most had both boys and girls as students, although some were set aside to train girls and one for boys. The secular education and the health care that often went along with schooling were welcome. The religious beliefs were often added to traditional Tlingit views but there was little awe of Christianity. One recent informant reminisced about her youth when she was one of a few English speakers in her native town. One Sunday she decided to sit on the side of the Presbyterian church where the non-English speakers sat to listen to the translation of the sermon. She thought she would test her English against that of the translators. To her surprise, as the minister told his Bible tale the translator told a traditional Raven story. The natives believed that the minister was telling Raven tales while the minister believed that the Tlingits were being enlightened by the Gospel. Both sides were apparently well pleased by the good sense of the other. The same woman tells of the general amusement that Tlingit felt at the Bible story of the flood. That sensible adults could believe that a mere forty days and nights of rain would cause a universal flood was too silly to believe for the Tlingit, who experience such rain often and take it in stride. The sanctity of a literal belief in the Bible was a virtue that the Tlingit were not apt to learn too quickly.

Morally, the missionaries were against potlatches (which invited rowdy behavior and discouraged permanent savings), the kinship system (since matriliny discouraged the Christian father role), house types (since communal houses encouraged matriliny and were considered unhealthy), the decorative labrets (since they were regarded as disgusting), all witchcraft and healing practices (since they were the antithesis of Christianity), and, of course, the sex-role patterning. The personnel of the missions, however, tended to provide examples that belied some of the teachings and especially those regarding female submission to male authority. Most local missions had from one to three missionaries; they performed the roles of minister, teacher, and nurse, and often one person had to hold all of these jobs. Married couples frequently took the minister-teacher roles, and when a husband died in the field, as history repeatedly records, the wife often stayed on in their mission. Other women came to Alaska as single women or widows and were put to work in the missions. It is not unusual to find women in positions of authority in the missions. Amanda McFarland is by far the most important Euro-American woman in the early mission history. She ran major missions and was the senior missionary overall during Sheldon Jackson's absences. Jackson noted that "all the perplexities, political, religious, physical, and moral, of the native population were brought to her for solution, and that her arbitration was universally accepted" (1880: 147). Even allowing for missionary optimism in this comment, history supports her general authority or respect. Maggie McFarland, the wife of Amanda's nephew, came to Alaska unmarried and, after her husband's death, took over his mission. She is remembered today as "the boss," a nickname the older residents of the town of her mission apply with both respect and the memories of a bit of fear. When the government officially took over the operation of schools, the missionaries continued to operate them under contract.

Missionary papers and books repeatedly record the adventures of these women. The epidemics that took their husbands and children, witch hunts, foul weather, and the various problems caused them by "paganism" plagued these women. As Wright noted at the time, "Timid women do not make good missionaries in Alaska" (1883:260). These women who came as missionaries provided strong role models. Whatever the preaching of domesticity, the living models of the best Christian women were public actors and powerful people.

That the domesticity argument was weak in affecting the Tlingit can be shown in the following examples drawn from 1888 through 1926. Although amusing today, they were written with the anguish of a missionary in great spiritual distress.

> After speaking of Shatterick's death (head chief of the Chilcats), [a parishioner] says, his widow (not quite as old as Methuselah, we suppose), sends a messenger to him [the parishioner] requesting him to write and ask up Chilcoot Jack's sons, we have 3 of them in the Home, the oldest not over eighteen years of age, that she may look at them and see if she wants either, or perhaps, all of them to take the place [as husband] of the *dear departed* (Anon. 1888:n.p.).

Said a Tlinget woman to the missionary who was urging her to marry her husband of many years according to American laws: "No! No want to get married! Because why? Because then James carry the pocket book." She evidently believed that the hand that pulls the purse strings rocks the world as well as the hand that rocks the cradle (Condit 1926:257).

One day [a "very quarrelsome couple"] had a fight in the road, so the council arrested them. They fined the man $2 and the woman $8 for disturbing the peace. The Indian woman carries the pocketbook so she paid her fine but let him go to jail. He was set to work on the road. But he is supposed to be a high caste man, but his father found him working on the road with a low caste man. So the council fined him $20 for breaking the caste law (Anon. 1924:257–58).

Obviously, the acceptance of mission teachings was selective. Those mission causes that were underlined by misunderstanding of or distaste for important elements of Tlingit culture were slowly, if ever, accepted, and those sermons that went against common sense or daily example were disregarded. There were no rewards for the taking of Euro-American sex roles and, indeed, there was much to be lost. The missions' most successful converts became Christian women, but they were active, in the image of the female missionaries, and often financially shrewder. It is ironic that Condit could note the "native woman's equality with man" but credit this to missionary teachings. It was "a transformation and a triumph for missionary effort" (1926:265). In fact, as shown, it was a continuity which endured despite the mission teachings. It was, in fact, a triumph for Tlingit individuality in the face of change.

Industrialists

The final interest group to be discussed is the commercial fishing industry. The earliest Alaskan commercial salmon canneries, the North Pacific Trading and Packing Company at Klawock and the Cutting Packing Company near Sitka, were opened eleven years after the purchase. In 1879, 12,130 cases of salmon were produced there (Freeburn 1976:162–63). By 1900 there were over forty canneries in Alaska and by 1914 there were that many on the southeast coast. The salmon industry has always been an uncertain one with the fluctuation in yearly salmon runs causing boom and bust years. Canneries, therefore, opened and closed with great rapidity (Browning 1974:43). The greatest number of canneries were operating in the summer of 1929 and the greatest amount of salmon was canned in 1936.

Of interest here is that such canneries provided local jobs for many native workers and continue to do so. They transformed the base activity of the subsistence economy into a base for the commercial pattern. The sexual division of labor was similar in structure in both realms. In both men fished and women processed the fish. Also, the scheduling remained essentially constant. As Gunther noted, the cannery owners demanded little change in employees' life styles. Some canneries, it is true, were placed away from traditional towns, causing employees to move to cannery camps for the season, but even this mimicked the traditional use of summer camps. The major distinction between commercial canning and traditional smoking and preservation for the evaluation of the status of women was that now canning was given a monetary value and, often, that value was less than that which was placed on fishing, the men's occupation. Men's work was worth more than women's in the reckoning of the new system. Cannery work, further, was not in itself especially enjoyable. It is hard work, as is fishing, but it did not provide the excitement and pride that fishing can. People will recreationally fish but few, if any, do canning for recreation.

The cannery industry at its heights provided in-season work for both men and women, but the men were more highly paid. Women continued to bring in wealth to their families in this way, however. Both sexes remained busy and contributed to the family in a familiar way.

CONTEMPORARY LIFE

The theme of the strong, autonomous Tlingit woman is quite alive in the modern society. The twentieth century presents many technical and economic changes from the earlier periods. In the new context, however, the old themes of sex-linked abilities and responsibilities persist. Women are still competent individuals who are steady, work oriented, and suited for handling wealth.

The theme of men and women sharing in economic endeavors continues although in a modern form. Technical advances have allowed the fishing industry to decentralize. Fish caught in Alaskan waters can now be processed to the south where the general overhead is lower. Also, poor fish runs in recent years have meant a decrease in the amount of fish caught and canneries have closed. This means that while the men's fishing jobs remain, many of the women's processing jobs are gone. Added to the preference of women for higher-paying jobs, this has created a new economic scheduling. Men have the more prestigious and lucrative jobs during the summer and provide the bulk of the labor in the subsistence area since freezers have lessened the need for smoking.

The year-round story, however, is the opposite. Commercial fishing is still the major employment of men. The season, which is now determined by the state Fish and Game Department as well as by the fish runs, extends from about May to October. Women still work in canneries during this period, but in fewer numbers, and many work the canneries as second jobs. The women in the area hold most of the year-round jobs which are Euro-American by nature. Office workers, postal workers, store employees, school employees, bank workers, and the like are usually women. One commonly reported reason for this is that women are steadier than men as they will not quit when the fishing is good in order to cash in on that industry; this is a strong theme. For example, one well-liked and highly respected man who had a college education was unable to find year-round work. All employers agreed that he was capable and reliable, but it would not be worthwhile for them to have his services for eight months a year when there were skilled women who would work for twelve months. This particular man now winters in Seattle, where he works, and fishes in Alaskan waters during the summer.

Seasonality—more precisely, the modern view of the seasons—has become central in the contemporary allotment of jobs. Because of this and other selection factors, the sexual division of labor here differs from both the traditional Tlingit system in detail and the usual Euro-American patterns. The theme of equal participation in the overall economy, however, is closer to the traditional ideal than to either the Euro-American ideal or the system of the earlier cannery days. It seems that as soon as it was possible to reject the inequality of the commercial fishing-and-canning system the Tlingit women did so.

Several employment schemes besides those of the fishermen and cannery workers fit well into both the Euro-American and Tlingit expectations. Dock and police workers and loggers, for example, tend to be men. Both societies allot positions that require physical strength to males. When a woman might occasionally take any of these jobs it would be considered worthy of comment. A neighboring village was noted for its policewoman, whose unusual and effective technique for dealing with the drunk and disorderly was to march into the bar, drag them out by their ears, and throw them into the bay to sober up. The fact that it was a woman doing this was said to have an extra sobering effect. She was not, however, ridiculed for this, but admired for being inventive. Sales jobs at stores, on the other hand, are generally taken by women, and this fits the Euro-American expectation of women sales clerks as well as the Tlingit concept of women in trade-oriented positions. Teacher's aide and health aide appointments also go repeatedly to women. Euro-Americans see subordinate medical and education jobs as naturally female and somewhat beneath the dignity of men. The Tlingit, on the other hand, see both positions as respectable and fitting into the general realm of education and health with which women have been long involved. In this case, however, men have also been active in these areas in the Tlingit world and will apply for such jobs. The overseeing boards, which are under non-native control, tend to ignore or discount such applications by men. In this, the sexual division is much more flexible among the Tlingit than among Euro-Americans.

This imposed employment differentiation has implications beyond the purely economic. Year-round jobs tend to be cash-oriented, involve more public relations, and generally are more Euro-American in style than the summer ones. Women in these jobs, then, tend to meet more Euro-Americans, learn their systems better, and generally have skills applicable to the non-Tlingit world. This is recognized and encouraged on the level of education as well. More women than men go on to post-secondary education from the local high school. Also the high school itself is a bit unusual in Euro-American terms since male students are expected to take home economics, and women, shop classes. A fisherman, it is noted, does not need an European education since it is the Tlingits not the Euro-Americans who are the expert fishermen; they therefore learn their skills best at home. A woman, however, can get a better-paying job in her realm with a good Euro-American education. This orientation provides a training in Euro-American skills that carries over to local-level politics. The town studied is officially a first-class city under Alaskan state law and has a mayor/city council form of government. The major elected officers are the mayor, city councilors, and school-board members. Their importance to the community stems from the grants they can bring in and the jobs they distribute, and a conscious effort is made to keep Tlingits in all of the important positions. The two single most important are that of mayor, a man, and school-board president, a woman. While the title of the former is more impressive in most Euro-American contexts, in this case it is the latter official who is more powerful; she has a larger budget and more jobs at her disposal. Both individuals hold offices in the myriad of town, state, and native corporation committees as well as those stemming from their clan obligations. There are many committees dealing with health, native land-claims money, education, fishing, and other business ventures. All such committees are composed of both men and women at all levels, and the individual who often represented this town during the Alaskan Native Land Claims disputes was a woman.[4]

Tlingit resistance to Euro-American sex-role models is also exemplified by the compatibility between the roles of mother and employee. First, despite the teachings of the missionaries, it is today a common opinion that a good mother cares for her children with financial, as well as emotional, support. One woman, the mother of six, was repeatedly criticized for not working during a time when jobs were plentiful. If she really cared for her children, it was said, she would work for them so they could have nicer belongings. Her presence at home and her doing housework were considered to be of little benefit. In other words, she was considered lazy and somewhat selfish. Secondly, there is no job in town which totally excludes the presence of children. Children regularly report to their parents at work; this is part of the flavor of the town and is considered normal. With older children responsible for younger ones, and given the general safety of the town, this type of control is usually quite sufficient. In addition, seasonally employed fathers can take responsibility for their children when they are not working, and there are neighbors and relatives who act as babysitters as well as a day-care center. Employment and children are compatible and Euro-Americans in this town have come to adjust to the pattern.

THE FUTURE

Speculation about the future is always dangerous, but is also irresistible. The Tlingit future, of course, depends to a large extent upon the Tlingit themselves, and, as always, it will be their reaction to non-Tlingit pressures that will count. The possible areas of conflict and pressure are myriad but some stand out; education, media, government pressure and land-claims money, and the state of the fishing industry are particularly important.

Schools actively teach Western concepts and models, some of which are welcomed and some disliked. As long as local communities control their schools such teachings can be modified. More and more students are attending colleges, however, and their influence may prove more problematic. It is an open question as to how the expectations and pressures of professors and students alike will affect the views of the Tlingit students in their first full exposure to the non-Tlingit world. The media also constitute a teaching tool television, radio, and motion pictures continue to portray women as subservient and somewhat silly. As long as these sources are perceived as portraying a non-Tlingit reality they will not be very powerful. As one woman recently remarked after seeing an episode of a television soap opera, "You whites are crazy, you know." It is not at all clear, however, that children are making the same distinctions.

Government projects and laws are becoming more immediate to Alaskans. The United States will no longer ignore the state that seems to have so much gas and oil. This can cause problems but the extent of the interference seems still a question for the future. The most obvious government project in the state, the oil pipeline, is far away and not of direct interest to the Tlingit. The Alaskan Native Land Claims settlement, however, is of major interest. Two influences on sex roles are worth watching. First, there is already pressure to change inheritance practices from matrilineal to bilateral; lawyers direct parents to write wills leaving their monies to their own children. Another point of interest will be the willingness of the non-Tlingit businesspeople to deal with Tlingit women in the corporations. If there is differential treatment of men and women in this realm the reaction will be particularly important to observe.

Were I forced to choose a single area as the most problematic and likely to cause the most widespread threat to Tlingit life at this time, however, it would be the condition of the fishing industry. Limitations on the numbers of fishermen allowed in Alaskan waters threatens the universality of fishing as the mainstay of Tlingit men. If they are forced out of this industry, wide-scale shifts in the employment patterns would have to take place. Where the sex-role patterns would fit into this is unanswerable at this point, but all aspects of Tlingit life could be disrupted.

Whatever external factors influence the roles of men and women in the future, it cannot be forgotten that Tlingit women are active, assertive individuals and have always demanded a say in their own future, and the future should not be any different than the past in this. The Tlingit, and Tlingit women in particular, are not pawns; they are actors and will continue to act to maintain their rights to employment and political activity.

NOTES

1. Data for this paper came from twenty-two months of fieldwork (including a thirteen-month span) in a Tlingit community in southeastern Alaska. This work had been supported by grants from the Ford Foundation (Dissertation Fellowship), and the Whatcome Museum Foundation (Melville and Elizabeth Jacobs Research Fund). I would also like to thank the members of the New York Women's Anthropology Conference for repeatedly stimulating exchanges of ideas. An earlier version of this paper was read at their conference on Women in Production and Reproduction in the spring of 1978.

2. In an avunculocal residence pattern, children live with their mother's brother. Among the Tlingit, boys were sent to live with a mother's brother at about ten years of age. They could then learn the rights and skills of men of their descent group. They could remain in this house for the rest of their lives. Wives moved in with their husbands.

3. Moieties are large, "bisecting" kinship units found in many societies. All Tlingit belong to either the Eagle or the Raven moiety. An individual belongs to the moiety of his or her mother. The key rule is that marriages are not allowed between members of the same moiety; thus, Eagles must marry Ravens. Each moiety is subdivided into a series of smaller, named kinship units referred to as clans. Clan members share rights to names, stories, emblems, fishing areas, and other property.

4. The Alaskan Native Land Claims refers to the recently won joint claim of all Alaskan natives (Indians, Aleut, and Inuit) to land and financial compensation from the U.S. government.

REFERENCES

Andrews, Clarence L. 1967. *Alaska and Its History*. Seattle: University of Washington Press.

Anonymous. 1888. No title. *North Star* Newspaper. Sitka, Alaska. 1 (5).

Anonymous. 1924. "Stories from a Real Home." *Women and Missions* 7:257–59. Presbyterian Church, Philadelphia.

Barnett, H. G., et al. 1954. "Acculturation: An Exploratory Formulation." *American Anthropologist* 56:973–1000.

Browning, Robert J. 1974. *Fisheries of the North Pacific*. Anchorage: Alaska Northwest.

Codere, Helen. 1950. *Fighting with Property*. Seattle: University of Washington Press.

Condit, James H. 1926. "Woman's Place in Alaska's Development." *Women and Missions* 9:257.

Dixon, George. 1789. *A Voyage Round the World: But More Particularly to the North-West Coast of America.* London: Geo. Goulding, Convent Gardens.

Drucker, Philip. 1963. *Indians of the Northwest Coast.* New York: Natural History Press.

———. 1965. *Cultures of the North Pacific.* San Francisco: Chandler.

Emmons, George T. 1916. "The Whale House of the Chilkat." *Anthropological Papers of the American Museum of Natural History* 19, 1:1–33.

Freeburn, Laurence. 1976. "The Silver Years." *Alaska Geographic.* 4 (4).

Gibson, James R. 1976. *Imperial Russia in Frontier America.* New York: Oxford University Press.

Gruening, Ernest. 1954. *The State of Alaska.* New York: Random House.

Gunther, Erna. 1972. *Indian Life on the Northwest Coast of North America.* Chicago: University of Chicago Press.

Hinckley, Ted C. 1972. *The Americanization of Alaska, 1867–1897.* Palo Alto, Calif.: Pacific Books.

Jackson, Sheldon. 1880. *Alaska and Missions on the North Pacific Coast.* New York: Dodd Mead & Co.

Jensen, Ronald J. 1975. *The Alaska Purchase and Russian-American Relations.* Seattle: University of Washington Press.

Jones, Livingston. 1914. *A Study of the Thlingets of Alaska.* New York: Fleming H. Revell Co.

Knapp, Frances and Rheta L. Childe. 1896. *The Thlinkets of Southeastern Alaska.* Chicago: Stone and Kimball.

Krause, Aurel. 1956. *The Tlingit Indians* (Erna Gunther, trans.). Seattle: University of Washington Press.

Kushner, Howard I. 1975. *Conflicts on the Northwest Coast.* Westport, Ct.: Greenwood Press.

de Laguna, Frederica. 1972. *Under Mount Saint Elias.* Washington: Smithsonian Institution.

Linton, Ralph. 1940. "The Distinctive Aspects of Acculturation" In Ralph Linton, ed., *Seven American Indian Tribes.* New York: D. Appleton Century.

Marchand, Etienne. 1801. *A Voyage Round the World Performed During the Years 1790, 1791, and 1792* (C.P. Claret Fleurieur, trans.). London: Port Mulgrave.

Okun, S. B. 1951. *The Russian-American Company* (B.D. Grekov, ed.; Carl Ginsburg, trans.). Cambridge, Mass.: Harvard University Press.

Sherwood, Morgan B. 1965. *Exploration of Alaska.* New Haven: Yale University Press.

Spicer, Edward H. 1961. "Types of Contact and Processes of Change." In Edward Spicer, ed., *Perspectives in American Indian Culture Change.* Chicago: University of Chicago Press.

Wood, C. E. S. 1882. "Among the Thlinkits in Alaska." *Century Magazine* 24: 323-39.

Wright, Julia. 1883. *Among the Alaskans.* Philadelphia: Presbyterian Board of Publications.

5 Forced Transition from Egalitarianism to Male Dominance:
The Bari of Colombia

ELISA BUENAVENTURA-POSSO[1]
SUSAN E. BROWN

Financed by Queen Isabella of Castile, Columbus landed in the West Indies in 1492 and claimed the Americas for the growing Spanish Empire. Colonizing first the islands of Santo Domingo and Cuba, the Spanish used these locations as bases for the conquest in 1521 of the great Aztec Empire and exploration into adjacent areas. Subsequently, extensive areas of South and North America were explored, while the military conquest of South America culminated in the fall of the vast Incan Empire. In the meantime, the Venezuelan region was explored from Santo Domingo in 1524, but no permanent settlements were successfully established there. The area was occupied mainly by pearl fishers, slave hunters, and the remains of an abortive attempt at founding an ideal Indian state by Fray Bartolome de las Casas.

In Europe, Charles of Ghent, grandson of the Spanish monarchs Isabella and Ferdinand and Flemish heir to the great Hapsburg Empire, became heir also to the Spanish throne. Uniting the growing Spanish Empire with the vast Hapsburg domain, Charles V became the most powerful regent in all of Europe. Choosing Spain as his most favored territory, he settled there in 1522. From Spain he waged long and burdensome wars, fighting France, Spain's traditional rival, waging continuing battle against the spreading Lutheran Reform, and resisting the infringing Turks. At the same time Charles V served as the official head of the Spanish Conquest in America. Its human and financial resources overextended by its numerous obligations, Spain soon became associated with the German trading and banking houses, seeking their financial, human, and technical resources. Spain soon became heavily indebted to the German banking houses, and in 1528 Charles V mortgaged the Province of Venezuela to the Welser banking house of Germany. He gave the Germans rights to the conquest of Venezuela as far inland as they could penetrate. In addition, the Welsers were given rights to exploit the mines and enslave all necessary Indian labor.

During the next eighteen years the province was wrought with devastation by one German governor after another. The first, and perhaps the most infamous of all, was Ambrose Alfinger, who quickly penetrated the region to establish the short-lived settlement of Maracaibo. Failing to locate sufficient gold, Alfinger established the colony on a base of slave trading, introducing two characteristically cruel innovations to the well-established commerce; these were the system of branding the captives with a hot iron, to avoid any mistake in identifying those he was going to export to Santo Domingo, and the chain gang. Destroying villages and killing all who opposed him, Alfinger plundered the region capturing slaves and coveting indigenous gold. Not content with the fortunes amassed, he continued in search of the famed El Dorado and was killed in a conflict with natives on the fringes of the great Chibcha Empire.

Followed by equally greedy governors, Alfinger but began what was to become a short but intense period of destruction and devastation. Motivated by the drive for wealth and commerce, the Germans failed to establish even one permanent settlement in Venezuela; yet from Coro, the one existing Spanish settlement, the effects of slave trading and the disease brought with initial contacts led to the decimation of the local indigenous populations and the resulting depopulation of most of the province.

As a result of vast abuses of power and their failure to fulfill the financial terms of their contract with the Spanish Empire the Welsers were expelled from Venezuela in 1546. From that date on the province was govered by Spain and was developed as an agricultural colony.

This study documents the imposition of a male-dominated hierarchy upon the traditionally egalitarian Bari. The Bari are tropical horticulturalists of northeastern Colombia and northwestern Venezuela whose social organization, as revealed by historical and ethnographic analysis, was fully egalitarian until the early 1960's. Today, the traditional egalitarianism persists only in the more isolated sectors of Bari society.

By "fully" egalitarian we refer to a society without classes that also exhibits full sexual symmetry. Individual autonomy is essential and, therefore, adults do not exercise authority over one another. Each person's labor is considered as socially valuable as another's; no differential access to resources exists, nor does the concept of the accumulation of wealth. Although exposed to imperialistic encroachment for nearly four hundred years, the Bari managed to maintain intact a great deal of their traditional social organization. It is only within recent years that we find Bari society succumbing to the powerful external forces encouraging the shift to male-dominated forms of social organization. Through these infringements of imperialistic, market society, the equal and autonomous position of Bari women is being undermined.

Before discussing recent transformations of the Bari social order and indicating how these changes have led to a degeneration of the autonomous and equal status of women, we will give a brief historical sketch of the Bari, and will document our contention that they traditionally exhibited a fully egalitarian form of social organization.[2]

HISTORICAL BACKGROUND

The Bari, commonly referred to as the "Motilones" or the "Motilones Bravos" are one of the least "acculturated" and least understood indigenous groups in Colombia. The Bari today probably number between 1500 and 1800 individuals (Pinton 1973: 138—39). While the exact origins of this group remain unclear, their language has been classified as belonging to the Chibcha stock, in contrast to the Carib-related languages of some of their neighbors (Rivet 1943; Rivet and Cesareo 1950).

Located at the time of the Spanish Conquest throughout the extensive Lake Maracaibo flood basin, the Bari today find themselves confined to a small area. Over four centuries their lands have gradually been usurped and the Bari forced to retreat to the 1000 square kilometers of inhospitable heavily forested and partially mountainous region they occupy today (Alcacer 1962: 28; Pinton 1973: 135). As we shall see, however, the invaders' struggle to gain control over indigenous land and labor was not an easy task. The Bari, in fact, more than any of their neighbors, persisted in their resistance to Spanish and subsequent Colombian and Venezuelan conquests.

In 1529, Alfinger began exploration of the Lake Maracaibo region. Within fifty years various indigenous groups of the area had suffered serious depopulation. As well as being directly enslaved, native populations were distributed to large landholders under the *encomienda* system. In exchange for labor, the Spanish landholders were to Christianize and care for the Indians. Overwork and lack of proper care under this system contributed to the decimation of native American populations.

Segments of the various indigenous groups from the Maracaibo region did survive these initial contacts. The history of one of these groups, the Bari, is related by the Spanish missionary Alcacer (1962). Through careful historical reconstruction, Alcacer details the various colonial interests working to gain complete control over indigenous lands of the region. The early colonialists were anxious to take over the Maracaibo flood basin for the commercial exploitation of native cocoa, cattle raising, and later the cultivation of sugar cane. The Spanish, however, encountered serious resistance from the Bari and other indigenous groups. The struggle to gain complete control over native land and labor was a long and difficult one, involving military campaigns as well as extensive missionary efforts. It was the Capuchin missionaries, who were given jurisdiction over natives within the Lake Maracaibo region.

By the end of the seventeenth century the expanding colonial agricultural society was infringing heavily upon Bari resources, and this period is associated with an increase in Bari raiding. The Bari frequently attacked landholders, workers, and others whom they encountered while fishing or hunting (Alcacer 1962: 71) and, at times, went out of their way to carry out special raids. By the beginning of the eighteenth century colonists had devised strategies aimed not only at maintaining but also at extending their control over Bari territory: local groups of neighbors and larger regional forces, sometimes accompanied by government troops, were organized into military expeditions against the Bari. With the general failure of these offensive tactics, however, small-scale self-defense groups were established among large landholders to patrol and protect their own haciendas and towns (Alcacer 1962: 72–83).

Between 1723 and 1771 the Capuchin missionaries seemed to have pacified and relocated into settlement villages most indigenous groups of the area, but the Bari, as a whole, remained outside of missionary influence (see Beckerman 1975: 98). In 1818, following Gran Colombia's independence from Spain, the Capuchin missionaries were expelled from the area, and the Bari were free to return to their indigenous ways of life. Their territory, however, had been reduced to a fraction of its original size. Interestingly enough while they did incorporate into their lifeways various elements of material culture such as metal tools, cloth, pots and pans, there were other items that the Bari did not adopt. For example, the Bari seem to be among the few indigenous peoples not to take on the use of alcoholic beverages or tobacco; neither did they accept the use of the canoe.

Late in the nineteenth century, Spanish Capuchin missionaries returned to South America and renewed their attempts at pacification, but it was not until 1914 that they made peaceful contact with a group of Bari (Alcacer 1964:

102). This same year marked the beginning of modern oil exploration in the region (Beckerman 1975: 151). Together, these two forces—missionaries on the one hand and petroleum concerns on the other—were to eventually penetrate and conquer the Bari. In 1936, at the outbreak of the Spanish Civil War, Capuchin activities ceased. But during the 1950s and the 1960s, renewed attempts were made to gain control over the "renegade" Bari. In this ultimately successful effort, petroleum interests and missionaries were joined by a growing number of homesteaders anxious to claim Bari lands as their own (Alcacer 1964; Jaulin 1973a). In 1964 both Colombia and Venezuela declared that the final "pacification" of the Bari had taken place. Missionaries, homesteaders, and petroleum concerns were all given relatively easy access to Bari lands, and as early as 1968 the vast majority of Bari groups were reported under missionary influence (Pinton 1972: 31). Today, petroleum explorations exploit much of the territory; some 5000 homesteading families are reported living in the general area (Garcia Herreros, in Olson and Neglia 1974: viii); and, in response to the continuing usurpation of Bari lands, the Colombian government set aside the remaining Bari territory as a national reserve.

The destruction that resulted from the 1964 truce reflects both the decimation of a population and the transformation of a culture. The Bari population dropped from 1800 individuals in 1964 to perhaps some 800 just a few years later; this drastic reduction is attributed to epidemics of smallpox and influenza combined with a decrease in fertility, all products of the contact situation (Pinton 1972: 31, 1973: 138; Jaulin 1973a). Recent estimates suggest that the Bari population is currently in the process of recovering its 1964 level (Pinton 1973: 138–39; Olson and Neglia 1974: 19). The cultural transformations undergone by the Bari since 1964, however, are less reversible. It is these changes which are our major concern.

BARI SOCIAL ORGANIZATION

Like many other forest horticulturalists, the Bari live in several autonomous groups. Each group utilizes certain areas for fishing, cultivation, gathering, and hunting without, however, having a concept of land ownership in the Western sense. Within these territories each group builds two or more large communal dwellings, usually several days' travel from one another. The entire group, from 40 to 80 persons, occupies one dwelling at a time and as a group periodically migrates to another existing house, or, when necessary, builds a new one (see Piston 1973: 141).

Within these dwellings, hearths are spaced along the major axis; each hearth is utilized by a small group which shares food and cooks together. The groups vary in size and composition, but generally seem to contain one or more families of procreation plus additional members. Spatial distribution within these communal dwellings is highly organized; each hearth group occupies a specific area along the walls of the dwelling behind its hearth where people hang their hammocks and store their belongings. Each individual's space is highly respected by all others and, as we shall show, this internal organization of the communal dwelling is crucial for the maintenance of egalitarian relations within the Bari social order.

Moving periodically from one dwelling to another, the Bari do not have permanent settlements. Their mobile existence reflect both ecological factors and social concerns. Tropical environments require that the land used for cultivation be allowed to periodically rest and regain fertility. The system of slash-and-burn agriculture—whereby an area to be cultivated is cleared, burned clean, used for a few years, and then abandoned to return to forest—allows for the utilization of the land base without destroying the soil. The land around each dwelling is cultivated for a period of time and then the group moves to another dwelling. Such mobility also serves to limit the stress on gathering, fishing, and hunting resources as well as to maintain sanitary conditions (Pinton 1972: 32). These ecological factors, however, do not fully explain Bari residential mobility and, as Pinton suggests, a more complete understanding calls for attention to social concerns. That is, the changing of residence allows for a restructuring of the internal organization of the house; it is through such moves that new relationships are established. Upon moving to a new house, individual hearth groups generally take up new locations within the house and thus make new pacts and alliances. The changing of houses also allows for the modification in communal-dwelling composition; some members may choose to stay behind or move in with another group altogether. If a move were made for purely ecological reasons, Pinton suggests, one might well expect the entire group to move; but stress on local resources is probably not the only motive for moving. Those who remain behind frequently find abundant resources and subsist perfectly well in the old location (Pinton 1972: 32–33).

With this brief sketch of residence and subsistence patterns in mind, we now turn to a more detailed examination of Bari social life. Our judgment that the Bari were fully egalitarian is based on the analysis of the following features of their social organization: leadership, social stratification, and decision-making processes; division of labor; ritual; and interpersonal relations and general social atmosphere.

Leadership, Social Stratification, and Decision Making
The hostility the Bari have exhibited in rejecting external infringements, however, finds no reflection in their internal social relations. Two points, then, should be made clear: (1) the aggressive and hostile behavior exhibited by the Bari towards the surrounding colonizing societies was a successful self-defense reaction to threats of usurpation and extinction and (2) the harmonious, classless, internal social organization characteristic of the Bari was not altered by

their fierce struggle for self-preservation. The first point needs little elaboration and can be summed up by Alcacer's statement that the Bari have the highest regard for peace and only fight out of extreme necessity—to defend themselves from attack and to recover possessions lost at the hands of outsiders (1964: 68). The second point deserves fuller attention for, while the classless nature of Amazon horticultural societies has been frequently reported, such groups are not generally described as harmonious and peace-loving. In fact, studies of South American groups that have been more extensively exposed to Western imperialism, such as the Yanomamo, the Mundurucu, and the Jivaro, indicate quite the opposite.[3] In such societies we find reported not only hostile relations with neighbors, but also a high degree of intragroup antagonism between the sexes, including such behaviors as verbal combat, the gang rape of women and woman beating.

The first written description of the Bari makes reference to the question of leadership and comes from Guillen, a colonial envoy who, with the Capuchin missionary Padre Fidel de Rala, made peaceful contact with the renegade Bari in 1772.

> They do not live subject to anyone's domination, and as I observed, they live in fraternal union, making decisions by unanimous agreement. Among them there are only a few individuals to whom more attention is paid because of their oratory skills. Being elders, they pass on the customs to the younger generation, illustrating their stories with narrations of feats and tragedies of past times. These histories they have stored in the library of the memory (quoted in Alcacer 1962:276).[4]

Guillen's observation is significant considering the fiercely antagonistic relations at the time between the Bari and the colonists. Furthermore, the same basic social atmosphere was maintained through the years; almost two hundred years later, Alcacer describes the Bari in similar terms.

> Among the Motilon there are no privileged classes. Everyone is equal and for everyone exist the same opportunities. The head of the group cannot be called a chief, and properly not even a leader, but can be characterized only as *primus inter pares*. The leader's tasks are very few and are reduced specifically to enforcement of the punishment of transgressors. Aside from this everyone enjoys absolute freedom within, of course, the required norms. Neither slavery nor servitude exists among them (1964: 66).

While Alcacer attributes to these leaders the responsibility for the sanction of inappropriate behavior, Alcacer himself later explains that the only means of social control among the Bari are such mechanisms as group pressure and public opinion. More rigorous data from the anthropologists Pinton and Jaulin indicate that Alcacer's "heads" did not have the power or authority to sanction behavior. Overall, in fact, they are even less "leading" figures than Alcacer understands them to be.

One of the most noteworthy attributes of Bari social organization—alluded to in both Guillen's and Alcacer's statements and later clearly enunciated by Pinton (1973), Jaulin (1973a), and Beckerman (1975: 27, 57)—is that the Bari neither tend to command others nor are given to carrying out orders from others. The most revealing documentation of this cultural norm comes from Jaulin's discussion of a Capuchin missionary's attempt, in the late 1960s, to establish effective positions of authority, "chiefs," among the Bari and thus organize them into a manageable work force. But the individuals designated as leaders, who were always men, were not willing to give orders, and, if they happened to do so, no one else felt obligated to obey.

> The priests enthroned one of the Indians from among them as "chief"—*Nyatobay*.... He was the one who should direct others in the cleaning and maintenance of the pastures, take charge of the cattle, attend to the visiting priests, look after the care of their dwellings and other domestic tasks as well as attending to the kitchen, etc. He was asked to make order reign within this new world, but certainly they did not demand that he do everything himself (Jaulin 1973a:59).

As things turned out, however, the new "chief" ended up doing almost everything himself, for the Bari do not give or take orders: "They have a great distaste for the entire matter and no Bari would be crude enough to demand anything of another person" (ibid.). This unfortunate "chief" had to take personal responsibility for the tasks without the power, or the desire, to ask that others assume or even share these responsibilities. He became, in other words, the servant of the other residents (:73).

What the missionaries did not seem to understand was that the Bari maintain special positions of responsibility without having chiefs, and in fact in the Bari language there does not exist a word corresponding to our concept of "chief" (Pinton 1973: 146). The position of *nyatobay* is one such position which has been misunderstood. Among the males within each communal house traditionally there exist two social positions of special responsibility, the *nyatobay* and the *isdora*. When a new dwelling is built, the *nyatobay* assumes responsibility for planning the floor structure and placement of the main supports for the dwelling. The *isdora* fills a similar function but digs fewer holes and places fewer poles for the major supports. The other future inhabitants of the house participate in the construction, particularly placing the exterior structure and roofing for the area of the house in which they will live (Jaulin

1973a: 60; Pinton 1973: 147—49). As with all Bari tasks, no orders are given or received during dwelling construction; each individual does her or his part. The *nyatobay* and the *isdora* have special responsibilities and carry out specific tasks themselves.[5] In addition, the positions of *nyatobay* and *isdora* are not permanent and those occupying them are replaceable. In fact, Pinton asserts that an absent *nyatobay* or *isdora* will immediately be replaced (1973: 146), while Beckerman states that a group does perfectly well without a *nyatobay* (1975: 7). Furthermore, as a single communal living group moves from one dwelling to another, the persons occupying these special social positions may well change (Pinton 1973: 146; Jaulin 1973a: 60).

The Bari exhibit another mechanism which serves to organize life within this communal setting. All house members fall into one of three named groups, *isdoashina*, *agbara*, and *duashina*, each group occupying a specific area within the house: the *isdoashina* in the east, *agbara* in the center, and *duashina* in the west of the house. The order established by this means is observed not only inside the communal house but also during various collective activities. For example, during visits to another group or walking along the path on a fishing trip, the *isdoashina* go first, the *agbara* second, and the *duashina* last (Pinton 1973: 144—45). These named groupings serve to organize Bari society and to guarantee that each individual has a recognized place within the order of things. Pinton makes very clear that these categories do not serve to stratify the society.[6] No special authority is attached to one's position and, as we later discuss, an individual or group of individuals may change position when the group settles in another dwelling (:145—46).

According to Pinton, the *nyatobay* quite often resides on the east side of the house and, therefore, is quite often, but not always, among the *isdoashina*. As we have mentioned, the *isdoashina* occupy the first position during any displacement of the whole group away from the dwelling, and because of this position of first in line they are always the first ones to come in contact with outsiders (1973: 144). Thus, the first *isdoashina* in line has, as Pinton states, been taken for, or instituted as, chief by the missionaries. What we are suggesting, then, is that social positions of responsibility did exist in the past and have been seized upon by missionaries and others in their attempts to establish permanent hierarchies within Bari society. Since these social positions did not provide the holder with even temporary authority, however, such attempts at social stratification have failed.

The Bari were not the only group to suffer from persistent attempts at colonial reorganization. All over the Americas, missionaries and government officials labored to establish viable hierarchies within the egalitarian indigenous societies they encountered. Special access to strategic resources was given to a limited number of persons, generally, if not always, males. These individuals were then expected to serve as brokers between the conquering interests and the hitherto "unorganized" native masses.[7] Given the intense efforts of colonial powers to stratify indigenous societies, it is noteworthy that even under missionary influence the Bari resisted and continue to resist the establishment of hierarchies or positions of authority.

Intimately associated with the question of leadership is that of group decision-making processes. From all available evidence, Bari decision-making processes are of a diffuse nature; decisions are made collectively by those women and men directly affected by the particular decision. Alcacer, for example, details how the entire residential group decides where they will build the new house (1964: 50–51). Jaulin confirms that Bari decision making is diffuse and specifies that it reflects the high value placed on both personal autonomy and the avoidance of conflict (1973a: 60).

Clearly, then, we can describe Bari social organization as classless, nonstratified, and fully egalitarian. In the simplest sense, there exist no bases on which to stratify the group. No individual or group has more access to strategic resources, including authority or knowledge, than another.

Division of Labor and Organization of Work

We find among the Bari a relatively simple and practical division of labor. Certain tasks are done by females, others by males, some by both sexes, some by children, and others together by the entire group. This assignment of tasks, as we shall see, is flexible. Generally, no strong taboos prevent one sex from carrying out, if necessary, tasks usually performed by the other.

> They try to be always busy, some of them working and cultivating their fields while others hunt. A few of the women follow their husbands while the others take care of the house and the infants. They sweep and clean the houses carefully, bring in water and wild fruits and prepare the day's food. They [the women] spend the rest of the day spinning cotton thread and cord to weave skirts and loin cloths to cover themselves and the men. They manufacture sisal cord and the men net it into hammocks for sleeping and make strings for the bows (1772, quoted in Alcacer 1962:276).

Compared with contemporary data, Guillen's description seems accurate, if limited. Let us broaden, with recent data, this picture of the Bari division of labor.

Many tasks, such as dwelling construction, fishing, and planting, are always carried out by women and men working together, each sex being responsible for a particular phase of the activity. Numerous other tasks—cooking, collecting vegetable foodstuffs, carrying items, and child care—are performed at different times and to varying degrees by both sexes (see Alcacer 1964: 62; Guillen 1772: 276; Pinton 1973: 150). Relatively few tasks are limited to one sex or another, and such restrictions as do exist most often serve to enhance the interdependence of the sexes. Women, for example, construct the looms, spin and weave, but men must be the ones to set up the looms on the ground. Men hunt with large bows, but women must be the ones to collect the fibers for the bow strings and women, not men, must bind the arrow canes in order that they dry straight. Men weave hammocks, but women collect and spin the necessary sisal.

Bari division of labor does not result in the work of any individual or group being more important than that of others. On the contrary, the Bari division of work serves not only to insure the completion of essential subsistence tasks, but also to create a meaningful place for each individual within society and to carry out socially productive and valued activities (Alcacer 1964: 31; Pinton 1973: 150).

In summary, we would stress that Bari division of labor does not divide society; no hierarchies are created, nor does the organization of work serve to create antagonisms between females and males. Instead, women and men's work is often communal and always complementary.

> At no moment of life do men affirm themselves as a group in opposition to women. On the rare occasions in which men get together without women (collecting the reeds for making arrow shafts, an important hunting trip) their getting together never appears as a collective activity, but rather is only a momentary association of independent individuals, all of whom are working for themselves and their families (:150).

Ritual

The Bari data illuminate a situation in which there exists full sexual symmetry not only in the daily subsistence activities but also within the ritual-ceremonial realm.[8] As noted by several authors, the Bari display few rituals, dances, or ceremonies. Los Cantos, the major Bari festival, appears to be one of few such activities, involving days of singing (and thus labeled *cantos* by Spanish speakers) and formalized exchange of personally manufactured goods. The singing is done in pairs by a visitor and the hostess or host. Thus, members of each sex sing songs telling of the items they manufacture. Women sing of the thread they spin and the clothing they weave; men sing of their bows and arrows.

From other accounts of the Cantos, we see that invited guests from other, often distant, communal dwellings participate in these festivals. Women and men invite to the festival other adults of the same sex with whom they have established special alliance relations. Ritually, the visitor and hostess or host sing to one another and exchange items each has made. Beckerman provides us with a later, but more detailed, account of such a traditional *Canto* celebration. On this occasion four women, six men, and their children came to visit the dwelling where Beckerman was doing research. The visitors arrived at night, and the next day was spent in a communal fishing project. Enough fish were caught so the entire following day could be spent singing. On the morning of the first day of singing,

> each of the guests climbs into a hammock, the men into the high ones and the women into the low ones, and lies on his back. A member of the host group of the same sex climbs into the same hammock and sits facing out, with his back to the guest....
>
> With no synchronization among the various hammocks, the singing starts....continues for several hours, and ends, quite abruptly, again with no synchronization among the various hammocks. One pair of women stops a full hour before anyone else, and one pair of men continues singing for two hours longer than any of the other groups.
>
> When the singing stops for the first hammock, the one with the two women in it, the host woman gives her guest a cotton skirt she has been holding in her lap. Then the host woman leaves the hammock and is replaced immediately by another host woman, and the singing resumes in that hammock. When the first pair of men stops singing they exchange bundles of arrows....The singing will go on for days or perhaps weeks, continuing until everyone in each group, host and guest, has sung with every adult of the same sex in the other group (1975:68-79).

Within traditional Bari society, then, the Cantos are important social occasions which serve many functions. Most particularly, they provide for the establishment and maintenance of alliances and communication networks between autonomous communal-living groups. Essential to our discussion is the fact that both women and men participate in this important traditional activity. Recent written descriptions of the Cantos call these festivals "El Canto de las Flechas" and make no mention of women's participation. Neither do they mention corresponding Cantos for women. We will discuss shortly this "disappearance" of female participation in the Cantos.

Interpersonal Relations and General Social Atmosphere

Traditional Bari social organization is based on, and supported by, self-sufficient groups living in separate communal dwellings. These residential groups are connected in many subtle and complex ways, even though they may be days' travel apart. Contacts between dwellings take the form of visits in which large numbers of people participate and which can last several weeks. During these visits--when the Cantos take place--new alliances and pacts are established, old ones are renewed, and information and goods are shared. Similar pacts and alliances are formed between persons within dwelling groups.

Little is understood about the Bari kinship system, but it is clear that all Bari stand in relation to one another as either *sadodi* or *ojibara*. *Ojibara* Pinton translates roughly as "ally" while she takes *sadodi* to mean "kin" or "family" (1973: 173–77). According to Beckerman *sadodi* and *ojibara* translate as consanguine and affine respectively (1975: 47). Both agree that the most strictly adhered to rule is that one never marry a *sadodi*. Some *sadodi* and *ojibara* relations are ascribed; one acquires them at birth. Other pacts of both *sadodi* and *ojibara* are made at various points during one's life without specific reference to geneological considerations. It is this system of *sadodi-ojibara* pacts and alliances which serves as the organizational principle linking all Bari in lieu of a geneological descent system.

> The *sagdojira-okjibara* system does not define moieties or any other concrete groups....The system is simply a complex of dyadic ties, which explains why it does not refer to actual groups, and also why inconsistencies are permitted which would make the formation of such groups impossible. A fair amount of attention is paid to existing relationships when new relationships are formed, and there is a good deal of order in the system. Nevertheless, the basic issue is one of a private, dyadic tie. There is probably no mechanism for compelling two people to make their tie consistent with anyone else's if they chose not to. A relationship between any two people is primarily their business, and not the affair of anyone else. Thus, here as everywhere else in Bari life there is a cheerfully *ad hoc* approach to the world (Beckerman 1975:49-50).

From the little data available it is clear that the *sadodi-ojibara* relations promote order without repression by establishing voluntary relationships between individuals. Special sharing, it appears, goes on between *sadodi*. Pregnant women go to give birth in the forest with a female *ojibara* (Olson and Neglia 1974: 44). Single persons interact in a more "formal" manner with an *ojibara* than with a *sadodi*.

In relation to the communal dwelling unit, *ojibara* and *sadodi* pacts are either inherited or established between neighbors; as a rule, adults of any given hearth group have adult *ojibaras* and *sadodis* of the same sex for their neighbors. Furthermore, this relative location of neighbors is preserved in displacements of the whole group, be this for a short fishing expedition or for a lengthy journey to visit another group.

Our own impression of Bari interpersonal relations as harmonious, egalitarian, balanced, and autonomous does not differ significantly from those of others who have written on the Bari. Guillen, for example, was impressed by the peaceful nature of this much-feared group. In 1772 he wrote, "Between themselves one does not see fights or even heated discussions" (quoted in Alcacer 1964:30). Two hundred years later other observers were to describe interpersonal relations among the Bari in a similar fashion. Pinton, for example, stresses the atmosphere of harmony and the purposeful avoidance of conflict within Bari society.

> This generalized reserve does not keep the atmosphere that reigns within the house from being warm and giving the impression of great harmony and very real understanding. We have never caught manifestations of discord nor overheard conversations carried out in a tone so intense as to make one believe there was a dispute; on the contrary, one has the feeling that everyone cooperates to avoid conflicts, at least in their outward manifestations (Pinton 1973: 172).

Pinton, Guillen, and Alcacer all associate the respect the Bari have for one another's property with their harmonious interpersonal relations. We were also impressed by the privacy and independence accorded to everyone—even while living within one large communal dwelling. Each family had its own space, recognized by others, where the members placed their hammocks and stored their material possessions. Each adult woman had a special area marked by her woven mat and upon which she carried out numerous tasks such as preparing food, spinning and weaving, making baskets, and the like. Other persons do not sit or stand on another's mat, nor does one sit or lie without invitation on another's hammock.

At first blush it might well appear to us that a certain tension should exist between collective and individual concerns. Are not individuals torn between their personal desires and conflicting collective concerns? This seems not to be the case. Personal autonomy, that is, the control of individuals over decisions central to their own lives and persons, is a characteristic feature of Bari interpersonal and group relations and contributes to maintaining their harmonious, egalitarian organization. Jaulin discusses this spirit of autonomy in the following terms: "The Indians essentially judge acts and do not coerce anyone. All of their social structure centers on the interplay of this freedom in relation to others and the full right and responsibility of one's acts" (Jaulin, 1973a:92). Indeed, it is the interaction between these groups of independent, autonomous individuals and families that allows for the egalitarian collective functioning of the group. Precisely because individuals are given freedom of choice about matters that affect them, the social order functions smoothly without coercion. Jaulin illustrates the value placed on personal and group autonomy by the example of Bari reaction to the extensive outside infringements he witnessed in the early 1960s.

> Within the families pertaining to one group, as well as among the groups themselves, no one invades another's jurisdictions. They can live together, be very good friends, visit one another, invite one another, marry each other and take different behavior with re-

spect to one or another thing and still remain compatible. One house declares war on the Whites, the other does not alter the peace, but not because of this would they cease to maintain good relations between themselves as long as the results of these diverse politics do not set them against each other (1973a:103).

Bari food-sharing patterns reflect the importance of autonomy and self-sufficiency. While some tasks, such as dwelling construction and double-dam fishing, by their very nature require group participation, each hearth group still remains responsible for its own subsistence. Sharing takes place within the hearth group, but appears limited otherwise (Alcacer 1964:57–58; Pinton 1973:149). In fact, Pinton suggests that the unsolicited offering of goods or services is in bad taste because it implies that the recipients are viewed as incapable of providing for themselves (personal communication). But, while the Bari do not automatically share things with one another, they have been consistently described as extremely generous when something is requested of them.

Another measure of personal autonomy concerns the sexual independence of individuals both before and after marriage.

Since marriage is not the only way to satisfy the sexual instincts, there frequently occurs, if not free love, a certain freedom of sexual intercourse sanctioned by custom, as long as those involved are not relatives. This happens with relative frequency between single persons as well as those married.... In the same way there are no laws to prohibit premarital sexual activities (Alcacer 1964:69).

Alcacer concludes that both wife and husband fulfill their own obligations and duties, "without worrying excessively, or almost at all, about what the other one is doing" (:72). For Alcacer this independence explains the lack of jealousy that exists in the face of the "relatively free sexual life they experience." Marital unions, as we might expect, are formed through the mutual consent of the partners. While these unions appear rather stable, unpleasant marriages are broken with little fuss.

In our own brief observation of the Bari we were impressed not only by the harmonious symmetrical relations between adults but also by the tenor of relations between adults and children. In our few weeks there, for example, we did not hear any recognizably harsh words directed toward adults or children. Children, although less so than adults, exhibited a considerable degree of responsibility and autonomy and from an early age, carry out useful chores. We were especially impressed with a seven-year-old girl whose mother had just given birth. This girl skillfully peeled large manioc tubers, washed the infant's clothes, swept the dirt floor with a small feather hand broom, fetched small amounts of water from the nearby stream, and did other essential chores. Yet she and other children, like adults, can refuse to carry out a specific task if they do not feel like doing it at that time. Infants and young children were given a great deal of attention and affection from adults, especially their parents and siblings. Neither mothers nor fathers, however, seemed to have their mobility encumbered by their children. Infant care does not significantly alter the activities of the mother. From an early age, infants are effortlessly carried about on their mother's back while she performs most of her regular activities, and the tasks of infant care, like other female activities, are frequently shared by other women of the hearth group as well as by both female and male relatives within the dwelling. Men, incidentally, do a large amount of childcare. When a mother goes into the fields, for example, infants and small children may be taken along or left with another adult staying at the dwelling.

Our picture of the Bari, then, is one of numerous autonomous communal living groups each comprised of autonomous hearth groups made up in turn of autonomous individuals. Each communal living group, while carrying on an intricate series of relationships with other such groups, acts independently without attempting to influence other groups' behavior. Hearth groups (frequently some sort of "family" grouping) each form an independent subsistence unit responsible for its own maintenance, and individuals, the basic units of these groupings, also exhibit the same type of control over their own lives.

WESTERNIZATION AND ITS EFFECTS ON BARI WOMEN

When Western capitalistic systems expand upon egalitarian communal societies, their actions involve the introduction and imposition of features such as the structure for general male dominance over females based materially on preferential male access to strategic resources; private ownership of land and a money economy; overall inequality in the form of differential access to privileges and resources which lead to the formation of socioeconomic classes; and an emphasis on the nuclear family, supported by a wage-earning male, as the ideal domestic unit. Wedded to their own experience of social and economic stratification, as well as to their concept of sex roles and statuses, such Western societies are unable to understand or accept the realities of a truly egalitarian society. Thus, outside contact with the Bari and their neighbors has been typically male-centered, elitist, and divisive.

Since the 1964 "truce," numerous transformations of Bari culture have occurred with particularly detrimental effects for women. In the political realm, other influences are working to create powerful, authoritative "chiefs" among the Bari, who do not themselves have even a word for "chief." Such newly appointed "chiefs" are, of course, all males. Changes in the economic realm have even more devastating effects for women. First, the forced breakup of the collective living unit and its replacement by the patriarchial nuclear family makes the female dependent upon a wage-earning male for subsistence items, which are now purchased with cash. Particularly important is the fact that males, and not females, are given access to the tools and skills necessary to acquire the newly desired cash. The introduction of male access to wage labor and cash cropping has brought with it a structure for male exploitation of female labor.

The breakdown of the collective living unit is also accompanied by the disintegration of communal subsistence activities such as double-dam fishing. In various ways, the collectivity is being destroyed in favor of a more individualistic mode of life. At the same time, many traditional female tasks are being eliminated through recent changes in Bari lifeways. Women's work is shifting from production tasks such as spinning, weaving, basket making, and food production to menial service tasks, such as washing clothes. In addition to these transformations, women's important traditional role in healing has been systematically usurped.

In the ritual-ceremonial realm we find that the characteristic sexual symmetry is being eroded to such an extent that, in those regions most influenced by colonial penetration, women no longer play a significant role in the only major ceremonial activity. Finally, all of these factors are almost inevitably creating a foreign and traditionally unheard of antagonism between the sexes.

In the following section we analyze these transformations of Bari society, and especially the impact of one aspect of intervention, the Motilon Development Plan. Begun in the mid-1960s this plan represents the most organized and successful attempt at absorbing the Bari into the contemporary industrial society, directly influencing a quarter, and perhaps up to one-third, of the Bari population. The plan has been well documented by its originator, a young North American missionary who made contact with the Bari in 1961 and, therefore, is an especially good focus for our analysis.

Important questions as to what might have occurred if the Bari had continued to resist pacification, and whether or not it would have been possible to implement another intervention plan which would have provided protection for the Bari while allowing them continued cultural integrity, lie beyond the scope of this study. Our object is not to evaluate the overall value of the actual Bari Westernization plan, but rather to analyze in detail its effects on women's status and, in doing so, document the creation of a male-dominated hierarchy within this traditionally egalitarian society.

The Creation of Male Chiefs

In an attempt to organize hierarchically the Bari, the Motilon Development Plan has instituted a *cacique* within each of the seven indigenous Bari autonomous groups. These seven men, designated as "chiefs," have been given Colombian citizenship and officially instituted as the leaders and representatives of those people living within their assigned territories. In addition, seven young Bari males have been assigned as assistant leaders to these "chiefs." Together with the *caciques* of each zone they serve on the Board of Directors for the Motilon Development Plan (Olson and Neglia 1974:117–20).

The attainment of Colombian citizenship papers for these fourteen privileged males means, legally, that they can become landholders and vote in Colombian elections. Although it is doubtful that the older males are aware of, or would even be interested in utilizing, these privileges it is still significant that only males have been given possibilities.

As for the success of the Motilon Development Plan in creating viable Bari chiefs, all available data suggests that the mature Bari continue to resist such impositions. It does appear, however, that one mechanism has been elaborated which might allow for the successful creation of such chiefs and involves the intensive socialization of young Bari males: at times these boys have been adopted by the missionary; in other instances he only formally sponsors and guides their education. The total result, however, is that a small group of chosen males are being sent to urban centers for higher education and eventual professional training. Already, some of these boys have been classified as sons of *caciques* who will in time become chiefs of the Bari. Thus, we are now witnessing a dual transformation by which certain young males are being given access to a strategic new resource, education, while females are not given parallel opportunities. In addition, at least some of these male students are already being given the title of *cacique*—as if it were a real and even inheritable Bari leadership position.

The Ursurpation of Women's Traditional Role in Healing

Traditionally, women played very important roles in Bari medicinal practices.

> Women play a fundamental role in Bari healing practices. They are in charge of the collection of plants [leaves] necessary for making the *potencias*....Once these leaves have been collected and dried they are ground into a powder and stored inside a gourd. Here they are available when someone falls ill and calls upon the *curandera* who hands out these *potencias* (Olson and Neglia 1974: 93).

It is clear that women collected, prepared, stored, and administered these *potencias*, which represent the principal element of Bari medicine. All sources agree that men never collected or prepared these medicinal plants, although at various points Olson and Neglia and Pinto (1973:150) indicate that males also serve as *curanderos*. Recently, however, significant changes have taken place among the groups most influenced by the Motilon Development Plan. Attempts have been made to eliminate the roles played by women in the healing practices, which are connected with the plan's carefully planned introduction of new medicines. The manner in which the medicines were introduced not only bypassed women's role as collectors, preparers, and administrators of traditional medicines but also placed the administration of medicine solely in male hands. For example, the early use of Terramicyn for the treatment of eye infections was introduced through male healers, as were the vaccinations brought for the Bari. It was also the intention of the Motilon Development Plan to try to train the sons of these male healers to be more modern medical practitioners (Olson and Neglia 1974:120).

The Encouragement of Male Exploitation of Female Labor and Forced Economic Dependency of Women

A recent intervention involves the encouragement of Bari participation in the market economy through the production and sale of surplus crops. The plan worked to encourage surplus production of traditional foodstuffs such as manioc, and plantains. Never concerned with selling food, or even storing it for long periods, the Bari lacked the notion of surplus production. For this new production, each hearth group employed its usual communal-cultivation procedures with the one modification that the men received instruction and facilities for the selling of surpluses (Olson and Neglia 1974:120–21). The result has been that individual males are now in control of the cash produced by the collective hearth group efforts. As unwittingly as it may or may not have been, this innovation provides the basis for male exploitation of female labor.

Bari entrance into and growing dependency upon the market economy brings about various interactions. New goods are introduced and subsequently desired and/or required by the Bari. Therefore, a need arises for money with which to purchase these goods. At the same time the Bari males are sought as inexpensive agricultural laborers. Today, numerous Bari men work, if only sporadically, for missionaries, homesteaders, and others, and through this activity only males gain access to the important new resource, money. Money allows them to purchase manufactured goods such as machetes, shotguns, cotton hammocks, clothes, and the like. Without access to cash, women must depend on men for necessary and desired manufactured goods such as clothing, shoes and boots, metal cooking utensils, and foodstuffs. Also, male participation in wage labor weakens the traditional subsistence system and alters domestic patterns. Since the men are away working in another's fields for weeks to months at a time, they are no longer able to fulfill their traditional subsistence tasks. Not only does the level of general nutrition suffer (Jaulin 1973a: 135–39) but, beyond this, the man's former work must be picked up by the women who remain at home.

The Modification of Women's Roles in Subsistence Activities

Another revealing sign of Bari cultural disintegration is given by the changes being brought about in women's subsistence activities. The impact of these modifications can be clearly seen by focusing on collective activities in which both women and men traditionally participate, and subsistence activities carried out only by women.

A communal activity of major importance among the Bari is fishing. Fish are a major source of protein, and, unlike hunting, fishing involves a highly organized group effort in which all members of the dwelling participate. The double-dam fishing technique, for example, involved a close coordination of women's and men's labor. Through this collective effort large numbers of fish are obtained in one day. Current economic and cultural transformations, however, are eliminating this form of subsistence activity. On the one hand, as men are removed from the communal dwelling to work as wage laborers this collective fishing stops. On the other hand, with the introduction of new technology, the traditional double-dam technique is being replaced by individual male fishing with weighted nets and motorized boats. The introduction of these new fishing methods has excluded women from this most vital, once collective, subsistence activity.

A second important collective activity concerns the construction of the communal dwellings. Again, we see a highly organized task in which both females and males participate, each performing roles assigned by sex. This effort represents a highly complex and organized activity with numerous implications for Bari social organization. Neither sex can build the house alone, everyone's contribution is essential. Women, for example, collect and prepare the palm branches used for thatching while men gather and place the frame poles. A major goal of missionary intervention, past and present, has been the replacement of these collective living units with individual, nuclear-family dwellings. In the case of the Motilon Development Plan the large communal dwellings are being replaced by small concrete houses. These units are constructed by Colombian laborers with the help of Bari male "heads of households." The women are thus also excluded from dwelling construction.

In addition, those subsistence activities carried out exclusively by women, and associated with the woman's space within the dwelling, are extensively affected by the new type of housing. For example, in the zinc-roofed houses, women no longer spin and weave. These houses do not facilitate these tasks since they are unbearably hot during the day and because their concrete floors make it almost impossible to set up and operate their looms. The decline in weaving is also linked to the introduction of manufactured cloth and the strongly encouraged abandonment of traditional dress, consisting of a short skirt for women and a breechcloth for men. Along the same line, hammocks formerly made by the men from sisal spun by women have been increasingly replaced by those produced industrially. These changes in dress and hammock preference, in turn, have dual effects. On the one hand, they are associated with a reduction in the female contribution to group subsistence, and on the other hand, they intensify Bari dependence upon the external market economy. Such modifications in dress also create some unpleasant and time-consuming tasks for women. Women are instructed that it is their duty to regularly wash these clothes. For this task they must obtain commercially made soap which can only be purchased in distant centers with money. These imperatives, combined with the totally unadaptive nature of this new clothing to the tropical forest environment, contribute to the fact that today the Bari are often seen wearing dirty, tattered clothing.

The diminished importance of women's collecting activities represents another important development. As already described, the Bari had an extremely flexible and mobile lifestyle, but they are now being forced into a sedentary existence by the construction of permanent individual dwellings, the effects of male wage labor, the encouragement of cash cropping, and other influences. Sedentarization along with the introduction of money and manufactured foodstuffs has led to a minimization of women's collecting activities, once essential to the Bari economy. The subsequent deterioration of Bari nutritional standards is an important side effect. Traditionally, the Bari women collected some twenty-three species of plant food (Pinton 1973:139). Today the groups exposed to extensive contact consume considerably fewer wild vegetables and fruits. As Pinton and Jaulin suggest, the traditionally well-nourished Bari now suffer a decline in the quality of their food intake. There has been an increased dependency on starchy staples such as manioc and plantains as well as new use of wheat, oatmeal, and oil. One might well ascribe an excessive weight gain by many Bari women to these dietary changes. Thus, the decline of women's collecting activities not only signals a further deterioration of female contributions to the subsistence base; it also is associated with a degeneration of physical well-being among the Bari (Jaulin 1973a:135–38).

The Breakdown of the Communal Residential Unit

As described earlier, the fabric of Bari social organization is woven together by formalized relationships between what we might call kin, *sadodi*, and non-kin, *ojibara*. Alliances established upon the basis of the *sadodi-ojibara* division provided each Bari with special relations to various individuals within their own communal dwelling as well as with individuals of other dwellings; at the same time, the entire Bari society was held together through such pacts.

The move to nuclear-family residential units promoted by the Motilon Development Plan disrupts this highly organized and intricately balanced form of social organization. With the disappearance of the communal dwelling unit there is necessarily associated a breakdown of the society's interpersonal and intergroup relations. Women in particular suffer detrimental effects from this atomization. The move to individual houses causes the isolation of adult women from each other and the subsequent weakening of their cooperative systems of meal preparation, cultivation and child rearing. [This cooperation was favored by matrilocality, a residence pattern in which closely related female kin are often found living within the same dwelling after marriage (Jaulin 1973a:132)]. On another level, the disruption of the communal living unit compounds the economic factors that destroy collective subsistence activities such as fishing and dwelling construction. Also, group communication and knowledge-sharing processes, important to the maintenance of such an egalitarian society, and facilitated by the traditional residence pattern, are eliminated or weakened by the transition to individual households.

Neglect of Women's Participation in the Ceremonial Cantos

The Canto celebrations represent an essential element in traditional Bari social organization. They offer the opportunity for communication and sharing between residential groups, and provide for the creation and maintenance of alliances and pacts with distant persons. For those groups most influenced by the Motilon Development Plan, the last decade has witnessed a significant shift in the structure and meaning of the Cantos. While traditionally both females and males participated in these celebrations, in recent years the Cantos have become known exclusively as male celebrations and are now called El Canto de las Flechas, which the development plan hopes to establish as the symbol of Bari cultural unity (Olson and Neglia 1974:117, 120—21; see also Pinton 1973).

In a similar vein we can add that the only known musical instruments among the Bari are reed flutes. While little data is available on the ritual or social significance of these instruments, it is well documented that the flutes are manufactured and played by the women (Pinton 1973:150). Flute playing, however, like women's participation in the Cantos, is rapidly being lost with the present cultural transformations.

Incipient Alteration of Egalitarian Relations Between the Sexes

During our brief visit with the Bari we were impressed with the egalitarian and gentle relations between women and men. Voices were not raised, anger not witnessed; commands belonged to another reality. Such elements of our own society as men's domination of women, sexual objectivication of the female, an ideology of basic human inequality, and sexism still find no equivalent in Bari society.

The current impositions of the market economy, combined with the growing infringements of Colombian and Venezuelan nationals and international missionaries, are, however, beginning to affect relations between the sexes. These relations, unfortunately, are as vulnerable to the forces of ethnocide as other cultural components, and women are beginning to resent men's exploitation of their labor. They dislike their new dependency on individual men for money and the goods money can buy. Thus, we heard of women complaining that their husbands did not provide them with adequate manufactured cloth and clothing. Also, we noticed that some Bari males who were in close contact with homesteaders have taken on their sexist behaviors. We witnessed, for example, two young Bari men referring in the presence of a potential marriage partner to her physical and sexual characteristics. Upon inquiring about the matter, we were told that such behavior is not socially acceptable among the Bari. In this case the young men were conversing with a male visitor from Bogota who they thought, no doubt, would appreciate their comments. While the Bari are very affable and sociable with each other, they do not impose themselves on others nor do they objectify individuals, sexually or otherwise.

In conclusion, we have shown traditional Bari society to be fully egalitarian. Under the circumstances, however, it is doubtful that this system of social relations will survive. Like many other native groups, the Bari have been, since the earliest contact with Western society, continually threatened with usurpation and extinction. Most recently, they have been under attack from homesteaders and petroleum concerns. The intervention of the Motilon Development Plan has perhaps saved the Bari from outright genocide. In the long run, however, the price they must pay for their survival may well be near total destruction of their culture. For although the adult generation in contact with the whites seem to passively resist much of the change imposed upon them, the new generation, particularly the males, seem to be somewhat eager to try the Western way of life. On the other hand, some observers assert that those communities of Bari who still remain in the more isolated places of the territory view whites with the same mistrust as before the 1964 truce and might renew hostilities with them in the not too distant future (Jaulin, personal communication).

The future of those Bari groups or individuals who continue to be exposed extensively to the Western culture and economic system seems decided. Slowly, they will be absorbed into industrial society, mainly as peasants, while a few Bari males will enter into slightly more privileged positions. Today, this process is well under way and the sexual equality and individual autonomy characteristic of the Bari are already in the process of disintegration.

NOTES

1. Both authors contributed equally to the writing of this article and the order of their names was decided by flipping a coin.

2. This study is based on an analysis and evaluation of all available published material on the Bari. In the summer of 1976, during a three-week visit with the Bari of the Iquiacarora and Sapha-Dana regions, we were able to corroborate some of the published descriptions as well as make observations of our own. We would like to thank Bruce Olson for facilitating our visit to the Bari and Solange Pinton and Robert Jaulin for discussing their research findings with us.

3. See Chagnon, (1968); Murphy and Murphy (1974); and Harner (1973).

4. All quotations originally in Spanish or French were translated into English by the authors.

5. In addition to these male positions, we were told that positions of special responsibility also existed among the women. Unfortunately, we learned of this only on the day of our departure from the Bari, and thus did not have the opportunity to explore the function of these special female positions. This is obviously a topic of great importance which has been heretofore ignored. The lack of information on these female positions is especially significant as it severely limits our understanding of the sexual symmetry of such responsibility positions. As in this case, outside observers consistently detail specific male positions within the society studied while never thinking to inquire about the comparable or related female positions.

6. While these categories do not stratify society, in Pinton's opinion the *isdoashina* has a "certain honorific character" (1973:146).

7. For a well-documented case study, see Leacock (1954; 1969) on the Montagnais-Naskapi of the Labrador Peninsula.

8. All too frequently, anthropologists recognize that women within egalitarian societies may have a sort of rough-and-ready practical equality but then, they explain, women are downgraded symbolically and ritually. Frequently, in the face of other evidence documenting female equality, this view of male dominance within ritual activity is drawn upon as decisive evidence of female subordination and inferiority. The validity of such observations should be carefully reviewed for various reasons. First, too often male participation in ritual or ceremonial activities is seen as primary and female participation as secondary. Secondly, ritual-ceremonial activity, just as other aspects of a culture, is tremendously affected by outside impositions and infringements. Specifically, female participation in such activities can be shown to have been eliminated after contact with male-dominated societies. Rarely are these forces of cultural disintegration taken into account when discussing ritual-ceremonial activity.

REFERENCES

Alcacer, Antonio. 1962. *El Indio Motilon y Su Historia.* Puente Comun (un dina Marcia), Colombia: Ediciones Paz y Bien, Seminario Capuchino.

———. 1964. *Los Bari, Cultura del Pueblo Motilon.* Bogota: Taller Editorial Procer.

Beckerman, Stephen. 1975. "The Cultural Energetics of the Bari (Motilones Bravos) of Northern Colombia." Ph.D. diss., University of New Mexico.

Chagnon, N. 1968. *Yanomamo: The Fierce People.* New York: Holt, Rinehart and Winston.

Guillen, Sabastian Joseph. 1772. "Testimonio." In Antonio Alcacer (1962), *El Indio Motilon y Su Historia.*

Harner, Michael J. 1973. *The Jivaro.* New York: Anchor.

Jaulin, Robert. 1973a. *La Paz Blanca: Introduccion al Etnocidio.* Buenos Aires: Editorial Tiempo Contemporaneo.

———. 1973b. *Gens du Soi, Gens de l'Autre.* Paris: Union General d'Editions.

Leacock, Eleanor. 1954. "The Montagnais 'Hunting Territory' and the Fur Trade." *American Anthropological Association Memoirs* 78.

———. 1969. *The Montagnais-Naskapi Band.* In David Damas, ed., *Contributions to Anthropology: Band Societies* National Museums of Canada Bulletin 228. Ottawa: Queen's Printer for Canada.

———. 1975. "Class, Commodity and the Status of Women." In Ruby Rohrlich-Leavitt, ed., *Women Cross-Culturally: Change and Challenge.* The Hague: Mouton.

———. 1977. "Women in Egalitarian Society." In R. Bridenthal and C. Koonz, eds., *Becoming Visible: Women in European History.* Boston: Houghton Mifflin.

Montoya, Javier. 1971. "Los Bari o Motilines del Catatumbo." *Franciscanum,* no. 37, pp. 34-53.

Murphy, Robert and Yolanda Murphy. 1974. *Women of the Forest.* New York: Columbia University Press.

Olson, Bruce 1973. *Por Esta Cruz Te Matare.* Miami: Editorial Vida.

Olson, Bruce and Angelo Neglia. 1974. *Una Raza Bravia: Estudios Socio-Antropologico de los Indio Motilones.* Bogota: Instituto de Desarrollo de la Comunidad.

Pineda, de, Virginia Gutierrez. 1975. *Familia y Cultura en Colombia.* Bogota: Instituto Colombiano de Cultura.

Pinton, Solange. 1965. "Les Bari." *Journal de la Societe des Americanists* 54: 247-333.

———. 1972. "La Maison Bari et Son Territoire." *Journal de la Societe des Americanists* 61:32-44.

———. 1973. "Les Travaux et Les Jours." In Robert Jaulin, *Gens de Soi, Gens de l'Autre.* Paris: Union General d'Editions.

Rivet, Paul. 1943. "La Influencia Karib en Colombia." *Revista del Instituto Ethnologico Nacional* 1, 1:55-87.

Rivet, Paul and Cesareo P. de Armellada. 1950. "Les Indiens Motilones," *Journal de la Societe des Americanists* 39:15-57.

6   Aztec Women:
The Transition from Status to Class in Empire and Colony

JUNE NASH

In the earliest encounters of Spaniards with the aboriginal populations of the Caribbean and mainland of Middle America, we find many comments remarking on the physical attractiveness, intelligence, and skills of the inhabitants of the New World. In the early years of Spanish colonization of the Americas, the Spaniards were motivated to populate the colonies with subjects faithful to Church and State. This led to the passage of liberal laws conferring citizenship on both women married to conquerors and their offspring, as well as to widespread conversion to the Catholic faith. Forced labor in the mines, fields, and factories took an enormous toll on the indigenous population, who were often forced to leave their villages and travel for days without provisions to far-off mines or plantations. These losses, combined with deaths from epidemics and armed encounters, resulted in reductions of the available labor force that threatened the economy.

When the Spaniards entered the central plateau of Mexico in 1519, they encountered a population with a highly developed city-state capable of recruiting and mobilizing an army and a labor force. State institutions coexisted with kinship-based *calpulli* which served to organize production of the commoners. The growing separation between an upper class of agnatically descended rulers and a commoner class was revealed in marital and reproductive behavior for the two groups. While commoners were expected to fulfill ideal norms of monogamy, the nobles practiced polygyny openly and common soldiers were permitted to indulge in licentious sexual behavior. This resulted in strained relations with Aztec allies and tribute-paying states. The break with traditions within the city-state, and beyond in the tribute-paying areas of the empire, threatened the stability of the society. At the time of the conquest, the Spaniards found ready allies among the Aztecs' tributaries who saw in them a means of gaining independence from the demands for female and male sacrifice victims, labor, and pawns, as well as payment in products.

Soon after the conquest by the Spaniards, however, the hope for liberation from the Aztec rulers turned to despair as the Indians found themselves caught in an empire that was far more demanding of the services of women and men, as well as of land and crops. In the violent transition from empire to colony, a mestizo race and culture was born.

Recent analyses of patriarchy enable us to understand the transition from aboriginal state hierarchies to colonial forms of domination in a new light. The assumption that patriarchy is a universal and transhistorical phenomenon based on biological reproduction (Millet 1971) denies ethnohistorical evidence on aboriginal society in the Americas (Leacock and Nash 1977) as well as other areas (Rohrlich-Leavitt 1977; Rohrlich-Leavitt and Nash, in press). When we trace the rise of patriarchy in specific historical epochs, we can analyze the particular and changing nature of patriarchy in distinct reproductive systems. Felicity Edholm, Olivia Harris, and Kate Young (1978) distinguish three different levels of reproduction systems. The first is reproduction of the social production in its totality. The second is human or biological reproduction. This is analytically separable from the third level of reproduction, that of the labor force, since under capitalism the allocation of labor is no longer linked to kinship.

By separating these three interrelated but analytically separable modes of reproduction, we can analyze the historical change involved in the transition from an autochthonous military and theocratic empire such as that of the Aztecs, to the imposition of colonial rule in New Spain. Both involved patriarchy, but there were important differences affecting the role of women. Even within the colonial administration, there were important differences between colonizing agents—the crown, the ecclesiastics, and the colonists—in their attempts to control marriage and biological reproduction, recruitment and allocation of the labor force, and the productive system.

In this chapter we will examine the changes in the status of women in production and reproduction that marked this transition. Our central thesis is that the emergent class distinctions that existed in Aztec society were reinforced in the early colonial period while, at the same time, they were deformed.

The Aztecs were a wandering tribe of agriculturalists and hunters who arrived in the central plateau of Mexico, the present site of the capital city, in 1248. Within a hundred years they developed a city state of priest-warriors ruling over an expanding empire. With the arrival of the Spaniards, the colonists reinforced some of the tendencies developing within Aztec society. The distinction that, in the last two centuries of their rule, the Aztecs were beginning to make between women as reproducers of nobility (*pipiltzin*) and women as reproducers of commoners (*macehuales*) (Zurita 1941:107) was incorporated in Spanish, colonial class society. Women as producers of legitimate heirs of the conquerors, and later settlers, were distinguished from those who produced Indians or bastard *mestizos* (of mixed blood). Offspring of the first class, whether born of Indian women or Spanish women immigrants, were the inheritors of the conquest; those of the second class became the laborers who produced the wealth for the colonists. The cliche that the Spanish Conquest was a conquest of women is only half true. On the one hand, women in the conquered and tribute-paying areas of the Aztec empire had already experienced enslavement and prostitution. On the other hand, since the Spaniards included only a few women—about a tenth of their numbers in the early decades—Indian women became wives and concubines of the conquerors and often enjoyed treatment preferential to that of the men.

Along with this reinforcement of class distinctions, there was an undermining of women's productive role. Women in Aztec society had many specializations as independent craft producers of pottery and textiles, and as priestesses, doctors, and merchants. Spanish development policy, as carried out by priests and crown administrators, diverted home production into male-operated craft shops and mills. In the *mestizo* and *creole* (Spaniard born in the New World) upper and middle classes, women were socialized to dependency in male-dominated productive spheres. To the extent that Indian culture persisted, women continued to reproduce a social system in which a kinship-organized labor force prevailed in semisubsistence activities.

WOMEN IN THE AZTEC EMPIRE

The Aztec empire was still in its formative stages when the Spaniards arrived on the mainland of Mexico in 1519. In the transformation from a kinship-based society with a minimum of status differentiation to a class-structured empire, we can see the relationships between male specialization in warfare, predatory conquest, a state bureaucracy based on patrilineal nobility supported by an ideology of male dominance, and differential access of men and women to its benefits.[1]

The constant diminution in the power of women can be seen in the record from the time of the Aztec migration, beginning about 820 A.D., until the establishment of their capital city in Tenochtitlan. In the course of their travels, described in the Codex Ramirez (see Duran 1964), a confrontation took place between their god Huitzilopochtli and his sister, Malinalxoch, that tells something about the changing authority of male and female leaders. Urging their followers to leave Malinalxoch behind, Huitzilopochtli is quoted as saying that they should conquer the people of Tula, the ancient Toltec capital, by the valor of arms and their courage rather than by the supernatural power over animals that his sister controlled.

In the first 100 years of their residence in the central plateau—roughly from 1248, when they entered Chapultepec, to 1325, when they moved into Tenochtitlan—the Aztecs transformed themselves from what Peterson calls "belligerent agriculturists" into an "organization of priest warriors" (Peterson 1959: 85). Structurally, this meant a shift from a tribe based on clans to a kingdom based on classes. Throughout their nomadic period and in the early years of residence in Chapultepec, the *calpulli*, or territorially based kinship group, provided the basis for governance in a council of elders, *calpullec*, who elected a chief in charge of war and another in charge of civil and religious acts (Zurita 1941:71-227). The corporate ownership of land by the *calpulli*, with redistribution in accord with the needs of each family, seemed to insure egalitarian relations. At least by rough indexes, women had equal rights juridically and in the economy. Men as well as women were punished by death for adultery (Clark 1938). Women were active producers as well as vendors, they possessed property and rights within the *calpulli*, and they were curers as well as priestesses. It is more than likely that matrilineal descent characterized the Toltecs and possibly early Aztec society. Soustelle (1962), states that "in former times, women had the supreme power in Tula," and in the beginning of the Aztec dynasty the royal blood flowed through the female line.

At the time Tenochtitlan was established in 1325, leadership of the tribe was still determined by the council of elders of the *calpulli*. The supreme leader, *tlacutlo*, was chosen from among them. He was called the "father and mother of the people,' and his vice-minister was called "Snake Woman."

Terminolgical reference to females at the highest levels, although the posts were occupied by men, suggests that women may have played leading political roles before the state was centralized.

The Aztec learned the skills of warfare from the Culhuacan and Tepanec armies, which they joined as mercenaries. During Itzcoatl's reign (1429-40) they overcame the Tepanec and distributed the land among state and military leaders and soldiers. After this victory the succession of a ruler was determined by the rising military aristocrats and the successor was chosen from among the male siblings or offspring of the king. (Katz 1972:147). Tribute and control over the lands of conquered people meant that the parasitic economy of war took priority over the productive economy of the commoners.

While women continued to have important roles in the domestic economy, they were excluded from the new predatory economy. Zurita (1941:165) describes the birth ceremonies in the late Aztec period. A boy was given a shield with arrows while the midwife prayed that he might be courageous in battle, while girls were given spindles and shuttles as a symbol of their future dedication to homely tasks.. While both boys and girls were admitted to the *calmecac*, the training school for the priesthood and bureaucracy, the military school was reserved for boys (Soustelle 1962:84–85, 103-4; Zurita 1941:165).

As men became specialists in warfare, women became the booty to be shared by the victors. When the Aztec conquered the other cities of the plateau and brought them into the empire as tribute-paying subjects, the soldiers seized the women of the conquered cities at will. This was one of the most common complaints the Spaniards heard from the people as they marched inland from Cempoali to Tlatelolco (Dias de Castillo 1965:;114; Romero Rosendez 1974:70, 128). The licensed sexual immorality of the soldiers and the polygyny practiced by royalty contrasted with the chaste and monogamous life of the peasants. The growing contradictions in their own society undoubtedly weakened the Aztec even before the Spaniards arrived.

Control over sexual reproduction, the reproduction of a labor force, and the productivity of women were in transition to patriarchal dominance. Noblemen had prerogatives in polygyny and extramarital liaisons denied the common folk. The sanction of death to bigamists was applied arbitrarily and reflected the transitional nature of the society. Contradictions between the ideological position asserting chastity and monogamy and the behavior of the ruling elite undermined the legitimacy of their rule. In addition to this, the huge number of offspring of the *pipiltzin* could no longer be absorbed into preferred positions as the field for conquest waned. They became a potentially disruptive force along with the severely taxed and oppressed commoners. On the eve of the Spanish conquest, the Aztec rulers had few supporters.

WOMEN IN THE COLONIAL PERIOD

The Spaniards who arrived in the first boatloads of settlers were prepared to take possession of the land and its people not only in the name of their monarchs, Queen Isabela and King Ferdinand, but in the name of the Christian god. The mission of Christianizing the natives legitimized the right to conquer. Spanish colonizers were encouraged to marry Christianized Indian women and far from being universally victimized by the conquest, some women took advantage of the opportunities offered by marriage or concubinage to the Spaniards during the first few decades of colonization when the scarcity of European women enhanced their value among the conquerors. Women responded selectively to Spanish rank, preferring governors (Konetzke 1972:26). The thirty Spanish women who came on the third voyage of Columbus were soon followed by other women. A law passed by the crown in 1530 stipulated that men who were married should bring their wives (Robles de Mendoza 1931:127), but some settlers found a way around this by purchasing a *composicion,* or waiver of sanction (Morner 1967:6). With immigration restricted to wives and daughters of colonists, women constituted only ten percent of all colonists in the first thirty years of immigration.

Biological Reproduction

Crown and Church vied in their attempts to regulate the marital and reproductive relations between the colonists and the aboriginal population. A royal decree of 1501 stated that a woman could not be retained against her wishes and, if a Spaniard wanted to marry, it had to be done voluntarily on both sides. Two years late, the Spanish governor of the islands was instructed to arrange mixed marriages in what Morner (1967:37) thinks may have been a form of experiment. In an attempt to weld the native chiefs more closely to Spanish colonial authority, Cardinal Cisneros, regent of Castile, instructed the friars in 1516 that Spaniards ought to marry the daughters of *caciques*, or native rulers, giving as a reason that the *caciques* would then be good Spaniards. Morner points to the obvious fallacy of the reasoning since the Arawak, aboriginal residents in the Caribbean islands, had matrilineal succession (ibid.).

As the Spaniards entered the mainland, new adjustments were made in response to the different social structures they encountered in the city states and empires they conquered. Upon their arrival in 1519, native chiefs on the coast spontaneously offered them girls as presents. Pedro Cortes was given Malinache, the daughter of the rulers of the Maya town of Paynala. She had first been given by her parents to Xicalango Indians in order to deprive her of her inheritance when a son was born to her widowed mother and new stepfather, The Xicalango in turn gave her to Tobasco Indians who conquered them and finally Cortes was to receive her. Recent studies have tried to overcome the portrayal of Malinache as a collaborator, progenitor of the *mestizo* spawn that lived under the stigma of illegitimacy (Kruger 1948). Her skill as a diplomat transcended the role of interpreter, as Bernal Diaz de Castillo (1965) reveals eloquently in describing the many encounters in which she thwarted attempts to massacre the conquerors and found allies for the Spaniards among the enemies of the Aztec. To interpret Malinache's support of the Spaniards against the Aztec as treachery ignores the historic relations of Indian tribes at the time of the conquest.[3] The Aztec were enemies of the southern tribes from which Malinache came and her own experience led her to expect little support from her parental group or the tribes who received her as chattel. Pan-Indian sentiment developed after independence, and it was a political force only in the time of the Mexican revolution.

The crown continued to try to order the form of the family and inheritance by offspring through legislation in the first half century of colonization. In 1530 legally married women who were widowed had the right to inherit an *encomienda* (tribute rights) provided that they marry again within a year of the death of their husband (Liss 1975:98). Rodriguez de Albuquerque reported in the sixteenth century that, of 692 *encomiendas*, 63 were granted to men with native wives, 19 were given to women, and 475 to single men (Pescatello 1976:139). The legal position of women in Spain was superior to that of English women since they had an equal share of all property acquired during a marriage whereas English women lost even their inherited property to their husbands. Wives of propertied Spaniards in Mexico, as in Spain, often acted as administrative assistants, second in command, while wives of the less well-to-do worked in the fields (Liss 1975:99). A decree of 1539 ordering an *encomendero*, or recipient of tribute, to marry within three years or, if already married but living alone to send for his wife, added to the urgency for men to find a mate and increased the options Indian women had. Until 1549 the crown continued to assert the primacy of the marriage bond in determining succession (Marshall 1939:164).

The significant change came in 1549 when racial origins became a factor, along with legally sanctioned marital unions, in defining rights of succession. The new laws stated that no *mulatto* (offspring of a black man and Indian woman, *mestizo*, person born out of wedlock was allowed to have Indians in *encomienda* (Mörner 1967:42). Mestizo and illegitimate became almost synonymous, and *mestizos* entered into lower-status roles in the society.

What were the conditions that brought about the changed attitudes toward sex and race categories by the middle of the sixteenth century? Without further research in primary sources, we can only infer the reasons from the data available on the population, the labor force and the economy. This will be discussed below in relation to the reproduction of the labor force.

Reproduction of the Labor Force

The original pattern of colonial relations was conceived as one in which Indians were supposed to be free vassals and subjects of the crown equal to the inferior stratum of Spanish society (Morner 1967:41). They were to be governed by their *caciques*, who were to be equal to *hidalgos* (Spanish landed gentry). The colonists, however, differed in their view of the new society from the start, and the *encomienda* was the mechanism by which they exerted demands on the Indian population that went beyond the designs of the crown (Wolf 1963). In the military interlude after the conquest, the division of conquerors and conquered was established in the rights over labor. Tribute labor granted in the *encomienda* was used and abused unmercifully in the mines, in agriculture, and in the factories that processed foodstuffs in the field (Bagu 1952: 100). The polarization of wealth and the hierarchy of political and economic power left little room for an expanding middle class.

The changed attitudes about *mestizos* and Indians are related to changing power relations among crown, colonists, and Church and to modifications in the interests within each group. In the early decades of the conquest, the crown wanted to stabilize colonies through marriage, regardless of ethnicity. This suited the colonists until the rising numbers of their own *mestizo* progeny threatened the prerogatives of a narrowing elite sector. As the interest shifted from producing heirs to recruiting a labor force, they tried to bring about changes in the laws governing inheritance and succession.

In the early colonial period, labor mobilization under the *repartimiento* (grant or division of Indian labor in exchange) corresponded to the preconquest payment of tribute in labor (Gibson 1964: 27), and oftentimes the same tribute list was used. Indian nobility played the role of intermediaries between Indian laborers and the Spaniards until the end of the sixteenth century. Some clerics were active in seeking reform in the labor system prior to colonization of the mainland, and, from the early years of colonization in the Caribbean islands, the colonists clashed with the clerics in regard to the treatment of the Indians. Vicar Pedro de Cordoba, for example, pressed for changes restricting the power of the colonists over labor, advising the king that Indians were forced into labor that amounted to slavery (Stoudemire 1970: 27). The Law of Burgos, passed in 1512, did not help much. Requiring that Spanish officials should look after the spiritual welfare of the Indians, it specified only that they be well-fed, provided with individual hammocks and clothing, and should neither be beaten nor used as beasts of burden. These early laws attempted, however, to restrict the exploitation of female and child labor: neither women nor children could be forced to work, and unmarried girls were to work with their parents.

This minimal protection was destroyed with the *corregimiento*, a system of rule by officials appointed by the crown. As a result of depopulation and the ensuing, forced concentration of remaining Indian populations, the Spanish system of hacienda, rancho, pueblo, and barrio was imposed on the countryside (Gibson 1964: 54). Spanish *corregidores* appointed by the crown demanded personal services of women to prepare food, fuel, and fodder, as well as the labor of men (: 95). The nearly unchallenged authority of the *corregidores* led to many abuses of female labor. For example, in 1720 the *corregidore* of Tlalmanalco was approving of all kinds of extortion imposed on subordinates, including the seizure of women.

Given the low technological level of Spanish colonial society, the need for a subordinated population to supplement tribute labor was clear from the early days of the conquest. Negro slaves were imported in the Caribbean islands from 1518, with 4000 entering in the first eight years (Morner 1967: 15). But the crown also tried other measures to bolster the declining Indian population. In 1528 it was declared illegal to keep an Indian woman from her husband when he was forced to travel many miles from his village to work in the mines or haciendas even if she wanted to remain at home (: 37). This was, clearly, an attempt to stimulate reproduction rates. Depopulation persisted, however, throughout the sixteenth century, as the following table shows (Rosenblatt 1954).

Indigenous Population (millions)

1519	25.2 (est.)	1580	1.9
1532	16.8	1595	1.4
1548	6.3	1605	1.1
1568	2.7	1650	1.5

The abysmal working conditions combined with the devastation of new diseases and plagues brought by the Spaniards reduced the aboriginal population to 6 percent within a century. At the same time, the Spanish population rose from 57,000 in 1570 to 114,000 in 1646. The interest in recruiting a labor force was clearly in conflict with interest in reproducing the labor force.

Legal and social restrictions limited mestizos' access to channels of mobility. Segregation laws enacted in 1536 and 1563 prohibited mestizos from living with Indians in villages (Morner 1967: 46). In 1570 mestizos were excluded from positions of protector of Indians, notary public, and *cacique*, and from 1568 they could not become priests except with some strong backing to prove they were legitimate and virtuous. In contradiction to earlier crown injunctions that Indian customs should be honored "except when repugnant to Spanish traditions," Spanish concepts of legitimacy and disinheritance of illegitimates were incorporated into law by 1580 (Borah and Cook 1966: 957). By the seventeenth century, social status was crystallized in a hierarchy linked to occupations (Morner 1967: 67).

Social Status and Occupations

Peninsular Spaniards	Bureaucrats and merchants
Creoles	Large landowners
Mestizos	Artisans, shopkeepers, tenants
Mulattos	Urban manual workers
Indians	Rural peasants

Because women were breeders of this population, their status in the ethnic categories, conditioned by their relationship to men as wives or concubines, determined whether their children entered or became marginal to a given occupational role. Throughout the colonial period they continually lost the edge they had at first in determining their own level of participation and that of their children. The significance of patriarchy in determining which offspring were to be part of the elite and which relegated to commoner status can be seen in the laws regarding illegitimacy. Five levels of illegitimacy were distinguished: *hijos naturales*, children born of commonlaw alliances; *fornezinos*, children born of adultery; *menzeros*, children born of prostitutes; *spuri*, children born of a commonlaw wife who has other men; and *notos*, children born in wedlock but not fathered by the husband. This was a far cry from the Aztec custom under which the death penalty for adultery applied, at least to commoners, up until the conquest (Borah and Cook 1966: 951-53). It was also contradictory to the missionary program, which stipulated that men must have only one wife and that sons should inherit (: 955). Most Indians married early, in response to both older custom and priestly pressure, and there was little illegitimacy. The more complex rulings by the crown affected the middle and upper classes as well as interethnic and interclass pairing (:963). A family life characterized by male dominance, submission of female to male and the double standard grew in this sector of the population (Penalosa 1968: 682).

The evolution away from an earlier pattern of interethnic marriage and incorporation of mestizo offspring into a caste hierarchy was confirmed in the crown regulations of 1778. Regulations requiring parental approval of unions and other restrictions to avoid "unequal" marriages attempted to control further integration of the population. Although mulattos, blacks, *coyotes* (offspring of Indians and blacks), and other *castas* were excluded from the regulations in law applying to *mestizos* and *castizos*, Indians were to be warned about the danger of marrying blacks or mulattos (Morner 1967: 38). However, despite the inferior rank that mestizos held in the caste hierarchy, they were more than twice as numerous as whites by the beginning of the nineteenth century and nearly equalled the Indian population. Over a century later, they were the dominant group numerically, double that of the Indian population and almost quadruple that of the white (Marshall 1939).

Population of New Spain (millions)

	1803	1930
Indian	2.5	4.6
White	1.2	2.4
Mestizo	2.4	9.0

Reproduction of Social Production

Although a fair amount of material is available on the reproductive role of Indian women, little is recorded about their productive roles in the society that was emerging in New Spain. In the Indian communities, we can assume, with men being drawn off in tribute labor the women did much of the agricultural work as well as the craft production and domestic chores that sustained the indigenous population and its way of life. The retention of preconquest modes of production in many contemporary Indian villages is almost synonymous with retention of production in the hands of women. Where pottery is made by the coil system rather than thrown on a wheel, where textiles are woven with a backstrap loom rather than with the Spanish "bed" loom or machinery, we can assume that the work is done by female labor. The factorylike production of pottery for a regional market by women of the Indian *municipio* of Amatenango, Chiapas, is an indication of the extensive contribution they make to production for exchange (Nash 1970). The retention of the same basic culinary arts in the preparation of tortillas, tamales, and beans is a tribute to the domestic productivity of women. The Spanish model of development ignored women's productive roles and incorporated men into craft production for the market. For example, the Flemish Franciscan Pedro de Gant set up trade schools for boys and taught them to work as interpreters, craftsmen, and teachers, while girls were taught only "the domestic arts" (Liss 1975). Despite this, women's productive efforts prevailed in the semisubsistence economy, and we can deduce some of the roles they played from their role in the current economy. Ethnologists who have gone beyond the superficial statement that women simply "take care of the house" have noted a far greater activity rate than can be deduced from the 10.5 percent participation rate in the labor force given in the census. Lourdes Arizpe (1977) points out that *campesinas* of Sierra de Puebla make liquor and hammocks, collect firewood, cultivate vegetables, collect fruit, grind corn, make tortillas and beans, and, in addition, provide medical services for their family and neighbors. They also provide education, nursing, and psychiatric attention and perform many other roles that may or may not be compensated but are rarely recorded. We can assume that this kind of productive activity, often carried out in preconquest patterns, continued unabated throughout the colonial period. Even superficial inventories of contemporary culture negate Woodrow Borah's (1964) statement that most of Mexican material culture is of European origin. If one were to weight traits in terms of the frequency and breadth of their distribution, it is quite possible that Indian traits might be shown to be the more pervasive. Corn, beans, and chile, the preconquest trinity of foods, are still basic subsistence for the masses despite the introduction of flour and rice. Foster has catalogued the many traits believed to be Spanish and found to be indigenous, as well as the reverse, in his survey of peninsular and colonial cultures (1960). Indian women, indeed, succeeded in reproducing a mixed culture, as well as a mestizo progeny, in the three hundred years of colonization and the century of independence.

CONCLUSIONS

We can see in the changing regulations governing marriage, inheritance, labor recruitment, and production the conflict between the crown, the Church, and the colonists in claiming control over women's reproduction of heirs and laborers. The creative role of women in shaping the emergent mestizo culture will be recognized only when the stigma of bastardization dictated by patriarchal power is removed. This has been partially accomplished as Mexican society has moved from a hierarchy based on castes to one based on class. The 1917 law on marriage grants women the right to divorce, equal authority in the family, and the right to work outside the home. But the stigma of illegitimacy and the real barriers to women's access to higher-level professions and business opportunities remain.

By separating the forms of reproduction involved in recreating a social system, we can analyze an historical transformation such as that of colonization more carefully. We can sort out the forms of patriarchy that persisted and those that were destroyed or transformed. This enables us to understand the conditions that reproduce patriarchy in order to overcome them. Thus, the half truth that the conquest of the Americas was the conquest of women can be restated in terms of an analytical separation of forms of reproduction. A more accurate statement would be that the conquest was not one of women, but of Indian male control over the reproductive power of women, with the result that Spaniards claimed the right to recruit the children born of their relations with Indian women as heirs or laborers. The advantages women enjoyed while their sex was in short supply were eroded as the caste society emerged. The patriarchal power of the male as head of the household was reinforced by his right, strengthened by crown and Church rulings, to determine the status of a woman's offspring. The creative role of Indian women and their mestizo offspring in producing a mestizo culture that brought together traits from the preconquest society and from Europe has been largely ignored. Undoubtedly, this lack of recognition is influenced by an androcentric perspective which equates women's productivity with biological reproduction. A priority in ethnohistorical research should be that of discovering the full contribution women made in the Americas and elsewhere.

NOTES

1. The following historical discussion is based, for the most part, on Sahagún (1938), Duran (1964), Zurita (1941), and secondary sources cited.
2. Despite their relative scarcity at the time, there is far more written about Spanish women than Indian women in feminist research on the colonial period. See for example Burges (1972), Villafane Casal (n.d.). Ann Pescatello (1977) has contributed toward a balanced picture in bringing the two ethnic groups into the same frame.
3. *"Somos todos hijos de la chingada!"* ("We are all children of the f— one"), the wail of the marginalized modern mestizo, symbolizes the patriarchal power to bestow legitimacy and position in colonial society. It is anachronistic since at the time of the conquest the denigration of Malinache, as a response to the caste structure, had not taken place.

REFERENCES

Arizpe, Lourdes. 1977. "Campesinas, capitalismo y cultura," *Fem* 1, 3:25-31.

Bagú, Sergio. 1952. *El estructural social de la colonia: Ensayo de historia comparada de América Latina.* Buenos Aires: Libreria "El Ateno."

Borah, Woodrow. 1964. "Race and Class in Mexico." *Pacific Historical Review* 23, 4:331-42.

Borah, Woodrow and Sherburne F. Cook. 1966. "Marriage and Legitimacy in Mexican Culture: Mexico and California." *California Law Review* 54, 2.

Burges, Analola. 1972. "La mujer pobladora en los origenes americanos." *Anuario de Estudios Americanos* 29:389-444.

Clark, James Cooper, trans. and ed. 1938. *Codex Mendocino* (Codex Mendoza), 3 vols. London.

Diaz de Castillo, Bernal. 1965. *The Conquest of New Spain.* London: Penguin Books.

Duran, Diego. 1964. *The Aztecs: The History of the Indies of New Spain.* New York: Orion Press.

Edholm, Felicity, Olivia Harris, and Kate Young. 1978. "Conceptualising Women." *Critique of Anthropology.* 3, 9:103-14.

Foster, George. 1960. *Culture and Conquest: America's Spanish Heritage.* Chicago: Quadrangle Books.

Gibson, Charles. 1964. *The Aztecs under Spanish Rule: A History of the Valley of Mexico 1519-1810.* Stanford: Stanford University Press.

Jimenez Rueda, Julio. 1970. *Historia de la cultura en México. El Virremento México.* Mexico: Editorial Cultura.

Katz, Friedrich. 1972. *The Ancient American Civilizations*, K. M. Lois Simpson, trans. New York: Praeger.

Konetzke, Richard. 1972. "El mestizaje y su importancia en el desarrollo de la población hispanoamericana durante la época colonial." *Anuario de Estudios Americanos* 29:389-444.

Kruger, Hilde. 1948. *Malinache; or Farewell to Myths.* New York: Arrowhead Press.

Leacock, Eleanor and June Nash. 1977. "Ideology of Sex: Archetypes and Stereotypes." *Annals* of the New York Academy of Sciences, vol. 285. New York: NYAS.

Liss, Peggy. 1975. *Mexico under Spain 1521-1556. Society and the Origin of Nationality.* Chicago: University of Chicago Press.

Marshall, C. E. 1939. "The Birth of the Mestizo in New Spain." *Hispanic American Historical Review* 19, 2:159-84.

Millet, Kate. 1971. *Sexual Politics.* New York: Avon.

Mörner, Magnus. 1967. *Race Mixture in the History of Latin America.* Boston: Little, Brown.

Nash, June. 1970. *In the Eyes of the Ancestors; Belief and Behavior in a Maya Community.* New Haven: Yale University Press.

Peñalosa, Fernando. 1968. "Mexican Family Roles." *Journal of Marriage and the Family* 30:680-88.

Pescatello, Ann. 1976. *The Female in Iberian Families, Society and Culture.* Westport: Greenwich Press.

Peterson, Frederick A. 1959. *Ancient Mexico.* New York: G. P. Putnam's Sons.

Robles, Margarita de Mendoza. 1931. *La Evolución de la mujer en Mexico.* Mexico City: Imprenta Galas.

Rohrlich-Leavitt, Ruby. 1977. "Women in Transition: Crete and Sumer." In R. Bridenthal and C. Koonz, eds., *Becoming Visible: Women in European History.* Boston: Houghton Mifflin.

Rohrlich-Leavitt, Ruby and June Nash. In press. "The Patriarchal Puzzle: State Formation and the Decline of Women's Status in Mesopotamia and Meso-America." *Heresies.*

Romero Rosendez, Alfonso. 1974. *Lo de Tlaxcala; Analisis imparcial de los sucesos acaecidos en epoca de la conquista.* Mexico City: Tallares de B. Costa-Amie, ed.

Rosenblatt, Angel. 1954. *La población indigena y el mestizaje en América*, 2 vols. Buenos Aires: Editorial Nova.

Sahagún, Bernardino de. 1938. *Historia general de las cosas de Nueva España.* Mexico City: P. Robredo.

Soustelle, Jacques. 1962. *The Daily Life of the Aztecs on the Eve of the Spanish Conquest.* New York: Macmillan.

Stoudemire, Sterling A., trans. and ed. 1970. *Pedro de Cordoba, Christian Doctrine for the Instruction of the Indians.* Coral Gables: University of Miami Press.

Villafane Casal, Maria Teresa. n.d. "La mujer española en la conquista y colonización de América." *Cuadernos Hispanoamericanos,* pp. 175-76.

Wolf, Eric. 1963. *Sons of the Shaking Earth.* Chicago: University of Chicago Press.

Zurita, Alonso de. 1941. *Breve y sumaria relación de los señores y las maneras y diferencias que habia de ellos en Nueva España.* Mexico City.

7 "The Universe has turned inside out... There is no justice for us here"

Andean Women Under Spanish Rule

IRENE SILVERBLATT

With the discovery and conquest of much of the Americas, Spain was at the helm of one of the world's largest empires. Yet in spite of its imperial power, Spain was dominated by other European nations. From the early sixteenth century, when Spain began to build its overseas empire until its collapse in the wars of independence three centuries later, Spain's dependency on the economically preeminent countries to the north increased. The history of Spain and of its possessions cannot be understood apart from the Iberian peninsula's contradictory role as satellite of Europe and center of an American empire.

It would be more accurate to describe Spain of this period as "the Spains." The marriage of King Ferdinand to Queen Isabela, which is supposed to mark the founding of the modern Spanish nation, belies the persistence in the Iberian peninsula of relatively autonomous political entities, nominally united through their allegiance to the Castilian dynasty. This pattern continued to characterize peninsula political development when Castile merged with the Holy Roman Empire upon the accession of the Hapsburg monarch Charles V (1516–56). The Spanish patrimonial political structure expanded as American colonies were attached to the crown of Castile as feudal or personal possessions. Spanish dynastic wealth and prestige grew in Europe with the expansion of Charles V's now "universal Empire," but control over these dominions was to a large degree illusory.

The conglomeration of political entities that made up the Iberian peninsula at the time of the conquest also housed distinct economic tendencies. While a town-based bourgeoisie oriented toward the development of trade and industry was emerging in Catalonia, a semifeudal aristocracy, exemplified by the Castilian knights, was concerned with expanding an economic structure rooted in herding and the export of wool and other primary products to northern Europe. The "reconquest" of the Iberian peninsula from the Moors, which was spearheaded by the nobility of Castile, coincided with the conquest of the Americas. The new wealth in gold, silver, land, and labor acquired in Spain's colonial possessions militated against the restructuring of Castile's semifeudal, land-based economy. At a time when other European nations—England, Holland, and France—were transforming their economies along the lines of capitalist development, Spanish feudal traditions were given a new impetus. To a larger degree than in other European nations, Spanish merchants strove to insure their status and economic security by investing their wealth in land government annuities, inherited public positions, and ecclesiastical benefices.

Spain's economic dependency on Northern Europe increased during the colonial period as peninsular industries were swamped by the influx of cheaper goods produced in France, Holland, and England. The gold and silver from the New World that wasn't used to support the interminable struggles between the Spanish monarchs and their European "heretic" rivals ended up in their adversaries' hands to compensate for Spain's balance-of-trade deficit with Western European manufacturing centers. By mid-seventeenth century, Spain's pretentions to European hegemony had failed; while by the end of that century even Iberia's control over its colonial empire had been substantially undermined.

The Spanish landed on Peru's northern coast in 1532, and began the process of conquest and colonization that drastically and irrevocably altered the lifeways of Andean people. Conquest was not new to the Andes; the Inca Empire which the Spanish encountred was the second large-scale imperial system to have subjugated coastal and *serrano* populations. But the experiences of the conquered populations under Inca and then under Spanish rule were radically different. Although the Incas formed a highly stratified society in which the elite enjoyed political and economic privileges denied the peasantry, institutions and norms rooted in the Inca precapitalist economy tempered the relationship between conquerors and conquered and provided peasant men and women with the insurance that their social and economic needs would be met. The mutual, albeit assymetrical, obligations which underlay relations between the Incas, with their capital in Cuzco, and the provinces were embedded in a shared cosmological structure in which relations between society and the forces of nature, and between man and woman, were conceptualized as being reciprocal and necessarily interdependent, and were ordered by a cultural ideal of balance and equilibrium.

The Spanish invasion imposed alien economic, political, and religious structures on Andean society. Oriented by an economic system in which production was governed by the dictates of the market, colonial institutions tended to break down the kin relations which underlay pre-Colombian economic organization. Buttressed by a world view in which nature and human beings were becoming increasingly defined in relation to their market value, and by a religious ideology that divided the world into competing forces of good and evil, colonial secular and religious authorities systematically attacked the ideological and religious foundations of Andean culture—now considered diabolic. However much they exploited Andean society as a whole, the structure that the Spanish brought to the Andes imposed a special burden on women. I propose to examine the particular oppression suffered by indigenous women through colonization, as well as the forms of resistance to that oppression that Andean women championed.[1] In order to understand these dual processes, we must first look at the position of women in Andean institutions and the impact on their role affected by the Inca expansion.

PERU BEFORE THE SPANISH

Social Relations of Production

In order to grasp the impact of the Inca conquest on the potentialities of Andean women[2]—a process which we will later want to compare with that imposed by the Spanish—we will begin by examining the ways in which the Cuzco elite affect preexisting social arrangements governing access to requisite factors of production.

Prior to the Inca conquest of the Andes, ultimate jurisdiction over productive resources—agricultural land, water rights, herds, and pasture lands—was vested in the *ayllu* (an ethnic community)[3] (Diez de San Miguel 1964:35,100; Murra 1956:151; Ortiz de Zuniga 1967:42). Membership in an *ayllu*, which was phrased in terms of kinship, provided its constituents with automatic access to the community's resources that served as a basis for subsistence (Murra 1956:53, 56, 151; Spalding 1967:63, 68). Economic activities within the *ayllu* were ordered by kinship bonds which underlay a network of culturally defined reciprocal obligations and responsibilities. These mutual obligations formed part of the social redistribution mechanisms, enforced by religious sanctions, which effectively checked individual accumulation of wealth and power.

Access to land in the pre-Inca *ayllu* was governed by a combination of systems involving the periodic reapportioning of land according to household size (Cobo 1964:2:121; Polo 1917a:68) and the inheritance of usufruct rights to particular fields (Murra 1956:57). Although the most well-known account of the distribution of *ayllu* land indicates that women relinquished their rights upon marriage (Garcilaso 1956:58), other data indicate that married women maintained independent usufruct rights to land (Guaman Poma 1956:2:125, 3:104, 125, 132, 181; Morua 1946:240). If modern data can shed any light on control over production, then we can grant that women had the ultimate say over the disposition of goods produced on their lands or derived from their herds (Stein 1961:54).

In addition to access to material resources, the ability to make claims on the labor of others was also required for the successful carrying out of economic activities (Murra 1975:125, 126; Cobo 1964:2:121). Wealth limited the ability of an individual to make labor demands because of the "generosity" with which these demands had to be reciprocated (Murra 1956:151). Kinship ties, as well as those acquired through marriage, ordered the process through which labor outside the immediate family was garnered.

Kin relations structured, in part, the social relations of production within local ethnic communities. The principle of parallel lines of descent, in which men conceived of themselves descending from a line of men, and women from a line of women, was one of the key rules ordering pre-Columbian Andean kinship (Zuidema 1972:17; Loundsbury 1964). Within this system, the basic structural unit was the sibling pair, in which either sex could be the point of reference or the genitor/genitrix of a descent group (Zuidema 1972:15). The parallel descent structure of the kin group marked out lines through which classes of material goods (as well as ritual objects and obligations) were transmitted (Zuidema 1972:17–19; Duviols 1971:373, 383; Morua 1946:427). Although it was not the only means through which rights to land and critical resources were inherited, parallel transmission did constitute an important mechanism both within the peasantry and the Inca nobility (Spalding 1967:126; Zuidema 1967:49–58; 1972:17–19).

Another rule which underlay pre-Columbian inheritance patterns was that of cross-transmission, in which the significant relations were those between mother's brother and sister's son, and between father's sister and brother's daughter (Zuidema 1972:18). Common to both these principles is the creation of links which are expressed in terms of corresponding gender markers—male or female. As we shall see, a paradigm of sexual parallelism also ordered political and religious relations in the Andes; and women's control over resources and the products of their labor provided them with the capacity to participate in these gender-specific organizations.

The *ayllu* (community) was endogamous, but within the *ayllu* marriage was permitted only between those descendents separated by more than four generations from a common ancestral pair (:17–19). While decisions regarding the appropriateness of a marriage resided with both parents, the mutual desire of both spouses was considered necessary for a union to take place (Cobo 1964: 2:248–49; Molina 1943:68; Morua 1946:240, 244; for contemporary practices, see Earls 1971; Earls and Silverblatt 1977). Brides sought the consent of their mothers since a portion of inheritance was activated at marriage. Although local marriage customs varied from community to community, in some villages it was the bride's mother who ritually received the first sets of gifts from the groom (Cobo 1964:2:249).[4] The equality of the relationship between spouses and between kin groups was expressed through ritualized gift giving, which at the same time bound both families into obligatory relations of mutual assistance and aid (Cobo 1964:2:248–46; Morua 1946:235, 240). Within the kin group itself, the designation of authority was based on order of birth, with no distinctions made in terms of gender (Guaman Poma 1956:3:111).

A higher-ranked group within some pre-Inca communities, known as *curacas*, could make a greater claim on the wealth and labor of their *ayllu* (Spaulding 1967:96–191; Murra 1956:67). The power and activities of the *curacas* prior to the Inca expansion are not well known,[5] and the role of women within this higher strata is even less well documented. There are indications that women *curacas* actively participated in the governing of their communities (Guaman Poma 1956:1:123–28; Cobo 1964:2:72, 84; Rostworowski 1962: 137); and according to some chroniclers women were the principal rulers of the cultures located on Peru's north coast (Anon. 1906:160; Collapiña et al. 1974:34). They enjoyed a privileged access to the material resources and labor of their communities (Diez de San Miguel 1964:107; Guaman Poma 1956: 2:69, 92, 3:104, 146) which was possibly phrased in terms of parallel descent (Oberem 1968:82, 83).

Probably the best known act that accompanied the expansion of the Inca Empire was its repartitioning of *ayllu* lands as a means of acquiring the surplus needed for the operation of the state. The Incas expropriated land from the *ayllus*, the produce of which was destined to support the empire's administrative apparatus and upper class ("lands of the Inca"), as well as the state religion ("lands of the Sun") (Rowe 1963:265; Moore 1958:17-48; Murra 1956:63).

The primary means by which the Inca Empire acquired surpluses was through demands made on the labor of the peasantry (Murra 1956:158; 1964: 430). Murra argues that the state revenue system was founded on the model used by the *curacas* who, prior to the Inca conquest, could make claims on the labor of their fellow *ayllu* members in exchange for "chiefly generosity" (1956:161). The governing norm of the *curacas*, which was later used by the Inca elite, was that the peasantry's production from its own lands was inviolable (Polo 1917a:67). The peasants farmed the lands of the state and of the state religion, wove cloth, were liable for *mita* service (a form of corvée labor) on public work projects and in the army, but their own production was never expropriated (Murra 1964:430).

From the perspective of the indigenous culture, male and female occupations—defined as interdependent and complementary activities—were conceptualized as forming the basic unit of labor required for the reproduction of Andean society. This conception also underlay the tribute system of the Incas: it was the household, and not the individual, that constituted the smallest entity liable for labor service to the state (1956:164). Thus, even though married men were registered in the state's census rolls—and therefore liable for *mita* service—the effective labor unit was defined as having a male and female component (:175; Cobo 1964:2:133). Similarly, although spinning and weaving were defined as "appropriate female activities," it was married peasant women who were responsible for weaving the cloth owed as tribute to the state.

Murra argues very cogently that in spite of the change in legal status of the community's resources—now defined as "dispensations" from Cuzco—the *ayllu*'s traditional rights to the use of its fields was not hindered (Murra 1956: 59–61). As long as lands for the state and state religion were set aside, and the community provided the labor for the cultivation of these fields, the Incas did not impede the *ayllu*'s self-sufficiency (:64). The basic resources required for the *ayllu*'s subsistence effectively stayed in the hands of the community and the community's arrangements governing land use remained intact. Thus, the customary right of women to claim usufruct rights to land and to make demands on kinsmen or in-laws for labor was not affected by the Inca conquest and its system of gathering tribute. In fact, special mechanisms were created to insure that women whose husbands were drafted for *mita* service were supplied with adequate compensatory labor (Garcilaso 1961:157).

Although the effects of the Inca conquest on the social relations of production within the *ayllu*—and its consequent impact on the economic potential of the majority of peasant women—was negligible, the capacity of women from Cuzco's upper strata to make claims to the empire's resources and surpluses equal to those of men is problematic. Part of the difficulty lies in our elementary knowledge of the complexities of Inca land-tenure practices (Murra 1975:20). With respect to women of the upper class, we face the additional problem that their rights to surplus production related to state lands (lands of the Inca); consequently, their effective access often lay hidden behind this category (see Villanueva 1970:46). This problem also exists regarding the religious lands (lands of the Sun), which were further subdivided to support cults to the empire's female deities—the Moon and the *Pachamama* (Earth Mother)

(Guaman Poma 1956:1:265, 3:132; Polo 1917a:56, 95; 1917c:50). Nevertheless, we are certain that a portion of the revenue from the state's lands went to maintain the *coya* (queen) (Guaman Poma 1956:2:253, 3:132); chroniclers and documents also verify that the *coyas* controlled certain lands, reserved for their personal use (Morua 1946:85, 87, 90, 94; Cieza 1959:240; Guaman Poma 1956:1:91–104), whose produce was probably employed to support ancestral cults after their deaths (Cieza 1959:247; Estete n.d.:393; Guaman Poma 1956:1:98). *Coyas* also had access to an emergent form of private property in land which was beginning to develop in the later stages of the Inca Empire (Rostworowski 1962:135–37, 141–59; Villanueva 1970:21, 35–37, 39, 46, 47, 51, 52). In keeping with Andean tradition, however, even though these land grants were made to an individual, the fields were worked, and the harvest enjoyed, by the members of the beneficiary's kin group—men as well as women (Cobo 1964:2:122; Polo 1917a:72).

It is difficult to determine, however, the relative access of men and women to these productive resources. We do not know if Inca men, who were primarily responsible for conquest, were thereby entitled to a greater share of the resources of subjugated populations. Moreover, it is possible that because of the occupational structure of the empire, men—who were the state's bureaucrats, administrators, and warriors—were more likely than were women to receive land grants rewarding their services to the Cuzco ruling class.

Politico-Religious Structures

The Spanish conquest of the Andes destroyed the religious-political organization of the Cuzco elite. The official state cults to the sun and the moon, as well as the Inca administrative and governing apparatus, were quickly dismantled by the Conquistadores and their cleric allies, but the politico-religious institutions of the peasantry were not so easily eradicated, and here I give priority to descriptions of local-level organizations. In contrast to the Spaniards, the Incas actually encouraged the groups they conquered to maintain worship of their native deities with the proviso that the Cuzco gods be venerated as more powerful, superior divinities. As was the case regarding the impact of the empire's tributary system on productive relations within the *ayllu*, the Incas, while imposing the worship of their gods, left intact the religious institutions and cults associated with conquered populations. What is more telling: the Inca, upon conquering an *ayllu*, took on the ancestors and deities of the conquered group as his own.

Several models or principles molded pre-Columbian Andean politico-religious relations: one of the more important structures was based on a paradigm of sexual parallelism. An excellent source of documents demonstrating how this model functioned in peasant communities, and the consequent formation of parallel gender-linked organizations is the Archivo Arzobispal of Lima in which suits brought by priest-inquisitors against practitioners of indigenous religion are housed. One account (Hernandez Principe 1923) describes the ancestral cults and religious organization of *ayllus* located in three communities in the Department of Ancash. Hernandez Principe includes lists of both *ministros* (male ministers) and *ministras* (female ministers) who were in charge of autochthonous religious activities. Thus, we know that female religious organizations existed (1923:28, 30, 34, 36—40; cf. Zuidema 1973).

An analysis of the masculine cults suggests that at least two principles governed the designation of "ministros." The first was succession from father to son: it appears that those who were responsible for the maintenance of ancestral cults often succeeded their fathers to office. The genealogies that structured the ancestral cults for each *ayllu* are, almost without exception, those of male ancestors. Female *huacas* (ancestor-deities) are mentioned as originators of *ayllus*, but they invariably give rise to a patrilineally phrased descent group. The predominance of male ancestors in the recorded genealogies suggests that Hernandez Principe's informants were men, and since a model of sexual parallelism structured Andean kinship relations, it is highly probable that a descent system described by a female would be matrilineally phrased. And, in all probability, the offices of a female ancestral cult would be transmitted from mother to daughter (BN:B1715). Second, the organization of the other "ministros," however, seems to be rooted in a system that was an antecedent of the *varayoq* or civil-religious hierarchies which form the backbone of governance in many contemporary indigenous communities (Zuidema 1973:23). The contemporary *varayoq* system is composed of a hierarchy of civil-religious posts whose officiants guard the morality of the community as well as regulate its agricultural and pastoral endeavors. The offices are achieved on a rotating basis with members working one year, and then "resting" in order to acquire the means to support the sponsorship of the next position in the hierarchy. These ranked posts function as a type of age-grade system which is phrased in terms of kinship: those who hold upper positions are "father-mother" to those below; those who hold lower posts are helpers ("younger siblings") of those holding higher positions (Earls 1973). The members of each rank hold a staff of office (*vara*) which symbolizes their position in this hierarchy. People who have gone through the *varayoq* system acquire prestige as the source of the community's wisdom and keepers of custom and tradition.

Hernandez Principe's information suggests that the female "ministras" also comprised a religious hierarchy which paralleled the male organization and whose organizing principles, at least in part, were similar to those of the *varayoq*. There is evidence of age-grading and ranking—both characteristics of the *varayoq* system—in the lists that Hernandez Principe records (1923:28, 32, 39). Some "ministras" had a superior status to others: these were designated *mayor* (elder). Lower ranks were also indicated, since some women were designated as helpers of those who preceded them on the list. Two women were specifically identified as "ministras" of particular *huacas* (1923:28), neither of which were mentioned in the text as being shrines of ancestors. Given the logic of sexual parallelism, this is highly suggestive that these *huacas* were the objects of adoration of a female cult, sponsored and organized by women.

Women's religious organizations responsible for the worship of female deities who represented the forces of creation and reproduction in Andean society were found throughout the empire (Guaman Poma 1956:1:105, 123, 127, 2:66, 69, 3:11, 22–24, 153, 250; Duviols 1971:370; Morua 1946:427; Perez Bocanegra 1631:111–15). One such cult, in Pimachi, was dedicated to the veneration of Mamasaras (corn mothers). Although Mamasaras are usually described as household amulets, in this case their worship formed the basis of an organization which integrated women from all the households of the community. Agricultural land was set aside to support the ritual complex devoted to Mamasaras, while vestments as well as offerings of silver were distributed by Maria Chaupis Tanta who was in charge of this cult (Duviols 1971:370). In accord with the model of sexual parallelism employed by the empire, the Mamasaras were conceived to be the sisters of the two major male deities of the community.

The visiting priest brought suits against several women in Pimachi, accusing them of being "confessors, dogmatists, witches, and mistresses of [idolatrous] ceremonies" (:385). The condemnations written by the priest clearly show that these "witches" had a female constituency. They were condemned as "confessors of women, whom they lead and instructed in the beliefs of their ancestors...and for having commanded that Indian women no longer adore our Savior Jesus Christ, but idols and *huacas*" (ibid.). There is also a suit which documents a cult to Guarmi Paso (Woman Moon), a goddess adored by women from several neighboring communities (:387). Here we have an example of a feminine sect which crossed community boundaries, articulating women from different *ayllus* in an organization rooted in the adoration of the moon.

This model of sexual parallelism, which ordered relations both within communities and between them, also structured the political-religious organization of the Inca Empire. The Incas could legitimize their political hegemony over Andean populations by stressing their supposed genealogical ties with the supreme deities of the state—the Inca with the sun and the *coya* with the moon (Garcilaso 1956:43–45, 47, 49; Cobo 1964:2:70). The official cosmology of the Inca Empire thus represents an ideological justification of a political hierarchy—conceived in terms of parallel matrilines and patrilines, headed by the Cuzco elite. Women's religious cults, transformed into institutions of a class society, would be under the dominion of the Queen, who would act as the representative of all womanhood. I have argued that these religious cults formed the basis of a political hierarchy which connected women of the Cuzco elite with those in the provinces (female *curacas* and peasantry) in a network that joined women throughout the empire. Evidence strongly suggests that a structure of dual authority existed, ordered along the lines of this paradigm of sexual parallelism (Silverblatt 1976, 1978).

Crucial to the creation of a network of mutual obligations which characterized the political organization of a society like the Inca Empire was the ability of the upper class to create bonds of obligations through "chiefly" largess. The *coyas* did have their own productive base or lands reserved for their use which provided them with the means to independently throw huge feasts—the hallmark of chiefly generosity (Morua 1946:85, 87, 90, 94; Cieza 1959:240; Rostworowski 1962:135—37; 141—59; Villanueva 1970:21, 36—37, 39, 46, 47, 51, 52). And, even though the majority of chroniclers imply that links between provincial communities and Cuzco's political apparatus were primarily made through men, there is evidence that Cuzco not only legitimized the power and privileges of women leaders of provincial groups, but that it ritually affirmed bonds with female *curacas* which linked the populations under their jurisdiction with the state's political machinery (Oberem 1968:82, 83).

The parallel structure of the politico-religious organization in the *ayllu* was only one of several principles that molded *ayllu* religious activity. Both men and women venerated a large number of *huacas* relating to various aspects of the *ayllu*'s social existence, as well as *huacas* that integrated several *ayllus* on the basis of common worship or ancestry. Most of the chroniclers and Spanish clerics suggest that the indigenous priests of *huacas* venerated by an entire *ayllu* or by several *ayllus* were male. Although these posts could be filled by women, the principal religious offices were performed for the most part by men, while women performed secondary functions as ritual assistants (Arriaga 1968:33—35). Although it is probable that men led community-wide cults to the Rayo—an indigenous deity of thunder and lightning associated with conquest and with the male ancestral spirits that resided in the mountains—statements like Arriaga's are difficult to evaluate because of the male bias of the priests and chroniclers as well as the parallel structure of Andean religious organization within which women sponsored their own religious cults.[6]

ANDEAN COSMOLOGY

The Inca Empire was a hierarchical and highly stratified society in which higher-ranked social groups were entitled to privileges not enjoyed by the peasantry. The Inca conquest marked the end of the autonomous existence experienced by the subjugated *ayllus*, and the difficulties of conquest in certain areas, as well as the rebellions of other vanquished ethnic groups, is testimony to their rejection of the Inca expansion and its concomitant impositions on local life. Nevertheless, the tribute system imposed by the Inca conquest, as well as its politico-religious institutions, were rooted in a model of reciprocity and redistribution developed by the pre-Inca Andean *ayllus* which imposed culturally defined limits on the kind and degree of exploitation to which conquered populations could be subjected by the upper classes. In addition, all Andean populations shared certain cosmological structures which expressed norms—

concerning the relationships between humans and nature, between individuals, between social strata, and between men and women—that generated expectations which were common to conquered and conquerors. The Incas' official cosmology, of course, served to legitimize their unequal power and rights, both in their eyes and—they hoped—in the eyes of the conquered. Nevertheless, by examining in more detail that official ideology we can better understand the Andean view of the relationships that governed the Universe—as well as the relationships that marked the interaction between the sexes—and thus be better equipped to comprehend the devastation caused by the Spanish conquest.

A dialectical view of oppositions, often phrased in terms of sexual parallelism, was a fundamental cosmological principle shared by Andean peoples; and this conception was formalized by the Incas as part of their official religious ideology. A description of the Temple of the Sun in Cuzco constitutes our major evidence of the empire's employment of a dualistic model to structure its cosmology (Pachacuti Yamqui 1950:227; for detailed interpretations, see Zuidema 1972; Earls and Silverblatt 1976a and 1976b; Isbell 1976). The central deity is Viracocha, the creator god of the Andes. Combining both male and female sexual elements, Viracocha contains all the forces that these elements symbolize: "the sun, the moon, day, night, winter, summer" (Pachacuti Yamqui 1950:220). As the founder of parallel lines of male and female deities who have as their descendents mortal man and woman, Viracocha "gives of his divinity" to the gender-specific modes of being which the concept of Viracocha embodies (Blas Valera 1950:136). The parallel hierarchy, with Viracocha at the center, unified in one system the cosmos; the Inca and Coya, who as "children of the Sun and Moon" were structurally equivalent to Venus of the Morning (male) and Venus of the Afternoon (female); the *curacas*, provincial nobility who were said to be the children of Venus (Duviols 1971); common man and woman, and the product of their joint labor—tools of production, *pata* (terraces) and food and other produce which is stored in the *collcas* (storehouses).

The dynamics implicit in this model were derived from the interaction between the intrinsically related and reciprocally defining entities symbolized as male and female. These forces stemming from the interplay between the model's male and female constituent parts were conceptualized as creating the driving energies of the universe. Thus, a fundamental cosmological structure which conditioned the Andean conception of the universe was in large part based on a dialectical view of the relations between the sexes (see Isbell 1978; but see also Silverblatt 1976, 1978).

We can also infer from the diagram that the interaction of men and women is expressed through their roles in social production. This evaluation is symbolized as the product of a culturally determined productive process—the technology of terracing and the goods stored in the *collcas*. The product of joint male and female intervention in nature was returned as sacrificial offerings to the deities who created human and cultural existence. This cycle of worship—the offsprings of products created by the interaction of men and women to the life-generating deities—insured the continued existence of social life. Although cultural norms existed which defined "appropriate" male and female tasks, these norms were submerged in a wider category of complementarity which expresses both the necessary interdependence of men and women to realize labor activities and the recognition that both male and female tasks were indispensable for the maintenance and reproduction of the household, the community, and the empire.

As "children of the Sun and Moon," the Incas tried to legitimate, through this cosmological structure, their power and privileges vis-à-vis conquered non-Inca populations. Their official ideology also incorporated the preferred position of the *curacas*, or provincial upper-ranked groups, However, although this model sanctions a political hierarchy, it also marks the reciprocal obligations owed by the higher-ranked political groups to those below them. Part of the dynamic intrinsic to this model embodies the mutual constraints effected and understood to exist between levels in the hierarchy (Earls and Silverblatt 1976b).

The normative ideal of balance and equilibrium governed the dialectical paradigm which structured pre-Colombian cosmology. *Viracocha* occupies the predominant position, representing the tensional unity, the equilibrium and synthesis of the opposing forces of the universe. The explicit expression of the Andean ideal is found in the term *ayni* (balance, or reciprocity). *Ayni* could be applied to various classes of relationships: husband-wife, *ayllu-ayllu*, society-nature, or the universe as a whole (Earls 1971; Earls and Silverblatt 1976a, 1976b). Relationships of balance (*ayni*) were not assumed or static in the Andean perception of the cosmos. The fact that *ayni* means both balance and reciprocity implies that human intervention was required to create an equilibrium in sociopolitical relationships, in relationships between humans and natural forces, and those between humans and the supernatural.

THE SPANISH CONQUEST

The history of Spain in the Andes is a history of the struggle between colonial forces which attempted to break down indigenous social relations and reorient them toward a market economy and the resistance of indigenous people to these disintegrating forces. The Spanish Conquest imposed radically different and alien economic, political, and ideological structures on Andean society. The economy of Spain, oriented toward the emerging market economy of Europe saw in its New World colonies the opportunity to accumulate great wealth. The economic institutions imposed on the colonies reflected the needs of the mother country to amass profit; the ideological underpinnings of these institutions embodied an evaluation of the universe—the nature of the relationship between man and nature, between social groups, between man and woman—that was totally alien to the conquered. The colonial process, thus, was an attack both on indigenous social relationships, which were structured by principles of reciprocity and redistribution, as well as on the ideology which molded and buttressed them. It was a battle to dismantle the structures that maintained pre-Columbian indigenous society and replace them with institutions which would bind members of the conquered population to the conquerors. The creation of a colonial society, the transformation of indigenous society, and its reorientation to European modes took centuries.

For within the constraints imposed by colonial rule, indigenous people struggled to defend pre-Columbian lifeways. The history of conquest is also the history of indigenous people struggling to contain, modify, resist, or adapt to the disintegrating forces unleashed by colonialism. The dialectic between the destructive external forces of colonialism and indigenous modes of organization and structures of defense will be the frame I will use to understand the transformations experienced by Andean culture and their concomitant effect on the position of native women.

WOMEN OF THE INCA NOBILITY:

Entering the Market Economy

We should remember that Spanish society at the time of the conquest was rigidly stratified, with feudal or feudallike structures predominating in competition with those of an expanding mercantile capitalist economy. These norms were brought to the Americas as a guide to the governance of the newly conquered Inca Empire, which was itself hierarchically organized. An amalgam of Inca and Spanish law and tradition—in practice weighted in favor of Spanish law—was applied by the conquerors in their attempts to reorganize the allocation and disposition of land.

The Spanish Conquest introduced to the Andes new concepts of property ownership and land tenure along with a complex legal system through which these forms were maintained and transmitted. Spanish property laws were rooted in rights of private ownership over land and its preferential inheritance by direct descendants of the owner. In accord with their own feudal traditions, the Spanish granted descendants of the Inca and provincial nobility certain privileges and rights which were denied to Indian "commoners" (*indios del comun*), thereby differentiating their capacities to participate in the commercial activities that marked the colonial economy. The privileges also created opportunities for members of the indigenous elite to make claims on the economic resources of Andean society which were denied them under Incaic structures of economic organization, and propelled their participation in colonial mercantilist activities.[7]

Indian nobles, for example, were allowed to claim personal property rights over land. Asserting descent from a particular Inca sovereign, members of the

162 Women and Colonization

Cuzco nobility began to lay claim to lands which were said to "belong to" that monarch. These personal claims made on the so-called "private property" of the Inca sovereigns conflicted, however, with the traditional norms governing the disposition of property effective during the Incanato. "Private property," as defined in Europe, did not exist in the Andes. Nor were fields pertaining to a particular ruler "inherited" by a descendent; upon the death of a monarch this land reverted to the control of the sovereign's entire descent group. Thus, with the imposition of Spanish property laws, certain members of the Inca nobility began to manipulate these new property forms to their own advantage. Female descendents of the Inca nobility were no exception; documents from the Archivo Departamental de Cuzco clearly show how women of the Cuzco upper class entered the land grab.

Female descendents of the Cuzco nobility were entitled to the privileges afforded by Spaniards to the indigenous elite and were therefore formally allotted agricultural fields by virtue of their noble descent. In the *reparticion* (allotment) of lands effected by the crown in the sixteenth century in the valley of Yucay (Department of Cuzco), indigenous noble women were formally granted agricultural lands which they could personally dispose of according to the dictates of Spanish law (AHU:Leg. 4, 5, 7). Also, as far back as the sixteenth century, women of noble descent began to enter into commercial transactions regarding the land thus claimed or inherited (ACC:Top. 8, Leg. 1; Top. 10, Leg. 21).

The process of the privatization of land—whether taken advantage of by the Spaniards or by men or women of the Inca nobility—severely affected both the native peasantry and Incaic institutions which supported women's religious authority structures. Lands which were destined, under the Incanato, to support female politico-religious organizations passed into private hands, thus curtailing a tradition which underpinned the independent religious and political activity of women, albeit of the Cuzco female elite (Villanueva 1970; AHU: Leg. 4, 5, 7). Indian commoners, often because of false claims made by the indigenous nobility, saw their land base (*del comun*, land granted to commoners and under communal jurisdiction)—which they desperately needed for their own maintenance as well as to pay tribute—being eroded. Thus, we find records of disputes between women who made private claims to land because of their noble descent and commoners who argued that these claims were not justified. And, as we shall see in the following section, women of the peasantry were more vulnerable to having their lands expropriated than men.

Indigenous noblewomen, like their male counterparts, occupied a contradiction-laden role in colonial society as privileged members of the conquered society. The ambiguity of their position is expressed in the dispute between Dona Paula Mama Guaco and the *india* Isabel. Declaring descent from the sovereign Topa Inga, Dona Paula Mama Nusta and Dona Madalena Mama Guaco, her mother (among others), claimed as their personal possessions the land of

Callixpuquio. These claims were contested by Indians of San Blas who asserted that they too had rights to these lands as the descendents of the *yanaconas* (state retainers) who worked them during the Incanato. (*Yanaconas* who cultivated fields ascribed to particular sovereigns were given lands for their maintenance.) Dona Paula Mama Guaco Nusta, in her declaration to the crown, complained that when she went to examine her property and that of her mother, she discovered some *indios* plowing her fields; "And a certain Indian, Isabel, dishonored me with insulting words ignoring the fact that I am the honorable wife of a Spaniard, and a woman of quality and nobility" (ACC:Top. 9, Leg. 5). By her own words, Dona Paula exposes the contradictory position of indigenous noblewomen. On the one hand, her claim to land is based on descent from the Cuzco nobility; thus, she conspicuously carries the Inca title Nusta. Her surname, Mama Guaco, reflects a relation to the Inca Queens. The passing down of surnames from mother to daughter, along parallel lines of descent, is a particularly indigenous (as opposed to Spanish) system of surname transmission. On the other hand, Dona Paula Mama Guaco asserts her superiority over the common *india* by emphasizing her marital ties with a Spanish male, which make her "honorable" and "of quality."

Spanish law, however, conflicted with Andean customs pertaining to the position of women in relation to land rights and tenure. According to Spanish law, married women were legally minors; therefore, all transactions involving goods that a woman inherited or brought into a marriage through dowry had to be conducted with the consent and permission of her male "tutor." Although women had customary rights over dowry goods, these goods became joint property upon marriage and the wife could not freely dispose of them. By Andean custom (which is still practiced today), a woman maintains independent rights over all goods, including lands, that she might inherit. The concept of joint or common property did not (and does not) exist.

Conflicts engendered by the contradiction between Spanish law and indigenous tradition surface in several litigations in which women protest the unilateral economic transactions entered into by their husbands. In Cuzco I found a case in which the husband of an indigenous noble woman, taking advantage of his position as her tutor, without permission sold land which his wife had inherited. The wife formally protested the validity of the sale, arguing that it was conducted without her knowledge (AUP:Exp. Siglo 18, Leg. 11-2). Perhaps no noble woman rejected the impositions of Spanish law more clearly than Clara Payco who declares in her will, "Even though I have no kinsmen, my husband has no right whatsoever over my lands" (ACC:Top. 10, Leg. 21).

The disadvantageous position in which Spanish law placed women is obvious. This must have been strongly felt by indigenous women who were accustomed to having ultimate disposition rights over their lands within the framework of Andean traditions and inheritance patterns. Interestingly, we find in some documents that indigenous inheritance patterns are maintained, albeit within the framework and constraints imposed by Spanish law. For example, in 1595, when lands were being formally distributed to the Indians of Yucay, Don Alonso Topa Cusigualpa, of noble descent, was granted lands for his personal use. Within the designation of lands under his name, we find that one *topo* of land was granted to his wife, Leona Tocto Sicsa, who had inherited this field from Beatris Sicssa (probably her mother). Thus, the Andean tradition of parallel transmission of rights to land—from mother to daughter— was recognized in colonial land allocation, even though the lands were distributed to this woman through her spouse in accord with Spanish law, under which a husband maintains tutelage over his wife's possessions (also see Zuidema 1967).

As in many colonial situations, privileged members of the colonized society will take advantage of new opportunities for personal gain which were nonexistent in precontact, traditional systems. These women descendents of the Cuzco elite were no exception. Yet we must remember that they were still subjugated members of a patriarchal colony. Even though the Inca queens were the renowned agronomer-geneticists of the empire, special schools established by the Spanish for the indigenous elite were open only to men; even though some of the world's most extraordinary weaving was produced by women of the Inca and provincial elite, their colonial daughters could never gain entry into indigenous artisan guilds; even though the *coyas* headed a political structure which united women throughout the empire, native noblewomen were denied positions established within the colonial governing apparatus for descendents of the Inca elite. The memory of the very different life experiences, potentials for action, and cultural evaluation of "womanhood" which existed in pre-Columbian society remained strong with these women. Thus, we shouldn't be surprised that Rowe, when describing colonial paintings drawn over two hundred years after the Spanish invasion, writes,

> In several of the women's portraits, their dress so accurately replicates Inca style, that if it weren't for the way in which the landscape was represented in the background, we would have to conclude that we were dealing with personages living at the time of the Conquest (1976:23).

Women of noble birth played crucial roles in the great indigenous rebellion led by Tupac Amaru and his wife Micaela Bastides (1781); the famous *curaca* Tomasa Tito Condemayta of Acomayo (Department of Cuzco), leading a brigade of women soldiers, successfully defended the strategic bridge of Acos against Spanish troops (Valcarcel 1947). Yet, paradoxically, but consonant with the contradictory position of privileged members of the indigenous elite, one of the severest attacks by indigenous followers of Tupac Amaru was against the houses and estates of Antonia Chuquicallata, a wealthy woman from the native nobility of Azángaro (Flores Galindo 1976:282).

Although such women were able to take advantage of the new sources of wealth opened after the Spanish Conquest, we must remember that we are dealing with the history of a tiny percentage of the indigenous population. The majority of the colonized were brutally mistreated under colonial institutions, and, even though both men and women suffered under the yoke of Spanish rule, we shall see that the burden placed on women was different and more intense.

WOMEN OF THE PEASANTRY

Economic Burdens

The Incaic and Spanish systems under which labor and tribute were garnered from the peasantry were as different as the principles which oriented their respective economies. Although the preconquest empire was a highly stratified society, production under the Incas was oriented toward the socially determined needs of that society. The surpluses required to support the empire's nonproductive members were acquired by taxing the labor of the peasantry under a system in which the state was obliged to feast and redistribute goods to peasant laborers while abstaining from directly expropriating any goods produced from their lands or herds. As under the tribute system, the state was bound to insure the well-being of those drafted for periodic corvée labor in the mines, army, or other public work projects. Built-in institutional and ideological mechanisms tempered the relationship between the state and the commoners, while the norms of reciprocity that operated in the kin-based *ayllus* insured that the fields of men serving in *mitas* were well tended. The fact that the minimal unit liable for tribute was the household was consonant with the Andean conception of the necessary interdependence of male and female labor activities and guaranteed that either the man or woman on whom tribute or labor obligations fell would be able to make demands on the labor of their respective kin or affinal groups to soften the burdens of services demanded by the state.

The goal of Spanish tribute and labor demands was intrinsically tied to a radically different economic system in which goods were produced not for use but for their exchange value on the European market. No built-in mechanisms existed to insure the well-being of the laborer, or to check or restrain the exploitation of nature. Both existed only as a means to accumulate wealth for the Spanish authorities, merchants, clerics, and the coffers of Spain. A Spaniard noted in the seventeenth century that "what is carried to Spain from Peru is not silver but blood and sweat of Indians" (quoted in Taussig n.d.:50).

In contradistinction to the Incaic system of tribute appropriation, under the colonial regime all indigenous males of "common origin" between the ages of 18 and 50 (regardless of marital status) were subject to tribute demands.

These demands took the form of labor service—primarily in the mines, or *obrajes* (proto-factories)—of personal labor service owed colonial authorities, and of taxes which were originally demanded in goods and later in money. The Church was entitled to charge a tithe; while priests also charged fees for the celebration of marriages, baptisms, and masses. All of these taxes imposed on the peasantry served to force the Indians to participate in the market sytem (Spalding 1974:116).

As Spalding has pointed out, in terms of the logic of the Andean system of revenue collection, the Spanish system was doubly exploitative. Even though the crown had expropriated lands that had been destined to support the Inca state and religious apparatus, it demanded that Indians pay for the maintenance of the new state religion (Catholicism) and of the crown from the produce of their own lands which, under the Incas, was inviolable (:50—52).

The Spanish system also ignored the deeply imbedded Andean conception of the household—embodying the necessary complementarity of male and female labor—as the minimal unit liable for tribute. Consequently, many Indians complained bitterly that their *curacas* (who were responsible for collecting tribute) were placing demands on single men "even though they had no women to help them" (Ortiz de Zúñiga 1967:73, 78, 79) and on widows and single women who were now also responsible for tribute in cloth owed colonial authorities (Diez de San Miguel 1964:75).

The Spanish system of acquiring tribute seems to have had many prejudicial effects on the economic capabilities of peasant women. Zuidema refers to a colonial document in which male members of an indigenous community wanted to abolish the traditional structure of parallel transmission rights to land because it was no longer compatible with the tribute system introduced by the Spanish (1972:20). Apparently, the produce of land to which a woman had rights could not be taxed by the Spanish. In this document, the *comuneros* were asserting that a man was using land inherited by his wife from her mother in order to pay his tribute quota, and were indicating their desire that women no longer maintain autonomous jurisdiction over the produce of their fields. This is just one example of how, as Spanish tribute demands increased, women's independent rights to land were being undermined (see also AHU: Leg. 2).

In addition, Spanish law, as well as the nature of the tribute system, undermined indigenous structures of social organization which were predicated on the principle of parallel descent. Intermarriage between spouses of different *ayllus* which occurred during the early colonial period (as opposed to pre-Columbian endogamy) often resulted in a double economic burden being placed on the shoulders of native women. Because of the nature and pressure of Spanish tribute demands, these women were pressured by both the *curaca* of their natal *ayllu*, in which they held land, and by the *curaca* of their husband's *ayllu* to contribute towards the royal tax (Diez de San Miguel 1964: 221). The Viceroy Toledo, attempting to settle conflicting claims made upon members of inter-*ayllu* marriages, stipulated that a couple must reside in the man's *ayllu* and that the children belong to the paternal kin group (Spalding 1967:122). Thus, the Spanish were strengthening patrilineal and patrilocal ties at the expense of those marked matrilineally and matrilocally and undermining parallel structures of descent and inheritance. Interestingly, in some cases *ayllus* themselves attempted to settle the potential conflicts that were derived from inter-*ayllu* marriages by reverting to or upholding this indigenous custom: woman's lands were to be inherited by a female heir and the man's by a male descendent.

The documents pertaining to inter-*ayllu* conflict (:126) support the argument that Andean women traditionally had independent rights to land which were not abrogated at marriage. If married women did not have independent access to land by virtue of their *ayllu* membership, there would be no basis for these inter-*ayllu* conflicts. They also point to the clash between Spanish law and indigenous custom and the ensuing process through which women's rights were undermined by colonial institutions. In terms of Spanish law women were legally minors and lands inherited by them were under the jurisdiction of their spouses; in addition, according to colonial law regulating land rights of commoners, usufruct rights were given to the male head of household (AHU:Leg. 3). Men were thus in a position to try to assume control over their wives' lands, an attempt which was fought by the *ayllus* (Spalding 1974:126) as well as by the women themselves (AUP:Exp. Siglo 18, Leg. 11-2; ACC:Top. 10, Leg. 21; BN:B1488). As colonization advanced in the Andes, indigenous men and women saw their communal lands encroached upon by Spanish and by the indigenous elite, who were building large agricultural estates. Because of the unfavored position in which women were placed by the colonial process, women were much more vulnerable to having their lands expropriated than men (BN:B1488, C3967; Guaman Poma 1956:2:144, 3:98).

From the beginning of the Spanish Conquest, women were brutally exploited by colonial administrators and *encomenderos* (recipients of royal land grants) who needed women's labor to produce goods—particularly cloth—destined for the colonial and European markets. The first forms of industrial labor draft emerged in the *encomienda* (estate) itself, when the *encomenderos* established a tribute in cloth. Many *encomenderos* introduced the practice of locking women in rooms and forcing them to weave and spin; these women were so exploited that in 1549 a royal decree was published prohibiting the continuation of this practice (Roel 1970:135). Because of the character of colonial institutions and the increasing pressures to augment tribute and to amass wealth, this decree, like many others issued to alleviate the burden of the peasantry, was effectively ignored.

One hundred and fifty years later, the judge responsible for indigenous affairs in Cuzco was imprisoned because he had a private jail in his house where he forced Indian women to weave (Esquivel y Navia 1901:185). Colonial magistrates (*corregidores*), who primarily saw their stay in the colonies as a way to make a fast buck, forced women to weave clothing for them for less than half the free market rate (Rowe 1957:163). Spanish tribute demands and taxes were so high that women saw themselves by necessity having to weave for the *obrajes* in their homes in exchange for grossly depressed wages, while their husbands and male kin were away working in the *mita* service (Roel 1970: 137). In addition, the wages paid to a *mitayo* (a man performing *mita* service) in the mines were equivalent to approximately one-sixth of the money needed to cover his subsistence requirements; since *mitayos* often were accompanied by their wives and children, Rowe suggests that one way in which the difference may have been made up was for the laborer's wife and children to work also (Rowe 1957:173),—but at wages which were certainly lower than the already depressed wages of their husbands.

The years following the Spanish conquest were marked by a tremendous population decline. The high incidence of native mortality, in addition to the fact that many males preferred to abandon their communities of origin rather than be subject to *mita* and tribute demands, meant that the *mita* and tribute burdens of those who remained necessarily increased. Since the *mita* and tribute quotas were not readjusted to account for demographic changes, the increased burdens in effect were met primarily by women (aided by the elderly and children). Thus, although according to Spanish law women were exempt from either paying tribute or from labor drafts, by the end of the sixteenth century and throughout the seventeenth and eighteenth centuries women, in practice, were paying tribute as well as performing labor services (Guaman Poma 1956:2:33, 64, 90, 133; Roel 1970:208).

More than any other source, the indigenous chronicler, Guaman Poma de Ayala, depicts in painful detail the systematic destruction of Andean institutions by the forces of Spanish Colonialism. Basing his critique of colonial society on a comparison with the quality of life enjoyed by indigenous people before and during Inca rule, he provides us with information detailing how indigenous institutions governing political, economic, and social life were transformed and perverted by the pressures of the colonial regime. Within this context, Guaman Poma outlines the vulnerable position in which Andean women were placed as the norms and structures which governed intersexual relations before the conquest—within which women and their labor were highly respected and valued—were eroded by Western values and institutions. Western institutions, particularly when applied in a colonial context, were especially brutalizing and dehumanizing in relation to colonized women (1956:2:220, 244, 251, 3:55, 98, 270). Indigenous women—married, single, or widowed—were forced to work under highly exploitative conditions for colonial administrators, landowners, magistrates, and clergy, who needed female labor for domestic service as well as for the production of goods to be sold in the market. Moreover, native political authorities, allying themselves with their Spanish masters to the detriment of the interests of their fellow *comùneros*, also began to abuse women in ways inadmissable in terms of preconquest Andean social relations (e.g., 2:61, 152—53, 3:75).

But the injustices suffered by indigenous women were not solely economic. It was not just that women's lands and herds were more easily confiscated, or that they were forced to work under near slave conditions for the Spanish or their native supporters, or that they increasingly bore the brunt of the crown's taxes or *mita*. Native women were also sexually abused (2:28, 127, 144). For a society in which premarital sex was encouraged but only under circumstances in which both partners consented and in which the relation between man and woman was conceived of as *ayni* (harmony), the rape and forced concubinage of women carried out by Spanish and indigenous authorities was an abomination. In Guaman Poma's eyes, the worst offenders were priests (1:49, 2:191, 144). Under the guise of teaching women catechism or delegating penance the clergy forced women to serve them as laborers, as mistresses, and as prostitutes.

> The priests want money, money and more money [so they force women] to serve them as spinners, weavers, cooks, breadmakers.... Women had honor...during the epoch of the Incas in spite of the fact that they were idolatrous, but now the clergy and parish priests are the ones who first violate them and lead them to sin (2:175, 3:34).

Tragically, colonial pressures also destroyed in many cases the relation of *ayni* that characterized the interaction of men and women, promoting a grotesque extreme of Western norms in which men "owned" their female relatives. Indeed, desperate to avoid service in the mines, men pawned their female relatives to Spaniards (e.g., Roel 1970:109).

Political Disfranchisement

Once Spanish control became entrenched in the Andes, colonial authorities were faced with the problem of how to modify the existing political and economic institutions of the peasantry to fit their needs. The indigenous *ayllus* were highly dispersed, making it difficult to collect tribute as well as to indoctrinate the conquered population in the religion of the conquerors. The Spanish were also aware of the dangers inherent to the colonial regime in allowing the *ayllus* to function as they did prior to conquest, since the *ayllu* structure would allow indigenous traditions to remain alive. For these reasons, in the mid-sixteenth century it was decreed that native populations be regrouped in nucleated settlements called *reducciones* (Roel 1970:94).

The Spanish imposed a system of indirect rule on the peasantry: they recognized *curacas* as leaders of their respective communities while also establishing local governmental and religious apparatus modeled after those of Spain. The *curacas*, like the Inca elite, were categorized at the same level as European nobility. Thus, they were released from tribute obligations; and, as opposed to the commoners who were entitled to usufruct rights in communal land, the *curacas* had the right to maintain private estates. In exchange for these privileges, the *curaca* was expected to insure that the demands made by colonial society on the peasantry be carried out—collection of tribute, meeting *mita* quotas, collecting goods and salary owed to the parish priest, construction and upkeep of the church (Spalding 1974:37). Through allegiances made with Spanish authorities, the *curacas* were able to take personal advantage of new channels of mobility and sources of wealth introduced by the colonial regime, often to the detriment of the community they were supposed to protect.

To the degree that the *curaca*'s authority was derived from the external colonial power structure, they were able to disregard Andean norms of reciprocity and mutual obligations which mediated the relation between *curaca* and governed—and consequently their relation with peasant women. Guaman Poma accused *curacas* of exploiting women's labor and abusing them sexually, as did Perez Bocanegra, who indicates that some *curacas* illegally charged women tribute and forced them into concubinage (1631:269, 271). Using various mechanisms at their disposal, *curacas* deprived women of their rights to land (AUP:Proto 1-2; ACC:Top. 8, Leg. 2). One channel open to *curacas* who began to increasingly participate in the colonial mercantilist economy was to convert lands under their control to monocrop production for the internal Peruvian market. In essence, *curacas*, abusing their function as official spokesmen for their community's resources, became quasi-feudal barons, and in this process the female members of their *ayllus* were most vulnerable to losing both water rights and land (BN:C3967).

Even though the colonial regime theoretically sanctioned preconquest mechanisms through which *curacazgos* were transmitted (Rostworowski 1961), colonial administrators did not recognize pre-Columbian parallel or dual hierarchies of authority in which female *curacas* had important governing and political functions, thereby eroding women's pre-Columbian rights to authority very early in the colonial period. The first Spanish to arrive in Peru wrote that women known as *capullanas* governed the ethnic groups of Peru's northern coast. Although it is not known how these offices were transmitted, it is probable that *capullanas* succeeded to office matrilineally. In litigations pursued in 1613 by a female descendant of the coastal nobility who was claiming rights to govern, testimony was gathered to prove that women were allowed to rule or hold office before the conquest. But if we carefully look at the testimony we find that while some witnesses assert in general terms that "women could hold office like men", others were already, in effect, citing Spanish inheritance patterns to justify a woman's ability to govern: if a *curaca* left no male heir, for example, then a female descendent could succeed him (Rostworowski 1961:29). Moreover, by 1625 Don Juan Temoche is registered as being the *"curaca* and governor" of Nariguala rather than his wife, Francisca

Canapaynina, who was the litigant in the 1613 suit. In other words, Temoche was exercising control of the office originally belonging to his wife, an indication of how indigenous traditions were slowly ceding to Spanish custom (ibid.).

The Spanish also established local political and religious institutions in communities which were modeled after municipal organizations existing in Spain. The civil apparatus consisted of the formation of a *cabildo* (town council) and the annual election of *alcalde* (mayor), *regidor* (deputy), and *aguaciles* (constable); in the religious domain the Spanish created a hierarchy of lay assistants to the parish priests—cantor, sacristan, and so on. As has been pointed out, there were advantages for those who decided to enter these positions and ally themselves with the provincial representatives of Spanish authority: exoneration from *mita* service and dispensations from tribute (Spalding 1974:37). Also, since the authority on which these offices rested lay with the external colonial power structure, those holding offices were, to some degree, outside of the traditional norms and obligations which regulated power and wealth in Andean society.

Although the purpose of the Toledean laws which decreed the formation of a Spanish style of indigenous government was to undercut preconquest political and religious institutions, the Spanish-imposed apparatus was quickly modified and adapted to these pre-existing indigenous structures. However, all positions in the political and religious organizations imposed by the Spanish on Andean *ayllus* were reserved for men. It should be clear, then, that even though the community governmental apparatus imposed by the Spanish was transformed by many communities in accord with pre-Columbian principles of politico-religious organization, the resultant synthesis was unfavorable to the continuance of parallel female religious authority structures. Whereas the municipal offices of the peninsula could be modified or reworked in terms of the masculine components of pre-Columbian religious and political organization, the pre-Columbian female organizations were provided with no equivalent Spanish forms to "legitimize" their existence. Not only did the Spanish effectively legitimate only masculine-dominated pre-Columbian political activities, but they also denied women access to positions within the formal religious and political apparatus with which the peasantry was supposed to govern itself.

Although the politico-religious institutions of colonial society militated against the maintenance of women's ritual organizations, it is important to stress that in various communities women (and men) discovered means through which these organizations and the ability of women to participate in formal structures were sustained. The Jesuit priest, Perez Bocanegra gives us some clues of the process through which some women who held native religious posts began to mesh their activities with Christian practices. Indians would confess to native clerics—who were women—before confessing to the Catholic priest. These women, who recorded the "sins" of their *ayllus* on *quipus* (knotted strings used as mnemonic devices), would then tell the confessant which "sins" selected from those of the entire community, to reveal to the priest (1631:11-13). Not only did the fact that women could be confessors horrify Perez, but that through concealing their "heretic" activities by sending people to confess to the Catholic clergy, native priestesses were reinforcing indigenous rites which embodied radically different conceptions of sin, guilt and responsibility. Women confessors were known as *hermanas mayores* (elder sisters)—a term that is used in modern communities to designate a superior rank within their civil-religious hierarchies. It would be interesting to speculate that these women were creating and participating in an emergent form of the contemporary *varayoq* system. Perez also documents the campaign mounted by the Church against practitioners of indigenous religion including the confessors; a campaign which, to judge by his instruction manual for priests working in the Andes, was particularly virulent in its attack against women (:14).

Although there is little archival material documenting these transformations and syncretic processes, female religious-prestige hierarchies associated with female saints or virgins are known to have existed in some contemporary Andean communities and are still functioning in others. In Chuschi (Department of Ayacucho), women remembered the functioning of a religious hierarchy of *cargos* (positions), sponsored exclusively by women for the celebration of Santa Rosa on August 30 (Isbell 1978). This festival appeared to be, in syncretized form, the pre-Columbian female festival to the Moon which was held in the month of September. In the communities of Huambalpa (Department of Ayacucho) and Quiquijana (Cuzco) a religious hierarchy similar to that of Chuschi still exists. In Quiquijana, until ten years ago, the ceremonies to Santa Rosa were very elaborate. They included ritual battles between women representing the upper and lower *ayllus* of the district as well as an initiation rite that was composed of special dances which young women performed with very large *varas* (staffs). These rites were curtailed by the priest, who was "appalled to see so many drunken women." At present, young women still sponsor the *cargos* to Santa Rosa but no longer participate in the ritual complex that characterized the festival in the past. In Sarhua (Department of Ayacucho), membership in the community's (*munidora* organization, now an ostensibly Catholic women's group, is inherited from mother to daughter—as were certain offices during the Incanato.

In other communities women do formally participate in civil-religious hierarchies. In Saraguro, Ecuador, women participate in the community's civil-religious hierarchy such that the women's positions dovetail with those of men (Belote and Belote 1973). Women jointly sponsor *varayoq* positions with their husbands in Huancasancos (Department of Ayacucho), as the *Libro de los Ayllus,* in which the names of all office holders are recorded, clearly indicates for 1920 (J. Earls, field notes). Although an explicit worship of sexually parallel deities is no longer present in the contemporary *varayoq* system of

Sarhua, its intrinsic structure is still based on a hierarch of offices divided along gender lines. The women of the *varayoq* system conceive of themselves as being semiautonomous from their masculine counterparts: they constitute their own hierarchy of positions, headed by the *alcaldina* (mayor) and followed by the *campina, regidora* (deputy) and *alguacila* (constable). The *alcaldina* commands great authority and respect in relation to her subordinates as well as the rest of the women of the community. As in the seventeenth century, those women who hold a superior position are known to those below them as *hermana mayor*.

Cultural Resistance and Cultural Defiance

The transformation of pre-Columbian organizations into prestige hierarchies associated with the Virgin, or into parallel political hierarchies within the contemporary *varayoq* system, is testimony to the strength and creativity of Andean women in the face of tremendous pressures exerted by colonial and later republican institutions. But in the sixteenth and seventeenth centuries, women found themselves doubly trapped. They were hounded by the Church as well as by indigenous governmental and religious authorities who allied themselves with the provincial representatives of the colonial regime. Their power deriving from allegiance to Spanish authorities, these local-level officials—who no longer felt bound by the mutual obligations and normative rules that maintained Andean social relations—threatened and abused women in ways which were opposed to pre-Columbian social and moral codes (Guaman Poma 1956:2:161, 167,168,170,3:30). Moreover, the local-level political and religious institutions imposed by the Spanish denied women direct access to the official channels of authority regulating community life. Declared Lucia Suyo Carhua, accused by the "extirpators of idolatry" of being a sorceress and priestess of heresy, "Now don't you see, the universe has turned inside out; for we are being persecuted" (AAL: Leg. 2, Exp. 4). It is no wonder that women tried to escape this world turned inside out, and no wonder that they tried to resist.

WOMEN AND THE DEVIL

The Weapon of Sorcery

Together with a lust for gold and silver, the Spaniards brought the devil to the New World (Taussig n.d.:43; see also 1977). As Taussig has carefully argued, the cosmovision of the late Middle Ages, which molded the ideology of the Spanish conquest, was based on a Manichean division of the universe into two opposed and competing principles: that of "good" upheld by the Christian servants of God; and that of "evil" supported by the servants of the devil. We must remember that to the Spanish conquerors, the devil was real and tangible, constantly battling to "dethrone" the Catholic god and the forces of good. The Church defined all indigenous religious practices as being inspired by the devil. Most of the early chroniclers, as well as the "extirpators of idolatry" refer to native religion as a form of devil worship—the devil spoke to the Indians through their *huacas;* the devil deceived them into worshiping mountains, the earth, springs, trees.

Much of indigenous religion and curing practices, therefore, became linked with sorcery, which in terms of Western thought of the late Middle Ages involved a contract with the devil. As in Western Europe of the fifteenth to seventeenth centuries which was shaken by intense witchhunts, the Church organized expeditions against "idolatry" in the Andes. To the dismay of the Church, idiolatry was still rampant one hundred years after Christian dominion and a new battle was engaged with the worshipers of the devil known as the "campaign to extirpate idolatries," spearheaded by the Archbishop of Lima. As indigenous religion was driven "underground" and native deities were equated with the archenemy of Christendom, the enemy of the Spanish oppressors, the continued worship of indigenous deities represented a cultural defiance and opposition not only to the Church but to colonial society as a whole (see Taussig n.d. :43-49).

According to the nineteenth century French historian Michelet, the devil in Western Europe was a figure which evolved from the paganism of French folk culture, rooted in a pantheon of natural spirits; towards the end of the Middle Ages, at a time of growing class and cultural conflict, the devil became an ally of the peasantry viciously oppressed by landlords and the Church (Taussig n.d. :49). Within the structure of late feudal society, it was peasant women who were most vulnerable, and thus women turned to the devil who was the principal entity in a pantheistic cult concerned with common problems of health and living (Michelet 1973: 21-61). In this period as well, the predominant cosmology of the West was beginning to symbolically associate all of "nature" with evolving cultural definitions of "the feminine": nature, like woman was capricious, emotional, unpredictable, something that had to be dominated, conquered, and controlled. As Leacock and Nash point out, this new definition of "nature" accompanied the emergence of capitalism and colonialism, in which "nature," like the colonies, became defined as an object that had to be conquered and controlled (Leacock and Nash 1977: 621).

Western cosmology, with its associations of women with nature, with paganism, and with the devil—the enemies of the Church and Civilization—built up an accompanying ideology concerning women in which women were defined as weak, incapable, more susceptible to the temptations of the devil, and thus in need of vigilance. Their "weakness" made them the potential mortal enemies of men, civilization, and God. This ideological evaluation of women was reflected in Spanish law in which women were defined as minors, needing protectors or "tutors" to carry out business transactions. When this conception was applied to the colonial situation in which Indians were similarly defined as minors and incompetents needing "protection," we discover a telling equation: in Spanish colonial law the testimony of two Indian males or of three Indian females was considered to be equal to that of one Spaniard (Testimonio 1950: 345).

But, on the other hand, if women were inherently weak and therefore susceptible to the temptations of the devil, they, in terms of the logic of Western thought, were more likely to be responsible for the black magic and sorcery that threated the foundations of Christendom. This conception of womanhood became an ideological justification for the Church's particular hounding of women during the witchhunts of the sixteenth and seventeenth centuries. This evaluation by the Church of the close relationship between women and the forces of evil (which was also an expression of the fear in which women were held) was transported to the Americas.

As Taussig has emphasized, very early in the colonial process the Manichean cosmovision that underlay the ideology of conquest was grafted onto indigenous religious beliefs. This dialectical process, which he calls "forced acculturation," entailed the institutionalization of the concepts of evil and the devil in pre-Capitalist cosmologies where such a dichotomy between "good" and "evil" had not existed before (n.d.: 40). As we have seen, Andean cosmology was predicated on a dialectical vision of the universe in which "opposing" forces were viewed as reciprocal, complementary, and necessary for the reproduction of the society as a whole. Within this framework, the maintenance of "balance" between social, natural, and supernatural forces constituted a predominant cultural ideal. Conceptions of sickness and disease were intrinsically related to this cosmovision, as sickness was produced by the breakdown of cultural norms and mechanisms regulating the balance between social groups, between society and nature, and between society and supernatural forces (Silverblatt and Silverblatt n.d.). Although it has been asserted that some form of "witchcraft" existed in the Andes prior to colonialism, it appears that concepts of sorcery, entailing pacts made with evil forces to injure others, is an outgrowth of the "forced acculturation" of ideas produced in the context of colonialism. Any cultural evaluation of Andean women involving their special relations with demonic forces was part of the same process.

It should not surprise us that several of the chroniclers, when discussing pre-Columbian religious activities, insist that witchcraft was practiced and that those "witches" who had powers to kill were almost always women (Morua 1946: 301; Polo 1916: 28, 29; Cobo 1964: 2:225). The Spanish commentators continue by noting that the knowledge and power of these native sorceresses was so great that even their own *curacas* and members of the Inca elite feared them.

While reflecting the suspicion of women that underlay the European ideology transported to the Americas and imposed on indigenous beliefs, these statements also reveal facets of the dynamics of the colonial process and its impact on native women. Defined by Europeans as being by nature more susceptible to demonic forces—forces which in the colonial context were equated with any and all indigenous practices and beliefs—Andean women, because of the male bias of colonial economic, political, and religious institutions, tended to turn to those traditional practices which were interpreted by the colonial regime as diabolic.

The dynamics of this process are unveiled in an ecclesiastical suit brought in 1697 against Francisca Carhuachoque, who was accused of using the powers she acquired through a pact made with the devil to injure a priest and kill a landlord (AAL: Leg.1, Exp.12). While denying the validity of a confession made under torture in which, because of the coercion of the court's interpreter, Francisca declared that the devil appeared to her in the form of a cat, she does admit to having made offerings to a snake (*culebra*) in a mountain spring (*puquio*) as well as to having harmed these two Spaniards. Although the Spanish viewed this admission as proof of a diabolic contract, from Francisca's perspective she was presenting an oblation to the Amaru. In Andean symbolism, the Amaru, who often takes the form of a snake residing in *puquios*, represents a destructive force that erupts when relations of balance and equilibrium are not maintained in the social and natural universe (Earls and Silverblatt 1976a). Thus Amaru has close associations in Andean thought with revolt and revolution. It should not surprise us that this persecuted woman was worshipping the Amaru for, by means of "sorcery," she was attempting to create the contitions through which the extremely "unbalanced" relations that characterized her life under colonial rule would be eliminated.

From the indigenous point of view, women became identified as the upholders of Andean culture and thus as the defenders of pre-Columbian lifeways in the face of the onslaughts of an illegitimate regime. As the *curacas* and other native allies of Spanish authority became increasingly entrenched and caught in the contradictory roles they occupied in the colonial system, they were bound to increasingly "fear" those women who replaced them—from the indigenous perspective—as the legitimate, albeit underground, representatives of Andean society. And even if it were the case, as Polo states, that Indians refused to divulge the names of these women to colonial authorities for fear of being bewitched (1916: 28), is he not perhaps also revealing that these women's identities were being protected by their indigenous companions because of their "powers" of cultural resistance to Colonialism?

WOMEN OF THE PUNA

Female Culture of Resistance

> They [Indian women] are overwhelmed by tribute demands and personal labor service, for this reason they are terrified and do not want to serve God or the King, and fleeing [the *reducciones*] they

Andean Women Under Spanish Rule 177

go and hide in the *puna* [high tableland where herds are pastured], and *estancias* (pasture area in the puna)....They do not confess, they do not attend catechism classes teaching Christian doctrine; nor do they go to mass. They do not even know who are their parrish priests, *corregidores,* or *curacas;* they do not obey their mayors, or their *curacas*....And returning to their ancient customs and idolatry, they do not want to serve God or the crown (Guaman Poma 1956:2:147).

By the seventeenth century, colonial institutions were firmly entrenched in Peru. While indigenous men often fled the oppression of *mita* and tribute by abandoning their communities and going to work as *yanaconas* (quasiserfs) in the emerging *haciendas,* women fled to the *puna* (high tablelands); often with difficult access and very distant from the *reducciones* of their native communities. Once in the *puna,* women rejected the forces and symbols of their oppression, disobeying both Spanish administrators and their own community officials. They vigorously rejected the colonial ideology which reinforced their oppression—refusing to go to mass, to participate in Catholic confession, and to learn Christian dogma. More importantly, women not only rejected Catholicism but they returned to their native religion and, as best as they could, to the quality of social relations of which this religion is an expression.

In the campaign mounted by the Church to extirpate idolatries in Peru women were persecuted not only as practitioners of the black arts, but also as priests leading the worship of outlawed indigenous heretic cults. We have noted that one of the most important "priestly" positions of pre-Columbian society entailed leading and directing the worship of *huacas,* the guardian-ancestors of the *ayllus.* Although prior to the conquest women were responsible for ceremonies devoted to female deities, the majority of the chroniclers who purport to describe pre-Columbian religious structures deny that women, for the most part, could serve as priests in these community-wide rituals which were dedicated to nonfemale deities. Manuscripts from the Archivo Arzobispal, however, indicate that in the seventeenth century women not only served as assistants in community-wide or *ayllu-*based religious cults to male ancestor-*huacas* (a secondary post which the chroniclers affirm that women could hold) but that they also could perform the role of chief officiants or priests in these ritual organizations. We must ask whether these documents reflect the role of women within preconquest ritual structures or whether the fact that women could act as priests in the colonial period was a function of the special conditions imposed on indigenous communities by the Spanish conquest.

In light of the previous discussion, I would contend that, because of the special constraints imposed on women by colonial institutions, women began to hold offices in indigenous religious organizations largely denied them during the pre-Columbian period. This is not to say that men stopped participating— either as priests or believers—in Andean religious activities for the traditions that the idol smashers tried to root out are still important to the Andean peasantry of today. But women in the colonial period were increasingly viewed by indigenous society as the defenders of ancient traditions and thus were encouraged to assume leading roles in the carrying out of native ritual.

By the seventeenth century, another underground religious structure was emerging in which virgins, dedicated to the service of *huacas*, were playing an increasingly important role in the maintenance of indigenous cults. It is well known that the *aclla* (called "virgins of the Sun" by the Spanish) exercised critical functions in Inca state religious activities; and the *aclla*, as an institution, only evolved with the development of the Inca Empire as a complex political system. The role of virgins in pre-Columbian local-level religious institutions was minimal (Silverblatt 1976). Yet the Archivo Arzobispal contains various references to virgins whose lives were devoted to the cults of local deities or who, because of marriage to a particular *huaca*, were said to become its sacred spokeswoman (e.g., AAL:Leg.2, Exp.4, Leg.3, Exp. 10; see also Arriaga 1968:36). As was the case regarding female priests, the role of virgins in native religious structures after the conquest probably reflects the development of an indigenous response to colonial pressures. An interesting and informative example is that of Francisca Guacaquillay who according to the testimony of Isabel Poma Cargua, Guacaquillay, the virgin niece of Don Alonso Ricary, *curaca* of Otuco:

> has never gone to hear mass, and the reason why is because she is not baptized and is dedicated to the idols and *huacas* and is a virgin...and although the priests asked about her when calling roll [for church attendance], Don Alonso and the foreman of the *ayllus* always excuse her, and she could never know carnally any man... and she only was concerned with making chicha for the *huacas*, and it is public knowledge that she is a virgin (ALL:Leg.4, Exp.18a).

Francisca Guacaquillay herself concurs "that [she] never went to mass, nor even once attended doctrine...[she] is not baptized, nor a Christian" (ibid.).

From these and other testimonies we glimpse a process through which native communities were desperately trying to defend indigenous religious activities in spite of the constant pressures exerted by Spanish secular and religious institutions. A critical component of this cultural defense was the designation of a young girl who from childhood was prepared and trained in the rites accompanying her society's outlawed religious beliefs. Francisca, whose mother was also a well-known "idolator-confessor," "ordered her *ayllu* not to worship God" and lived an underground existence. Whisked away to the *puna*, Francisca lived as isolated as possible from the contaminating elements of Spanish society. At thirty-five years she was not baptized; she never entered church; she had no contact with Spanish authorities; she was never violated by Spanish men.

In the village of Otuco it appears that the dedication of virgins into the service of *huacas* was a critical component of the community's growing attempt to defend native culture. Approximately thirty years earlier, only Francisca Guacaquillay was designated to be a virgin-priestess, but by 1656 four more young girls, all under ten years of age, were being initiated into indigenous religious lore, under the tutelage of Francisca Guacaquillay. Each of these girls, who represented the four *ayllus* of which Otuco was composed, was being carefully trained in the "rites and ceremonies that the consecrated *india* commands" (AAL:Leg 4, Exp. 18a). Thus, we can observe a process in which the dedication of virgins into the service of autochthonous deities was part of an expanding native religious structure, evolved under the exigencies of the colonial reality, the purpose of which was to defend indigenous traditional life.

The return to native religion and the increasingly important role women played in its maintenance was one form of cultural resistance and defense. Women hiding in their small homes in the Andean tablelands refused to allow their children to be corrupted by Spanish culture. Women hid their children from baptism "for fear that the priest would exile them from their native *ayllus*—they as well as their female companions—in order to compel them to enter forced labor service" (Guaman Poma 1956:2:183). Mandatory exile work in *obrajes* was one of the most common punishments meted out to women who were accused of witchcraft and engaging in native religious practices (AAL:Leg. 1, Exp. 10).

Guaman Poma also gives us a clue to the emergence of a female society in the *puna*; a society that resisted and defended itself against the oppression of colonialism. Sometimes women became so desperate at seeing their culture destroyed that they preferred to commit infanticide than allow a new generation to suffer at the hands of priests, colonial magistrates, Mayordomos, or their own native functionaries. But women who practiced infanticide killed only their male children (:2:182; see also Roel 1970:110). Perhaps revealing their complete despair at seeing themselves abused not only by male representatives of colonial authority, but by male members of their own culture, women attempted to re-create the "female component" of Andean institutions, as well as the social and ideological mechanisms through which order and balance were maintained in the Andean universe.

The creation of an underground female culture of resistance in the *puna*, marked by a return to the ancient traditions of pre-Columbian society is glimpsed in the account of three elderly women fleeing from the persecution of an infamous cleric and extirpator of idolatry, Francisco Avila.

> These women, since they were Christians, declared...that they knew nothing about *huacas*. In spite of having said this, [Avila] made them, as well as other Indian women, mount llamas where he beat them until they bled...these women, overcome by the torture and pain, were obliged to confess that they did adore *huacas* in or-

der that the priest would stop torturing them. The women lamented, "Now, in this life, we women like those men [Castillians whose ancestors had been pagan] are christians; perhaps then the priest is to blame if we women adore the mountains, if we flee to the hills and *puna,* since there is no justice for us here (Guaman Poma 1956:3:265).

CONCLUSION

In contemporary Andean culture, the *puna* is considered women's territory and is the center of women's society. In this isolated tableland where they pasture their herds, women occupy the preferred spatial positions in the "geometry" of ritual organization when rites are celebrated to the mountain spirits (Wamanis). The *puna,* close to the home of the Wamani, is also associated with the "wild and savage" when metaphorically compared with the "masculine" village—the locus of "civilization." But the physical manifestations of "civilization" in this male domain exemplify the history of colonial domination of the Andes: the church, the municipality, the jail. And so we find a paradox. The male members of the *varayoq,* who are obliged to guard the morality of the village, are afraid to go to the *puna.* "If the women in the *puna* do not like what we are doing, they will stone us and make us return to our village." But on the other hand, the *varayoq* add, "The women in the *puna* are living in the ways our ancestors lived years ago, they are defending our customs, they are defending our culture."

NOTES

1. I am grateful to the Doherty Foundation for supporting ethnographic and ethnohistorical research in Peru from June 1975 to June 1976 as well as the Wenner-Gren Foundation for supporting investigations on the role of women in Inca society from January 1977 to December 1977. I would also like to express my appreciation to the Organization of American States which funded my research in Peru on women in Andean society during the colonial period from January 1978 to December 1978. I owe special thanks to Billie-Jean Isbell, and to my *companeras* of ALIMUPER who are struggling to create a better world for women in Peru. All translations from the Spanish are mine unless otherwise noted.

2. For a more extensive account of the role of women in pre-Columbian economic, political, and religious structures see Silverblatt 1976 and 1978.

3. The word *ayllu* in its basic form means "family." However, it can be extended to include political units based on territorial organization as well as political units based on principles of descent (cf. Earls 1971). The size and nature of the unit that the *ayllu* specifies is always determined by local context and history; *ayllu* can refer to a nuclear family, a local ethnic community, subdivisions within an ethnic group, or an entire empire. It is very difficult to know with certainty what constituted the political and social organization of pre-Inca ethnic units. Nevertheless, in general terms, the schema presented here is representative of the politicoeconomic organization of the Andes prior to the Inca conquest.

4. Such is still the case in the contemporary community of Sarhua, where the "wife givers" and "wife takers" are women—the sisters of the bride and the sisters of the groom, respectively (Earls and Silverblatt 1977).

5. During periods of hostility and intercommunity conflict, *curacas* led their constituents in war (Morua 1946:47) and had a supervisory role in the internal functioning of the community (Ortiz de Zúñiga 1967:1:36, 46; Spalding 1967:174). In some communities, prior to incorporation into the empire leaders were only chosen as needed, resuming their customary *ayllu* status after their designated task was completed (Ortiz de Zúñiga 1967:2:66; Morua 1946; 47).

6. For further details on women's religious roles in the broader community, see Avila (1966:115), Avedaño (1904:380), Arriaga (1968:31, 35, 168), Cobo (1964:2:225-29), Molina (1943:83), and Morua (1946:286).

7. See Spalding (1974) for a detailed analysis of the new opportunities for mobility and wealth open to the indigenous elite.

8. Suits in which women were accused of bewitching Spanish authorities, priests, and their indigenous allies often indicate that these "witches" had, prior to their condemnations, been unfairly treated by colonial and indigenous office holders.

REFERENCES

AAL. Archivo Arzobispal de Lima.

ACC. Archivo Colonial de Ciencias. Archivo Departamental de Cuzco.

AHU. Archivo Historico de Urubamba. Archivo Departamental de Cuzco.

Albornoz, Cristobal. 1967. "Instruccion para descubrir todas las guacas del Peru y sus camayos y haziendas." *Journal de la Societe des Americanistes* 56:17-39.

Anonymous Discurso. 1906. "Discurso de la sucesion y gobierno de los Yngas." Ed. Victor M. Maurtus, in Juicio de Limites entre el Peru y Bolivia, *Prueba Peruana*, vol. 8, pp. 149-65. Madrid.

Arriaga, Pablo Joseph de. 1968. *The Extirpation of Idolatry in Peru*. Lexington: University of Kentucky Press.

AUP. Archivo Urubamba, Protocolos y Expedientes. Archivo Departamental de Cuzco.

Avedano, Hernando de. 1904. "Relacion sobre la idolatria." In J. T. Medina, ed., *La Imprenta en Lima*, vol. 1. Santiago.

Avila, Francisco. 1966. *Dioses y Hombres de Huarochiri*, Castellano Jose Maria Arguedas, trans., Lima.

Belote, Linda and Jim Belote. 1973. "The Fiesta Cargo System in Saraguro Ecuador." Paper presented to the annual meeting of the American Anthropological Association, New Orleans.

Blas Valera. 1950. "Relacion de las costumbres antiguas de los naturales del Piru." *Tres Relaciones de Antiguedades Peruanos*. Asuncion.

BN. Biblioteca Nacional de Lima.

Cieza de Leon, Pedro de. 1959. *The Incas of Pedro de Cieza de Leon*, Victor Von Hagen, ed. Norman: U. of Oklahoma Press.

Cobo, Bernabe de. 1964. *Historia del Nuevo Mundo*, 2 vols. Madrid.

Collapina, Supno, y Otros Quipucamayos. 1974. *Relacion de la descendencia, gobierno y conquista de los Incas*. Lima.

Diez de San Miguel, Garci. 1964. *Visita hecha a la provincia de Chucuito...en el ano 1567*. Lima.

Duviols, Pierre. 1971. *La Lutte Contre les Religions Autochtones dans le Perou Colonial: L'estirpation de l'idolatrie entre 1532 et 1660*. Appendice Documentaire. Lima.

Earls, John. 1971. "The Structure of Modern Andean Social Categories." *Journal of the Steward Anthropological Society*. 1, 1.

———. 1973. "Andean Continuum Cosmology." Ph.D. diss., University of Illinois, Champaign-Urbana.

Earls, John and Irene Silverblatt. 1976a. "La Realidad Fisica y Social en la Cosmologia Andina." In *Proceedings of the Forty-first International Congress of Americanists*. Paris.

———. 1976b. "Sobre la Instrumentacion de la Cosmologia Inca en el Sitio Arqueologico de Moray." Paper presented at the Colloquium on Mesoamerican and Andean World Views and Social Organization. Universite de Provence, Aix-en-Provence.

———. 1977. "El Matrimonio y la Autoconstruccion de Alianzas en Sarhua (Ayacucho, Peru)." *Bulletin de l'Institut Francais d'Etudes Andines* 6, 1-2.

Esquivel y Navia, Diego de. 1901. *Anales de Cuzco* (1601-1749). Lima.

Estete, Muguel de. n.d. *Noticia del Peru*. Biblioteca Peruana, 1st series, vol. 1. Lima.

Flores Galindo, Alberto. 1976. "Tupac Amaru y la Sublevacion de 1780." In Alberto Flores Galindo, ed., *Tupac Amaru II, 1780*. Lima.

Garcilaso de la Vega. 1956. *The Incas,* Alain Gheerbrant, ed. New York.

Guaman Poma de Ayala, Felipe. 1936. *Nueva Cronica y Buen Gobierno.* Travaux et Memoires de l'Institut d'Ethnologie, vol. 23. Paris.

——. 1956. *Nueva Cronica y Buen Gobierno,* Luis Bustios Galvez, trans. 3 vols. Lima.

Hernandez Principe, Rodrigo. 1923. "Mitologia andina." *Inca* 1, 1.

Isbell, Billie-Jean. 1976. "La otra mitad esencial: un estudio de complementaridad sexual." *Estudios Andinos 12: La Mujer en los Andes.* 5, 1., No. 1.

——. 1978. *To Defend Ourselves: Ecology and Ritual in an Andean Village.* Institute of Latin American Studies, University of Texas, Austin.

Leacock, Eleanor and June Nash. 1977. "Ideologies of Sex: Archetypes and Stereotypes." In *Annals of the New York Academy of Sciences,* vol. 285, *Issues in Cross-Cultural Research,* Leanore Loeb Adler, ed. New York: New York Academy of Sciences.

Lounsbury, Floyd. 1964. "Some Aspects of the Inca Kinship System." Paper presented at the International Congress of Americanists, Barcelona.

Michelet, Jules. 1973. (orig. 1939). *Satanism and Witchcraft: A Study in Medieval Superstition.* A.R. Allinson, trans. New York: Citadel Press.

Millones, Luis. 1976. "Religion y poder en los Andes: Los curacas idolatras de la Sierra Central." Seminario de Ideologia y Religion, *Primera Jornada del Museo Nacional de Historia.* Lima.

Molina de Cuzco, Cristobal. 1943. *Relacion de las fabulas y ritos de los Incas.* Lima: Los Pequenos Grandes Libros de Historia Americana.

Moore, Sally. 1958. *Power and Property in Inca Peru.* New York.

Morua, Martin de. 1946. *Historia del origen y geneologia real de los Incas,* Constantino Bayle, ed. Madrid.

Murra, John. 1956. "Economic Organization of the Inca State." Ph.D, diss., University of Chicago.

——. 1964. "Una apreciacion etnologica de la visita." In Garci Diez de San Miguel, ed., *Visita hecha a la provincia de Chucuito....* Lima.

——. 1975. *Formaciones Economicas y Politicas del Mundo Andino.* Lima.

Oberem, Udo. 1968. "Amerikanistiche Angaben aus Dakumenten des 16 Jahrhunderts." *Tribus* 17:81-92.

Ortiz de Zuniga, Inigo. 1967. *Visita de la Provincia de Leon de Huanuco,* vol. 1. Huanuco.

Pachacuti Yamqui Salcamaygua, Juan Santa Cruz. 1950. "Relacion de antiguedades deste reyno del Peru." *Tres Relaciones Peruanos.* Asuncion.

Palomino, Salvador. 1971. "Duality in the Socio-cultural Organization of Several Andean Populations." *Folk* 13:65-88.

Perez Bocanegra, Juan. 1631. *Ritual formulario e institucion de curas para administrar a los naturales....* Lima.

184 Women and Colonization

Polo de Ondegardo, Juan. 1916. *Errores y supersticiones: Linaje de los Incas; Ceremonias y ritos.* Coleccion de Libros y Documentos Referentes a la Historia del Peru. Series 1, 3:1-45.

——. 1917a. *Relacion de los fundamentos acerca del notable dano que resulta de no guardar a los indios sus fueros.* Coleccion de Libros y Documentos Referentes a la Historia del Peru. Series 1, 3:45-188.

——. 1917b. *Instruccion contra las ceremonias y ritos que usan los indios conforme al tiempo de su infidelidad.* Coleccion de Libros y Documentos Referentes a la Historia del Peru. Series 1, 3:189-203.

——. 1917c. *Del linaje de los Ingas y como conquistaron.* Coleccion de Libros y Documentos Referentes a la Historia del Peru. Series 1, 4:45-95.

Roel, Virgilio. 1970. *Historia Social y Economica de la Colonia.* Lima.

Rostworowski, Maria. 1961. *Curacas y Sucesiones.* Lima.

——. 1962. "Nuevos datos sobre tenencia de tierras reales en el Incario." *Revista del Museo Nacional* (Lima) 31.

Rowe, John. 1957. "The Incas Under Spanish Colonial Institutions." *Hispano-American Historical Review* 37:155-99.

——. 1963. (orig. 1946-50) "The Inca Culture at the Time of the Spanish Conquest." In J. Steward, ed., *Handbook of South American Indians*, vol. 2. Bulletin 143, Smithsonian Institute, Bureau of American Ethnography.

——. 1976. "El movimiento nacional Inca del siglo XVIII." In Alberto Flores Galindo, ed., *Tupac Amaru II, 1780.* Lima.

Silverblatt, Irene. 1976. "La organizacion femenina en el Tawantinsuyu." *Revista del Museo Nacional* (Lima) 42.

——. 1978. "Andean Women in the Inca Empire." *Feminist Studies* 4, 3.

Silverblatt, Irene and Helene Silverblatt. n.d. "Andean Folk Medicine: A Cultural and Historical Perspective" (ms.).

Spalding, Karen. 1967. "Indian Rural Society in Colonial Peru: The Example of Huarochiri." Ph.D. diss. University of California, Berkeley.

——. 1974. *De Indio a Campesino.* Lima.

Stein, William. 1961. *Hualcan: Life in the Highlands of Peru.* Ithaca, N.Y.; Cornell University Press.

Taussig, Michael. 1977. "The Genesis of Capitalism amongst South American Peasantry: Devil's Labor and the Baptism of Money." *Comparative Studies in Society and History.* 19, 2.

——. n.d. "The Devil and Commodity Fetishism in South America."

Testimonio...de la Audiencia de Lima. 1950. *Revista del Archivo Historico del Cuzco*, no. 1.

Valcarcel, Carlos. 1947. *La Rebelion de Tupac Amaru.* Mexico City.

Villanueva, Horacio. 1970. "Documentos sobre Yucay en el siglo XVI." *Revista del Archivo Historico del Cuzco*, no. 13.

Zuidema, R. T. 1967. "Descendencia paralela en una familia indigena noble del Cuzco." *Fenix* 17:39-62.

———. 1972. "The Inca Kinship System: A New Theoretical View." Paper presented to the annual meeting of the American Anthropological Association, Toronto.

———. 1973. "Kinship and Ancestor Cults in Three Peruvian Communities. Hernandez Principe's Account of 1662." *Bulletin de l'Institut Francais d'Etudes Andines* 2, 1.

8 Daughters of the Lakes and Rivers:
Colonization and the Land Rights of Luo Women

ACHOLA PALA OKEYO

Kenya colony came out of British efforts to confirm hegemony over East Africa in opposition to the Italian and German influence in the area. The declaration in July 1895 of the East Africa Protectorate over the area between Zanzibar and Buganda concluded Britain's formal acquisition of what was later to become Kenya.[1] The area had a strategic importance being on the route to India and in the vicinity of the Suez Canal. Because strategic considerations initially outweighed economic ones, there was not a clearly worked out strategy for exploiting the wealth of the country to the benefit of Britain. One of the first investments made by Britain was the construction of a railway to link the seaport of Mombasa and the seat of the Kabaka of Buganda, a distance of some

700 miles. The building of the railroad required semiskilled labor and this was expropriated in the form of "coolies" from India, also a British colony. In order to make the railroad and the colony profitable, more radical strategies had to be devised. Through the initiative of Charles Eliot (1905) the first commissioner of the East Africa Protectorate, white settlers were invited from South Africa, Britain, Australia, New Zealand, and Canada to exploit the country's natural resources in commercial agriculture. For Eliot a major condition for the desired development of commercial agriculture was a stable white-settler community protected by an ideology of racial segregation called "separate development."

Since the colony was to pay for itself through agriculture, the administration decided early that the land and labor needs of the settler community would be met by alienating these factors from the native peoples, who were living in autonomous socioeconomic groupings based on subsistence agriculture and livestock keeping. The choice to develop the colony by means of agriculture, managed by white settlers exploiting African labor, entailed the disenfranchisement of Africans and the entrenchment of white control over human and natural resources of the area. The enforcement of new rules and procedures governing the deployment of human and natural resources undermined those bases upon which the economic independence of local communities rested and introduced race as a major criterion for determining access to resources, including land.

In this pursuit, an important aspect of colonial policy was the reservation system, that is, the limitation of land available to Africans, Indians, and Europeans based upon legislation. By 1926, the demarcation of African areas (reserves where Africans were required to live) was concluded by the establishment of Native Reserves. This was a logical sequel to the 1915 Crown Lands Ordinance which in effect made Africans tenants-at-will of the British crown (Ogot 1974:271). The effect of the reservation policy was to restrict the internal migrations by Africans which were still in process when the area was annexed by Britain in 1895. Together with the 1915 enactment, it denied Africans the opportunity for expansion and access to some of the best agricultural land in the country. Despite these legal enactments, customary land tenure and patterns of land use were allowed to continue in the African areas. This was because the reserves were to play the role of supporting a stable African labor force to serve the export sector which was dominated by commercial agriculture under white-settler control. The transformation of African economy and society which followed was to be inextricably bound up with the development of European areas. Policies designed to boost settler agriculture and labor requirements in turn placed constraints on the reserves. In the process, subsistence farming and customary land tenure stood in the same relationship to Africans as did commercial agriculture and individualized land tenure to European settlers.

The "appropriateness" of subsistence farming for Africans was often overemphasized and justified on the grounds that Africans loved their land and wanted to maintain their farming traditions without interference. In effect, able-bodied men were siphoned off to work in the European sector, while women, older men, and young children remained hostages in the reserves. African culture, tradition, and economic and political institutions were co-opted to aid the administration of political control and economic exploitation. Colonial policy in the African areas vacillated between progressive and regressive phases. When commercial agriculture could not pay its way, African agriculture was sometimes improved in order to prop up the ailing settler economy. When, however, the latter gained momentum, African agriculture was forced to revert to a purely subsistence role.

This chapter discusses the interrelationship between land tenure and social structure in the context of the Luo community in West Kenya.[2] In particular, it examines the impact of the individualization of land tenure on the traditional precolonial landholding unit (the lineage) and on the position of women. Since Luo women play a key role in the rural economy, especially in food production and reproduction, they are a major category of producers whose land rights are bound to be affected by changes in land tenure. Although previous research has shown that women are central to the Luo subsistence economy (Owen 1933; Pala 1977), the question of women's land rights has not been fully discussed in the context of the impact of changing land tenure on the Luo community as a whole.

Traditional Luo customary land tenure can be described as corporate in that proprietary rights to land reside not in the individual but in the group. The principle of inalienability also reinforces the emphasis on equal access to land for subsistence production. Individual men and women enjoy a multiplicity of use rights in land which are wide-ranging and well defined. For instance, each household has a precise knowledge of where fields, pastures, and homesteads are located and to which their use rights apply. Generally speaking, males inherit land or are potential successors to land passed down from father to son. Females have usufructory rights to land by virtue of being a daughter or a wife. Landholding rights are acquired by virtue of affiliation to the landholding group by birth, marriage, residence and clientship.

The land-tenure reform[3] currently being implemented in Luo areas has its origins in the colonial period. At that time, the economic development of Kenya was predicated upon a theory of inequality between Africans and Europeans. Therefore, development in the reserves, or the "nonscheduled areas" as they were sometimes called, was restricted to the minimum required to support a stable labor force for the European or scheduled areas. Separate development of the two areas and the orientation of agricultural and land-tenure policy in favor of the white-settler community was supported by legislation. Increasing population pressure and land shortage led to political protest on the part of Africans which forced the colonial government to reformulate its policy on land tenure and agriculture. In 1952 a dramatic shift in land policy, which came in the wake of the Mau Mau rebellion, extended the theory of inequality to within the African communities themselves. A policy formulation in 1954 by Swynnerton aimed at creating an African middle peasantry to protect the settler community from the heat of African political protest. The impact of the Swynnerton plan varied from area to area; as far as the Luo community was concerned, land consolidation did not take place in a systematic way before 1963, other than in a few pilot schemes. The land-tenure reform has been carried through to the postindependence era (since 1963), and with it the basis of inequality regarding access to land from the colonial period.

Throughout this study, special emphasis is placed on the historical connectedness of socioeconomic and political factors which have contributed toward individualized tenure in Luo community. Four propositions are explored: first, Luo customary land tenure system is a product of the combined impact of changes in the mode of livelihood—in particular, the transition from transhumant pastoralism to a mixed economy with emphasis on agriculture when Joluo migrated from southern Sudan to settle in West Kenya. Second, increased reliance on agriculture brought the Luo woman into the center of production, since her labor and the labor of her children became necessary for agricultural work. In addition, the woman's economic position was enhanced by the fact that the house (*ot*), which is the minimal unit of production and of which she is head, became a major channel for the transmission of agricultural land between male agnates. Third, demographic pressures following the sedentization of the population introduced greater precision in the control of land by lineages (corporate landholding descent group). Fourth, colonial reservation policy—with demands for space to build schools, churches, commercial and administrative centers, and roads, usually on land alienated from the community—exacerbated conflict in customary tenure. And the institution of individualized land-tenure reform extinguished women's rights in land by nullifying the corporate landholdings that had guaranteed their rights.

THE COMMUNITY

Geographical Location

In Kenya, Joluo live in three administrative districts of Siaya, Kisumu and South Nyanza located in the northeastern shores of Lake Victoria. Three ecological zones characterize the area. First, the lakeshore savannah zone (3700–4000 ft.) has a minimum annual rainfall of 20–35 inches and a maximum of

40 inches; second, the star-grass zone (4500–5000 ft.) has a fairly high and stable annual rainfall (60–70 inches) which supports commercial agriculture and high population densities. The third zone is the "intermediate," or higher-rainfall savannah at 4000 to 4500 ft. elevation and has moderate rainfall—over 45 inches (see de Wilde 1967:122–23).

Much of Luoland, therefore, is to be found in the zone with low and irregular rainfall. In my research in Kisumu and South Nyanza (1974–75), I found that the Luo economy has been subject to recurrent drought and famine of varying magnitude since the 1870s (Pala 1977:207–17, App.). These ecological factors indeed affected the pattern of colonization of Luoland. As a region of Kenya colony, Luoland was not settled by white immigrant farmers. Rather it provided a labor pool for the white-managed commercial agriculture in the highland areas further east (see Ogot 1963; Whisson 1964; and de Wilde 1967).

Origins of Joluo

Joluo are part of a larger group of Luo peoples who originated (1000 A.D.) in the Bahr-el-Ghazal area in southern Sudan (Crazzolara 1950, 1951; Ogot 1967; Cohen 1974; cf. Okot 1971). A common linguistic and cultural heritage links the Joluo with other Luo peoples who today live in southern Sudan, Uganda, northeastern Zaire, and northern Tanzania along the reaches of the Nile, which furnished their migration routes from the "cradle land" to their present locations (see Okot 1971:9–37). Linguistic evidence also substantiates the relationship (see Greenberg 1966:85–129; Sutton 1974:82–83). Historical sources further indicate that by about 1400 Luo peoples began to emigrate from southern Sudan in several directions owing to a number of related factors: overcrowding, overstocking, and internal disputes arising from pressure on the land. The overriding cause of Luo migrations, therefore, seems to have been a search for pastureland and water since their traditional economy was a pastoral one. According to Ogot (1967) Luo peoples moved out of the "cradle land" in several stages, the third and last of which accounts for the southern Luo settlements in Kenya and Tanzania. The first of this stage settled in the Nyanza Gulf area between 1490 and 1600 (see Ogot 1967; Cohen 1974). Pastoralism remained important to the traditional Luo economy until 1800, but sedentary agriculture and some fishing have since become increasingly central to the economy.

The traditional settlement pattern of Joluo in Kenya is a series of homesteads, often comprising two and sometimes more, generations of families, surrounded by euphorbia hedges which have traditionally served as a windbreak. Even where there is no hedge the pattern of housing still symbolizes the structural relationship (including seniority and decision making power) between fathers and sons, mothers and sons, wives and husbands, as well as between co-wives.

Social and Economic Structure

Patrilineal kinship ideology, segmentary lineages, and exogamy remain central internal principles of Luo social organization. For purposes of inheritance of property, including land and cash savings, descent is traced through the father's line. Relationship to the father and, through him, to paternal kin affect an individual's jural rights which still fall under customary law. It is customary for a married couple to reside after marriage with the man's patrilineage and not with the woman's kin group. Allegiance to, and mutual support from, maternal kin is stressed, however, and there are many instances where they provide land and other material assistance to individuals.

While the dominance of a patrilineal ideology is suggested by postmarital residence patterns, property rights, and the status of children, women occupy an important structural position in the Luo lineage system. As mothers and wives and to a lesser extent as daughters their productive and reproductive roles are crucial for the continuity of the lineage, a core concept in Luo social structure. While these roles unequivocally testify to the structural importance of women among Joluo they also represent contradictions and conflicts in power relations between men and women as political and economic actors within the context of the lineage system. For example, children, especially males, are crucial to the continuity of their patrilineage and strengthen a woman's position in the patrilineage; for this very reason, a woman tries to endure even a bad marriage because if she accepts divorce she loses the children as well. Children belong by customary law to the father (i.e., to his patrilineage), and separation rather than divorce is the norm when a marriage proves to be too stressful to either of the parties.

The house (comprised of a woman and her natural children) is the minimal economic unit in Luo economy, but economic cooperation characterizes the homestead, which is headed by a man, where land and various farm operations like plowing may be shared. A homestead usually consists of members of an extended family—a man, his wife or wives, and children or several men of the same patrilineage with their families. Only where a homestead is coterminous with a house does it constitute a minimal unit of production.

In the recent years, especially since the late 1940s, there has been a considerable amount of spontaneous migration from Siaya and Kisumu Districts to South Nyanza District. Because Siaya and Kisumu were the first districts to be settled by Joluo, population increases began to be felt in these areas, especially in the medium- and high-potential zones, where subsistence agriculture became increasingly important. Internal rural migrations in this period can be interpreted as a process of conflict resolution at two levels: at the level of population-to-land ratios, it was a way of resolving demographic pressures, and, at the level of social structure, it was a resolution of conflict between male agnates who would be competing for the inheritance of scarce resources, especially land. (For evidence from Luo oral history, see Crazzolara 1950:33, 37–39,

62–66; Ogot 1967:163–64). Therefore, the availability of land to which people could go and settle also seems to have militated against a centralized state system with differentiation based upon political and economic power.

LAND ACQUISITION AND SETTLEMENT

The bulk of land held by rural Luo households today has a history that dates back nearly five centuries when Joluo first settled in the Lake Victoria basin. Oral history documents the acquisition of land by four major methods: first, land could be acquired through warfare and conquest. Second, land could be claimed on the basis of first clearance and settlement. Third, it was possible to obtain land through clientship; typically, a client (*jadak*) was a man who was separated from his immediate kin group and had to seek to use land belonging to another group. Finally, land could be acquired through the inheritance of usufructory rights to land previously held by one's domestic group.

Joluo seem to have initially preferred to settle on the expansive lakeshore savannah where the low-lying grasslands afforded wide-ranging opportunities for grazing cattle, and the lake and rivers in the area provided opportunities for fishing. The patterns of early settlement, together with the subsistence economy based upon fallow cultivation and livestock keeping, both contributed to shaping customary land tenure. It is, therefore, important to outline briefly the structure of traditional Luo farming systems and its implications for land tenure.

TRADITIONAL FARMING SYSTEMS AND LAND TENURE

Oral historical sources state that, in the early days of migration and settlement in the Nyanza region of Kenya, Joluo practiced fallow cultivation; family groups migrating into the area cleared land and built their homesteads together to fortify them for protection against other groups. They also dug their garden plots adjacent to each other in order to synchronize their farm operations (sowing, weeding, and harvesting). The main advantage in the proximity of garden plots was the possibility of protecting the crops from pests. According to the fallow system of cultivation, strips of land were cleared and cultivated for three to five planting seasons and then left to revert to bush for an equal number of seasons before it was cultivated once again. All farm operations were done on the basis of family labor which was largely made up of women and children since men were in charge of livestock.

It seems that the emergence of the fallow system can be placed between 1500 and 1700. This coincides with the period when Joluo were losing cattle in epidemics and were shifting to a greater dependence on agriculture. Fallow cultivation and the necessity to insure that the crops of the family group were not totally destroyed by pests led to the pattern of land tenure in which family groups had scattered plots. Furthermore, differences in soil types made it necessary for each family group to acquire tracts of land in different areas in order to maximize the growing of different crops. Indeed, a look at any Luo kin group today in the rural areas will reveal that the settlements of different segments of the group correlate with soil types. This pattern of settlement was a guarantee that members of a kin group, which was also a landholding group, had access to land with different potentials. They could therefore exercise their use rights to all the land held by all members of the group. Needless to say, the pattern of land tenure which emerged from such ecological and social-legal constraints seen from an individualist standpoint is one of fragmented holdings. Viewed from a corporate group's point of view, however, it insured every member's rights in land needed for subsistence cultivation and grazing. Land fragmentation became a critical choice in the need to diversify production, decrease the risk of crop failure, and insure equity in access to land. In this context, then, fragmentation of land was an asset and not an obstacle to agricultural development as it later came to be seen by the colonial administration.

SOCIAL STRUCTURE AND LAND TENURE

Although available sources do not establish a precise correlation between lineage formation and land tenure, it is important to understand those endogenous factors which defined the normative basis of landholding before the integration of Joluo into a money economy and a settlement colony with an emphasis on the private ownership of land.

The paucity of economic research describing traditional Luo economy in the pre-emigration period (1000—1400 A.D.) in the Sudan makes it difficult to state precisely what the relationship between social structure and systems of property holding were. It seems, however, that the Luo segmentary lineage structure was already well developed before the adoption of a sedentary agriculture mode of livelihood. Landholding, therefore, became structured by the rules of property holding (mainly livestock) already in operation within the lineage system as Joluo began to settle in the Nyanza region of Kenya.[4]

Over the years, the principles of complementarity of lineages, cognatic filiation, exogamous marriage, age, and sex have remained operational in the definition of property relations among Joluo. They not only continue to set limits to rules and procedures governing access to land and livestock (traditional property), but they also extend to the realm of cash, thereby affecting patterns of income redistribution among Joluo both in rural and urban Kenya.

Although cognatic filiation (relationship traced through ascendants of both sexes) sets the furthest limits of rules and procedures governing access to land, the principle of agnation (descent through the male line), represented in the segmentary lineage system, is the more crucial operational concept. A Luo lineage is a corporate, exogamous, agnatic descent system comprised of persons who trace descent to a common male ancestor and can demonstrate linkages between them to the ancestor by a genealogical chart. Through kinship fiction, however, client households can be incorporated into any given lineage segment; that is, the lower-order lineages are subsets of the upper-order ones. At each structural level the lineage segments are equal and opposed to each other (see Evans-Pritchard 1940:192–93). Southall (1952) identifies two sets of Luo lineages. The first are corporate landholding units which arise from the establishment of lineage segments and their subdivisions; their segmentation is based upon genealogies but is often modified by such factors as landholding status and political power. The second are lineages which can potentially emerge when specific occasions demand it but otherwise remain a latent basis of grouping.

Luo women are structurally more important and more effective in their family of procreation that that of origin. As wives and mothers they are heads and organizers of the minimal unit which is a potential lineage segment. In this regard, women in their daily and economic and ritual participation are the demonstration par excellence of the segmentary lineage principle. As a lineage wife, a woman occupies the structural position which will, potentially or in reality, differentiate one lineage from another. In a polygynous marriage it is the maternal principle in reference to the mother as head of house that differentiates one potential lineage segment from another. The segments are ultimately represented in households in the polygynous compound especially those with sons. Women, therefore, are fundamental to the structure of segmentary lineages because their reproductive and productive activities combine to reproduce and sustain the developmental cycle of the family within the lineage system. It is for this reason that lineages spring from women and even long after they are dead some women remain lineage eponyms. Women's security of land tenure under customary law is in essence rooted in their structural role as lineage wives, which has ramifications throughout the traditional social structure. The normative emphasis on the agnatic principle is part of an ideology whose main function is to preserve corporate rights in land under the control of men and to eliminate the possibility of alienation of land by any one member of the corporate group.

In theory, patrilineages are localized and share a common land base, but the evidence on the ground is that segments of maximal lineages are often dispersed all over the area that is known as Luoland. The determinants of this dispersal still need further research, but I found that, while demographic pressure and consequent internal migration may explain why family groups move from one area (thereby jeopardizing their rights in a particular piece of land), migrations at this level may be a function of social cohesiveness. In other words, those who leave and those who remain represent two integral aspects of the problem of lineage consolidation. Persons migrate in order to join those members of their lineage who have a larger land area and are therefore stronger politically because the size of lineage lands is ultimately a reflection of the number of men who control the land. They also migrate as a reflection of the perceived lack of cohesiveness with the rest of the lineage group. After they have settled an alternative piece of land they can expand through marriage and be more autonomous. What is interesting is that the cleavages between those who remain utilize descent traced through the mother. Upon settlement in the new land, however, the agnatic principle and corporate rights in land become operational once again.

For a woman, marriage carried more security of tenure in land than being unmarried; this was chiefly because a woman's structural position was much stronger as a wife than as an unmarried girl. Her economic responsibilities were considerably enlarged by marriage because of her role in the house (*ot*). The house as a concept is broader and offers more analytical insight into women's proprietary rights and productive roles than does the notion of household. As a minimal component of a lineage segment, the house, comprised of a married woman and her natural children, represents the starting point of the developmental cycle of the Luo family. It encapsulates its current status as a property-holding unit by virtue of the birth of sons and anticipates its internal structural changes which are expected to occur when sons marry, move out, and set up their new houses. A woman and her natural children together constitute the minimal productive unit with the woman carrying the responsibility of feeding the family.

As a wife, a woman held usufructory rights to land under the corporate ownership of her husband's patrilineage. These rights defined access to communal grazing grounds, farmlands, water supply, and hills where firewood could be collected, as well as access to fish and naturally growing fruits, vegetables, and herbs. They were enjoyed by all wives of the patrilineage or those women within a neighborhood, with common pasture and water as well as fuel sources. More precisely, a woman could use land in the direct patrilineage for growing crops and vegetables. Individual women do not have the right to allocate land, but the principle of corporate land ownership, which proscribed the alienation of land, reinforced the security of their use rights.

A man had use rights in land by virtue of being a member of a patrilineage. While he, as an individual, could not alienate land, he held allocative rights in land along with other males in his patrilineage. Marriage also helped him to acquire an allocation of land for his own household. Prior to this, an unmarried man is subordinate to his father and men of older generations who make decisions concerning the disposal of land.

Inheritance of Land

Individuals—men or women—inherit only use rights in land while the corporate descent group (the lineage) retains the right to dispose of land. The allocation of land to wives and sons is a complex mechanism and depends in part on the position of a wife (first, second, or third, etc.); the position of a son in relation to full siblings who are part of his mother's house and/or other sons of his father by other preceding or subsequent marriages; and the personal relationship between a husband and wife or father and son. In other words, the seniority of a wife or a son affects the allocation of land that she or he may expect to have. In addition, the more sons a woman has the more land she expects her house to control. A first wife may receive an allocation of land at marriage either from her husband if he has already been allocated land or from her father-in-law. A second or a third wife receives her allocation from her husband who may do this by subdividing land originally allocated to his first wife. The last-born son invariably inherits use rights to land which had been hitherto farmed by his mother after all the subdivisions were made. Although it is only use rights in land that are inheritable, in operational terms this system leads to subdivision of holdings in such a way that individual men have discrete plots of land over which their use rights apply. As much as the number of sons affects the land sizes originally acquired by settlement, the survival of sons to the age where they can inherit land also tends to imply greater subdivisions of the holdings. If for some reason a man and his family migrate from one place to another the rights in land revert to the descent group for reallocation. If, however, he or his sons or grandsons should choose to return they can reactivate use rights in lineage lands since they can substantiate their claims in land by genealogical linkages.

COLONIAL IMPACT

Land-tenure reform was probably the last phase of attempts by the British colonial administration to rationalize the integration of native peoples of Kenya, Joluo among them, into a colonial socioeconomic structure. The extent to which colonial policy affected relations between Africans and the land can best be seen in the context of local communities.

Serious plans by the British to colonize Luo economy and society were not implemented until 1899. Joluo, however, had technically become subject to the British crown by the declaration in 1895 of the East Africa Protectorate. Military expeditions, epitomized by the attack on Uyoma, Sakwa, and Seme lineages in December 1899, marked the beginning of the integration of Joluo into the colonial economy (see Hobley 1900, Collard 1900, Johnston 1901, Ogot 1963).

According to Hugh Fearn (1961), the Luo economy stagnated in the period 1903–30 and accelerated its growth from 1931 to 1953. In brief, efforts by the colonial administration to bring the Luo peasant economy into the cash economy and to diversify it were very slow and ineffective in the pre-1931 period. The choice of cotton as an experimental cash crop in Nyanza within the framework of the indigenous land-tenure system between 1903 and

1922 achieved little or no change. Although the administration blamed the slow progress of cotton growing on lack of enthusiasm on the part of the Luo, Fearn suggests that the relatively unsuccessful career of cotton in Nyanza, compared that in Buganda, where the crop had been simultaneously introduced, could be explained by at least six other factors: the location of experimental stations in savannah areas with little rain; the supervision carried out by newly appointed chiefs who were generally unacceptable representatives of an alien power; the introduction of cotton on communal plots contrary to Luo crop farming; the difficulty of fitting cotton into the Luo cropping pattern which, unlike the Buganda banana (perennial) cycle, depended on annual crops such as maize and millet and in which pastoralism still played a significant role; the lack of official policy on cotton which had to wait until 1923 for formulation; and the lack of capital among African peasant farmers (:70–72).

In addition to the cotton campaign, the colonial regime was at pains to implement an administrative infrastructure to facilitate the control and exploitation of local resources among Joluo. Consequently, by 1902 headmen appointed in accordance with the Village Headman Ordinance were empowered to collect taxes and enforce the campaign for labor needed on public works. The Native Authority Ordinances, enacted between 1912 and 1922, legalized forced labor, requiring a man to provide six days of unpaid work for each quarter for public works, but the people resented working for no pay and payment was instituted. As it turned out, however, the increased hut and poll taxes paid by the men ended up subsidizing their wages for public works. By 1921 the Native Registration Ordinance legalized a pass system requiring every male worker to carry proof of employment signed by his employer (Fearn 1961:51–52).

Evaluating the impact of British administrative policy in Central Nyanza from 1900 to 1960, Ogot (1963) points out two effects of indirect rule on Luo social structure. First, the selection of chiefs from dominant lineages increased social differentiation between lineages based upon political authority and reward systems over which local people had no control. Prior to colonization, Luo maximal segmentary lineages exercised political authority which was regulated within the descent group itself through an age-class system. In their new capacities as locations with a chief, paid by the colonial government, the collective political authority of lineages was severely challenged: the chief was no longer responsible to the collective will; instead, he implemented directives from the colonial government. Second, the administrative machinery contributed to an even more rapid transition from a semimigratory pastoral mode of livelihood to a sedentary agricultural one. This sedentization led to further subdivision of lineages and aggravated land-tenure problems. Joluo were accustomed to solving conflicts over land and power by secession or migration. Reduced opportunity for these mechanisms compounded political and economic disputes within the descent group (:252–53).

Apart from laws concerning labor, taxation, and administrative machinery, there were others governing access to land and settlement as well as military service, which had further repercussions on Luo economy and society. The 1926 Native Reserves Ordinance, together with the hut-and-poll-tax regulations, was to contribute to male migration in search of wage-earning jobs in the European areas in order to raise money to pay their taxes. Women remained in the reserves to tend the farms and to produce and feed new generations of the male labor force. For this very reason, female migration in search of wage-earning work outside the reserves was limited. From age 16, men were liable to be conscripted for forced labor, and World War I demanded more male recruits. Between 1917 and 1918 nearly 9000 men were conscripted from Kisumu District, and at least 2000 cattle were appropriated, in addition to other food supplies. Besides, the poll tax was increased to subsidize war efforts (Ogot 1963:258). The effect of this process was to involve men more and more in the cash economy while keeping women in the nonmonetized subsistence-farming role.

In my view, Fearn's explanation of the pre-1931 stagnation by the heavy Luo dependence on subsistence farming—livestock, agriculture, and fishing—and the lack of major cash needs requires qualification. The colonial administration was not particularly interested in raising agricultural productivity in the reserves because of the need to satisfy labor demands from the settler farmers; if the reserves were to become more economically viable, the male labor force would be diverted from European farms. One illustrative episode may be cited here. During his term as Provincial Commissioner of Nyanza in 1907–1910, John Ainsworth introduced a number of agricultural and economic projects in the province. He provided Joluo and others in Nyanza with opportunity, inputs and technical assistance to grow cotton, ground nuts, simsim and improved maize. Keen interest was expressed by the people and the chiefs assisted in getting new roads and tracks constructed. By 1913 Nyanza, which had not made prior effective use of the railroad, was cited as "the best customer." The Europeans criticized Ainsworth on the grounds that his activities "discouraged the flow of labour to settled areas" (Ogot 1963:255). In other words, the continued impoverishment of the reserves was an absolute necessity for the settler and colonial profit-making.

From 1931 to 1953, according to Fearn, a number of factors contributed to the stimulated growth of the economy of Nyanza. There was the discovery of gold in Nyanza and notably in Kakamega in 1931 which led, by 1935, to employment for 13,450 African males (1961:137). The gold mining seems to have peaked in the period between 1934 and 1939 and was on the decline after 1941, production having been affected by the outbreak of World War II in 1939. Second, the tea industry in Kericho District by 1947 employed 17,000 Africans (:151). Third, the Asian sugar concerns in Miwani-Muhoroni area were employing 3000 Africans by 1947. In addition to employment, trade and marketing are also noted by Fearn, particularly the trade in maize which was conducted in trading centers licensed by the African District Council. Cooperative societies also served as a means of increasing the involvement of Africans in the monetary economy between 1940 and 1950. Joluo participation in the cooperative movement was confined to maize but their success does not compare favorably with that of the coffee cooperatives in Kisii Highlands. Women tended to participate in the sale of small quantities of produce in the so-called "bartering areas." Women were also quite active in the Nyanza Egg Service set up between 1947 and 1949. It is estimated that at the time of the 1945 Cooperative Societies Ordinance at least 60 societies were registered. The dropout rate was high, however, and by 1953 only 20 were running (Fearn 1961:212). Africans became more engaged in transport trade while the introduction of the *posho* mill also improved the household consumption of ground maize flour. Luo fishermen who prior to 1930 did not have dhows were by 1950 fishing in dhows they owned either singly or collectively and were engaged in commercial trade in fish.

According to Heyer, the stimulation of growth in the African areas during this time is explainable by the fact that the settler economy, badly hit by the depression of the 1930s, required less labor. It also had to seek subsidy from African agriculture (Heyer 1975). In other words, the apparent growth of the subsistence sector was a temporary measure for further exploiting the reserves to the advantage of the settler-export community.

Prereform State Intervention and Changes in Land Tenure

Available evidence indicates that conflict in customary land rights was exacerbated by colonial state intervention either by direct legislation governing access to land or by indirect means through agricultural land and labor policies. In an evaluative study of problems of land tenure and land use among Luo and Kalenjin farmers in a Kenya sugar-settlement scheme, Okoth-Ogendo (1977) identifies population pressures and state intervention as two sources of change in customary land tenure and details the response of the tenure system to them. Although Okoth sees these as two separate sources of conflict, in reality both emanated from colonial state policy. He points out that rising populations in the reserves following World War II put considerable pressure on customary tenure institutions with two consequences: land shortage with resultant competition for land within the corporate landholding units, and rapid deterioration in the quality of land. The weakening of corporate control of land challenged traditional authority controlling both the allocation and use of land. It also encouraged much litigation within the descent group as well as within the families. Deteriorating soils also rendered obsolete the system of fallow cultivation, which had been the chief method of preserving soil quality and replacing soil nutrients. This population pressure was at least in part created by the reservation policy which set legal bars to expansion and settlement outside of ethnically demarcated reserves.

According to Okoth-Ogendo, the customary tenure system responded in two ways to these demographic and administrative pressures. First, corporate landholding descent groups adopted greater precision in methods of settling boundary disputes. Second, family heads assumed greater autonomy in decisions regarding cultivated land while grazing rights remained extensive and communal (:10–11). It can be seen then how population pressure posed by the reservation system began to narrow the bases of landholding in the Luo community from the larger kin group to the house line.

IMPACT OF LAND-TENURE REFORM

The decision to formulate a precise policy for changing the basis of landholding in the African areas grew out of developments and contradictions within the colonial system. An important theme in a settlement colony like Kenya was not only to insure a stable, self-supporting, low-paid labor force, but also to maintain political and economic behavior, both within the settler community and in the reserves, which would enhance the stability of that labor force. Therefore, it soon became necessary for the administration to evaluate the future political implications of population pressure in the reserves. State intervention first took the form of resettlement schemes. However, the option soon proved untenable and policy shifted toward land preservation, particularly measures to deal with soil erosion (Okoth-Ogendo 1976:160–61). It was evident, not too long after, that this conservationist approach to the African agrarian problems could not provide a satisfactory solution.

Reviewing agricultural research in Kenya from 1939 to 1963, Ominde (1973) puts colonial agrarian programs for African areas in a wider context. He points out the bias in research and extension work in favor of commercial settler agriculture. Extension work and research in the commercial sector was concentrated in entomology, plant pathology, genetics of important crops, and livestock improvement. In the African subsistence areas, however, the solution to agrarian problems was seen in terms of how to remedy soil erosion and land fragmentation. It can be concluded, therefore, that any shift in agricultural and land policy which might appear to improve the African subsistence sector was calculated only to provide a modicum of improvement that would avert industrial unrest, a much feared eventuality.

The 1950s saw a concatenation of a number of important political and economic events which pushed the question of land-tenure reform to the fore. The resettlement and conservationist approaches to land-tenure problems had virtually failed, and articulate native peoples were demanding their human rights as they attacked the pillars of colonial society—the Church, forced and low-paid labor, land and agriculture, school education, and cultural alienation. A growing demand for access to land found its most cogent formulation in the Land and Freedom Army movement climaxed by the armed, anticolonial

Mau Mau revolt in 1952 (see Ngugi 1964; Kenyatta 1965; Barnett and Njama 1966; Rosberg and Nottingham 1970). In October of that year the government declared a state of emergency over the country, banned the Kenyan African Union, and arrested its leaders and over 120 key members of the predominantly African political platform. Land-tenure reform was to be implemented, therefore, in the wake of political confrontation under emergency conditions.

The Evolution of Land-Tenure Reform Policy: The Concept

According to Okoth-Ogendo, land-tenure reform in the African areas went through three phases: the agronomic, the administrative, and the legislative (1976:162–67). The agronomic phase was informed by the view that soil depletion in the African areas was a result of a bad land-tenure system. According to this view, the customary land-tenure system was an obstacle to improved farming because it encouraged land fragmentation and land disputes. In addition, the customary inheritance pattern encouraged the subdivision of holdings into subeconomic units, and individualized tenure was seen to be ipso facto a means of fostering agricultural growth. It is upon these views that the Swynnerton Plan (1955) was based.

The administrative phase was precipitated by rising political tension in the struggle for political and economic resources of the country between the colonial administrator-settler-evangelist bloc and the Africans. It is in this period that colonial attempts to change the land-tenure practices in the African areas went beyond isolated experiments to a systematic scheme of land consolidation. Access to individual titles to land would create, as Swynnerton saw it, an African middle peasantry which would cushion the settler community from political agitators. These so-called agitators were characterized by L. S. B. Leakey, a well-known archaeologist, as "A band of young men armed with immense patriotism and a little learning, who made the first slogan of their party 'We must be given back the land that the white man has stolen from us'" (Leakey 1952:67).

The main objective of the legislative phase of the tenure reform was twofold: first, to formulate and enforce rules and procedures to protect individual tenure and, second, to give legislative support for the newly created middle peasantry in order to block anticipated local challenges to landholding under the new rules. In line with the theory of "separate development," such legislation was designed to pit the middle peasantry against the rest of local people rather than challenge the basis upon which the settler community owned land.

Okoth-Ogendo (1976:164–67) also reviews the legal history of the legislative phase. The promulgation in 1956 of the Native Land Tenure Rules marks the beginning of this phase which was to continue into the postindependence era. The 1956 legislation found its first application in those reserves where economic inequality had been translated into political protest, a most immediate challenge to the colonial regime. Subsequent formulations and reformulations of measures to control access to land were unanimous in one theme: the replacement of oral, customary tenure rules with statutory ones, regardless of equity considerations between households, within the descent groups, or between men and women. And "The effect of these provisions was that after 1959 registration operated to defeat all existing rights and interests under customary law" (:166).

Implementation of Land-Tenure Reform in Luoland

As far as Luoland is concerned, the agronomic, administrative, and even legislative phases of land tenure reform did not find their full application in the colonial period. Political conditions were not right. Articulate Joluo were already protesting land consolidation which they saw as a political tool which was then being used to defuse anticolonial activities among the Agikuyu in Central Province (Odinga 1967). Consequently, government initiative in implementing land-tenure reform in Luoland was so cautious that it was constrained to take a voluntary and experimental, rather than radical approach.

The Swynnerton recommendation continued, however, to be advertised in schools, in public meetings organized by chiefs, and in the sessions of the African District Council (ADC). The tenor of this propaganda was that the major obstacle to agricultural development in Luoland was the customary land-tenure system because it led to land fragmentation, incessant litigations, and the division of land into noneconomic units. It was, in short, a disincentive to an aspiring "better farmer." Land consolidation was seen to be the cure-all for agricultural stagnation.

Between 1956 and 1962 there was virtually no progress in land reform. Work which began on a voluntary self-help basis with scanty staff in 64 sublocations in 1958 dropped to only two sublocations by 1962 (Sytek 1966:5). Budgetary cutbacks, lack of personnel, and resistance on the part of Joluo all affected the progress of the land-tenure reform. In addition, the administration had chosen *jokakwaro*, a group of people descended from a male agnate above the level of grandfather, as the initial group whose land rights were to be adjudicated and consolidated. As it turns out in the segmentary lineage system *kakwaro* can refer both to a large or small descent group depending on the reference point. As a descent group, its rights in land overlap and are governed, as shown earlier, by a complex set of rules and procedures. As such it was not possible to expect a self-help group to be based on the *kakwaro* concept. Apart from two experimental areas in Gem and Nyakach, Kenya's independence arrived before any extensive implementation of land-tenure reform in Luoland occurred.

The Current Situation

When Kenya gained independence in 1963 the legislative phase of African land-tenure reform was still in progress. The new government undertook to carry through the reform substantially unchanged. It seems that by 1968 the core legislations governing the land tenure reform were fairly well set out. (Mifsud 1967; Okoth-Ogendo 1976). The legislation elaborates on three stages of the reform deriving from the 1956 Native Land Tenure Rules and subsequent enactments: the *adjudication* process, the objective of which is to ascertain customary rights in land; *consolidation*, the aggregation of adjudicated parcels; and *registration*, which in the Kenyan situation is a systematic compulsory vesting of the individual with absolute proprietorship of land and the security of a title holder entered in a state-maintained register. The Luo areas, however, with few exceptions, have not been able to realize land consolidation, primarily because of land shortage.

The Impact of Land-Tenure Reform on Women

Since the overall objective of the land tenure reform is to secure individual tenure under statutory law and to facilitate the possibility of individual use of land as collateral, it is important to assess the implication of this process for others whose customary rights in land had been usufructory only. In Luoland women and men under 18 fall into this category. As indicated earlier, the impact of colonial land and labor laws on men was to force them out of the reserves into low-wage employment outside. Women, on the other hand, were by the same logic constrained to remain in the reserves, primarily to produce food and to reproduce and nurture the male labor force for the export sector. Male absenteeism in the area is concentrated in the 15—49 age group, that is, able-bodied men. As of 1962, this group accounted for some 24 percent of the male migrants from the higher areas and up to 40 or 50 percent in the lakeshore savannah areas (de Wilde 1967:127—29, 153—54). Female migration to wage work outside the Luo areas is minimal. For this reason women continue to be the most stable group of adults in rural Luoland. The point is that the security of their tenure in land under customary or statutory law is of particular relevance to the economic development in the area.

Data from a study conducted by the author in 1974—75 (Pala 1975) describe a typical situation of Luo women with respect to land rights in the tenure reform. A portion of the field research surveyed 135 in-marrying females (lineage wives) on the current position of women regarding land tenure. We were interested in the following issues: women's access rights to land; how they acquired the land they are currently using; how they use the land; who holds the right of allocation of the land they are farming; the status of women's cultivation rights in relation to men's allocative rights; whether some or all of the land they are using has been bought or sold recently; whether their land is being registered, and, if so, in whose name; and how decisions are made regarding the sale, use, or exchange of land.

In response to the first question concerning the amount of land over which respondents have cultivation rights, 23.0 percent said that they have access to at least one parcel and not more than three parcels; 46.0 percent reported access to between three and five parcels; and 23.0 percent said they had access to between six and nine parcels. One respondent reported access to twelve parcels, and one said she had more than 15 parcels to cultivate.[5] Five respondents (3.7 percent) said they were landless.

From this, it can be concluded that 91.9 percent of the respondents have access to land ranging between 1.5 and 4.5 hectares. Only 2 respondents (1.5 percent) have land between 5.7 and 7.5 hectares. Furthermore, only these latter two respondents reported that their land is consolidated all around the homestead. The rest have parcels scattered in different sections of lineage lands. This means that *none* of the respondents had enough land to qualify for the agricultural loan scheme meant for small farmers in Kenya.[6]

The scheme required that each applicant must have proof of access to a minimum of 15 acres (6.1 hectares) and a maximum of 20 acres (8.1 hectares) to qualify for a subsidy. Our data on landholding underscore the fact that most peasants in this area cannot hope to expand the potential of their land through government assistance. This is true even if we allow for the possibility that—owing to perceived problems surrounding land availability, the indigenous tendency to underplay the value of property (animals, land, produce) in public discussion, and the fact that respondents are women who are land users rather than persons with the right of allocation—the land sizes quoted by respondents may be slightly smaller than those recorded by the land adjudication officers for purposes of land registration.

This brings us to the notion of landlessness. Five respondents reported being landless but, on further investigation, they turned out to have access to land ranging between 0.5 to 1 hectare. Why then should they describe themselves as "landless"? There are two possible interpretations of this notion. First, it can be seen as a perceived precariousness of access rights which may derive from, first, the registration of land in the name of males, thereby, in effect, alienating women's access rights to land. Traditionally, such access rights depended upon the fact that individual males were not able to alienate land, even though as members of the landholding patrilineage they had the rights to allocate land. Moreover, anticipated cash needs—taxes or children's school fees—may force those with little land to lose it all through sale to those who have money to buy it. Second, landlessness may reflect women's recognition of the fact that they cannot expand their acreage. This is a particularly important point when considered as a prognosis of future land problems in the area. A married woman, as we have seen, represents a house, the embryonic stage in the developmental cycle of the domestic group. The resources she has in hand constitute her perception as to what her sons could inherit in the future when they take wives and set up new houses. Thus, in terms of future options for her children, a woman who has 0.50 hectares of land at the moment is justified in saying she has no land. In Dholuo, *onge* ("being without") is often used to refer to scarcity, particularly of important resources such as water, grass cover for cattle, and land, when it is perceived that the resources will not last for long. Thus, when the women answered *"Aonge lowo"* ("I have no land"), it can be said that they were both describing a condition of scarcity and anticipating future problems of land shortage.

After the question of land sizes, we were interested in determining the sources of the land cultivated by the respondents: whether it was all derived from lineage sources or whether part was bought or borrowed for use from friends and/or relatives. Of the respondents, 67.4 percent said that they are *wuon lowo* to all the land that they are cultivating—this means that they are recognized users of that land by virtue of their structural position as lineage wives; 14.8 percent reported a similar status for three-fourths of the land they were cultivating; and 1.5 percent and 14.8 percent were *wuon lowo*, respectively, for one-half and one-quarter of the land they were farming. When asked to identify the source of land they are cultivating, 96.3 percent responded that they acquired the land through a relative by marriage and named husband, husband's father or mother, and 3.7 percent said that the land they are tilling came partly from a lineage source and part was bought. These two responses, read together, mean that the majority of respondents actually till only lineage land and that there is some possibility of the exchange of land within the lineage group so that some respondents have access to more land than they actually have from their direct land-allocating group; and this is why land registration is likely to be a disadvantage to the lineage group if, after the registration of plots, individual titleholders limit the customary exchange of short-term use. This point is suggested by the pattern of responses to a question concerning the source of borrowed land: 93.3 percent of the respondents stated that land has been borrowed from a relative by marriage.

At the time of the field investigations (1974–75), most of Kisumu and South Nyanza Districts were undergoing the second phase of a legal process which would eventually lead to the change from corporate rights to land, based on the lineage, to rights based upon individual tenure. This would mean that individuals (invariably males) who have attained majority age (18 years) at the time of registration would be given title to particular plots of land. In the event that an individual was under age at the time of adjudication, the title would be held in trust for him by his father, his mother (if the father was dead), or his elder brother until he could have it transferred to his name at the appropriate time. Such a title would give him a theoretical and, in practice, a legal right to dispose of the land by sale or any other means without necessary recourse to the elders of the patrilineage, who would ordinarily have the power of veto in matters of alienation of land by individuals. It seemed important, therefore, to inquire how far the process of land registration had been implemented and whose names were actually being entered in the land register.

To the question of land registration, 97.0 percent said that their land is already registered. When asked in whose name the land is registered and their own relationship to the registered owner, 51.9 percent said that their land is registered in their husband's name; 25.9 percent reported the registered owner to be their son; 7.4 percent said that their land is registered in the joint names of their husband and son; 6.0 percent reported joint registration in their name and their son's name; and only 5.9 percent reported that land is registered in their own names.

The striking point in these results is the manner in which land is being transferred to an almost exclusively male, individualized-tenure system which leaves no provision concerning how women's access rights are to be defined when the reform is completed and the new tenure system becomes operational. Of all the respondents, 85.2 percent reported that their land is already registered in the name of their husband, son, or jointly in the husband's and son's names. If we add to this those respondents who have land registered jointly in their own name and their son's name (since the land will eventually go to the son), we find that 91.1 percent are eventually to depend on land whose registered owner is a male relative. In practice, these women would probably still enjoy their cultivation rights to land as lineage wives, but the status that guarantees their rights is being superseded by the new stipulation which gives individual men the right to alienate the land from which their female relatives (wives, mothers, and sisters) expect to draw their livelihood for several years to come.

Although it may be too early to predict the outcome of this process with a great deal of precision, there are, in our view, at least two trends which could develop. In the first instance, young unmarried men who have reached the age of majority but who have no opportunity for paid employment will tend to sell the land which is registered in their name, leaving their parents to try and eke out a living on very small strips. In the course of our field study, we observed some instances of this trend and were often told by woeful mothers that they were unable to restrain their children from "losing" all the land for money which lasted for a very short time. This is the same situation as that which occurs when parents sell their land to obtain cash for school fees, even though at a great loss to themselves. Alternatively, it is possible to expect the registered owners to honor the use rights of their female relatives, thereby causing little insecurity to them. This trend, however, is likely to be jeopardized by the fact that land is not readily available and, in addition, employment opportunities for these families are very limited.

Two categories of women are most threatened by this transformation. The first are those women who come from families with little or no off-farm incomes, so that their cash needs are generally met by the sale of livestock, land, or agricultural produce. The second are those women who have only daughters and/or are widowed. They are invariably defined by the land-adjudication officers as those who do not need much land. If we look ahead five or ten years, women in these two categories might lose their land rights because of the manner in which land ownership and use rights are being redefined in the tenure-reform process.[7]

This problem is compounded by the manner in which the law operates, its technical language and its application at the local level which obscures the peasants' understanding of the implications of legal regulations affecting their lives. In our sample, the respondents knew only that land was being registered "because the government says so." They were unaware of the mechanics of the land-tenure reform program and were therefore not in a position to intervene in processes which are clearly inimical to their well-being. Furthermore, in the local area, the group that was constituted to assist in the adjudication of land was entirely male. These men argued that, by custom, women did not take part in land disputes and, therefore, it was reasonable for such a group to be all male. During the time this research was carried out, the advisory group, which was constituted to advise the adjudication officers on customary land rights, was all male. As such they were seldom able to give advice that would lead to the strengthening of access rights to land by women. This is because they have overemphasized the structural points of allocation and inheritance of land at the expense of use rights, in which women cultivators stand to be most adversely affected by the tenure reform.

The house is the locus of female autonomy—whose legitimacy derived largely from the socioeconomic and legal status associated with marriage. One of its main functions has been to differentiate between sons as to which ones inherit what land and livestock. In view of the land-tenure changes discussed above, it seems that one of the outcomes of the land-tenure reform program is the diminution of the status of the house and its head, the woman. The new scheme is directed at identifying the individual males in a patrilineage who are likely to inherit the property (land) of that patrilineage. Thus, it speeds up the developmental cycle of the house and renders the house essentially unnecessary from a proprietary point of view. In this way it isolates women from their sons, for whom, in the past, they would have been guardians of property until their marriage. This new approach to land tenure may also tend to redefine the lineage, no longer as an expression of corporate rights in land, but more and more as an ideology of kinship, not necessarily realizable on a territorial basis. In any case, the overall effect will likely be to diminish the proprietary function of the house and thereby reduce the basis of female autonomy.

All of the women interviewed are cultivators. They depend for their livelihood on the land. They grow agricultural crops and vegetables which are largely used for home consumption and are sometimes sold to buy small household items, such as sugar, paraffin, soap, and matches. When asked what they use land for, 48.2 percent said that they use their land for raising crops for food (i.e., for the household); 33.3 percent reported using their land for raising crops both for home consumption and for sale. What, in fact, is happening here is that 95.6 percent use land largely for subsistence-crop production, but will sell some produce in order to raise cash for buying household goods. Some of them also use land for grazing livestock. The main crops grown for consumption are maize, millet, elusine, beans, cowpeas, greengrams, and pumpkin. Cassava and sweet potatoes are the major root crops grown. Three of the respondents grow sugar cane for sale, nearly one-third grow sweet bananas, and a similar proportion grow cotton for sale.

CONCLUSION

The chapter has attempted to discuss the process of land-tenure change and how that process has affected social organization in the context of one local community in the Kenya Luo community. By examining land-tenure changes in the social history of the community, it attempts to identify new bases of landholding which have been emerging over the decades of the twentieth century. Special emphasis is placed on historical factors that have contributed to the change from corporate, lineage-based, land-tenure systems to an individualized one and the resultant cleavages between men and women and within the descent group. It is contended that the cleavage between men and women regarding the control of land was particularly intensified by the institution of land-tenure reform under the colonial and postcolonial state systems.

Three conclusions may be drawn here. First, the transition of the Luo community from a pastoral to an agrarian community placed the domestic group with its head, the woman, into a more central role in production. It appears that in the presettlement period (1000—1400) Luo peoples living in the southern Sudan pursued transhumant pastoralism in which men controlled both the ownership and management and livestock. During this period agriculture seems to have been peripheral, and women's contribution to the economy was limited to childbearing and -rearing and domestic work. With the transition in the fifteenth and sixteenth centuries to agriculture, some sections of the Luo community became sedentary. With this control of agricultural land became important and the lineage began to define the structure of land tenure, including pasture and water supply. During this period the labor of women and children became critical to agriculture, and the rights of women in land became anchored in their role within the lineage as wives and mothers. For it is in these two roles that their contribution to the economy of the house was greatest and lasted for the greater part of their lives.

The second conclusion of this chapter is that the integration of the Luo economy and society into a colonial system had the result of distorting the population-to-land relationships, as well as the structure of the access to land, in a very special way. On one level, the reservation system led to increased demographic pressures on land because it left no option for expansion outside the reserves. Customary tenure adjusted to this artificial population crisis by redefining and restricting the corporate holding of land in such a way that the larger lineage control of land was in some areas reduced to family control. On another level, the reduction of corporate holding also jeopardized women's usufructory rights which had previously benefited from the flexibility and multiplicity of rights in corporate landholding. The trend toward the individualization of tenure which was thus set off was further exacerbated by the institution of land-tenure reform which, in effect, negates customary principles of landholding and land use. The reform translates corporate, allocative rights in land (the final authority to dispose of land) into individual male titles to land and creates uncertainty as to the legal status of women's usufructory rights in land. Thirdly, the assumption that customary usufructory rights of women will somehow coexist with individualized statutory tenure is questionable because customary and statutory rights are different and, in theory, mutually exclusive. It may be predicted that over the next five to ten years the basis and practice of corporate landholding will be eroded and that women as a group will be virtually deprived of their security which had hitherto been protected by the principles of corporate descent and land tenure. In this process the lineage becomes subordinated to the nation-state because the latter assumes authority over resource allocation. By the same logic the house could lose its proprietary control and, therefore, the proprietary link between the mother and son within the house and that of the father and son within the lineage could be severely challenged.

NOTES

1. For basic sources on colonial land, labor and administrative policies in Kenya, see Bennett (1963); Mungeam (1966); Dilley (1966). More recent studies include Brett (1973); Ogot (1974); Wolff (1974); Leys (1974); van Zwanenberg (1975); Heyer et al. (1975); Lugard (1923) outlines British policy of indirect rule.

2. According to the latest national census, Joluo (Kenya Luo) numbered 1.5 million, the second largest community in Kenya out of a population of 12 million. In everyday life Joluo identify themselves as *jonam* ("people of lakes and rivers"), hence the title of the chapter.

3. Much of Luoland is in the transition period between the operation of customary and statutory land rights. Some areas originally used as pilot schemes in Gem and Nyakach locations have come under individualized tenure; others are not yet adjudicated. The subsequent use of the past tense in connection with customary tenure is based upon the fact that in theory the land tenure situation has been technically changed at law even where in practice customary tenure still applied.

4. This conclusion is based upon genealogical information collected in 1974–75. The genealogies are complete for 13–15 generations, which approximates to the first Luo settlements in West Kenya in 1490 estimated by Ogot (1967), and then taper off.

5. "Parcel" is the term used by land-adjudication officers to describe a discrete piece of cultivated land. In the course of the interview session, it be-

came evident that, while respondents had a very precise count of how many parcels of land over which they have cultivation rights, few of them could give us an accurate measurement of their land sizes in hectares. On consultation with a land lawyer, H. W. O. Okoth-Ogendo, we were able to approximate the average size of a parcel to be 0.5 hectares (approximately 1.2 acres). Since there is a certain amount of variation in actual parcel sizes, this estimate must be seen as a broad indicator only.

6. The GMR (Guaranteed Minimum Returns) Loan Scheme (no longer in effect) has its origins in the Increased Production of Crops Ordinance of 1942, a war measure intended to satisfy the cereal needs of the British Empire by inducing white settlers to plant maize, a crop they would not voluntarily grow because it was less profitable than other crops. It was extended to Africans in 1960 when the Kenya (Lands) Ordinance of 1960 ostensibly abolished all the structural discriminatory regulations affecting Africans. Ironically, the majority of peasants did not really have access to the necessary aggregated agricultural land to enable them to participate in the GMR. Thus, the extension of the GMR to Africans implied the creation of an African elite based on landholding and served as a constraint on peasant farmers, hindering their participation in development. The GMR operated by guaranteeing the farmer a credit equivalent to the resources expended in growing a crop on a 20-acre plot when the farmer can prove that expenditures exceeded returns.

7. In several instances I talked to land-adjudication officers and asked them why an overwhelming number of women were not being registered with land in the new scheme. In every case their answer was "because it is customary: men own land and women do not own land." Okoth-Ogendo suggests that there is some conceptual confusion between *ownership, right of allocation,* and *access rights.* In the precolonial system of landholding, women were guaranteed use rights to lineage lands because their tenure was supported by the structural principle which defined a wife, among other things, as a person who was entitled to land for production as long as she maintained that relationship with the patrilineage. The right of a man to allocate land is not equivalent to the right to alienate land which the tenure reform is bringing into operation.

REFERENCES

Allan, William. 1967. *The African Husbandman.* Barnes and Noble.

Barnett, Donald L. and Karari Njama. 1966. *Mau Mau from Within.* Modern Reader Paper Backs.

Beattie, John H. M. 1959. "Rituals of Nyoro Kingship." *Africa* 29, 2:134–45.

Bennett, George. 1963. *Kenya: A Political History, The Colonial Period.* London: Oxford University Press.

Brett, E. P. 1973. *Colonialism and Underdevelopment in East Africa: The Politics of Economic Change, 1919–1939.* London: Heinemann.

Butt, Audrey. 1952. *The Nilotes of Anglo-Egyptian Sudan: Ethnographic Sur-*

vey of Africa, East Central Africa, pt. 4. London: International African Institute.

Charnley, E. F. 1966. "Some Aspects of Land Administration in Kenya." Paper presented at the World Land Reform Conference of the Food and Agriculture Organization (FAO), Rome (RU:WLR-C/66/20).

Cohen, D. W. 1974. "The River-Lake Nilotes from the Fifteenth to the Nineteenth Century." In B. A. Ogot, ed., *Zamani*. Nairobi: East African Publishing House.

Collard, Charles E. 1900. "Military Report of the Expedition Against the Wa-Usakwa, Wa-Uyoma, and Wa-Semi People." *Foreign Office Series*, (F.O. 2/297.) London: Public Record Office.

Crazzolara, J. P. 1950. *Lwoo Migrations*. The Lwoo, Pt. 1. Verona: Missioni Africane.

———. 1951. *Lwoo Traditions*. The Lwoo, Pt. 2. Verona: Editrice Nigrizia.

———. 1954. *Clans*. The Lwoo, Pt. 3. Verona: Editrice Nigrizia.

Dakeyne, R. B. 1960. "The Pattern of Settlement in Central Nyanza in Kenya." *Australian Geographer* 8:183-91.

Dilley, Marjorie Ruth. 1966. *British Policy in Kenya*. London: Frank Cass & Co.

Dupre, Carole E. 1968. *The Luo of Kenya: An Annotated Bibliography*. Washington, D.C.: Institute for CrossCultural Research.

Eliot, Charles. 1905. *East Africa Protectorate*. London: Edward Arnold.

Evans-Pritchard, E. E. 1940. *The Nuer*. Oxford: Oxford University Press.

———. 1949. "Luo Tribes and Clans." *Rhodes Livingstone Journal*, no. 7.

Fearn, Hugh. 1961. *An African Economy: A Study of the Economic Development of the Nyanza Province, 1903-1953*. London: Oxford University Press.

Food and Agriculture Organization of the United Nations. 1971. *Report on Customary Land Tenure and the Development of Agriculture* (FAO No. RP 14). Rome.

Fortes, Meyer. 1971. "The Developmental Cycle in Domestic Groups." In Jack Goody, ed., *Kinship*. Hammondsworth: Penguin.

Greenberg, J. H. 1966. *The Classification of African Languages*. Bloomington: Indiana University Press.

Heyer, Judith. 1975. "The Origins of Regional Inequalities in Smallholder Agriculture in Kenya, 1920-1973." *East Africa Journal of Rural Development* 8 (1, 2).

Heyer, Judith, J. K. Maitha, W. M. Senga, eds. 1976. *Agricultural Development in Kenya: An Economic Assessment*. Nairobi: Oxford University Press.

Hobley, Charles W. 1900. "Report on the Uyoma Expedition Near Lake Victoria." *Foreign Office Series*, F.O. 2/297. London: Public Record Office.

Johnston, Harry H. 1901. "General Report on Uganda, 1901." *Foreign Office Series*, F.O. 2/462. London: Public Record Office.

Kenyatta, Jomo. 1965. (orig. 1938) *Facing Mount Kenya*. New York: Vintage Books.

Leakey, L. S. B. 1952. *Mau Mau and the Kikuyu*. London: Methuen & Co.

Leys, Colin. 1974. *Underdevelopment in Kenya: The Political Economy of Neo-colonialism 1964-1971*. Berkeley: University of California Press.

Maina, J. W. 1966. "Land Settlement in Kenya." Paper presented at the World Land Reform Conference. Food and Agriculture Organization (FAO), Rome (RU:WLR-C/66/20).

Mifsud, Frank M. 1967. *Customary Land Law in Africa*. Food and Agriculture Organization of the United Nations Legislative Series, no. 7. Rome: FAO.

Mungeam, G. H. 1966. *British Rule in Kenya: 1895-1912*. Oxford: Clarendon Press.

Ngugi, James [Ngugi wa Thiongo]. 1964. *Weep Not Child*. London: Heinemann.

Odinga, Oginga. 1967. *Not Yet Uhuru*. London: Heinemann.

Ogot, B. A. 1963. "British Administration in Central Nyanza District, 1900-1960." *Journal of African History* 4:249-73.

———. 1967. *History of Southern Luo, Vol. I: Migrations and Settlement 1500-1900*. Nairobi: East African Publishing House.

———. 1974. "Kenya Under the British, 1895 to 1963." In B.A. Ogot, ed., *Zamani*. Nairobi: East African Publishing House.

Okot, p'Bitek. 1971. *Religion of the Central Luo*. Nairobi: East African Literature Bureau.

Okoth-Ogendo, H. W. O. 1976. "African Land Tenure Reform" in Judith Heyer, J.K. Maitha, and W.M. Senga, eds., *Agricultural Development in Kenya: An Economic Assessment*. Nairobi: Oxford University Press.

———. 1977. "Problems of Land Tenure and Land Use in the Nyanza Sugar Belt." University of Nairobi (mimeo).

Ominde, S. H. 1968. *Land and Population Movements in Kenya*. London: Heinemann.

———. 1973. "What Do We Know in the Social Sciences." In S. M. Mbilinyi, *Agricultural Research for Rural Development*. Nairobi: East African Literature Bureau.

———. 1975. *The Population of Kenya, Tanzania, and Uganda*. Nairobi: Heinemann.

Owen, William E. 1933. "Food and Kindred Matters Among the Luo." *Journal of East Africa and Uganda Natural History Society*, nos. 49-50:235-49.

Pala, Achola O. 1977. "Changes in Economy and Ideology: A Study of Joluo of Kenya with Special Reference to Women." Ph.D. diss. Harvard University.

———. 1978. "Women's Access to Land and Their Role in Agriculture and Decision-Making on the Farm: Experiences of Joluo of Kenya," Discussion Paper no. 268. University of Nairobi, Institute for Development Studies.

Parsons, Kenneth. 1971. "Customary Land Tenure and the Development of African Agriculture." Land Tenure Center, Reprint no. 77. University of Wisconsin-Madison.

Rosberg, Carl G., Jr., and John Nottingham. 1970. *The Myth of Mau Mau: Nationalism in Kenya.* New York: Meridian Books.

Sheffield, James R., ed. 1967. *Education, Employment and Rural Development.* Nairobi: East African Publishing House.

Southall, Aidan. 1952. *Lineage Formation Among the Luo.* Memorandum 26. London: International African Institute.

Sutton, J. G. 1974. "The Settlement of East Africa." In B.A. Ogot, ed., *Zamani.* Nairobi: East African Publishing House.

Swynnerton, R. J. M. 1955. *A Plan to Intensify the Development of African Agriculture in Kenya.* Nairobi: H. M. Stationery Office.

Sytek, William L. 1965, "Social Factors in Land Consolidation in Central Nyanza." East African Institute of Social Research, Makerere University Conference Papers.

———. 1966. "A History of Land Consolidation in Central Nyanza 1956-1962." East African Institute of Social Research, Makerere University Conference Papers.

Whisson, Michael G. 1964. *Change and Challenge: A Study of Social and Economic Changes Among the Kenya Luo.* Nairobi: Christian Council of Kenya.

deWilde, John C. 1967. *Experience with Agricultural Development in Tropical Africa,* 2 vols. Baltimore: Johns Hopkins Press.

Wolff, Richard D. 1974. *Britain and Kenya, 1870-1930. The Economics of Colonialism.* Nairobi: Trans-Africa Publishers.

Yudelman, Montague. 1964. *Africans on the Land.* Cambridge, Mass.: Harvard University Press.

vanZwanenberg, Roger. 1975. *Colonial Capitalism and Labour in Kenya, 1919-1939.* Nairobi. East African Literature Bureau.

9 Women and Men, Cloth and Colonization:
The Transformation of Production-Distribution Relations among the Baule (Ivory Coast)

MONA ETIENNE

European interest in West Africa can be traced to antiquity, although direct contact was limited and its extent is not well known. Until the fifteenth century, West African goods reached Mediterranean Europe via the trans-Saharan trade, developed by the Carthaginians before their conquest by the Roman Empire. It is believed that Dieppois merchants established trading posts along the Upper Guinea Coast between 1364 and 1413, but early French overseas expansion focused on the Mediterranean and coastal North Africa. Maritime contact with West Africa developed only in the fifteenth century, when Portugal emerged as the foremost European colonial power, and the Atlantic seaboard became the first zone of regular contact between Europe and Africa south of the Sahara. The Portuguese traded along the coast for ivory, gold, spices, cloth, and slaves. They established coastal forts and missions, as well as sugar plantations and a cloth-dyeing center (using African dyeing methods) on offshore islands. There was some inland penetration.

Toward the mid-sixteenth century, the annexation of Portugal by Spain, growing interest in the Americas, and new sources of wealth in the Far East drew European attention away from Africa. With the expansion of the plantation economy in the Americas, however, the slave trade along the West African coast was renewed and reached unprecedented intensity in the eighteenth century. Some six million West Africans were shipped across the Atlantic. Because European traders acquired slaves almost entirely through agreements with African rulers and entrepreneurs and confined their activity to those stretches of the coast that were geographically and politically most accessible, direct contact remained primarily coastal and ultimately was concentrated along the seaboard from the Gold Coast eastward and southward to the Cameroons. The demands of the slave trade nevertheless affected inland peoples throughout West Africa, causing raiding, wars of conquest and flight migration.

Progressive abolition of the Atlantic slave trade in the first half of the nineteenth century contributed to the renewal of "legitimate" trade and a new interest in West Africa as a source of foodstuffs and raw materials for industrial Europe, but did not immediately lead to inland penetration and conquest. For the most part, African entrepreneurs continued to satisfy the demands of European traders. Inland products reached the coast through established and adaptable trade networks, and palm oil—in high demand during the nineteenth century—was produced by coastal peoples. Again, the absence of direct colonial intervention did not preclude an indirect impact of European contact on the interior, as well as the coast. It influenced productive activity and consumer needs and notably intensified the importance of domestic slavery. Most West African societies nevertheless maintained their sovereignity vis-à-vis European powers and some increased their prosperity, albeit at the expense of others. Coastal traders interacted autonomously with their European counterparts; coastal rulers commanded respect and controlled by treaties the establishment of trading counters by European firms. This situation was to change radically in the last quarter of the nineteenth century.

European industrial and economic expansion took on new momentum in the second half of the nineteenth century. The need for raw materials and foodstuffs increased, as did the need for markets for manufactured goods and opportunities for capital investment. At the same time, improved technology in naval construction rendered formerly difficult parts of the West African coast more accessible and made expanded trade more feasible by making transportation more rapid and far less costly. (The first British steamship arrived in West Africa in 1851, but the steamship did not affirm its ascendancy over the sailing ship until the 1880s). The steamship and heightened demand for products and markets brought newcomers to West Africa and perturbed preexisting trade relations, creating rivalries among both Europeans and their African partners. The ensuing economic disorder was compounded by the "Great Depression" (1873—95) and a deterioration in the terms of trade to the detriment of primary producers, making Africans less amenable to European demands. These rivalries and this discontent sometimes materialized in violent conflict, leading trading firms, primarily British and French, to call for the intervention of their home governments.

These pressures coincided with new developments in European political rivalries. France, a major colonial power in the seventeenth century, had by the end of the Napoleonic Wars (1815) lost its most valuable overseas possessions and spheres of influence to Great Britain (although it retained Senegal, its earliest West African colony). Renewed colonial efforts had led in 1830 to the conquest and occupation by settlers of Algeria and, after 1843, to annexations in the Pacific. But France remained far behind Great Britain, both in industrial and economic development and as a world power, a situation that was not improved by the Franco-Prussian War (1870) or internal political conflict. In the early years of the Third Republic (1871—1940), colonialism was to become a weapon in the struggle within the ruling class between the republican vanguard of industrial capitalism and more conservative elements, allied with the Church and remnants of the aristocracy.

The last quarter of the nineteenth century was marked by intense rivalry among European powers—and the United States—to gain control of the rest of the world. By establishing effective occupation as a ground rule for official annexation, the Conference of Berlin (1884—85) precipitated the "scramble" for Africa, with Great Britain and France the principal competitors. When partition was completed, France had acquired the greater part of West Africa. Inland penetration and conquest, actively pursued from the 1880s on, ended in the early years of the twentieth century.

This classical period of European imperialism stands in contrast to the dominant forms of overseas expansion in the past: on the one hand, scattered trading posts and spheres of influence and, on the other (outside of West Africa), settlement colonies. Europeans no longer transported Africans elsewhere to exploit their labor, as in the slave trade, nor did they send expatriates to alienate and exploit African land, as in settlement colonization. Instead, they promoted a more systematic form of exploitation by using

African labor to extract wealth from African land according to the demands of the colonial power, resorting to military force when necessary.

In France, lucid protagonists of this exploitation, who understood that short-term costs would bring long-term benefits, asserted themselves against the protests of the working class and the opposition of the old-guard bourgeoisie. In Ivory Coast, which became a colony in 1893, early administrators were representatives of the new ruling class—republican, anticlerical, and conscious of the economic goals they implemented. In the Ivory Coast hinterland, the proud and prosperous Baule, who had until then profited by coastal trade without ever encountering a European, rapidly experienced the full impact of the new colonialism, undisguised by missionizing and deterred only temporarily by their own resistance.

The Baule are a population of about one million occupying some 35,000 square kilometers in the center-east of Ivory Coast, beyond the pale of precolonial Islamic penetration from the north, well inland from the coast and marginal to West African kingdoms and major trade routes.[1] They are believed to have emerged as a cultural entity in the seventeenth and eighteenth centuries and their origin is very heterogeneous: preexisting Mande-Dyula, Voltaic and Kru elements, and groups of Akan immigrants, the first we know of from Denkyera and then, toward 1730, from Ashanti. The Akan, sometimes by conquest, sometimes peaceably, assimilated—or were assimilated by—the previous inhabitants of the region. Although many came from state societies, they failed in their attempts to constitute—or reconstitute—a state. Effective centralization of authority was limited in scope and short-lived; political formations were subject to rapid change; stratification was never clearly defined or rigidly established (see P. de Salverte-Marmier 1965; P. de Salverte-Marmier, M.-A. de Salverte-Marmier, and P. Etienne 1965; Chauveau 1972a, 1972b, 1973; Weiskel 1976, 1977).

Because neither the coast nor the hinterland was easily accessible, we have no eyewitness accounts and little secondary information concerning the Baule before the end of the nineteenth century. For the same reason, they were affected only very indirectly by the Atlantic slave trade. It is probable, however, that the genesis of Baule society as we know it was strongly influenced by the violent impact of the slave trade on the Gold Coast hinterland, where slave raiding and political rivalry within and between African states sent unprecedented numbers of migrants westward to a safer region. The reconstruction of Baule history also suggests that active trade relations with the Akan heartland to the east existed until the intensification of European trade along the Ivory Coast in the nineteenth century diverted Baule trade southward. The Baule are believed to have exchanged cloth and gold, and perhaps captives, for firearms and other European goods, which reached the hinterland of the Gold Coast (now Ghana) at a much earlier period. With the development of the palm-products trade in the nineteenth century, coastal populations directly to the south increased their production, and with it their purchasing power, and became desirable trading partners, offering and receiving much the same goods as those exchanged in the eastward trade.

The colonization of the Baule, documented by Weiskel (1977), began in 1893, when the French officer Marchand conquered Tiassalé, a trading post on their southern border, and then penetrated inland. Impressed by Baule prosperity, he recognized the economic potential of the region. At first amenable to new commercial relations and willingly responding to the demand for wild rubber that marked the early years of colonization, the Baule reacted violently from the very beginning to French attempts to interfere with their productive relations by mobilizing their labor or that of their captives. The French did not immediately pursue total military conquest, both because it was made difficult by Baule techniques of guerrilla warfare and because collaborative arrangements were reached whereby the colonial administration limited its demands and the Baule acceded to them. Until 1908, phases of armed conflict alternated with phases of relative peace and prosperity.

By 1909, however, the situation had changed: the economic status of the colony was unsatisfactory and, in any case, economic control was necessary if the potential of Baule land and labor was to be exploited. The new governor, Angoulvant, having provoked a revolt by tax reforms and attempts to force the Baule to produce cash crops under administrative and military control, obtained support for total conquest, which he pursued by systematic search-and-destroy missions. The last Baule resistance was overcome in 1911. In 1912, the railroad reached Bouaké, an early military outpost in the heart of the Baule north, now the second largest city in Ivory Coast.

BAULE SOCIETY IN THE PRECONQUEST PERIOD

In spite of their conquests and their resistance to colonization, the Baule do not appear as a people of warriors. Farming was and still is the essential productive activity; hunting and gathering, although secondary, were more important in the past. Crafts, now marginal, were essential in precolonial times and cotton-cloth production was particularly important. Uncultivated vegetable fibers were used for certain purposes (baskets, mats) and bark cloth was used for bedding. The continuing ritual importance of bark cloth as a gift from husband to mother-in-law "to replace the mat her daughter wet as a baby" may be a reminder of earlier times, but we find no clear evidence, as we do for other peoples, of a time when the Baule went unclothed or wore only bark cloth or raffia.

Marriage seems always to have been characterized by considerable freedom of choice, even in cases of childhood betrothal; there was no bridewealth, but only brideservice and symbolic gifts, primarily of consumable goods.[2] Descent, in the past as in the present, was cognatic, although the inheritance of wealth, including captives,[3] and of positions of authority was generally matrilineal. Because of the cognatic principle, group membership was indeterminate and depended both on the informal power relationship between maternal and paternal kin and on individual choice. It also depended very much on women, who, as mothers, tended to determine de facto group membership of children by attaching them to the domestic group with which they themselves elected residence.

These structural factors seem to have played a decisive role in determining the autonomy and mobility that are still characteristic of Baule people in general and Baule women in particular. Correlative with this autonomy and mobility we find between women and men, or between juniors and elders, no indication of clearly established relationships of subordination-domination and no mechanisms whereby husbands or elders could systematically appropriate the surplus production of wives or juniors, although in practice they might sometimes profit by it. (Even captives—at least the captive-born as opposed to those newly acquired—could control property during their lifetime.) The obligation to increase the sacred treasure of the kin group could perhaps have served such a purpose; it seems, however, to have weighed most heavily on the kin-group head and those who hoped to succeed to this position.

Land, the source of all subsistence, was available to all and all were subsistence producers, but durable wealth, especially in the form of gold and cloth, was important. Moreover, not only were there local barter of subsistence products, ritual gift-giving, and non-commodity exchange of prestige goods, both among the Baule and with neighboring societies, but there were forms of trade that can be defined as commodity exchange in the context of a noncapitalist society.[4] There was a system of gold weights and gold served as currency (see Chauveau 1972b; Meillassoux 1974: 263–75, 286). To control distribution of a product therefore could have real economic implications, not merely prestige value, as would be the case if production were only for subsistence use and ritual exchange.

Very schematically, this is the context of an analysis that will attempt to describe one limited instance of the impact of colonization on the relations between women and men.

All productive activity in Baule society was based on the sexual division of labor. In the case of some essential subsistence products, production was entirely the responsibility of one or the other sex and the producer was the "owner" of the product or, in other words, controlled its distribution. In the case of other products, both sexes contributed to production, each being in charge of specific tasks or phases of the production process; the sex that was considered to have initiated the process and taken responsibility for it "owned" the product or controlled its distribution. In both cases, the wife or husband who controlled an essential product had to provide for the subsistence needs of the other spouse and their children. When one sex controlled the product but the other had shared in its production, this latter could also receive a share of any surplus in exchange for his or her labor.

Thus, Baule marriage appears very much as an association between a woman and a man, not only for purposes of reproduction and childrearing, but also for purposes of production—the two being, of course, closely related. Although no social or supernatural sanctions rigidly enforced the division of labor and a woman or man could, if necessary and possible, occasionally do the work of the other sex, this division of labor was clearly defined, maintained, and perpetuated by the socialization process. Possible deviation was further restricted by sex-specialized competence in tasks that required complex skills. Marriage, therefore, gave each person a necessary partner of the other sex or, to borrow Siskind's formulation, it served to "define rights to the appropriation of objects of production for one's self and to the appropriation of the product of the opposite sex" (1978:863). At the same time, the partnership in production constituted the material basis of the conjugal relationship, and also of the relationship between the kin groups of the spouses.

Two products were both labor-demanding and vital to subsistence in Baule society: yams and cloth. Yams were the basic crop and, although survival was objectively conceivable without them, it would have been considered a miserable existence. To eat only cassava was "famine."

Cloth, too, was essential to everyday life. Although children were clothed only to protect them from chilly weather and men might wear only their breechcloth maintained by a waist band for farming work, the untailored cotton cloth (*tanni*) covering the breechcloth and falling below the knees was a minimum that clearly marked the transition from puberty to womanhood. Later in life, additional *tanni*—one for carrying a baby—were the mark of the married woman. The draped or wrapped cloth was worn during leisure hours and in public places by all adults. (To go naked or with only a breechcloth in public places is one symptom of madness among the Baule and even casual observers note the extreme modesty of men as well as women.)

Both yams and cloth required the labor of both sexes in the different phases of production. In the case of yams, it was the man who initiated production and took responsibility for it; he also controlled distribution. In the case of cloth, it was the woman who initiated production, took responsibility for it, and controlled distribution.

As suggested above, although cloth is not nourishment, if we define needs by a people's own values—and so we must—it was as essential as yams in the context of subsistence. Beyond subsistence, both products played an important role in precolonial Baule society in that they were exchanged on various occasions and thus marked the establishment and perpetuation of social relationships between individuals and groups. Gifts of yams by the man marked the phases of what was a very gradual marriage process. Helping to nourish a young wife-to-be, especially during pregnancy, was an obligation in establishing rights—as husband and father—as was contributing labor to the production of in-laws' yams. Cloth was equally indispensable in establishing the conjugal partnership. In defining marriage, older women today rarely fail to describe the production and distribution process, specifying the mutual obligations of wife and husband. Here, too, affines were involved: *tanni* were exchanged reciprocally between parents of the wife and husband.[5]

The Importance of Cloth

While the yam—a perishable foodstuff—remained primarily confined to the subsistence sector,[6] the woman-controlled product, cloth—no doubt because of its durability—circulated more widely and played a greater variety of roles.[7] Once the production process terminated, surplus production—what was not needed for everyday family use—became, with gold and gold ornaments, the most valuable type of property produced by the Baule themselves. It was given at funerals, sometimes buried with the deceased, displayed on special occasions, and conserved in the sacred treasure that was guarded by each kin-group head. Thus, within Baule society, besides its subsistence function, cloth had an essential function in what can be considered the ritual and prestige sector.

Even more important, unlike yams cloth was not confined to intrasocietal relations, but was very important in relations with people of neighboring societies. For example, it was traded directly with the Guro for iron and cattle, and with other groups for captives. It is not always clear whether this direct trade with neighbors can necessarily be characterized as commodity exchange.[8] To the south, however, and especially at Tiassalé, cloth served to acquire salt, guns, and gunpowder from coastal peoples who traded directly with the Europeans. These commodities, although prized by the Baule themselves for their use value, were also traded, again with the Guro and other peoples, for iron, captives, and other goods. To the north, Islamic conquerors furnished captives in great numbers in exchange both for Baule gold and for guns and gunpowder acquired with gold and cloth (see Chauveau 1972a, 1972b, 1974). Therefore, besides its subsistence, ritual, and prestige functions, cloth was important in long-distance trade and seems clearly to have served as a form of currency and/or commodity.

Cloth was, of course, also art in that esthetic appreciation was decisive in determining the value of Baule cloth. But, as has been frequently noted for non-Western societies, no object was "art for art's sake" independently of its utilitarian or ritual function.

That the original distribution of such a valuable and polyvalent product was the woman's domain inevitably gave her power and autonomy both in the conjugal relationship and in Baule society in general. Further, since women participated even in long-distance trade, either directly or by delegation,[9] there is no reason to believe that the emergence of a precolonial form of commodity exchange would necessarily have resulted in their losing control of cloth when it entered that sector.

There were, however, in the production process itself, possibilities for the man to minimize the woman's control of the product. As we shall see, they opened a breach in the subsistence model that would later become a radical breakdown.

The Production and Distribution Process

In order to understand the transformations introduced by colonial conquest and penetration—as opposed to contact—it is necessary first to examine the production process and the way in which it established the woman's rights over the product, as well as the mode of distribution on the domestic level, that is, on the level of the household, which is also the production unit.

The Baule practiced rotational bush-fallow cultivation, in which settlements are fixed and land is cultivated for one to three years—with annual rotations, successions, and crop mixtures (intercropping)—and then left fallow for four to ten years to restore fertility. A plot would originally be prepared for yams. The initial and heaviest work of clearing it, breaking the ground, and preparing mounds for planting, as well as staking of the young plants, was the man's job. Although he received assistance from the woman in burning and clearing away the brush and in planting, this initial phase of labor was his responsibility and this is the reason given for his "ownership" of the yam crop.

A man, however, always prepared a plot for a given woman, generally his wife, though sometimes his sister, mother, or other kinswoman. The Baule were polygynous, but, when a man had more than one wife, each co-wife would have her separate plot. That a plot was "for" a woman meant (1) that the yam crop was to feed her and her children, as well as the man, for whom she cooked; (2) that she would do female tasks, such as weeding and helping to plant and harvest yams on this plot; and (3) that the plot was hers to exploit by intercropping between the yam mounds and also after the yams were harvested. She used this last right to grow cotton, always an intercrop, as well as various other intercrops and secondary crops (condiments, corn, cassava, rice).

Because she had this use right over the yam plot, and because she initiated, tended, and took responsibility for these crops, the woman had ownership of the end-product and could dispose of it unreservedly, once family subsistence needs were taken care of. All of these raw products, with the exception of cotton, were also transformed by the woman herself—in cooking. In the case of cotton, the first phase of transformation was the woman's responsibility. She cleaned the cotton, carded it, and spun it into thread. Thus, she owned this thread. She also made vegetable dye (indigo) to color it. But only men did weaving and sewing. She therefore turned the skeins of cotton over to her husband, who wove them into bands and sewed the bands together to make *tanni*.

The man wove according to the woman's instructions relative to her estimation of the necessary repartition between immediate family needs and other uses, although they discussed this together. Because he was simply accomplishing one phase of the labor process *for her* and even though he well knew which cloth was for himself, he would turn over to his wife all of the final product and only then receive from her his lot.[10] This, then, was the model for the domestic or home production of cloth. It also exemplifies the model of reciprocity and interdependency in the marriage relationship, a combining of individual rights, cooperative labor, and responsibility for the other's needs.

The question we must ask at this point, before examining postconquest changes, is whether the model was always the reality. Did it always happen that way or were there other possibilities? Clearly, there could be no guarantee that a woman would produce and spin exactly the amount of cotton that her husband could or would weave. A woman who produced large quantities of cotton thread could be married to a man who was a mediocre or unenthusiastic weaver; a man who was an expert and dedicated weaver could be married to a woman whose production of thread was insufficient to satisfy his productive capacity. This imbalance could open a breach in the model of wife-husband production and could eventually create opportunities for men to control the product of their weaving, even if they did not control the raw material. They could form partnerships with other women, even strangers, or obtain thread from these women in other ways. In the case of a partnership, it is likely that a man who was an expert weaver and who approached a woman who had a large surplus of thread would sometimes be able to bargain with her to his advantage. An old widow who spent much time spinning and had no man to weave for her would be glad to get cloth for her needs in this way, and the man would be able to appropriate more of the surplus production, as he no doubt would if he used the thread of some dependent woman, such as his own captive. If he could purchase thread—or even cotton—outright, he could control the product completely, but there is no indication that this practice, if it existed, was widespread.

Women, too, could profit by the imbalance in wife-husband productivity and the breach in the subsistence model, depending on the availability of cotton thread and the extrafamilial demands of weavers. Further, according to the same principle that governed other areas of production, the daughter, younger sister, or other dependent kinswoman of an adult woman assisted the latter, contributing her production to that of her elder. The junior partner would receive either part of what she had produced (cotton or thread) or part of the final product (cloth) for her personal use. There was in this relationship the opportunity for the older woman to take advantage of the younger woman's surplus production. Finally, an adult woman—married or unmarried— could have a yam plot prepared "for her" by a kinsman or by her male captive and, like the wife who worked her husband's plot, use it to grow cotton that she would spin into thread and have woven for her. Informants emphasize the spinning-weaving relationship as a marital obligation and it is not clear, outside of the marital relationship, to what extent a woman was obliged to give her thread to spin to the man whose yam plot she grew cotton on. If there was such an obligation, it would have been especially strong when the man was unmarried or, relative to his productive capacity, insufficiently supplied by his wife or wives. When he was the woman's dependent, particularly her own captive, she could certainly gain an advantage, whether by disposing freely of her thread or by appropriating more than the usual share of the finished product, the general rule being that the mistress—or master—controlled the surplus production of a captive.

Opportunities for women or men to appropriate each other's surplus production, therefore, depended on particular circumstances and precise relationships. It was, however, the finished product that circulated outside the domestic sphere and it was the man who finished the product. This suggests that any opportunity to break away from the wife-husband partnership could tip the balance in his favor and that any systematic deviation from the domestic production model in general could favor men's control of cloth. Such a deviation seems to have existed.

One can say that there was no specialization in Baule society in the sense that all craftspeople were also their own subsistence producers, relying on others, kin as well as captives, to tend their crops only partially or occasionally when they were not available. There was, however, semispecialization in the sense that certain crafts—for instance, goldsmithing—were not known by all.[11] This was not the case for weaving, a craft of all adult men, but, besides the general variability in expertise, certain types of cloth among the most sought after were specialties, both regionally and individually. Itinerant weavers, especially during the dry season, when agricultural work was light, would go from village to village, weaving to order, as would male dyeing specialists.[12]

This semispecialization and the importance of cloth in the prestige sector certainly could facilitate and encourage any tendency on the part of the weaver to gain control of the product, eventually by gaining control of the raw material. Further, although the prestige function of cloth and this kind of specialization do not in themselves imply commodity exchange,[13] commodity exchange, as I have shown, clearly existed—with cloth as an important item—and certainly served as a motivation to control it.

These factors—the durable value of cloth in the prestige sector, its function in commodity exchange, and the female-male production relations that were not strictly confined to the wife-husband relationship—created a breach in the subsistence model. This breach could not, however, in and of itself lead to a total breakdown of existing production-distribution relations, removing the control of cloth from women.

What about the fact that weaving differs from spinning in offering a wider range of expertise and variability, an infinity of esthetic possibilities? (Basic designs were traditional but, inevitably, there were innovations.) In a word, as perceived by a Westerner, weaving is an art whereas spinning is a simple, monotonous, and repetitive technique. Should not the fact that he was the "artist" have favored control of cloth by the man? This, however, was not the Baule perception, in spite of their capacity for esthetic discrimination and its confirmation by the value attributed to Baule cloth throughout the region. What they perceived was that without the original cotton, without the spun thread, no weaving, no woven cloth, splendid or ordinary, was possible. That is why the woman, who grew the cotton and spun the thread, controlled the product.

THE POSTCONQUEST PERIOD

The preconquest contact period certainly accentuated the importance of Baule cloth both in the prestige sector of the economy, since there were greater opportunities to accumulate wealth, and as a commodity in long-distance trade. Although neither the Baule nor their cloth were directly involved in coastal trade with Europeans, they did, as indicated above, take part in this trade indirectly but actively, the Baule furnishing cloth to coastal peoples who were in direct contact, using it as currency to obtain European commodities both for their own use and for trade with other groups. For cloth production at least, this involvement apparently resulted in changes that were for the most part quantitative. One of the factors that were to determine radical qualitative change, the introduction of imported cloth, was present during that period but was not widespread and, in itself, could have only a limited impact on Baule production relations.

What would ultimately be decisive was colonial conquest and penetration. Several precise changes introduced in the differenc economic sectors were to converge and complement each other in breaking down the precolonial production-distribution relationship, divesting women of their control over an essential and valuable product. One must see these changes as interrelated and intermeshing, mutually reinforcing each other. They will, therefore, be examined in what seems to be the logical order of their importance rather than in the strict chronological order of their occurrence.

Colonial Penetration and the Breakdown of the Precolonial Production-Distribution Relationship

Although European cloth and perhaps thread—other than what may have been obtained by unraveling cloth—were introduced by preconquest trade (Boser-Sarivaxévanis 1969, 1972a), imported thread seems to have been used only occasionally and partially in the oldest existing specimens of Baule cloth—dating back no further than the late eighteenth or early nineteenth century (Boser-Sarivaxévanis 1972a:13; 1972b:53). Museum specimens collected in 1910 and examined by R. Boser-Sarivaxévanis (1972a:179–80) are all made with native thread, except for some decorative use of factory-made thread. Many later specimens, however, are composed mainly of factory-made thread (:179 ff.)

Colonization rapidly provided new opportunities to acquire factory-made thread. In 1923 a textile factory was established by R. Gonfreville just outside of Bouaké (M.-A. de Salverte-Marmier 1965:6). Producing both cloth and thread for the local market, "Gonfreville," as it came to be called, grew into what is practically a "company town" and in 1973 was still the largest textile factory in Ivory Coast.

Weavers could purchase Gonfreville thread with cash, thus freeing themselves from dependence on their wives' home production or on the production of other Baule women, making the woman's role in cloth production appear inessential and her control of the product unjustified. The availability of Gonfreville thread, decisive in destroying precolonial production relations, also contributed to what was to become a flagrant disproportion between women's spinning and men's weaving, a disproportion confirmed by recent sales figures of the textile industry.[14]

Although factory-made thread favors the weaver's control of his product, its growing use has not been simply a question of availability and of choice on his part. There is a real scarcity of homespun thread, determined by causes other than lack of demand. If we examine the agricultural sector, the reasons for this scarcity become clear. It is not that the Baule no longer produce cotton or that Baule women no longer contribute to its production. On the contrary, as we shall see, the Baule produce more cotton than ever and the role of Baule women in the production of both cotton and thread is still essential, but, mediated by cash and the capitalist commodity economy, it has become invisible.

As early as 1913, shortly after conquest and before the establishment of Gonfreville (Pezet 1965:4), the colonial administration wanted cotton for export purposes. Women's surplus production from intercropping could not satisfy this demand (Benetière and Pezet 1965:12). New varieties were introduced—at one point Gonfreville provided the seed (:24)—and new agricultural techniques aimed at improving production both qualitatively and quantitatively were imposed (Pezet 1965; Benetière and Pezet 1965:12; Ripailles 1965: 63).

Attempts to force the Baule to grow cotton as an unmixed crop proved that they were more knowledgeable than the colonizer; crowded cotton is destroyed by parasites. In spite of the "war effort" (World War II), postwar production figures made it clear that the choice was between intercropping, with its limited yield, and insecticide treatments, permitting the development of cotton as a high-yield unmixed crop. Furthermore (especially since forced labor had recently been abolished), higher yields were necessary to bring the higher revenues, relative to input, that would encourage farmers to grow cotton as a cash crop (Royer and Boutillier et al. n.d.:9–10). As a result, a heavy technical-assistance apparatus was instituted for research, for intervention during the different phases of production, and even for marketing (Pezet 1965; Benetière and Pezet 1965; Ripailles 1965). From sowing to selling, cotton became the focus of agricultural development experts, the principal buyer being Gonfreville (Pezet 1965:24).

There were also attempts to make cotton a first-year crop. They tended to be unsuccessful both for technical reasons and because the Baule preferred to save the best soil for yams (Pezet 1965:9–10; Benetière and Pezet 1965: 25). Cotton was therefore developed as a second-year main crop on previously exploited yam plots. As we have seen, the second-year use of the yam plot, like intercropping, was traditionally the woman's right. Cash-crop cotton, however, because it involved considerable preparatory work, could be considered a new beginning. Furthermore, this preparatory work, like the following phases of labor, was directed by agricultural experts and their extension agents. Just as the colonial administration—when it demanded that more cotton be produced—had addressed its demands to men, early and later agricultural experts and their male extension agents, when they introduced new techniques, addressed their teaching to men. It is, therefore, not surprising that cash-crop cotton, like other cash crops, became the man's domain.[15] At the same time, especially in the more densely populated areas, the takeover of second-year exploitation of the yam plot for cash cropping, by intruding on their use rights, could divest women of their means of production or, more precisely, of their object of production.

History confirms that it was not simply on their own initiative that Baule men came to control cash, cotton, and cloth. What has finally worked to their advantage began as a serious disadvantage. Until 1946, when forced labor was abolished, cotton production was one of its main goals. Quotas were established and physical violence was used to oblige villagers to cultivate "collective fields" of cotton (called by them "the commandant's cottonfields"). Besides force, taxation, the first act of the colonizer following conquest, served as a serious incentive. Cotton, like other products, could serve either as payment in kind or as a means of acquiring the necessary cash, since it was paid for, though badly.

As in agricultural development and forced labor, the colonizer did not generally intervene directly to collect the head tax, but specified the goals to be attained and used native agents and the native hierarchy (manipulated, of course, by the colonial administration) as intermediaries. Whether it was because of the way in which orders were given, because the 'head of family' concept was convenient, or for other reasons related to precolonial wife-husband obligations, the man became responsible for his wife's head tax. To be the primary target of taxation made the acquisition of cash a vital need for men, rather than for women, tending to justify and reinforce their control of cotton as a cash crop.[16]

While the burden of taxation made cash a necessity for men and while cotton grown by them, willingly or unwillingly, provided the necessary cash, the expanding commodity economy also made cash useful to purchase the Gonfreville thread that was both advantageous and indispensable in replacing homespun thread. At the same time, cash-crop cotton made Gonfreville thread more available and contributed to making homespun thread less available. There were, however, in the agricultural sector, still other changes that reinforced men's economic position.

Besides cotton, other cash crops such as cocoa and coffee, were introduced for export purposes. They, too, became men's domain. With the growing need to feed urban populations, the yam itself sometimes became a cash crop, the entire harvest being sold wholesale after enough were set aside for subsistence needs and turned over to the adult women of the family. Here again, the right of each woman to "her" separate yam plots tended to be alienated. Cocoa and coffee—coffee is particularly important as a source of income—have not been the focus of as much technical intervention as cotton; but they are perennial, not annual plants and can therefore compound the alienation of women's use rights by giving a new meaning to permanent rights over land, whereas in the past only use rights and rights over crops existed. Eventually, this shift in meaning of land rights, combined with the use of wage labor, could eliminate women's use rights completely.[17]

Wage labor, however, is still the exception rather than the rule among the Baule. With the development of cash cropping, women have remained active in agricultural production. Because men's cash income is now as necessary to them as to their husbands, women continue to fulfill the conjugal obligation to assist a spouse, pursuing such tasks as weeding and harvesting for which they were traditionally responsible. The harvesting and shelling of coffee beans are particularly arduous and time-consuming tasks.[18] The principle of retributing a spouse for her or his labor remains operative and women receive some share of the profits. Because they do not control cash crops, however, they are dependent on the men for their reward. Their remuneration tends to be arbitrary, and disproportionately low when compared both to labor input and to the monetary value of the product.

Perhaps more important, the labor time devoted to men's cash crops is not available for other activities. Intercropping of cotton and other products on the yam plot continues, as does second-year production of foodstuffs necessary for subsistence. Surplus production of cassava, peanuts, and other women's crops can be retailed or even wholesaled in small quantities at the local marketplace, but women often do not have time for their own agricultural production, just as they do not have time for carding and spinning cotton. These productive activities, quantitatively, financially, and by their economic function, have become far less important than those controlled by men.

In conclusion, the scarcity of homespun thread and the widespread use of factory-made thread, resulting in women's loss of control over handwoven cloth, are two related aspects of what has been a fundamental transformation of production relations. The impact of this transformation was to be compounded by another intrusion of the expanding commodity economy: the widespread marketing of industrial commodities in general and of factory-made cloth in particular. Like other commodities, factory-made cloth will inevitably be more available to men insofar as men control more cash.

Baule Cloth and Factory Cloth

With cash cropping and/or labor migration,[19] men's time too has become less available for other productive activities and weaving is no longer a routine activity of all adult men. It persists, however, as a leisure activity, especially since it can be pursued during the dry season when there is usually a lull in agricultural labor. Among older people in villages less affected than others by the commodity economy, the spinning-weaving relationship is still considered a conjugal obligation, although it may be reduced to the strict minimum. On the other hand, for the most expert weavers, handwoven cloth can be an important source of income.

As imported cloth, Gonfreville cloth, and now the cloth of other local textile factories has become widely available, it has tended to replace Baule cloth for everyday use and less important gifts. Gonfreville even makes imitations of handmade cloth and of handwoven bands that can be sewn together to make a *tanni*. This enhances the prestige value of authentic Baule cloth, more appreciated than ever as a symbol of wealth and for ceremonial occasions, both among the Baule (see P. Etienne 1968:813—17) and among other Ivory Coast peoples.

Thus, in both the subsistence and prestige sectors, cloth now circulates as a commodity. Subsistence need—that is, the everyday necessity to clothe one's body—is satisfied by the factory-made commodity, while handmade cloth itself has become almost entirely a commodity, with its circulation restricted to the ritual and prestige sector,[20] losing its function as a subsistence product that both served a basic need and consolidated the relationship between wife and husband. If precolonial commodity exchange of cloth opened a breach in the subsistence model, colonization and capitalist commodity exchange alone could lead to this total breakdown, transforming all cloth into a commodity and divesting Baule cloth of its primary subsistence function.

A corollary of this transformation is that "art," in the form of weaving, has become dissociated from functional or subsistence production. Baule cloth has long been appreciated for its beauty and variety, but, as long as it was also an everyday necessity, this dissociation could not occur. Because art and life were one and because woman's labor was the indispensable origin of the production process, the considerable skill or "art" required of the weaver could not radically affect her control of the product. Thus, we see that at the same time that art tends to emerge as a separate domain—distinct from everyday life and reflecting the generalized subordination of Baule society to the colonizer's commodity economy—it emerges as a male-controlled domain, reflecting the generalized subordination of women to men.

WOMEN AND CLOTH TODAY: ALIENATION AND THE REVERSAL OF A RELATIONSHIP

A major consequence of the changes analyzed above has been the reversal of the relationship between women and cloth; once an object that women controlled because it was their product, cloth has become, in a sense, an object that controls them. Much of what has been described here could have been systematically described in terms of alienation, the concept being applied in its different connotations to the different aspects and phases of the process analyzed.

The Gonfreville textile factory is one instance in which the concept of alienation imposes itself, so flagrant and obvious, almost ironical is the changed relationship between producer and product. In 1950 the factory started employing Baule women (M.-A. de Salverte-Marmier 1965:6, 9) and has continued to employ them extensively in several departments as wage laborers (:6–12). Thus, on the most manifest level, simply as factory workers they are alienated from their own product in the immediately given context of capitalist production. This alienation, however, is founded on a more complex historical process of alienation. The very production process in which Baule women sell their labor to produce thread and cloth has been a key factor in destroying a production process in which they controlled the same product.

The alienated labor of Baule women also appears in other phases of the new process, since they contribute to growing cash-crop cotton for Gonfreville cloth and thread; here the productive activity itself is much the same as in the past, but its meaning and function are entirely different. Meanwhile, traditional, woman-controlled production of cotton, by intercropping, and of thread continues but has become practically a remnant of the past, playing no essential role in the economy. Further, what primarily motivates women to sell their labor for wages is the need to acquire the cloth they once produced and, in a sense, to regain control of this product by controlling their own cash.[21] Thus, multiple processes of alienation converge with the Baule women as their focal point or subject.

Alienated production means the producer's control of the product is replaced by the product's control of the producer. In the case of the Gonfreville factory worker, the relationship between woman and cloth has been visibly reversed in this way. If we move from the sector of production to the sector of consumption—and we must in a commodity economy that radically dissociates the two—this same reversal of the relationship between woman and cloth manifests itself. Control of the consumer by the product is, of course, a generalized characteristic of the modern capitalist commodity economy. In this case, however, we will see that it is particularly striking—a magnified and oversimplified illustration, almost a caricature, of the more general relationship.

Although handmade cloth is now confined to the prestige sector, subsistence needs being satisfied by factory-made cloth, the latter also occupies an important position in the prestige sector. All the values and functions previously attributed to the one have been extended to the other. To clothe one's body is a necessity. To have cloth in quantity and quality beyond the mere necessity of clothing one's body is a constantly pursued goal. For women in particular, the brightly colored cloth specially designed for the African market and imported from England or Holland—and the less valued local-factory cloth—is the most sought after commodity. Whenever possible, it is bought in six-yard lengths necessary for a complete three-piece outfit. It is generally worn unsewn by villagers and is often machine-stitched and tailored, more or less elaborately—usually by male tailors—for townswomen. Except for schoolgirls, very few women, even among the educated, wear European-style dresses.[22] Women also hoard this factory cloth along with the handmade cloth and gold objects that have always constituted treasured property. Whether worn or hoarded, cloth is coveted and continues to represent wealth and status.

As did handmade cloth, factory cloth also tends to materialize the relationship between woman and man, and especially between wife and husband. But now this materialization of the personal relationship takes another form. Instead of emerging from the cooperative production process with one spouse's labor being restituted by the other's gift of the final product, it is mediated by the commodity economy. The principles of wife-husband cooperation in production and of compensating the participating partner for her or his labor remain operative, but the woman is the participating partner for products that bring cash and cash has become indispensable. The equilibrium of an economy where both sexes had control over essential products—and these could be acquired in no other way than through the woman-man production partnership—has disappeared, as have the rules governing distribution in a context where labor produced use values rather than commodities. At the same time, cash and cloth have become interchangeable, although it is cloth that tends to measure the value of cash, rather than the reverse. (A woman who receives a sum of money will estimate its value by the amount of cloth she can buy more naturally than she will estimate the value of cloth by its purchase price.)

Thus, the woman who contributes her labor to her husband's production of cotton or coffee will receive cash or cloth in amounts which she considers arbitrary and which, in fact, very much depend on the man's "generosity." Abusively low remuneration is facilitated by the man's knowledge that the woman cannot reciprocate, as she could when she too controlled essential products. As a result, the wife-husband production relationship is becoming a constant source of conflict. Because the production relationship has always been the foundation of marriage, and because cloth and cash now tend to be the measure of a husband's affection and respect, the whole personal relationship is also conflict-laden.

Inevitably, many women prefer to remain unmarried and all seek to acquire their own cash, whether at Gonfreville, on southern coffee and cocoa farms, or in town, through wage labor, petty trade, or sometimes prostitution (see P. Etienne and M. Etienne 1968). Whether in prostitution, the preconjugal relationship, or marriage itself, a woman may try to appropriate the man's advantage by constant demands for cloth and cash, but this hardly restitutes her autonomy. To pursue wealth is not entirely new. In the past women also traded and sought to acquire gold and captives, as well as prestige cloth woven by experts, and they were not always anxious to marry.[23] What is new is a transformation of the woman-man production relationship that replaces interdependency by dependency in the most essential areas of subsistence. Here, as in the Gonfreville factory, the relationship to the object cloth is reversed. Women no longer control cloth but are controlled by it. This formulation is more than an elegant abstraction. When we move from the interindividual relationship and the general production-distribution relationship to women's relationship to the political power structure in contemporary Ivory Coast, the way in which cloth has become, if not the controlling agent itself, at least the means by which control is exercised, is clearly perceptible.

Ivory Coast women—and Baule women in particular—played an important and very active role in the struggle for independence.[24] The national party (Ivory Coast is a one-party state) continues to rely heavily on women's support without always maintaining adequate communication to justify their mobilization on various occasions. When such mobilization is necessary, cloth is distributed. For example, when the party wants to organize a mass demonstration to welcome a visiting head of state, cloth is produced in a local factory especially for the occasion—often with portraits of the Ivory Coast president and the visitor—and is distributed to the women, especially to those who are known supporters of the party and influential in the community. Here, besides motivating the women to take part in the demonstration, the cloth serves as a uniform for politico-esthetic purposes. In other circumstances, cloth is distributed as a reward for services rendered or expected. The traditional point of reference for this practice is to be found in the principle of materializing a relationship and rewarding labor. Cloth, because it has always served this purpose, and because it is highly valued and sought after, is an excellent vehicle, made even more appropriate by its display function. As in other areas, the modern power structure uses traditional models and values astutely. What colonization and the capitalist commodity economy have taken from Baule women, the state now returns—in a different form and in different circumstances.

Cloth has become a prime motivation for supporting the party and the focus of attention for the recipients. The women themselves experience this relationship with ambivalence, sometimes appearing entirely absorbed in the pursuit of cloth as a party handout, sometimes expressing with bitterness the feeling of being manipulated by gifts of cloth. They do not explicitly formulate the contrast between present and past as I have done here.

They do however perceive it and reflect it in their behavior, often going through the motions of an activity that, once essential, has become anachronistic, while actively engaged in more realistic pursuits. One case illustrates this contradiction: that of a very old woman who, from early colonial times, had adapted to change with intelligent opportunism, becoming the "native wife" of early administrators, serving as an intermediary in their dealings with the population, acquiring wealth and prestige that were maintained in the postindependence period, when she shifted her allegiance to the new government and its party, for whom she continues to play much the same role that she had played for the colonial administration, seeing for her purposes very little difference between the two. Throughout a life that began before colonization, she has maximized every opportunity available to an illiterate woman and avidly collected factory-made cloth. Yet she continues to spin her cotton in her town compound, explaining that young kinswomen in her village grow it and that she returns each year to collect it and to give the thread to kinsmen for weaving—pointing with pride at this activity that in the past defined a woman's social reality, no doubt getting some profit from it in the present, but pretending to ignore what she obviously knows: that the spinning she carries on almost obsessively has meaning only in reference to a world that is becoming obsolete.

NOTES

*This chapter is a revised version of an article originally published in *Cahiers d'Etudes africaines* XVII (1), 65, 1977:41–64. Some of the more specialized footnotes have been omitted and references have been updated. I thank Christine Gailey, Eleanor Leacock, and Susan Vogel for revision suggestions.

1. Where specific references are not given, the source of my data is fieldwork in 1962 and 1963 among rural Baule of the Bouaké region, sponsored by the Ivory Coast government's Ministère du Plan, and in 1974-75 among urban Baule of Abidjan, supported by grant No. 3067 from the Wenner-Gren Foundation for Anthropological Research. I am grateful to the Ivory Coast government (Ministère de la Recherche scientifique) and to the University of Abidjan (Institut d'Ethnologie) for their authorization to pursue research in Abidjan. I thank Jean-Louis Boutillier, Ariane Deluz, Nicole-Claude Mathieu, and Claudine Vidal for contributing their suggestions to the original version of this chapter.

2. Young women legitimately could—and did—reject the man they had been betrothed to in childhood. Exceptions to the general rule concerning bridewealth occurred in marriage with members of neighboring patrilineal societies and in one type of marriage practiced by the wealthy and noble (see P. Etienne and M. Etienne 1971:172–73).

3. *Captives*, a term I prefer to *slaves*, were numerous and important in Baule society. They were to all appearances assimilated through marriage and were never a separate caste or class, but their status was transmitted matrilineally and, in the matriline, was never lost.

4. There were, however, no large towns and no local or regional marketplaces, but only borderland markets or trading posts. (see Chauveau 1972b).

5. Meillassoux stresses the importance of cloth as bridewealth among the Guro (1974:195, 216). It is interesting that in Baule marriage this valuable durable product is exchanged reciprocally between affines. Meillassoux also says that the Guro woman gives her skeins of thread to her husband or to others (:194). This would mean that she does not control the end-product.

6. At trading and gold-prospecting centers in general, and, during the 1890s, in the war-ravaged regions to the north of the Baule—where captives could be bought with cassava—foodstuffs did function as commodities, but these were exceptional circumstances.

7. Leacock suggests the importance of the study of cloth and notes the physical and functional characteristics that make it a potential commodity par excellence (1975:613–14).

8. According to Meillassoux, cloth was not traded directly for captives between Baule and Guro (1974:267). Further, in some instances at least, Baule-Guro trade cannot be defined as commodity exchange, but rather had sociopolitical functions (:266–67). Craft production in the two societies was similar and cloth was traded in both directions.

9. Baule trade was of the "expedition" type, as defined by Meillassoux (Chauveau 1972b:6). Both women and men could mandate another individual, generally a dependent—son, daughter, other kinsperson, even a trusted captive—to carry out this unspecialized and often dangerous activity for them. The same was true of gold prospecting, a related activity. The grandmother of one of my informants had been sent south by her mother to trade cloth. She returned with both gold and captives.

10. See P. Etienne for a somewhat different explanation of distribution rights and for an interesting comparison between the wife-husband and the client-craftsperson relationship (1968:796; 1971:241).

11. These craft specialties could be learned from a stranger or transmitted by a parent or kinsperson of the same sex.

12. Women, however, prepared indigo and did certain types of dyeing. See Boser-Sarivaxévanis for a technical study of West African weaving and dyeing (1969, 1972a, 1972b, 1975). She documents the remarkable complexity of dyeing techniques, whether of cloth or of thread, and the unusual variability, sometimes within the same cultural group, of the gender assignment of this craft (1969:194–95).

13. It is important not to confuse "prestige sector" and commodity exchange—and also not to assume, as does Weiskel (1977), that it was necessarily the most valued cloth that circulated as a commodity. An informant showed me a very old piece of ordinary, undyed cloth, with the remark: "This [not the richly woven *tanni*] is what we used to get salt and guns at Tiassalé." It is significant that ordinary, undyed cloth, which women most clearly controlled, could circulate as a commodity or as currency.

14. Already in 1945, of 162 tons of thread produced by Gonfreville, 77 tons were sold to Baule weavers (Benetière and Pezet 1965:24). In 1963 weavers purchased 72 million francs worth of factory thread, whereas women's homespun cotton was valued at only 8 million francs (Fride 1965:204).

15. Boserup notes the generality of this phenomenon—the control of cash crops by men—in developing countries and relates it to the intervention of experts and development agents (1970:53–57). It is my experience that they

are not unaware of women's rights, but simply ignore them or are sometimes consciously determined to transform women into the helpmates of men, in spite of observations that point to the low revenues of women as a source of conflict between the sexes (see M. Etienne and P. Etienne et al. 1965b:107; Fride et al. 1965:153).

16. Boserup notes that taxation in the colonial context was meant to serve more as a means of drawing the colonized into the cash economy than as a source of income (1970:19). She sees its relationship to cash cropping, but not to the takeover of cash crops by men.

17. The changed meaning of land rights can also lead to the sale of land, generally to the disadvantage of women (see Boserup 1970:57-61). The Baule, however, are buyers rather than sellers of land. Women, *provided they have the financial means to begin with,* can thus regain an advantage. Some of my urban informants owned coffee and cocoa farms in the regions south of Baule country. Wage labor, too, can sometimes work to the advantage of women. A woman can ask for land, if it is available, and control the product, if she can find a dependent man to work for her (or do all the work herself). Wage laborers, a convenient substitute for captives, can serve this purpose. Further, when men use wage labor—generally for coffee in the wealthier villages—women can sometimes devote more time to their own crops and even get husbands to help them, again *provided that land is available.* These are, however, exceptions to the general rule that cash cropping and wage labor (by promoting cash cropping) tend to alienate women's land rights.

18. Pounding foodstuffs is a woman's task, but men do take part in the pounding of coffee beans.

19. Both women and men from unforested regions, which are unfavorable for growing coffee, especially if other cash crops are not highly developed (Michotte 1968), often work seasonally on southern coffee and cocoa farms belonging either to members of their family or to strangers (see P. Etienne and M. Etienne 1968; P. de Salverte-Marmier, M.-A. de Salverte-Marmier, and P. Etienne 1965:59-82). There is also urban migration, but seasonal migration particularly affects crafts, since it occurs during the dry season, which was traditionally devoted to craft production.

20. The principal economic activity of one urban woman informant was to buy Baule cloth in rural villages and sell it to well-off employees and civil servants, going from office to office to vend her wares. Some women sell factory cloth at the market place, but they by no means control this sector as do Ashanti women in Ghana.

21. Women in the sample studied by M.-A. de Salverte-Marmier are all of rural origin; almost all live in nearby villages and they are for the most part unmarried (1965:9, 16-19). They devote a considerable portion of their salary to the purchase of cloth (:15).

22. Men, too, attribute great importance to their clothing. In town and often in the villages, European-style clothing is worn for work and on everyday occasions. Brightly colored, draped factory cloth or hand-woven *tanni* are worn for leisure and on special occasions.

23. It is said that noble and wealthy women did not marry. This refers more to a de facto than a de jure situation and is related to the fact that virilocal marriage prevents a woman from succeeding to positions of authority.

24. In 1949 they marched on the prison of Grand-Bassam to liberate political prisoners and many were maimed and injured in a violent encounter with colonial troops (see Diabaté 1975). The demonstration used as a model a Baule women's ritual, *adjanu*, a precolonial form of symbolic warfare that can be directed against village men or against enemies. The power of *adjanu* is both verbal and visual; its visual weapon is nudity.

REFERENCES

Benetière, Jean-Jacques and Pierre Pezet. 1965. "Histoire de l'agriculture en zone baoulé." In Côte d'Ivoire, Ministère du Plan, *Étude régionale de Bouaké, 1962-1964*, doc. 2. Abidjan.

Boser-Sarivaxévanis, Renée. 1969. *Aperçus sur la teinture à l'indigo en Afrique occidentale*. Basel.

—. 1972a. *Les tissus de l'Afrique occidentale: méthode de classification et catalogue raisonné des étoffes tissées de l'Afrique de l'Ouest*. Basel.

—. 1972b. "Les tissus de l'Afrique occidentale à dessin réservé par froissage." *Ethnologische Zeitschrift Zürich* 1:53-59.

—. 1975. "Recherche sur l'histoire des textiles traditionnels tissés et teints de l'Afrique occidental." *Verhandlungen der Naturforschenden Gesellschaft in Basel*. 86:301-41.

Boserup, Ester. 1970. *Woman's Role in Economic Development*. London: Allen and Unwin.

Chauveau, Jean-Pierre. 1972a. *Les cadres socio-historiques de la production dans la région de Kokumbo (pays Baoulé, Côte d'Ivoire)*. I: *La période précoloniale*. Petit-Bassam (Abidjan): ORSTOM.

—. 1972b. *Note sur la place du Baoulé dans l'ensemble économique ouest-africain*. Petit-Bassam (Abidjan): ORSTOM.

—. 1973. *Note sur la morphologie matrimoniale de Kokumbo (pays Baoulé, Côte d'Ivoire). Perspective historique*. Petit-Bassam (Abidjan): ORSTOM.

—. 1974. "Note sur les échanges dan le Baoulé précolonial." Paper presented at the Bondoukou Colloquium on Peoples Common to the Ivory Coast and Ghana, Jan. 1974.

Côte d'Ivoire, Ministère du Plan. 1965. *Étude régionale de Bouaké, 1962-1964*, 4 vols., 11 docs. Abidjan.

Diabaté, Henriette. 1975. *La Marche des femmes sur Grand-Bassam*. Abidjan, Dakar: Les Nouvelles Editions africaines.

Etienne, Mona. 1976. "Women and Slaves: Stratification in an African Society." Paper presented at the 75th annual meeting of the American Anthropological Association, Washington, D.C.

Etienne, Mona, and Pierre Etienne, et al. 1965a. "L'organisation sociale des Baoulé." In Côte d'Ivoire, Ministère du Plan. *Le peuplement. Étude régionale de Bouké, 1962-1964*, vol. Abidjan.

———. 1965b. "Essai de monographie d'un village de savane: Diamelassou." In Côte d'Ivoire, Ministère du Plan, *Étude régionale de Bouaké, 1962-1964*, doc. 4. Abidjan.

Etienne, Pierre. 1966. "Phénomènes religieux et facteurs socio-économiques dans un village de la région de Bouaké (Côte d'Ivoire)." *Cahiers d'Études africaines* 6:367-401.

———. 1968. "Les aspects ostentatoires du système économique baoulé." *Économies et Sociétés* 2:793-817.

———. 1971. "Les Baoulé face aux rapports de salariat." *Cahiers OSTOM* (ser. Sciences humaines) 8:235–42.

Etienne, Pierre and Mona Etienne. 1967. "Terminologie de la parenté et de l'alliance chez les Baoulé (Côte d'Ivoire)." *L'Homme* 7:50-76.

———. 1968. "L'émigration baoulé actuelle." *Cahiers d'Outre-mer* 21:155-95.

———. 1971. "'A qui mieux mieux' ou le mariage chez les Baoulé." *Cahiers ORSTOM* (ser. Sciences humaines) 8:165-86.

Fride, B. 1965. "Les activités industrielles et artisanales: le secteur secondaire." In Côte d'Ivoire, Ministère du Plan, *L'économie. Étude régionale de Bouaké, 1962-1964*, vol. 2. Abidjan.

Fride, B. et al. 1965. Éléments pour une monographie du village de Kouakou-Broukrou." In Côte d'Ivoire, Ministère du Plan, *Étude régionale de Bouaké, 1962-1964*, doc. 5. Abidjan.

Leacock, Eleanor. 1975. "Class, Commodity, and the Status of Women." In R. Rohrlich-Leavitt, ed., *Women Cross-Culturally: Change and Challenge*. The Hague: Mouton.

Meillassoux, Claude. 1974. *Anthropologie économique des Gouro de Côte d'Ivoire* (1st ed. 1964). The Hague: Mouton.

Michotte, Jean. 1968. *Mouvements migratoires et développement économique dans la zone dense à l'ouest de Bouaké*. Adiopodoumé, Ivory Coast: ORSTOM.

Pezet, Pierre. 1965. "Le coton dans la zone baoulé." In Côte d'Ivoire, Ministère du Plan, *Étude régionale de Bouaké, 1962-1964*, doc. 6. Abidjan.

Ripailles, C. et al. 1965. "Les activités et la production agricoles: le secteur primaire." In Côte d'Ivoire, Ministère du Plan, *L'économie. Étude régionale de Bouaké, 1962-1964*, vol. 2. Abidjan.

J. Royer, J.-L. Boutillier, et al. n.d. Enquête agricole par sondage dans le cercle de Bouaké, juillet 1954–janvier 1955. Abidjan: Côte d'Ivoire. Service de la Statistique et de la Mécanographie.

Salverte-Marmier, M.-A. de. 1965. "Les ouvrières de l'industrie textile." In Côte d'Ivoire, Ministère du Plan, *Étude régionale de Bouaké, 1962-64*, doc. 9. Abidjan.

Salverte-Marmier, P. de. 1965. "L'organisation politique et la structure territoriale." In Côte d'Ivoire, Ministère du Plan, *Le peuplement. Étude régionale de Bouaké, 1962-64*, vol. 1. Abidjan.

Salverte-Marmier, P. de, M.-A. de Salverte-Marmier and P. Etienne. 1965. "Les étapes du peuplement." In Côte d'Ivoire, Ministère du Plan, *Le peuplement. Étude régionale de Bouaké, 1962-64,* vol. 1. Abidjan.

Siskind, Janet. 1978. "Kinship and Mode of Production." *American Anthropologist* 80: 860-872.

Weiskel, Timothy C. 1976. "L'histoire socio-économique des peuples baule: problèmes et perspectives de recherche." *Cahiers d'Études africaines* 16: 357-95.

——. 1977. "French Colonial Rule and the Baule Peoples: Resistance and Collaboration, 1889-1911." Ph.D. diss., Oxford University.

10 Desert Politics:
Choices in the "Marriage Market"

DIANE BELL

Intensive European colonization of eastern Australia from 1788 onward quickly brought disease and violence to the original inhabitants. Aborigines in the arid areas of central Australia were little affected until the 1870s and were not removed to missions and government settlements until the 1940s, although news of European goods, disease, and the visits of the occasional missionary, miner, explorer, and scientific expedition preceded intensive contact. In general nineteenth-century explorers' accounts asserted that the country was uninhabitable and useless, while noting that the native inhabitants were remarkably healthy and vigorous. For millenia these people have survived and reproduced themselves in one of the severest environments this planet offers.

But only when their intricate accomodation was in the process of disintegration were the desert communities studied by modern, professional anthropologists. Much of my information is drawn from people now living in a totally changed manner.

From the journeys of the earliest European explorers—Stuart in the 1860s, Gosse in 1873, and Warburton in 1873—to the struggle for land rights in the 1970s, race relations in central Australia have been fraught with violence and characterized by European denial of Aboriginal community autonomy and by continuing dispossession. Warburton's journal signals the beginning of dispossession: on June 26, 1873 while 48 kilometers north of Waterloo Well in central Australia he wrote, "found two sacred stone boards, 15 inches by 6 inches with decoration hidden in a hole on top of a hill—took them" (1875:18-82).

European colonization of the desert areas really began with the first influx of workers building the north-south telegraph line in the 1870s and the slow construction of the railway from Port Augusta northward to Alice Springs. Curious about this activity and attracted to new commodities (among them tobacco), Aborigines repeatedly visited the settlements which sprang up around the telegraph depots such as Barrow Creek, established in 1872. Read and Japaljarri suggest that they did not intend to stay, but other factors—drought, labor demands, and violence—intervened (1978:141). Conflict arose when European-introduced cattle wandered into the hills in search of water, despoiled and depleted the Aboriginal hunting grounds, and were speared by Aborigines. A disput over the distribution of rations at Barrow Creek station also led to an Aboriginal attack in which two Europeans and an unknown number of Aborigines were killed; govment-sponsored punitive parties in turn killed a much larger number of Aborigines. Public opinion expressed in February 1874 by the *Adelaide Advertiser* insisted, "Retribution, to be useful, must be sharp, swift and severe." This kind of action and sentiment persisted well into the twentieth century.

From about 1900 onward widespread mining activity has also disrupted Aboriginal lives and despoiled their lands. Gold rushes to the Tanami area in 1910, to the Granites in 1932, and wolfram finds at Hatches Creek in 1913, drew Aboriginal people into areas of new settlement and provided some employment. In the report of the Northern Territory Chief Warden and Surveyor, for the year ended June 30th 1918, it was stated that at the time of inspection 23 of the 40 Hatches Creek employees were Aboriginal—an exceptionally high employment rate for Aborigines now or then in the mining industry (see Hagen and Rowell). Payment, as in the pastoral industry, was not in cash, but in food and clothing rations. Such payment, despite government legislation and the granting of equal pastoral wages in 1965, continues at certain stations even today. Aborigines are still underemployed and underpaid in central Australia: mining is increasingly a threat to their lands.

The second wave of pastoral expansion in the 1920s again brought violence well remembered by many living central Australian Aborigines today. The "Coniston Massacres" of 1928, for example, are a well-documented, though certainly not an isolated, example of frontier violence in the twentieth century (see Harting 1960; Peterson et al. 1978). In 1917 Coniston station (ranch) was established. By 1924 a severe drought had set in which forced Aborigines and cattle into competition for the same water resources. Two local Europeans were killed by Aborigines in 1928. Official reports of the punitive expeditions acknowledge that 31 Aborigines were killed; Aboriginal oral tradition suggests as many as 200 deaths. My own geneological research supports the higher claim.

As pastoral expansion alienated the best-watered lands and violence forced Aborigines to retreat to the safety of marginal areas and institutions, survivors came to depend more and more upon rations obtained from missions and government depots. As a consequence of the 1940s assimilation policy, many Aborigines were forcefully removed to new centralized settlements, often far from their own territory.

My older Aboriginal friends, who spent their childhood in the arid center, the last frontier for Europeans, have experienced in a lifetime the effects of colonization which elsewhere were spead over two centuries. Victims of forced resettlement, missionary repression, overt settler violence, and the more insidious social violence of government policies (see Rowley 1970:201-21, 255-87), these desert people still preserve a distinctively Aboriginal lifestyle. Policy reforms and some limited recognition of land rights during the 1970s has had minimal effect on Central Aborigines as a whole. But some groups have achieved a degree of self determination: by leaving the artificial conditions of settlements, they have now begun to establish "homeland centers" in their traditional country where they can pursue a more congenial lifestyle (see Bell 1978a).

INTRODUCTION

The dual and conflicting images of women cherished by European members of frontier culture—the honoured mother and ridiculed whore—have, I suggest, created an illusion for Aboriginal women.[1] Many have grasped the opportunity to make new and superficially powerful choices based on their perception of (and tuition in) this colonial culture, but they have not achieved the hoped for increase in status. The indigenous culture encouraged women to perceive themselves as autonomous beings: their autonomy is a myth in the colonial situation, but this view has sustained women in a rapidly changing world. In fact, the male bias of that world has constrained and restricted Aboriginal women, limiting them to the dishonored image. All subjugated people have limited opportunities but Aboriginal women have been doubly disenfranchised by being deprived of a satisfying self-perception of their role as mothers and providers.

One "community" is discussed here in detail while a comparative comment is offered for a second. The first, Warrabri, is a government-controlled settlement, lying between the main towns of Alice Springs and Tennant Creek in the Northern Territory. Some 350 Warlpiri[2] and Warramunga people (whose country lies to the west of Warrabri) and 300 Aljawarra and Kaititj people (whose country includes Warrabri and land to the east) must coexist at Warrabri. Europeans provide education, health, law and administrative services. Tensions in this mixed community encourage violence and drunken brawls among Aborigines: hostility between Aborigines and Europeans is more insidious because it has no overt release.

Warrabri was established in the 1950s to accomodate the Warlpiri and Warramunga transferred from Phillip Creek Baptist mission where the water supply had proved inadequate. Kaititj and Aljawarra also drifted into Warrabri from nearby cattle stations. In neither case was the Aboriginal population properly consulted as to the location of or move to the settlement. Warrabri Warlpiri were simply trucked into country with which they had few dreaming ties (see below).

The second community, the Yalata Aboriginal Reserve is located in the far west of South Australia. Yalata is a Lutheran mission where 400 Aborigines speaking western-desert dialects (Pitjantjarra, Jangkuntjarra, and Andagaringa) now live. Missionaries and employees of the government's federal and state departments of health, education, and welfare provide a buffer between the Aboriginal population and the wider Australian society.

Both Yalata and Warrabri residents have suffered from the restrictions supervisors attempted to place on parent-child relations and ritual activity. Employment opportunities were extremely limited; settlement maintenance tasks and seasonal jobs in the cattle industry were not sufficient for the growing populations on these settlements. Instead of training and real work, officials only provided rations and "welfare" payments and, more recently, standard pensions and benefits. For both the Yalata and Warrabri people the expansion of the European pastoral industry meant the disruption of their hunting-and-gathering mode of subsistence, displacement from land, and some loss of identity.

In attempting to analyze the impact of colonization on Aboriginal women at Warrabri, I have focused on marriage in the hope of achieving some time depth. My analysis utilizes, in addition to my own fieldwork, statistics collated by Meggitt (1965). A time depth of fifty years is provided by the recollections of Warlpiri and Yalata women. Marriage, I argue, has always been a matter for political decision making, whether in relations between husband and wife or involving many others, in such areas as the staging of rituals. Colonization has provided new political arenas which may be exploited, with varying degrees of success, by men and women alike. But in the male-dominated European frontier society Aboriginal women have fared less well than their menfolk. Alterations in marriage patterns indicate some of the subtleties and complexities of these imposed changes.

Ethnographic Comment

This brief sketch of the desert culture of the Warlpiri is merely an outline: fuller descriptions are provided by Meggitt (1962) and Munn (1973), although, as will become evident in my analysis, I disagree with these ethnographers about the role of women in marriage arrangements. All aspects of Warlpiri society, from the gathering of vegetable food to high ritual activities, derive form and meaning from the sustaining and complex notion of the dreaming (*jukurpa*)—now sometimes translated as "power" by literate Aborigines—which is both the creative era when the world was given form, shape and meaning and the power of people today to preserve harmonious relationships as established in terms of the law in the dreamtime past. While the ancestral heroes and heroines traveled through the country, they created different physical features such as waterholes, rock formations, and the flora and fauna. Part of their spiritual power still resides in these sites, tracks, and country in general.

"Country" is a critical dimension of identity for desert Aborigines, male and female, all of whom count themselves as the patrilineal descendants of particular ancestors. Living Aboriginal men and women hold a sacred trust to maintain the life force of the country to which they belong by virtue of dreaming associations which are reckoned through both the matriline and patriline. For particular dreamings, small, shallow exogamous patrilines, the owners (*kirda*), stage rituals which celebrate their place in the world of nature. In so doing the *kirda* call upon the children of the senior women of the patriline, the *kurdungurla*, to assist. These are the workers who assist the owners. In turn owners will be workers at the ceremonies of the dreamings owned by those whom they call workers. This reciprocity pervades ritual organization and enactment. Both men and women hold rituals based on their dreaming affiliation. Sisters are considered owners throughout their lives, jointly with their brothers, fathers, and father's sisters, and are all known by the term *kirda*. This fact is hazily reported (and understood) in male-orientated ethnography (see Meggitt 1962:203; Roheim 1933).

Men and women stage independent ceremonies and are also present on occasions in a secondary capacity at each other's rituals. Those men's rituals at initiation which are closed to women and children serve to instruct the teenage male initiate in the way of the dreaming of his father i.e., of his patrilodge. Women's ceremonies, closed to men and children, ritualize life crises, but other rituals, segments of which are seen by men and children, celebrate ties to the land through the patriline. The significance and themes of these latter ceremonies (*yawalyu*) have been inadequately understood by male anthropologists who have focused on men's spectacular rituals and dismissed women's rituals as of concern to women only (for central Australia, see Roheim 1933; Munn 1973).

The sex-segregated world of ritual is both a reflection and rationalization of the division of labor in the economic sphere where women reliably gather vegetable food and hunt small game, and men somewhat more unreliably hunt larger game and gather vegetable food. Seminomadic in their hunter-gatherer mode of subsistence—until as late as the 1930s and 1940s for some—desert people have experienced dramatic upheavals in the shift to a sedentary lifestyle. The underlying complementarity of the sexual division of labor has been fundamentally affected by the incorporation of Aborigines into the cash economy in settlements, and women, whose right to an independent economic base is not generally recognized by governments, have fared rather more badly than their menfolk in the economic upheaval.[3]

One focus of women's solidarity and autonomy, in the past as now, is the single women's camp, the *jilimi*. Here live widows who have chosen not to remarry, the estranged wives of violent husbands, women who are ill or visiting from another country, and all their dependent children. In fact, any woman who wishes to live free of the conflicts of heterosexual society may seek refuge in the *jilimi*. Married women who are living with their husbands congregate in the *jilimi* during the day to talk and plan visits, family affairs, and ritual matters. The *jilimi* is taboo to all men, who often must travel long, circuitous routes to avoid passing nearby.

Initiation rituals and marriage arrangements are closely intertwined. The indigenous marriage model ordained that the circumcisor, chosen by the boy's family, promised to find a wife, either his own daughter or a girl in the same kinship status, for the initiate (see Peterson 1969). The circumcisor's wife became the mother-in-law for whom the boy must provide meat and other goods for the rest of their lives. Girls were thus betrothed in infancy or before birth and grew up knowing the identity of their future husband, to whom they would go after puberty. The most preferred marriage was with a mother's mother's brother's daughter's daughter or son ("mmbdd/s"). The next preferred marriage was with the "father's sister's daughter or son" ("fzd/s"). All other marriages were, in the past, considered incorrect; polygyny was an ideal, but is now realized less frequently for eastern Warlpiri.

There are no political leaders as such in desert society, although there are ritual bosses for individual dreamings. As men and women grew older and more learned in the law, they became more important in decision making. Desert society was a gerontocracy in the wider sense of the word, as government by old people. The kinship system, considered in conjunction with the exogamous patri- and matrimoieties and the endogamous generation moieties, allocates to each person an unique, though not necessarily equal, place within the society. The subsection system provides a shorthand version of this complex of relationships and statuses but each specific instance of a person's responsibility is reckoned through specific kinship links (see Meggitt 1962).

Women and Colonization
The influx of European settlers, primarily men, into the desert areas in the 1870s generated three-way conflicts, among Aboriginal men and women and the settlers which were played out against the backdrop of colonial violence. *The Adelaide Advertiser* suggests that one of the stated possible causes of the Aboriginal attack on the Frew River Station in 1891 was the 8 to 10 Aboriginal women who were camped there (July 11, 1891). Cohabitation with local women was said to have been a contributory cause for the killing of Brooks, the first European casualty of the Coniston tragedy. Often, European males who sought sexual access to Aboriginal women gave only a small gift to the woman and a larger one to her male kin. Women today will often attribute past instances of frontier violence to the differential perceptions of Aboriginal and European men concerning their respective rights in Aboriginal women. European males, in paying for sexual services, believed they controlled the woman. Aboriginal men were roused to violence when their women didn't return.

The primary reason women gave for going in the past to their European partners was economic although, more recently, women argue that European husbands are desirable because they are less prone to violence and alcohol.[4] Meggitt's account of the Warlpiri people mentions women who had cohabitated with miners in the 1920s (1962:25). A number of aged Warrabri and Yalata women said in the 1970s that in their youth they bore children to European men. Most such women had then lived near railway towns, the telegraph stations, or on cattle stations. Some unions with Europeans, based on genuine affection, were long enduring. However, the earliest memories of the elderly Warrabri women emphasize that a specific motivation was to obtain European foods for themselves and useful tools and other articles (particularly tobacco) for their communities.

Referring to European men and Aboriginal women on the remote cattle stations in South Australia and the Northern Territory early this century, R. and C. Berndt (1964:511-512) wrote as follows:

> In a very few instances liaisions of this kind may have had their source in genuine affection between the man and the woman concerned. More often they were asymmetrical arrangements, which flourished as they did because the Aborigines' demand for material

>goods and introduced foods, including beef, outstripped their ability to satisfy it by other means, such as employment: and because their traditional permissiveness in regard to some extra-marital relations provided a loophole which could be expanded without too much difficulty. What it amounted to in many cases was a triangular situation in which a young woman lived almost simultaneously with her Aboriginal husband and with a white man, who had in practice more rights over her than her husband did because of the tremendous discrepancy in status between the two men.... Aboriginal women, in this situation, had more avenues open to them than their menfolk did to enhance their status: not merely through straight-forward employment but also through sexual association and even, occasionally, marriage with members of the dominant population (Berndt and Berndt 1964:511-12).

A liaison with a European man occasionally continued after the European bride arrived to join the owner or manager, a situation which has given rise to some well known novels and short stories, the most popular being *Coonardo* by Katherine Susannah Prichard.

For Aboriginal women these domestic experiences obviously provided access to areas of European society which were not available to their menfolk. It is not unusual to find that one's older informants have had such sexual liaisons with European men. Consequently, they may have a good command of English and an appreciation of aspects of European life, but what they learned was scarcely of a middle class lifestyle and was nearly always restricted to domestic matters.

Naturally, some of the knowledge acquired about the way in which marriages are arranged and maintained in English-speaking society was passed on to other women. More recently, such knowledge has been reinforced when Aborigines have the opportunity to view films (mostly American) depicting the Western concept of romantic love as the basic reason for marriage. This concept was alien.

CENTRAL AUSTRALIA: MARRIAGE MODELS

Since Meggitt's (1962; 1965) pioneering analyses of the social structure and marriage patterns of the Warlpiri of Central Australia, these marriage arrangements have been subject to reinterpretation by Long (1970) and Peterson (1969) and to a structural-symbolic analysis by Munn (1973). A persistent preoccupation in these works is the manner in which oppositions generated by the social separation of the sexes, by secular and sacred concerns, and by matri- versus patrilineal principles are structured, balanced, and represented. While recognizing the political nature of marriage and ritual alliances, these analysts have underplayed or ignored the relations of husband and wife and male and female as power struggles in which either party may attempt to exploit, manipulate, or advance his or her position. The emphasis in the anthropological literature on male control of women and the dominance of older men (as expressed in promised marriages and polygyny) has obscured the power exercised and sought by women as wives, co-wives, widows, and mothers of initiates.

Munn (1973) has demonstrated, through her presentation of Warlpiri graphic representations, how the husband/wife relationship is the pivot of many exchanges but located men at the apex of the symbolic order. In her analysis it was the men who held the keys to cosmic order (:40). In examining the mesh between beliefs about procreation and social structure, Peterson suggested that marriage arrangements were one working out of the tension between agnatic (father's) kin and uterine (mother's) kin; he concluded that the matrilines organize the secular concerns, such as marriage, and the patrilines, religious ritual (1969:27).

Although fuller than that available for any other Aboriginal groups, the literature on Warlpiri marriage suffers from a male bias which has short-circuited real analysis of women's attitudes to and perception of marriage (see also Goodale 1971:53; Hamilton 1970:20). Analyses from a male point of view cast women as the major cause of fights, as economic assets, as commodities, or as the pivot of domestic exchanges, but not as politicians in their own right (see Van Baal 1970:289). Here I suggest that if we examine marriage from an Aboriginal woman's point of view, we find her experience to be one of evolving serial monogamy. As women enter marriages subsequent to their first arranged .narriage, they exercise a greater degree of choice. Women are thus entering into different marriages, for different reasons, at different times in their lives. From a Warlpiri woman's point of view, we also find the mother whose son is going through initiation to be maneuvering in a manner similar to that of the men during their lodge ceremonies associated with initiation. Both women and men attempt to establish relationships which are to their advantage. Women *did* have room to maneuver and they *were* aware of this potential in political terms. This awareness has persisted in a situation where women may avail themselves of new allies and pursue new strategies in the vastly changed reality of mid-twentieth-century Warlpiri politics. This does not, however, mean that the overall status of Aboriginal women has improved, since the context is now the colonial society of the settlements. In fact, woman's status has been severely undermined.

WARLPIRI: THE COLONIAL ILLUSION

For the eastern Warlpiri,[5] the real impact of colonization followed quickly behind the telegraph lines. Ration depots, then missions, and finally a government settlement were established to accommodate the dispossessed and dislocated eastern Warlpiri and Warramunga. Frontier culture was more intrusive and devastating for the eastern Warlpiri than for the Yuendumu people of Munn's research and Hooker Creek people described by Meggitt. (It was earlier and closer to a mining town which boasted "booze and the boys"). Nonetheless, the critical difference between the eastern (Warrabri) and the western (Yuendumu and Hooker Creek) Warlpiri forced settlements was the distance the former were from their traditional dreaming sites. Limited access undermined the strength of identity and the intensity of ritual life. The impact of this difference is more apparent now than 20 years ago. In 1976-78 Warlpiri boys were still initiated at Warrabri, women's rituals were alive and well. In comparison with the western Warlpiri, however, the eastern people are not as defiant in their belief in the superiority of their culture and language; they are generally less resilient and less likely to oppose the wishes of European supervisors. Warrabri men and women still visit their traditional country but not as frequently as in the past or as the western Warlpiri. Peterson's (1969) analysis of marriage indicates cult-lodge affiliation amongst western Warlpiri at Yuendumu is a major organizational factor in initiation. For the eastern Warlpiri, who are far from the sites which provide for continuity and renewal of lodge rituals, the correct staging of ceremonies is extremely difficult and sometimes impossible. Therefore, correct marriage arrangements are also more difficult to contract in such circumstances. It is not surprising that Warrabri Warlpiri marriage patterns differ markedly from western Warlpiri as Meggitt (1965) has shown.

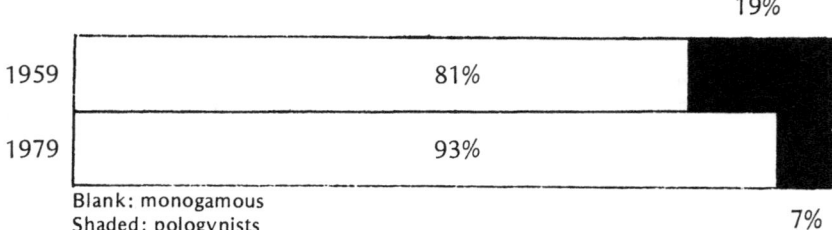

FIGURE 10.1
Warrabri Warlpiri: Men's Marriage Patterns; 1959—Meggitt (1965: 149); 1979—Author's Field Data.

Dramatic changes are apparent in the 20 years between Meggitt's fieldwork and mine. Warrabri, a new settlement during his stay in Warlpiri country, is now 24 years old and still desperately divided by complex factions. Land rights have become a reality for some western Warlpiri but the eastern Warlpiri of Warrabri remain far from their traditional country. Alcohol has become a major problem on all Warlpiri settlements. Bilingual education thrives at Yuendumu and Hooker Creek, and Aboriginal Councils, which were established in the 1950s, are now playing an increasing role in the running of their own affairs.

In the face of upheaval, dislocation and disruption, Warrabri Warlpiri have clung to critical aspects of their law as established and maintained since the dreamtime. On the one hand, they recognize that the changes of the last 50 years have irrevocably damaged their law but, on the other, they fiercely insist that their law has not changed. Figure 10.1 indicates that the trend to monogamy which Meggitt (1965) noted for 1959 has become more pronounced in 20 years. The ideal of polygyny may well be under threat but the rule of correct marriage is still, Warrabri Warlpiri insist, being adhered to. By manipulating their own category of what constitutes a correct marriage Warrabri Walpiri have, it seems, created their own illusion of strength and persistence of their law. The 1959 total of preferred (mmbdd/s) and alternate (fzd/s) marriages does not differ significantly from the 1979 total, as Figure 10.2 illustrates. The sharp distinction, in 1959, between preferred and alternate marriage is in 1979, less sharply drawn so that either marriage is now considered equally correct.

This willingness to stretch the scope of correctness is an ongoing process. It is possible that in the future the category of correct marriage may include marriages other than the preferred and alternate forms. In 1979 Warrabri Warlpiri women identified a third choice marriage with a mother's mother's brother (mmb) as acceptable although not preferable, as is the mmbdd/s or fzd/s. Perhaps in another 20 years this marriage will be absorbed into the correct category, and the Warrabri Warlpiri claim that they marry "straight" can be sustained.

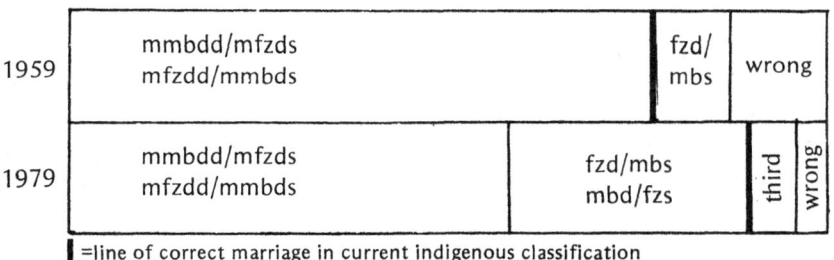

| =line of correct marriage in current indigenous classification

FIGURE 10.2

Warrabri Warlpiri Marriage Choices, 1959—Meggitt (1965: 165); 1979—Author's Field Notes.

The colonial situation has made available new political forums which have been elaborated and exploited by Aboriginal men in distinctive ways. Men have derived some advantage from the male chauvinist bias of frontier culture. They can rely on police, who are poorly trained to cope with the special problems of Aboriginal settlements, not to interfere in "domestic" brawls for all the same reasons that make police in our society loath to interfere. On settlements where drunken brawls involve Aboriginal women as victims, this "blind eye" of the police is worrying for women. They often wish men to be taken into protective custody but the police are reluctant to do so. Although the majority are explicitly racist, police are also men on the frontier and, on occasions, survival strategies involve throwing in one's lot with Aboriginal men. Police rely on their Aboriginal trackers and guides in uncharted and poorly watered country. In this shared world, minimal though it is, Aboriginal and European men may share jokes and women. Some black/white liaisons endure—most are violent. For many Europeans, Aboriginal women are barely distinguishable above the flora and fauna. The services of Aboriginal women can thus become the subject of ribald joking for Aboriginal and European male alike.

The government does not look favorably upon social security claims from women for unemployment benefits, nor does it grant widows and supporting mothers' pensions to second wives without tedious and prying investigations. From police and the government Aboriginal women can expect little assistance in preserving their once dignified and independent lifestyle. In the past their economic contribution was the basis of respect but, now that women must rely on police and governments to assist them, their independence is diminished. In place of respect they now face ridicule and rejection from European officials.

The perception of women, both European and Aboriginal, solely as sex objects is encouraged by frontier culture (where men outnumber women). Women are treated as either workhorses or whores and are occasionally cherished as wives who must be protected from the brutality of frontier culture. (This last option has not been available to Aboriginal women). In some respects Warlpiri women do appear to have been advantaged by the cessation of such practices as infant betrothal. Missionaries at Phillip Creek in the 1940s forbade these practices and offered sanctuary to any girl who wished to defy the demands of an older husband. Unfortunately, when they left the closed world of the mission's segregated dormitories and entered into the wider world, they found that they were ill-prepared for the demands of men. There was little work to support them in the style that the missionaries had led them to believe was the lot of young ladies. Rather than entering a marriage for which they were gently prepared from infancy, the mission virgins were abruptly thrown into marriage with angry husbands who, having been denied their rights through mission intervention in their lives, often vented their anger on them.

WOMEN'S MARITAL CAREERS

To document marriage from a woman's point of view and to indicate the potential for women's politicking in marriage arrangements, I shall begin by tracing through the marital careers of three women and then discuss the marital choices which a woman may make.

I have suggested that we see marriage for women in terms of serial monogamy. Women's marital careers then fall into different periods. In the first she is the promised wife but not abused; she learns the role of a wife. In co-wifeship she has first a role model in an older women and later, as the older wife, she has support in the rearing of her own children. In second and subsequent marriages, she expresses her desires and preferences more clearly as she achieves greater maturity and status in the community. In her final marriage or retreat to the *jilimi*, she achieves companionship, economic security and ritual status (and if she seeks it sexual satisfaction).

Promise and Choice for a Nupurrurla
"Molly" Nupurrurla[7] is the eldest daughter of an important Warlpiri man who has spent many hours explaining to her the intricacies of the dreaming that he follows and that as an adult she could also celebrate. Her mother and her mother's mother were also ritually important women who instructed her in the ways of their dreamings. Now in her mid-forties Molly is a widely recognized ritual expert. She is intelligent, quick to learn, witty, and well traveled. When I first met her in 1976, she was living in the *jilimi* close to her parents' camp and was pursued by every eligible man in Warrabri. Now she is married to a man her own age and living away from Warrabri.

Her first marriage, which was to a much older man, was, according to her, a "promised" union. As it is improper to name the recently dead, any reference to her mother or late husband would have caused her pain so I did not seek details of its arrangement. As this spouse belonged to a patrilodge with which her father and not her mother is associated, one may speculate that the father's line organized that marriage. Molly was junior co-wife with a woman some 15 years her senior. After the husband's death the widows continued to be close friends and today enjoy many shared jokes and ongoing friendships with various men. As Molly was still young when widowed, she was again married to a man some years her senior, related as a distant, classificatory "brother" to her late husband. She says this was a happy marriage and describes both husbands as "good." Although she remained childless, Molly sponsored several of her dead sister's sons through initiation and cared for the children of her brother's eldest daughter. In this marriage she opposed a junior co-wife and her husband respected her wishes.

When this second husband died several years ago, she completed her strict mourning and then retreated to the *jilimi*, where she was when I met her. Freed of the constant worry of child care, Molly had devoted much time to improving her ritual knowledge and performance. By the time she entered her period of mourning she was already very knowledgeable. Her residence in the *jilimi* gave her further opportunities to increase her ritual status because all women's ritual activity is initiated from the *jilimi*.

Molly's dead husband's brother began pressuring her to marry him. He invited her to stay with him and visibly glowed when with her. She visited but objected to ever becoming a co-wife. Molly had no dislike for the woman who was his wife but wanted to avoid the jealous fights which could occur, as she was still being actively pursued by several Warrabri men. She avoided permanent liaisons with these men by claiming she was not yet through her mourning but enjoyed the freedom she had in various affairs.

Eventually, Molly's deceased husband's brother issued an ultimatum. She was to stop her flirting and marry him or he would never allow her to be released from the final stages of mourning. (During the final period of mourning a woman may have affairs but she may not enter into a permanent union until the brothers of the dead husband have performed certain rituals which leave her free to remarry.) She countered his threats by developing and sustaining an affair with a man who lived hundreds of miles from the brothers. Her family and friends were distressed and shook their heads, and her new husband was afraid to meet her parents. In drunken outbursts he would beat her, but her parents would not intervene as long as the couple stayed away from Warrabri. The women of the *jilimi* sent messages to say she was welcome to return but, although she did, it was only for a short time.

After about nine months the marriage settled into a much easier relationship. He no longer beat her and she was free to travel to visit her parents. The couple now plan to move her relatives closer to their new camp, miles from Warrabri. The one relative who was delighted from the very beginning was the mother of the man. She now had a daughter-in-law with whom she could talk and in whom she could find support. In ritual performance they cooperate as *kirda* (owner) and *kurdungurla* (worker).

Promise and Love for a Nungarrayi

"Joan" Nungarrayi is the daughter of ritually important parents. She is a woman in her late twenties with three children and a playboy husband in his late thirties. Like many women of her age, Joan is literate; her favorite reading is the "Dear Abby" column in women's magazines which she buys or borrows whenever possible. Occasionally, she pondered the difference between the marriages discussed by European women and her own—she has much to consider. In the past she has spent long periods separated from her husband who is a "second choice" spouse in that he is her mother's brother's son. This is her first marriage and considered correct by Warrabri Warlpiri. Most of the jealous fights between her and her husband concern her sweetheart from her school days. She explained to me she would have married him but she couldn't wait, so she married a Jupurrula as her father wished.

Consequently, her children have dual subsection affiliation—one from her and one from her husband.[8] This causes many tensions as the father wants the children reared near his family and Joan wants to stay near the protection of hers. When asked about the fights in her marriage she explained it was the same for all other marriages like hers because in a really important dispute settlement (she had recently been through one where she was severely beaten for adultery), she could not appeal to her mother's brothers to help as they were also her fathers-in-law. Joan, however, sometimes jokes that at least she has the support of other women, unlike the women she reads about in her women's magazines.

When her husband recently left Warrabri to take up his younger promised wife at his mother's camp 100 miles from Warrabri, Joan moved into *jilimi* and has remained there ever since. In her opinion, her husband's violence towards her would increase if she became a co-wife; she would be first wife, but with a girl she hardly knows and with whom she has no close ties. Her husband no longer beats her for suspected infidelities with her sweetheart; he has, however, attempted to take the children with him, but she protested and won. One day perhaps, she says, she will marry her sweetheart.

Promise, Choice and the Single Life for a Nakamarra

"Sue" Nakamarra is the ritual boss of important Warlpiri dreamings. Now in her sixties she lives in the largest and busiest of the Warlpiri *jilimi*. She maintains a lively interest in the opposite sex but prefers to remain single. She has adult sons and daughters who are married with adult children. Her grandchildren and great-grandchildren are frequently in her care, and she often camps near her eldest daughter's family.

In her marital career she had been the promised wife of a man who has now been dead some twenty years, the wife of a man closer to her own age, and sweetheart to many. She remembers the first time she wore clothes and the problems of prostitution, half-caste children (Rowley 1970:341—64), and brutality for Aboriginal women in mining towns like Tennant Creek. Much of her ribald joking now employs expressive phrases and gestures learnt from miners who teased, taunted, and propositioned her.

In her youth she sustained wounds, which crippled her for months at a time, as punishment from her husband for her open affairs with young Aboriginal men. During her first marriage, spoken of as a "good" marriage, she became senior wife with two close "sisters" as co-wives. As the daughters of two patrilineal parallel cousins, these women shared the same dreamings and many experiences in the past as now. Their co-wifeship was, like the life in the *jilimi*, one of cooperation. Their bond as "sisters" preceded and has outlived the marriage and husband.

Having raised her children, lost her first husband, engaged in several affairs, and lived on the fringes of Tennant Creek, Sue now lives in the Warrabri Warlpirl *jilimi* and devotes herself to ritual concerns, reminiscence, and speculation about future love affairs.

A Girl's First Marriage: The Promise

This marriage has been the subject of most anthropological attention; given the interest in analyzing the institutions of polygyny and gerontocracy, this is not surprising. It is the marriage in which male dominance appears to be most starkly drawn. It is the marriage most clearly hedged in with ritualized and verbalized constraints. Certainly, for male anthropologist and informant alike, it is a more spectacular marriage than the later, more casual marriages of a woman to a man close to her own age. As Reay (1963:24) argues, arranged marriages did account for the majority of first marriages for girls, but not for men who were more likely to marry older widows before they received their young promised wives.

Drawing on western Warlpiri ethnography, Peterson (1969) has offered a convincing argument that it is the boy's matriline which organizes his marriage choices. He does not, however, discuss what women are doing and thinking while men are engaged in their ritual politicking and arranging. Further, while it is clear that the young girl, often promised in infancy or before birth, has little choice in arranging her first marriage, this does not mean that she is abandoned to a lecherous old man. As Rohrlich-Leavitt et al. argue, this idea reflects incestuous fantasy among Western men rather than any actual state of affairs in Aboriginal society (1975:116).

Older men recognize that younger women are not necessarily going to be satisfied with an aging and perhaps impotent man. A degree of licence is in the interests of the old man as well as the girl; he does not want to have his inadequacies become the subject of public comments, and young wives do threaten to embarrass men in this way. As long as she is discreet and does not neglect her duties, he will tolerate her affairs. Nonetheless, he seeks her affection and loyalty as well as duty, for many of the men's love songs explicitly encourage a young promised wife to love her husband.

Both Goodale (1971) and Kaberry (1939) depict marriage for a young girl as an extension of her caring family environment. The expression they quoted most frequently, which describes the relationship of young wife to an older husband is "He took me like a daughter. He grew me up." From her co-wife the young girl learned the economic and social responsibilities of being a wife. If anything she is more likely to be exploited by the older wife, who may see her as an economic asset, rather than by the older husband. Reay cites an example of a Borroloola woman in 1960 asking for a co-wife to assist in the rearing of children (1963:25).

If a young wife felt in any way abused or maltreated she could appeal to her maternal uncles for assistance. The arrangement that placed her in the marriage also entailed a series of checks and balances and obligations on the husband as well as rights in his wife's services. This was made plain to me when I read to several groups of women an article which had appeared in the *National Times* (Davenport 1977). It contained lurid stories of abuse of younger girls by older men and was designed to sensationalize and trivialize Aboriginal culture. The older women objected on several counts. They asked for the writer's credentials and promptly dismissed him as an ignorant white man. Then they exploded in rage and indignation: "We are not things. Who told him this? We have rights. We have feelings. No man can use us like that. We have fathers and brothers and uncles to protect us. No man can use us like that." But what about the old days? "Even better then. Our mother could help us and there were no police to laugh at us for what we did."[9]

It is my impression that European authorities at Warrabri have sometimes unwittingly aided and abetted Aboriginal men in the ritual politicking and pursuit of traditional punishments, but rarely allowed women the same assistance. For instance, local courts, at their discretion, now hand over certain offenders to male elders for "tribal" punishment. Such distribution of power and authority to older men in a society is intelligible to our court system but I doubt that a judge would turn a rapist over to the "mothers" and "aunts" of the victim. An accused rapist now is normally removed from the community as soon as possible on the grounds that if he remains there will be violence. (Police will not use protective custody at the request of a woman to prevent possible violence.) Older women say that women would indeed take violent action. They believe European men have made it easier for young Aboriginal men to escape from a rape accusation. Rape is everywhere a less serious offense to men than it is to women, and Aboriginal women recognize this bias. Women are further disadvantaged in that they are less familiar with the court situation and police procedure than are men—many of whom have worked as trackers, informants, and interpreters—and are also more likely to be tried for various offenses.

But the web of rights and relationships which surround a girl's first marriage are not only the result of arrangements made by male members of the boy's matri- or patriline, but are also the result of female politicking. During the public segments of male initiation in the week prior to circumcision, the women participate in two night-long dances separated by three or four nights of shorter performances. Afterwards, the men stage the spectacular "night of the long poles" performance, when the circumcisor (a father-in-law whose wife is a member of a particular matriline) is publicly announced. Although close kin of the initiate may suggest names of several potential circumcisors, no woman will claim to know his identity until the ritualized public statement is made by the men. On this occasion a number of women playing key roles in the initiation ritual are formally placed in various relationships to the initiate and members of his marriage lines. The actual mothers-in-law and the sisters of the initiate are from then on placed in strict avoidance relationships to the initiate which are over and above that of classificatory mother-in-law and a man's younger sisters.

The ramifications for women of the choice of circumcisor are thus extensive. But what do they really know of the male decision and can they influence it at all? The women have danced throughout the night before the men's public statement. In the early hours of the morning, the initiate's mother, who has during previous nights danced with and cared for the firestick, passes it to the woman she wishes to have as mother of her daughter-in-law. This, the women insist, is a decision taken independently of the men. The gesture occurs while the men's backs are turned to the women's (and, incidentally, behind where a male-oriented anthropologist must sit in order to observe closely the "really important" behavior of the men). It is a gesture made first by women to women and then communicated to the men as the women line up in the matrilines of the mother and mother-in-law, dance towards each other in mock attack, and then join forces and dance along beside the men.

Women emphasize the importance of being present to bear witness on this occasion; according to my informants, all sisters of the person to whom the stick is passed are, in fact, implicated in the nomination. Unless one is present at the passing of the stick, one cannot be nominated as a mother-in-law: one woman told me of how she slept through the passing of the stick and her sister received the stick; another related that she had stayed home to mind a child and thus missed her chance. All impressed upon me the need to be present and awake. This is partly because the choice, like that of the circumcisor, is not absolutely known until the public statement. Women who had been unable to attend a full night's dancing would often ask me who took the stick, and many conversations involved speculation as to who might receive it. Men would comment to me that I was a big help—by attending and staying awake I was able to tell others.

Before the boys can be "captured" and initiation begun, actual mothers are consulted by the maternal uncles of the boy. I have seen women, alleging that their sons are immature, dismiss the men's suggestion that they be initiated: this objection has been accepted. However, as the readiness of her son for initiation symbolizes a mother's ability to rear children to adulthood, and since it is to her economic advantage and a prestigious status to have initiated sons, no woman is likely to refuse for more than a season or two; in fact, no one could remember a case. Once mothers have agreed to proceed, the relevant males assume responsibility for much of the ritual. The women prepare food for these assemblies but also stage their own rituals independently of the men. These are basically *yawalyu* rituals (noted earlier) but focus on the country of the mother and the women visitors present during the period of public dancing prior to circumcision. The mothers maneuver to have present those women with whom they wish to establish exchange relationships and women with whom they already have ritual relations.

Thus, while men are inviting certain ritual partners to be present for the initiation of their sons, their wives are also selecting and inviting those women they wish to attend. Mothers of initiates invite women of their own patrilodge dreaming (i.e., sisters and father's sisters). These women are *kirda* or joint owners of the mother's clan dreaming. "Daughters" of the *kirda* are also included because they act as *kurdungurla* (workers) for these rituals. The *kurdungurla* are, however, not only related as "daughters" of the *kirda*: they may also be potential "mothers" of the girl who will become daughter-in-law of the mother of the initiate. The anthropological emphasis on men and their mothers-in-law has obscured the women's view: in reality, one does not lose a son but rather gains a daughter. The mother of the initiate potentially has a ritual relationship with the woman who will be mother of her son's bride. The relationship between the mother of the boy and the mother of his future wife is *wankili* (a reciprocal). It is a close relationship based on friendship which may precede the marriage of their children. Women sometimes translated the kin term to me as 'mate'. (Figure 10.3).

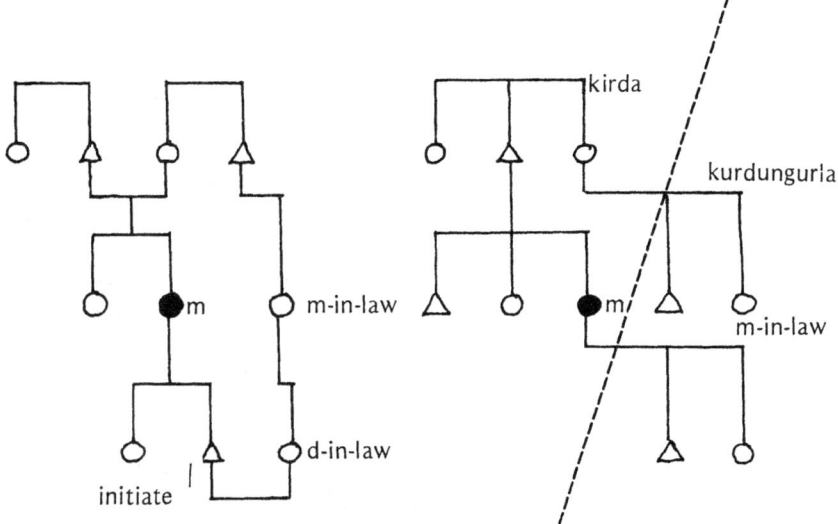

FIGURE 10.3
Kin and Ritual Relations at Initiation for Women
(constructed by the author)

Warlpiri women seem prepared to withhold permission (or perhaps passively resist an unwanted choice by staying away or falling asleep) in order to establish a favorable relationship with a specific woman they would like to see as mother-in-law to their son *or* daughter. Not only are women politicking with their son's initiation, they are also engaged in establishing an exchange of daughter-in-law for son-in-law with a woman they now in English call "mate." A dutiful daughter-in-law is a great comfort and asset, and a good son-in-law provides security in old age. Women have much to gain through the relationships established during initiation rituals.

As women make public their nomination of mother-in-law before the men announce their choice of circumcisor cum father-in-law, the possibility arises that women may influence the men's choice (or at least perceive it as a result of their influence). Women claim that they make their choice independently but, of course, the mother and father of the initiate are also husband and wife who may have domestic discussions as may the mother and her brother, being full siblings. Ideally, women's choice of mother-in-law and the men's of father-in-law should be an actual married couple with suitable offspring, but this is not always the case. There is also the possibility that women may make a choice perceptibly different from that of the men, and the system allows them to publicize this before the men have stated their preference. If, indeed, women did make a choice substantially different from that of the men, the boy would, in theory, have two promised wives—one who was the "daughter" of the mother-in-law and one the "daughter" of the father-in-law, the circumcisor. In rapidly changing situations, such as that at Warrabri, this possibility would allow a boy, as he grew older, room to maneuver. He could marry either girl and still contract a correct marriage.

How these ambiguities are resolved in practice is rather difficult to establish. One must allow for retrospective reinterpretation of both existing marriages and the details of the arrangements, which were made many years ago. Such marriages can not provide a reliable data base to statistically calculate which choice, men's or women's, prevails. I do doubt, however, that confusions occurred often in the past. Rather it is the children with dual subsection affiliation, borne of the second- and third-choice marriages over the last 10-15 years, who are creating the new tensions apparent at initiation time. If the boy is of an important matriline, his maternal uncles and mother will conspire to nominate a wife who will confirm his subsection affiliation as correct for descendents of the matriline. If, on the other hand, the boy is of an important patriline, his father and his father's brothers will conspire to have the boy reside in their country before initiation and thus confirm his subsection affiliation as correct for a descendent of his patriline. If neither the patriline nor the matriline prevails, the boy may have two possible wives.

Subsequent Marriages: The Choice

In keeping with the demographic pressures generated by polygyny, one could expect a widowed woman to be subject to the levirate, but, although this is a male expectation, it is frequently flouted successfully by women. If her first husband was a promised spouse and 15-20 years older than she, a woman may expect to be widowed any time from her mid-thirties onward. She may still be fertile and have dependent children; most certainly, she will still consider herself attractive and, if the pursuit by men of her age is any indication, she is also considered attractive. Once she has gone through the prescribed period of mourning, which includes speech taboos and withdrawal from all heterosexual situations, she is considered eligible for remarriage. A young woman may not wish to endure these social and sexual hardships for too long and may attempt to have the older men release her from the speech taboo. For younger women this is becoming a common practice because they have spent so much time out of the care of their mothers during school years that their grasp of the complex and rich sign language—which had been used by some older women during periods of speech taboo for as long as a decade—is weakened. Rather than risk the possibility of women breaking the taboo through ignorance or defiance, the men comply, thus shortening the mourning period for younger women; the demands of employment (as when a young widow is also an active worker in a school or hospital in her community) also hinder the lengthy observance of a speech taboo and withdrawal from all heterosexual contacts.

Today, as in the past, those widows who remain in mourning for two or more years go through a ceremony in which the dead husband's actual and classificatory brothers attempt to arrange a further marriage for the widow with a member of their own patriline. Many women do not wish to enter into a marriage with such men as it makes them feel "too sorry," and may aggravate family frictions which possibly emerged in the previous marriage. Most often the choice of a brother of the dead husband simply runs counter to the desires of the widow. "I have feelings," she will assert, usually with the backing of positive action. If she has already chosen her next husband she may be busily working love rituals (Bell 1978b) to insure the match or she may be prepared to elope with him (with or without love rituals) and endure a period of ostracism. In the past, as now, it appears that if a couple eloped and successfully eluded the pursuing spouses and in-laws, they would be free to rejoin their own community after a decent interval of survival alone in the desert. As long as that marriage did not violate any incest taboos, such a union would be accepted and in several years would be considered a correct marriage. The recounting of such elopements and the woman's defiance becomes a matter of pride for the couple and sentimental pleasure for other women. If, however, the marriage seriously violates the moral code, the couple are unlikely to elude the pursuing parties, nor would they be excused after verbal censure.

Pursuit parties can now use cars and trucks and, although the couple may also have a vehicle, they are confined to the few existing roads and are more likely to be followed for greater distances than in the past, when all traveled on foot. Once caught by an enraged husband, the eloping male normally yields and the woman receives the bashing. Women are again disadvantaged as few have driving licences or access to vehicles. It is therefore more difficult for them to escape an angry husband unaided than it is for a man to escape an angry wife.

One reason a woman readily gives for not wishing to marry a brother of her late husband is that this man already has a wife. (This is not an objection to co-wife status per se, as a senior wife often asks her husband to take a younger wife.) It is usually a statement by a mature woman who could become senior wife but is secure in her own judgement and the knowledge that she has other options. Many widows argue that they have had enough of jealous fights; their older husbands probably accused them of many infidelities and they do not want to incur such recriminations again.

If, however, the dead spouse's brother does not have a wife, or is married to the widow's close classificatory or actual sister, she may consider remarriage within the same patriline to be advantageous. If she is the mother of adult children, she has the support of her son-in-law and daughter-in-law. And she also has the option of remaining in the *jilimi*. This does not mean deprivation or hardship: to residents of a single women's camp, old-age pensions now provide a solid economic base and obligatory gifts from sons-in-law supplement older widows' incomes. Young widows may also be employed for cash wages which are shared in the camp. A widow may have love affairs so long as these are not permanent liaisons while she is in the early stages of mourning. In fact, many liaisons in the later stages of mourning provide an avenue for women to encourage men to release them formally from onerous taboos. When these liaisons become more permanent unions, the woman will not have the support of kin she had as a promised wife, but as a mature woman with adult children she commands respect and exudes confidence in her own independence.

I have deferred discussing eastern Warlpiri women's attitudes and beliefs about love, marriage, and divorce until the range of possible behaviors of women were spelt out. Women choose and enter a number of different marital states at different times in their lives. As a young promised wife she may flaunt her sexuality and enjoy extramarital affairs while accepting her duty; indeed, she may learn to appreciate the charms of an older husband as he woos her with gentleness and love rituals. Such arranged marriages often develop into obviously happy and satisfying unions for both parties and are claimed by older women, as they sentimentally enumerate examples, to be the preferred and admired arrangements of this society even today. Yet this is the kind of marriage which Europeans most deplore and try to prevent. In the past missionaries attempted to prevent the "abuse" of young brides by offering them sanctuary, but male, European officials often now choose to support older men's claims to younger wives and may do so simply by not intervening. In 1977 at Hooker Creek, older men prevented some young girls from returning to school in Alice Springs by airplane. White officials did not defy the old men, deeming this a "tribal matter," yet they apparently did not perceive that the girls' attempt to prolong their single state by escaping to school was equally a tribal matter, involving rights that could not now be enforced without support by officialdom. In the past a reluctant bride could still return to the camp of her mother and find support. Today, young wives do not always have this option and most mothers and officials are reluctant to support this "disobedience." Many Europeans are now loath to interfere with incidents defined as "tribal." Of course, this aids men, who may beat their wives without rebuke by officials.

In deciding whether to remain single, woo a younger or older man, marry her dead spouse's "brother," or force early termination of mourning, a woman must weigh the advantages and disadvantages. By defying relatives she risks loss of protection; by remaining single or marrying where she pleases, she increases her self-esteem and ultimately gains acceptance of her chosen status.

I suggested earlier that women and men did not perceive marriage to a younger woman to be the only preferred form. Older men or older women, widows and widowers, may court each other, and such choices are considered sound and good. A man may also pursue an older woman even though he has a young wife or the possibility of claiming one. This is not prompted merely by a greed for women, but also by a desire to marry a woman who has high social and ritual status and who can participate as a mature partner. Women do not consider that aging diminishes charms, and I frequently heard men declare that they would prefer a mature widow to a young troublesome wife. (See Table 1).

TABLE 1.
Average Age Difference of Spouses
(for husband older than wife) by Age of Woman

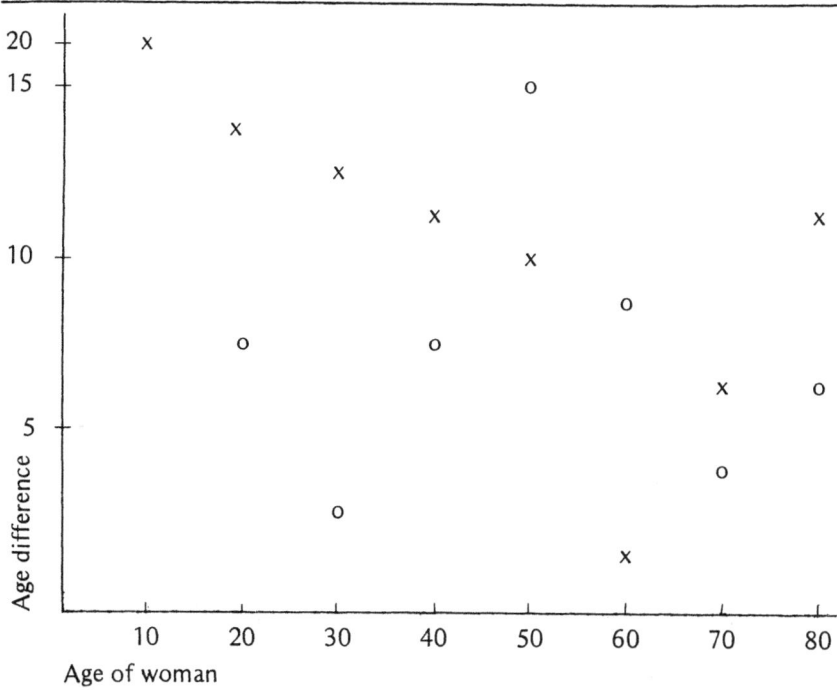

x Meggitt 1959 (1965:159).
o Bell 1979

    Women may also seek much younger men. This is a common consequence of the systems of polygyny and gerontocracy, but it is not a union which younger men today consider themselves obliged to enter. Perhaps the marriage model in which male seniority and authority are intertwined finds more ready acceptance in European society than in Aboriginal society, which permits a number of different age arrangements. As I have stated, older widows have always been able to live in the *jilimi*, so they do not choose a younger husband from duty or necessity. Both parties are motivated only by mutual attraction. Several of the most satisfying marriages at Warrabri are of this kind and are approved by other women, but if any friction occurs women will shake their heads and say, "Well what do you expect? He is too young for her" (Table 2).
    There is a new category of unions, a consequence of contact rather than an indigenous form: the marriage of young men to young women. This is statistically the most fragile kind of marriage and is recognized as such by women. In recent years, unions with Europeans have taken a number of young women out of their communities. In towns such couples face a new community with different checks and balances; these marriages are short-lived in most cases.

TABLE 2.
Graph of Age Difference against Wife's Age (for wife older than husband)

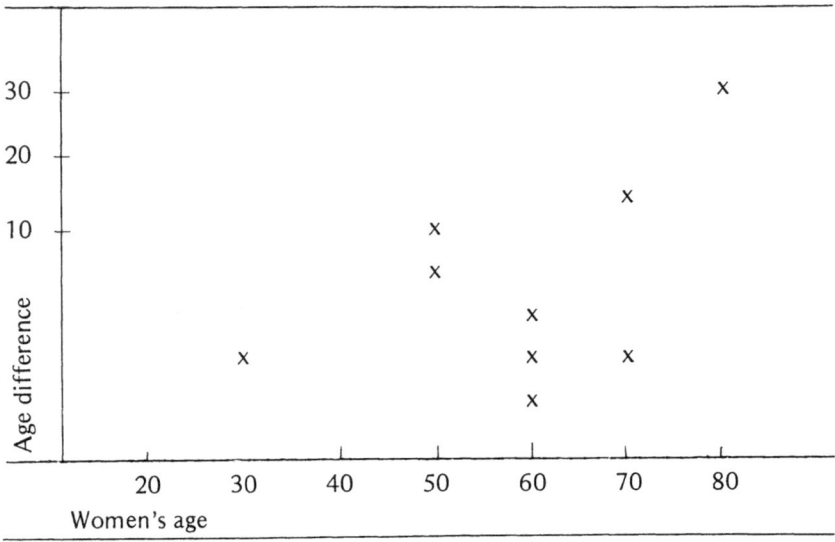

Bell 1979

I have stated that the *jilimi* is always an option for women who do not wish to live with men.[10] A resident woman of such a camp may have affairs but, like the promised wife, she does not bring her lover home. Older women in the *jilimi* are usually ritually important, and the care and maintenance of ritual paraphernalia consumes much of their time. If a woman and her husband are both very old, she may choose to live in the *jilimi* but would still be considered his wife. There are a declining number of co-wives and an increasing number of widows who are choosing to remain single. Co-wives often continue to live together after the death of their husbands or their separation from them. Their bond is one of close sisterhood and thus precedes and even survives their marriage.

I have classified marriages here in terms of the age of spouses. The range of marriages and stated reasons for making certain unions at Warrabri is as extensive as one would expect in any community of that size. People marry for love, for property in the form of ritual knowledge and status, to escape from home, to have children, for companionship, and because they are led into it. People also separate for a range of reasons. Younger women run away to the towns; older women retreat to single women's camps. Women tire of husbandly violence or troubles with the neighbors. By concentrating on the rules which govern first marriage, anthropologists have stripped Aboriginal marriage, and women in particular, of a range of emotions and initiatives which they certainly possess and exercise.

A COMPARATIVE COMMENT: YALATA, SOUTH AUSTRALIA

In the 1920s and 1930s news of the new railway and European goods drew Aborigines from 400 miles around to Ooldea where a Baptist mission was later instituted. In the 1950s the Aborigines were moved from Ooldea to Yalata, some 100 miles to the south and outside their own traditional country. In comparison with the Warrabri Warlpiri, Yalata women are in some ways further along the road of accomodation to colonization. They are living away from traditional land and although they occasionally make journeys to visit sacred sites, they are for all intents and purposes dispossessed and landless.

Itinerant European male employees in the cattle and mining industries and "doggers" (dingo hunters) provided Yalata women with their first glances of colonial culture. In her history of the Pitjantjarra at the Ernabella Mission of South Australia, Hilliard comments on the doggers: "Most of them lived with native women, rearing half-caste children, and in some cases, caring for them well. Others had no conscience about abandoning their little ones when the time came to move on" (1968:82).

The children fathered by European men created only minor problems in Aboriginal camps where women could return without shame. Older Pitjantjarra women assert that in the past a woman and her children would have been taken back with a warm welcome. Such women could join, or rejoin, their promised husbands, who would take responsibility for the children even to the extent of initiating and betrothing them in the customary manner. These children did, however, create problems for welfare departments (see Rowley 1970:236) which saw the hope of future generations of Aborigines in the education of the "half-caste" children. Welfare officers and police would raid Aboriginal camps and forcefully remove any lighter-colored children. Old women at Yalata tearfully recount that they have children, last heard of in Adelaide.

In the early days at Ooldea, the United Aboriginal Mission maintained separate dormatories for boys and girls and attempted to eradicate "heathen practices," such as male circumcision and subincision, and to prevent polygyny and infant betrothal. Polygyny, or at least its outward show, did decline and today there are only a couple of men with more than one wife, and even they do not live openly with both wives. The Lutherans do not try to forcibly change the beliefs and customs; the forces of change operating in school and through the media are more subtle.

Despite the destruction of their subsistence mode and the dispossession of their lands, women still perform secret ceremonies (White 1970, 1975), and men circumcision and subincision rites. A young man is promised a wife by his circumcisor and must then wait for her to reach the age of marriage. Not infrequently young girls object to marrying older men and gain support of mothers who quote the legal minimum marriage age under Australian law. Such women may have the ideal of love marriages and the advantages of monogamy in mind for their daughters. When young men and women have affairs and insist upon marrying, a girl may seek and find support from her mother and female kin. After a display of anger and even violence from the girl's fathers, mother's brothers, disappointed grooms, and close male kin, the sweethearts may triumph. This is most likely if the man to whom the girl was promised already had a wife; once again women would quote Australian law.

In order to comply as far as possible with Aboriginal law, the men will then arrange for the girl's father to circumcise her sweetheart, and after he has been duly circumcised and subincised, the pair will be allowed to marry. In this case they will probably have a proper church wedding, rather than the so-called "tribal" marriage of their parents. But this does not seem to make the marriage any more lasting. The girls' "mothers" and some female kin may give them support, but their "fathers" and male kin will not support them in the way they would have had the marriage they arranged been consummated.

CONCLUSION

Although differences between the 1959 and 1979 marriage statistics for Warrabri Warlpiri indicate that marriage patterns are indeed changing, it is important to remember that these postcontact changes extend over the past 80 years and include facets of male-female interactions that are not amenable to statistical analysis. This chapter has explored how the changes are perceived by the Warrabri Warlpiri, constrained within the colonial context and characterized by anthropologists.[11] In analyzing marriage from a woman's point of view, I have suggested that women's role in marriage arrangements has been misrepresented and that this has restricted our understanding of the changes wrought by European colonization of central Australia.

In spite of the violence, the dispossession of Aboriginal land, and traumatic upheavals, the Warrabri Warlpiri maintain their belief in the persistence and continuity of their law. The accommodation of an increasing number of alternate (second-choice) marriages within the category of correct marriage sustains such beliefs. Women, however, have experienced this change in terms of increasingly fragile marriages, such as "Joan's," where the support of kin is less readily available. Marriage is related to other forms of solidarity, to wider kinship networks, and to the identification of men with men and women with women. The bases of these various forms of solidarity have been differently affected for men and women in the colonial situation. Women, I have argued, have been the losers. Once economically self-sufficient and ritually autonomous as a sex, women are now dependent on support from governments which do not recognize their previously independent role. Women are forced to the periphery of frontier society from where their only access is sexual.

I have suggested that for Aboriginal women, their marriage expectations and choices have changed. In marrying younger and attempting to sustain monogamous unions, young women today seek to emulate the model of subsequent marriage for older, mature women in the past and to derive advantage from the perceived benefits of love marriages. Instead of security and support they have encountered violence and instability. Because Aboriginal woman's primary contact with frontier society has been sexual, her attempts to conform to the colonial image of wife has been to her further disadvantage. She is increasingly bereft of support, recognition, and protection in both worlds.

In focusing upon woman's perceptions, attitudes, and roles in marriage arrangements, I have described a process wherein the rational, knowing actor makes choices and decisions. The further assertion that such behaviors are political derives from the power-structured nature of male-female relationships whereby one group of persons attempts to control another. Sexual politics are about enforceable choices or, as Millet states, about "a set of strategems designed to maintain a system" (1969:23), and this chapter has outlined various strategies utilized by women in the arena of ritual politics. The institutionalized forms of the control of power differentials entailed in male-female relationships, such as those expressed in terms of polygyny and gerontocracy, do not constitute the totality of the experience of male-female relationships either in or out of marriage.

Arenas in which women are now attempting to enforce their choices are constrained, however, by a male-dominated colonial society. The European usurpation of effective political roles in Aboriginal society—apparent in the forceful removal of people from their country, the establishment of artificial settlements, and the appropriation of valuable resources—Aboriginal men have been denied full status as responsible individuals. Instead, they have been gradually incorporated at the lower levels of the new power structure. This has not been the experience of Aboriginal women. In subsuming the parallel political and social forms of desert culture, European frontier society has denied legitimacy to women while according limited recognition to men in the new social order. Aboriginal men have identified as men in being able to drive vehicles, sit on councils, and assist police. Their new models of marriage and male-female relationships, forged within the violent brutalizing context of colonization in Central Australia, emphasize dominance and control. Their anger has turned toward women and their expression of male solidarity takes the form of interpersonal violence. Women, on the other hand, remain on the periphery of the new political order; their models of male-female relationships and marriage, based on their tuition in the colonial society, emphasize love and security.

The colonial situation posits, makes mainfest, and reinforces the idea of the individual as the choice-making actor. For Aboriginal women this has proved to be an illusion. As individuals they have ever diminishing powers to enforce their choices because their various bases of solidarity have been eroded. The *jilimi*, to which women retreat, is one arena where their need for solidarity, separate from men, can best be realized. Here solidarity is based on a hierarchy where age means access to knowledge and where an acceptance of the centrality of the category of "woman" submerges the individualistic construction of the person in the formation of sexual solidarity.

Our understanding of these changes has been based on recent anthropological data refracted through the eyes of male-oriented anthropologists and organized in terms of models that stress marriage as a marked event. From a woman's point of view—in which the expectation is one of serial monogamy—marriage is a continuing process of the constitution of relationships which flow and change through a life course. Gerontocracy, polygyny, and arranged marriages are all stressed in the ethnographic literature, but I have argued that these must be balanced against knowledge of women's strategies. Unchallenged male control is presented by male-oriented anthropologists as an enduring dimension of Warlpiri marriages, in both the past and present. In this view women are reduced to objects. Characterizations of marriage in terms of the control of labor and children and the objectification of women reveal the ethnocentricism of anthropological concepts based on an understanding of male-female relations within the capitalist ideology which is superimposed upon Aboriginal society.

In this chapter I have argued that if Aboriginal women's perceptions of the choices and options available to them are ignored, the highly political nature of marriage arrangements is obscured. The colonial frontier has moved rapidly from the mid-twentieth century. In 1959 the Warrabri Warlpiri were, for Meggitt, characterized by a low incidence of polygyny. In 1979 I found a willingness to absorb alternate marriages into the correct category and a substantial proportion of women choosing to live in the *jilimi*. Will the Warlpiri ethnographer of 1999 find monogamous Warlpiri or a high incidence of bachelors?

NOTES

1. This chapter began as a joint enterprise but, because of her field work and family responsibilities, Isobel White withdrew as co-author. The sections on the Aboriginal women of Yalata are based on her notes which she generously made available to me. I am grateful to Doug Jervis for the photographs, the Australian Institute of Aboriginal Studies and the Australian National University, Canberra, for funding; Bernard Cohn and Nicolas Peterson for their comments on an earlier draft; Graham Harrison for assistance with statistics; Jim Urry who prepared the tables; Diane Sutton who typed the manuscript; and all the women who shared their lives with me in the field. I appreciate and cherish the support and criticism of Diane Barwick and Caroline Ifeka who shared the ten frantic days in which the first draft of this chapter was written.

2. Throughout, I have used the orthography of the Warlpiri (Walbiri) bilingual program at the Yuendumu school, as this is the orthography of literate Warlpiri of the future. Warlpiri people also live at Yuendumu (800), Hooker Creek (850), Papunya (200), Warrabri (350), Willowra (200), and on nearby cattle stations and in Alice Springs or Tennant Creek (150).

3. Hamilton argues that women at Maningrida, Arnhemland, have been offered an "illusory equality in exchange for complete subservience to a white-controlled economy and the brutalizing value system which supports it" (1975:179). See also Larbalestier (1977) and Barwick (1970).

4. Reay (1963:42) adds that the Aboriginal wife of a European male enjoys more leisure time than as the wife of an Aboriginal male.

5. The 'eastern Warlpiri' is my own designation for those Warlpiri who now live east of the Stuart Highway. Meggitt deems that the Warlpiri nation was divided in the past into 4 communities (1962:5). Settlements have disrupted these residential units. The eastern Warlpiri do, however, recognize themselves as different from the Yuendumu and Hooker Creek Warlpiri in that their speech is "softer."

6. Aboriginal women are eligible to apply for widows' pensions, supporting mothers' benefits, old-age pensions, and unemployment benefits, but are thwarted and hindered in their applications for benefits by illiteracy, bureaucratic bungling, and sometimes the attitudes of European male officers.

7. I have used real subsection names and fictitious given names in the case histories. See Meggitt (1962:61-2) Munn (1973:17) for an account of subsection names.

8. According to many informants, today the current procedure in the case of a second-choice marriage is that the subsection of the child is reckoned as if the mother had married correctly, that is, the father's subsection is disregarded. In actual practice this does not occur and children are often called by members of one subsection by their father's family name and those of the other by their mother's.

9. Women have emphasized the protective role of men; but, in other contexts (e.g., rape), they emphasize female strategies.

10. This is in direct contrast to Goodale's (1971) study of Tiwi where the possibility of unmarried women does not exist.

11. The trends in Warlpiri marriage patterns identified by Meggitt (1965) are, in his analysis, indices of acculturation. Long has countered that "acculturation is a process, one symptom of which may be a decline in polygyny rather than a factor determining change in marriage behaviour" (1970:206). In distinguishing between family structure and familial culture, Marie Reay offers a framework in which to think about the changes. Assimilation, she argues, is not an undirectional process (1963:42). Superficially, Aboriginal family structure may now approximate more closely to the White frontier society models than in the past, but the Aboriginal family retains its distinctive culture. Like the women of Warrabri in the 1970s, the women with whom Marie Reay worked in the Northern Territory in the early 1960s had contracted marriages which were as much a result of contact as of indigenous models.

REFERENCES

van Baal, J. 1970. "The Part of Women in the Marriage Trade: Objects or Behaving as Objects." *Bijdragen* 126, 3:289-308.

Barwick, Diane. 1970. "And the Lubras are Ladies Now." In Fay Gale, ed., *Woman's Role in Aboriginal Society*. Canberra: Australian Institute of Aboriginal Studies.

Bell, D.R. 1978a. "For Our Families: The Kurundi Walk Off and the NgurrantijiVenture." *Aboriginal History* 2:31-62.

———. 1978b. "Love and Marriage: How Well Do They Go Together?" (ms.). Australian Institute of Aboriginal Studies, Canberra.

———. Berndt, R. M. and C. H. Berndt. 1964. *The World of the First Australians*. Sydney: Ure Smith.

Davenport, Michael. 1977. "Tales of Modern Tribalism." *National Times*, June 4.

Goodale, Jane C. 1971. *Tiwi Wives*. Seattle: University of Washington Press.

Hagen, Rod and Meredith Rowell. 1978. *A Claim to Areas of Traditional Land by the Alyawarra and Kaititja*. Alice Springs: Central Land Council.

Hamilton, Annette. 1970. "The Role of Women in Aboriginal Marriage Arrangements." In F. Gale, ed., *Woman's Role in Aboriginal Society*. Canberra: Australian Institute of Aboriginal Studies.

———. 1975. "Aboriginal Women: The Means of Production. In Jan Mercer, ed., *The Other Half: Women in Australian Society*. Ringwood, Victoria: Penguin.

Hart, C. W. M. and Arnold R. Pilling. 1960. *The Tiwi of North Australia*. New York: Holt, Rinehart and Winston.

Hartwig, Mervyn C. 1960. "The Coniston Killings." B.A. thesis, University of Adelaide.

Hilliard, Winifred. 1968. *The People in Between: The Pitjantjatjara People of Ernabella*. London: Hodder & Stoughton.

Kaberry, Phyllis M. 1939. *Aboriginal Woman: Sacred and Profane*. London: Routledge and Kegan Paul.

Larbalestier, Jan. 1977. "Black Women in Colonial Australia." *Refractory Girl*, nos. 13-14:42-53.

Long, Jeremy. 1970. "Polygyny, Acculturation and Contact: Aspects of Aboriginal Marriage in Central Australia." In Ronald M. Berndt, ed., *Australian Aboriginal Anthropology*. Nedlands: University of Western Australia Press.

Meggitt, M. J. 1962. *Desert People: A Study of the Walbiri Aborigines of Central Australia*. Chicago: University of Chicago Press.

———. 1965. "Marriage among the Walbiri of Central Australia: A Statistical Examination." In R. M. Berndt and C. H. Berndt, eds., *Aboriginal Man in Australia*. Sydney: Angus and Robertson.

Millett, Kate. 1969. *Sexual Politics.* New York: Avon.

Munn, Nancy D. 1973. *Walbiri Iconography: Graphic Representation and Cultural Symbolism in a Central Australian Society.* London: Cornell University Press.

Peterson, Nicolas. 1969. "Secular and Ritual Links: Two Basic and Opposed Principles of Australian Social Organization as Illustrated by Walbiri Ethnography." *Mankind* 7:27-35.

Peterson, Nicolas, Stephen Wild, Patrick McConvell, and Rod Hagen. 1978. *A Claim to Areas of Tradition Land by the Warlpiri and Kartangarurru-Kurintji.* Alice Springs: Central Land Council.

Prichard, Katherine Susannah. 1961. *Coonardo.* Sydney: Pacific Books Angus & Robertson. (orig. 1929).

Read, Peter, and Engineer Jack Japaljarri. 1978. "The Price of Tobacco: The Journey of the Warlmala to Wave Hill 1928." *Aboriginal History* 2:140-48.

Reay, Marie. 1963. Aboriginal and White Family Structure: An Enquiry into Assimilation Trends. *Sociological Review* (n.s.) 11, 1:19-47.

Roheim, G. 1933. Women and their Life in Central Australia. *Journal of the Royal Anthropological Institute* 63:207-65.

Rohrlich-Leavitt, Ruby, Barbara Sykes, and Elizabeth Weatherford. 1975. "Aboriginal Woman: Male and Female Anthropological Perspectives." In Rayna R. Reiter, ed., *Toward an Anthropology of Women.* New York: Monthly Review Press.

Rowley, C. D. 1970. *The Destruction of Aboriginal Society.* Canberra: Australian National University Press.

Warburton, P. E. 1875. *Journey Across the Western Interior of Australia* (H. W. Bates, ed.). London: Sampson Low, Marston, Low and Searle.

White, I. M. 1970. "Aboriginal Women's Status: A Paradox Resolved." In F. Gale, ed., *Women's Role in Aboriginal Society.* Canberra: Australian Institute of Aboriginal Studies.

———. 1971. "Aboriginal Women in Transition." In *Seminars 1971.* Centre for Research into Aboriginal Affairs, Monash University.

———. 1975. "Sexual Conquest and Submission in the Myths of Central Australia." In L.R. Hiatt, ed., *Australian Aboriginal Mythology.* Canberra: Australian Institute of Aboriginal Studies.

11 Stability in Banana Leaves:
Colonization and Women in Kiriwina, Trobriand Islands

ANNETTE B. WEINER

Although some variation exists in scholarly definitions of the geographical boundaries of Melanesia, the culture area usually is recognized as including the mainland of New Guinea and the smaller island groups of the Admiralties, the Bismarck Archipelago (including New Ireland and New Britain), the Massim (with the Trobriand Islands situated to the north), the Solomons, Santa Cruz, the New Hebrides, New Caledonia, and Fiji. Following Pacific explorations throughout the sixteenth and seventeenth centuries, the various islands comprising Melanesia were apportioned among French, Dutch, German, British, and Australian powers. In many parts of Melanesia, however, the reputations of the "fierceness" of the villagers, and the treacherous geographical terrain (especially in the interior of New Guinea) kept early exploration and exploitation to a minimum.

By 1814 the Dutch had firmly established their claim to the western half of mainland New Guinea. Dutch New Guinea (now West Irian) was ceded to Indonesia in 1963. German trading companies were situated in the northeastern part of New Guinea (including the Admiralties and the Bismarck Archipelago) by the latter half of the nineteenth century, while the southeast (including the Massim) was occupied by the British. In 1906, British New Guinea, called Papua, was transferred to Australian control and in 1921, as a result of World War I, German New Guinea became Australian Mandated Territory. Until recent independence, Australia has governed the entire eastern half of New Guinea, including the outer island groups, as the Territory of Papua and New Guinea.

During the early colonial period, beginning about 1850, the Massim, a ring of coral-based and volcanic islands—about 160 islands and over 500 islets—played a prominent part in the economics of Papua. Whalers, traders, planters, and recruiters for sugar plantations in Queensland rapidly infiltrated the islands. The possibilities of gold sent hundreds of men exploring the Massim to search out claims, most of which, however, remained rather small. European and Asian markets, eager for copra, rubber, bêche-de-mer (a type of sea slug important in China for use in soup), and pearls kept traders, prospectors, and planters operating in the area. But, gradually, with changes in the world market and difficulty in obtaining both extensive local labor forces and ownership of land, commercial economic production decreased until by the end of World War II, the Massim was no longer a significant economic center.

Subsistence cultivation, primarily of yams, taro, and bananas (with fish and pigs as protein sources), continues today as the common mode of production in the Massim. The early "boom" did nothing to advance modern communication and transport systems, and few local populations or individuals shifted to commercial enterprises. Within specific island populations, however, changes did occur that were disruptive to traditional ritual life, residential patterns, and certain kinds of trade and exchange systems. The missions (entering the scene as early as 1840) were often more influential than commercialization in causing the abandonment of traditional activities. Since the emergence of Papua New Guinea as an independent country in 1975, a growing resurgence of local-level autonomy has occurred throughout the Massim with an intensification of traditional modes of production.

The Trobriand group, situated in the northernmost part of the Massim, includes the islands of Kiriwina, Kitava, Vakuta, Kaileuna, and over 100 uninhabited coral islets. Kiriwina, a low-lying coral atoll, is geographically the largest and politically the most central, about 30 miles long and 10 miles across at its widest part. The total population of the island group, now about 10,000, has increased steadily since the turn of the century. The Trobriands not only had a colonial history of traders, missions, and government, but they have had a rather dramatic anthropological history as well. In 1904, C. G. Seligman collected data from Kiriwina as part of his ethnographic survey of the northern and southern Massim (1910). What seemed especially significant to Seligman was the system of rank and inherited chiefs that appeared far more formalized and elaborated in Kiriwina than in any other Massim island. Ten years later, Kiriwina, and the Trobriands in general, were to become even more significant anthropologically following the field research of Bronislaw Malinowski. With Malinowski's extensive publications on a wide range of topics such as Trobriand kinship, matriliny, exchange, magic, myth, and garden production, the Trobriands became one of the most "sacred places" in the history of anthropology. Many of Malinowski's interpretations were to become the basis for general theoretical principles as well as the subject of long-standing scholarly debates.

What initially astounded me upon my arrival in Kiriwina was the striking similarity between a Kiriwina village in 1971 and Malinowski's descriptions and photographs of the same village in 1922.[1] Although superficially some things had changed (an airstrip, tourists, some Western clothing) everything else was as if nothing had changed. Yam houses still occupy the most prominent place in each village, and yams remain the most important food crop, having extensive economic and political value. When properly stored, yams last for 4 or 5 months without rotting. During this time, raw yams may be exchanged for a variety of other kinds of commodities. Taro plays a secondary role, both as food and as an object of exchange. Sweet potatoes (grown exclusively by women), squash, beans, tapioca, breadfruit, bananas, sugar cane, and greens serve to supplement the preferred diet of yams and taro. Catches from both open-sea and lagoon fishing sites, organized by men living in coastal villages, supply most of the protein in the diet. Both women and men own and raise pigs, but the pig population is small and pork is eaten only for feasts or as a result of special exchanges. Coconut and *areca* (betel) palms surround each village; each palm is individually owned. Slash-and-burn cultivation is practiced with women and men working together during the clearing and planting phases. Men and women also tend food and taro gardens, but men are responsible for the cultivation of yam, or exchange, gardens, which they work for other villagers.

The production from food gardens is never displayed, but at harvest men present the production from the yam exchange gardens to other men, and these yams are loaded into the yam houses. Yams from the exchange gardens are presented to specific kin relations, such as a man's sister, his daughter, his father, his older brother, and his mother's brother. Through distributions of yams at harvest, men are able to create and maintain networks of relationships with individual women and men.

The hamlet is the basic unit of residence, with contiguous hamlets comprising a village. Usually one man controls the hamlet and garden lands marked in the name of his lineage (*dala*). Land divisions are bounded by genealogical sanctions which must be traced back to the original matrilineal founders. Barring the loss of land through compensation payments, theft, or the demise of a particular lineage (*dala*), inheritance of land control should pass from an older brother to a younger brother and then, in the next generation, to a man's sister's son. But each hamlet "manager" has the right to determine exactly who his heir will be, and he also has the right to allocate use rights to land to others who are not members of his *dala*. The most important hamlet manager (often a man of rank) within a village will organize and control the communal activities in which all villagers participate, regardless of hamlet affiliation. But the head of a village never controls the *dala* property (e.g., land, names, body and house decorations) and mortuary distributions of the hamlets.

Most marriages occur between individuals who live in different hamlets in the same or in neighboring villages. But the few chiefs who are polygamous have a much wider range of affinal connections. Although women reside in their husbands' hamlets, geographically, economically, and politically, women are never very far from their own blood kin. Avunculocal residence occurs only in those cases when a young man may in the future inherit the right to control his own *dala* land at his mother's brother's death. But most men remain in residence with their fathers. Male-male relationships are of extreme importance for residence, land use, land control, access to material resources, and special kinds of knowledge, such as magic spells. The most significant of these relationships must be reaffirmed continually through annual distributions of yams. Female-male relationships are equally important and these relationships, too, must be "fed" annually with yams.

JOSHUA'S MESSAGE

One afternoon during the summer of 1976, while engaged in a return period of field research in northern Kiriwina Island, I had a brief encounter with an unmarried Kiriwina man in his late twenties, who was employed as a medical assistant at the small hospital at Losuia, the administrative center for the subdistrict. Thinking back to my conversation with Joshua (not his real name) today, I realize that the few sentences we exchanged about Kiriwina women frame the issues raised here.

On the particular day of our encounter, I had been walking to Losuia along the one vehicular road bisecting the northern part of the island from the beach area at Kaibola, south to Losuia on the lagoon. I was hoping that my walk would be interrupted by the return trip of a medical truck that earlier had gone north toward Kaibola to pick up a patient. As I anticipated, after I had gone about two miles the truck came along and gave me a ride to Losuia. Joshua was driving, and having never met each other before, we chatted at length about who we were. Joshua had not lived in Kiriwina since he was twelve when he was sent to secondary school, then to training college, and then to work elsewhere in Papua New Guinea. He had just been transferred to the hospital in Kiriwina a few weeks prior to our meeting.

As we bounced along over the deep ruts in the coral-graded road, we passed a hamlet crowded with several hundred women. By this time in my research I was well aware of what was going on in the hamlet, having attended a score of such gatherings myself and even having participated directly in some of the proceedings. Turning to my new acquaintance, and in retrospect probably attempting to establish for him my "knowledge" of Kiriwina traditions, I said that a mortuary distribution (*sagali*)[2] was going on and that women were "throwing their wealth (*doba*)." "Ah, very good," he said, "you already know about women's wealth." Smiling, I nodded, but my satisfied feeling of being well-informed was only momentary. Immediately, Joshua became serious and said, "We have to get those women to stop throwing their wealth, because they take our money. If the women would stop needing so many baskets of wealth [bundles of strips of dried banana leaves and brightly colored banana fiber skirts], then men would have plenty of money to pay for other things."

I remember feeling rather shocked and dismayed by Joshua's attitude. What went through my head rapidly was the thought that Joshua had been away too long and had learned to think in Western capitalistic terms. His attitude was based on involvement in a competing economic system that has its own imperatives. Of course, from that perspective Joshua was right. Women did take men's wealth in order to increase their own wealth. Mortuary distributions of women's wealth are an enormous drain on the flow and accumulation of all kinds of other goods. But the drain on resources each time a death occurs must be understood as an integral part of the entire internal system of exchange, linking women's wealth to yam production and other forms of male activity.

I believed then, as I still believe today, that the strength and resiliency of Kiriwina traditions have their roots in women's *sagali*, the mortuary distribution of bundles of banana leaves and skirts, organized, produced, and controlled by women. To take away women's wealth and to alter the procedures of mortuary distributions and payments would force the most drastic changes in the status and roles of women *and* also in the status and roles of men. Not only would women become economically disadvantaged, but Kiriwina men would lose their base of political power. (Men might create another base of power, but it would be in a very different form.)

I am not the first anthropologist, however, to predict the loss of male political power. After Bronislaw Malinowski's seminal field research in the Trobriand Islands between 1915 and 1918, he predicted that because of mission and government interference, the power of the chief (Touluwa) and many traditional activities, such as formal exchange procedures and polygamy, would soon completely disappear (Malinowski 1922:465).[3] But Touluwa died in 1930, and his successor, Mitakata, appears to have had a very prestigious career. Despite mission influence, Touluwa and Mitakata managed to keep the system of polygamy for chiefs very much alive. Malinowski's assessment of the decay of tradition, however, was based on his observations of men. He never wrote much about women's activities, except to point out the high status of women and to note that women played an important role in mortuary distributions of food (e.g., 1929). Although in one photograph in *The Sexual Life of Savages* (Malinowski (1929:1A) a Kiriwina woman is sitting with a small basket of her wealth, Malinowski never published any mention of women's wealth. (Seligman [1910] also noted the important status of Trobriand women.)

From the perspective of men, Malinowski correctly noted the importance of polygamy for chiefs as well as the tradition in which men make annual yam gardens for their sisters. As I describe elsewhere (1976:201–7), when a chief marries a woman, four of her male relatives (usually her brothers, her father, and her mother's brother) agree to work an annual yam garden for her. When a woman marries a man who is not a chief, then only one kinsman makes a garden for her. Thus, chiefs have access to more resources than other men, an advantage that is compounded by polygamy, since men of no rank are not polygamous. What Malinowski and other anthropologists ignored was the role that women's wealth plays in these yam distributions. Because a man receives yams from his wife (through her male kin), he must contribute his own wealth to aid her in accumulating women's wealth when one of her own kin (or her father's kin) dies. All married men participate in these transactions involving women's wealth. What Malinowski never understood was the drain on a man's wealth directly attributable to his wife's economic activities. Therefore, the power of any man is directly connected to the power of his wife; that is, women and their wealth (and not just the institution of polygamy) play an important role in stability and change.

In another way, Malinowski faced difficulties in predicting the effects of colonization. The first mission station (the Methodist Wesleyan Church) was established along the lagoon in 1894, and the government administration post was set up at Losuia in 1907. Arriving in Kiriwina in 1915, Malinowski would have been confronted by many immediate changes. Yet, because of his narrow time perspective, he probably would not have been too sensitive to the Trobrianders' resiliency in the face of changes over long periods of time. For, Kiriwina has shown enormous resistance to fundamental cultural changes while in many other parts of the Massim (see, for example, Damon 1978 on Woodlark Island; Berde 1974 on Panaeati Island; Young 1971 on Goodenough Island), indigenous responses to Christianity, Western trade, and the enforcement of Western law have been more disruptive.

In 1950, when Harry A. Powell did fieldwork in Kiriwina, the villagers were recovering from the aftermath of American and Australian troop camps established on Kiriwina during World War II (Powell 1956). But according to Powell's studies (1960, 1969a, 1969b), many traditional aspects of yam exchanges, the position of chiefs, harvest ritual, and *kula* [the interisland exchange network first studied systematically by Malinowski (1920, 1922)] were still going on in a vital way. Although Powell never discussed women's wealth, in a brief segment of a film he made (1950), Kiriwina women are shown distributing bundles of banana leaves.

More recent films on *kula* and politics made in the early 1970s (see Weiner 1978a for a discussion of these films) visually convey the tenacity of cultural traditions. In a wonderfully provocative sequence in the film *Trobriand Cricket* (Leach and Kildea 1975), a few Kiriwina men sit talking about the way villagers consciously remade British cricket (introduced in the early 1900s by missionaries) into their own unique Trobriand Island game—a game now played for high political stakes. Watching a few men discuss with great vigor the way they "rubbished" the British game and made it into their game, an audience receives an immediate sense of the resiliency mentioned above.

Throughout the past 100 years of contact, the shifts in and impingements on the Kiriwina system of exchange brought about by the interests and activities of traders, government, and missions have not caused any major significant changes in the basic structural features of the exchange system. This does not mean that change has not occurred (see Weiner 1976:25–37). For example, warfare has stopped; chiefs no longer have sole control over a range of resources (see Weiner 1980); education has proven a valuable economic asset for older men whose children send back money from their jobs in other parts of the country; tourism accompanied by extensive sales of woodcarvings peaked in the late 1960s and early 1970s; and political movements, cooperative stores, and local government councils have come and gone. But throughout a history of shifting economic circumstances women's wealth has not suffered a decrease in value.

The production and distribution of women's wealth operate as a buffer, absorbing and adjusting changes in the economic activities of men. Further, the processes of exchange, involving women and their wealth, not only serve as a buffer to Western economic intrusions but, as Joshua knew, drain off most kinds of men's wealth. Therefore, the history of women's wealth over 100 years of contact has been a history of inflation—for women. The greater the opportunities for men to accumulate any kind of wealth, the greater becomes the number of baskets of women's wealth that "wealthy women" demand.

My immediate shock at Joshua's words occurred because he sounded so righteously, correctly Western and because he knew what no "outsider" living in Kiriwina since contact had known. If the "outsiders" ever understood (or ever noticed) anything about women's wealth, they never recorded anything about it. Begun in 1890, the *Annual Report on British New Guinea* documents various aspects of Trobriand culture written by early missionaries, visiting administrators, and resident magistrates (e.g., Bellamy 1913; Gilmour 1905; Moreton 1905); The reports by Bellamy and Gilmour especially document a variety of economic activities (see also Austen 1945 on pearling and other economic developments), but no one discussed women's wealth. Through these documents and the work of anthropologists, Kiriwina became well known for its yam production, participation in *kula*, paramount chiefs, and sexual practices, but not for its "wealthy women" and their banana leaves.

In retrospect, it seems that the ignoring of women may have influenced events. No one from "outside" ever intruded on the economic role that women played, because no one ever knew that banana leaves had an economic value. But when Joshua spoke to me that day about women's wealth, I realized that the collapse of this tradition, which up until now has withstood a variety of Western influences and intrusions, may only come about if a younger generation of Kiriwina children, educated in a Western tradition, come to believe that banana leaves are unworthy of respect and prestige and therefore unworthy of economic support. Joshua's stern words—words learned from another culture—suddenly made me aware of this possibility.

Women's Place

This chapter, however, is not about the future. Rather, it is about the past from a perspective that illustrates the way women's wealth—protected from "outsiders'" interests—served continually to integrate new kinds of Western wealth, as well as individual economic growth, into the traditional exchange system. According to my informants, women's wealth was important prior to contact, and the introduction of new sources of wealth for men gradually inflated the specific economic value of each bundle of banana leaves. In this regard, the Kiriwina situation appears to be unique, both in the Massim and in the larger Melanesian culture area.

But the early literature hints that women elsewhere in Melanesia may have played significant economic roles. More recently, a few ethnographic cases illustrate that the roles of women need to be much more carefully defined—in the given culture's, rather than our, terms (e.g., Faithorn 1976). For example, "mat money" was described very briefly by Codrington (1891) as an important object manufactured by women in the New Hebrides, and there are some suggestions that mat money was essential for pig transactions. Deacon left us with descriptions of women's secret societies in Malekula, New Hebrides, which seem to have been as impressive as men's secret societies. Women had to pay high-ranked women in order to proceed through the various ranks of the society and attain certain rights and insignia. Thus, women must have had access to wealth objects in order to make such payments, and some women reached positions of high rank and great power (1934:478–97). Deacon further reported that men feared these women of high rank because a man could lose his own high position in the men's society if he came in contact with women's insignia and because women of high rank were thought to have such power that a man might die from its effects (:487).

On Panaeati Island in the Massim, despite severe cultural repercussions from missions, women still make significant mortuary payments of yams (which they have grown), thereby securing land for their sons (Berde 1974). The New Guinea Highlands is an area consistently described by both male and female anthropologists in terms of the polluting effects of women and the strong ritual segregation between women and men (see Allen 1967; Langness 1967, 1974; Meggitt 1964; Read 1952). This ritual antagonism has been used to define women's roles as private, without any public status and with women playing nothing more than a peripheral part in men's political exchange activities. But recently, Darryl Feil (1978a; 1978b) described the central place that Enga women occupy in the highly political *tee* exchanges.[4] Enga women make their own decisions regarding pig transactions involving pigs that they themselves own and control. Feil's study differs significantly from research with other groups of Enga where we have been told that women do not own pigs and have no significant place at all in the *tee* exchanges (see Meggitt 1964, 1972). The neighboring Melpa women have also been described by Marilyn Strathern (1972) as "producers" of pigs rather than "transactors," as men are called. According to Strathern, Melpa women feed and care for pigs, but they do not play any formal part in men's political transactions.

Complex issues are raised by these contradictory ethnographic data, and any in-depth discussion is beyond the scope of this chapter (but see Weiner n.d.a.). Part of the problem obviously results from changes brought about by the contact situation and the subsequent loss of ethnographic information about the past. Yet another part of the problem relates to the assumptions anthropologists make about the roles of women in the present and in the past (see Leacock 1978). In Melanesia the issues are complicated further because, in many cases, women may have controlled objects of exchange that were not considered by observers to be worthy of study. Only very recently are we beginning to understand that unlikely elements such as semen (see Kelly 1976 on the Etoro) or sago grubs (see Ernst 1978 on the nearby Onabasulu) may be significant objects of exchange, in these cases for men. Traditionally, Melanesian exchange has been studied as transactions involving shell and stone valuables, pigs, vegetable foods, and women.

By concentrating attention on what overtly seems economically important, we ignore, for example, Deacon's reference that in Malekula marriage transactions piles of women's mat skirts were exchanged for piles of food

(1934:147). In the New Guinea Highlands, the Melpa present women's net carrying bags—symbolized in native terms as "fertility" and the "womb" (Strathern 1972:14—15)—in marriage and mortuary transactions. Among the Dugum Dani, in important male transactions women's net carrying bags must accompany the giving of male valuables (Heider 1970:156, 161). Further, Dani women manufacture salt, which appears as an extremely important object of exchange in securing shell valuables and stone axes (:29, 44—46). These scattered references in the literature, however, are very difficult to weave together into any kind of coherent scheme of women's place (see Weiner 1976, n.d.a.). Both Heider and Strathern state that male informants say that net bags are unimportant. My conclusion, however, is that mat money, net bags, women's skirts, and bundles of banana leaves may not make women political leaders, but regardless of women's political or economic roles these kinds of objects—if attention is given to the way they operate, whom they are given to, and what they symbolize—may take us deeper into more comparative and less biased analyses of the place of women *and* men in the societies we study. From this perspective, the Kiriwina example seems especially significant.

BUNDLES AND SKIRTS

Elsewhere I describe in detail the hundreds of transactions constituting mortuary distributions as well as the specific interactions between women and between men in terms of the distribution of bundles and skirts (1976:chs. 3, 4). Here I summarize briefly the relationship between women and men in conjunction with the two most important material components of these relationships—yams and women's wealth.

In Kiriwina, women manufacture bundles of strips of dried banana leaves (*nununiga*) through a long process which involves drying sections of a banana leaf, and later tying individual strips together at one end to form a whiskbroom-like effect. (Bundles are about ten inches long and eight inches wide at their widest.) Women also fringe sections of banana leaves and weave these into skirts. Fringed banana-leaf skirts, dyed red and beautifully decorated around the waistband with geometric designs in pandanus, are also classified as wealth (*doba*). Skirts have an exchange value and a use value, but bundles of banana leaves have an exchange value only. Although old and dirty bundles may be stripped apart for use in the manufacture of skirts, I was told that in most cases, bundles were simply discarded when they became too old and dirty to use.

Finished bundles, stacks of natural banana leaves, and leaves already fringed into skirt fibers may be exchanged (*valova*) for other commodities. By far the most numerous exchanges occur with the finished bundles. For example, a woman may purchase a stick of trade store tobacco for cash. She then takes the tobacco to another villager who wants tobacco, but the payment for the tobacco now must be transacted in bundles. In 1976, one stick of tobacco (selling in the trade store for ten *toya*, about 1.3 cents) was equivalent to ten bundles. (Since that time, tobacco prices have almost doubled, but I do not have any data on the accompanying increase for bundles.) In collecting my own stock of bundles, I was instructed by my women friends to purchase tins of fish and meat because "too many villagers already can find tobacco." As word circulated that I wanted bundles, women who wanted tins of corned beef came to me with bundles. In these transactions the equivalent exchange value was also based on one bundle equivalent to one *toya*. A constant demand for bundles exists, and both men and women are always trying to think of new items either to make or to buy for "resale" in order to accumulate more bundles. The largest single transaction I observed was a return of 1800 bundles for the payment of a pig.[5] Each part of a butchered pig is equivalent to a specific number of bundles, and the amount of bundles for a pig seems to move in accordance with the market price of pigs.

Women told me that before the Europeans came it was much more difficult to get bundles. There were fewer "new things" around, and the possibilities of finding interesting items were more limited. Manufactured objects such as earrings, combs, baskets, and mats could be used for exchange in bundles. Yams would be exchanged for manufactured objects, and the objects then further exchanged for bundles. But these things were not as quickly consumed as trade-store food and tobacco. Therefore, in the days prior to contact, the dependency on new or rare items from other islands was much greater. From trading expeditions and from *kula*, "foreign" imports such as special face paint, white mats, feathers, lime spoons, and betel nuts would have high value for villagers unable to obtain these things in other ways. Just as in today's situation, where villagers without cash have access to trade-store commodities through exchange of bundles, so too, in the past, villagers unable to travel, without trade partners, or without kin connections still had access through bundles to some of these imports.

Betel nuts, coconuts, and fresh fish may be traded for bundles. But prior to contact, betel nuts and coconuts had less circulation through bundles. Only villagers of rank owned betel and coconut palms and pigs. R.L. Bellamy (1913), the first resident magistrate in the Trobriands, initiated a huge program of coconut planting which for the first time gave nonrank villagers access to their own coconut palms. Gradually, with increased Western economic activity, villagers also began to plant their own betel (*areca*) palms. But it was as late as the 1950s when the high-ranking chief, Mitakata, declared that everyone could own pigs.[6] Therefore, prior to these changes, villagers had access to pork, betel nuts, and coconuts for their own consumption only through direct exchange relationships with villagers of rank (see Weiner 1976) or through trade in bundles. Traditionally, women of rank and women married to men of rank were presented with many more avenues to accumulate women's wealth.

At least by the 1880s, however, and probably earlier, as a result of trade in woodcarvings to ships' crews, diving for *bêche de mer* and pearls, and the sale of garden produce to Europeans, access to certain kinds of Western goods became more and more common. Payments by Europeans generally were made in tobacco, rice, axes, and knives, but tobacco seems to have been the most frequently used commodity for trade. An indigenous tobacco was grown, but smoking never reached the proportions that it did with the advent of trade-store tobacco. According to a few women informants, until recently tobacco constituted an important item for trade in bundles. Now, however, with more cash available, most villagers usually have ways to find tobacco to smoke. This was the reason I was advised to buy tins of fish and meat. These items cost more than tobacco, and many villagers cannot afford to buy them in the trade store.

Today, when women gather in large numbers, especially at mortuary distributions, one always observes some women who simply come to trade various commodities for bundles. At these times women often try to think of things that children want. I was instructed to take candies and just to sit with my basket open: "The children will see your candy and run and ask their mothers to get them some." I have seen women with items ranging from balloons and chewing gum to octopus meat and special kinds of sea shells, all displayed in anticipation of increasing their stores of bundles. The inventiveness never ceases: one night I watched two married men cook biscuits (with ingredients purchased in the trade store) over an open fire. The next day they took the biscuits to other villages, "selling" each one for five bundles.

In fact, watching men think of ways to get bundles for their wives was my introduction into the relationship between men and women's wealth. One day a close friend asked if I wanted to buy his new carving. He said that he knew it was not very good because his eyesight was too poor for him to carve properly. But his wife's brother had died, and he had to get cash in order to help his wife accumulate bundles. I watched men work for months—going fishing, selling garden produce to the Europeans, selling carvings, cooking biscuits, trading off pigs—all in an effort to get bundles for their wives.

Although women are always involved in the manufacture of bundles and skirts, they must engage in trade for bundles with other commodities if they want to accumulate large amounts of bundles. Men, however, are the major sources of cash for trade-store goods, and commodities such as pigs, "imports" from other islands, fish, and even biscuits of their own invention. Behind every wealthy woman is a man—her husband—who has taken his own wealth and labor and converted them into bundles for her. From this perspective Joshua's remarks were quite accurate. Men give everything they have to women for their bundles. Obviously, the next question—that which Joshua did not consider—concerns why men should continually support women with their wealth.

It took many months of observation and discussion before I was able to piece together the key relationship between women's wealth and yam production. As I noted earlier, men produce special harvests of yams annually for their married sisters. These yams are loaded into their sisters' husbands' yam houses. Each man has the right to use the yams placed in his yam house.[7] When Malinowski described these harvest transactions, he found it difficult to understand why men worked for their sisters, rather than for their own wives. The difficulty, as I already suggested, lies in part in not understanding women's place in the exchange system.

Men work a variety of gardens throughout the year, including a garden which supplies their wives and children with daily food. Among the most important gardens a man works will be the yam garden for a married sister. But because the presentation of yams is made in the name of a woman, the woman's husband is obligated directly to her rather than to her brother. Thus, this transaction must not be understood as an exchange between men only. Each time someone who was a member of a woman's natal kin group (*dala*) dies, she must distribute her own women's wealth at the *sagali*. Although women work hard to manufacture their own wealth, the work is slow. In order to have many large baskets of wealth, women need additional wealth obtained through others. Therefore, a woman's husband, because he received yams from her brother, should work for his wife, converting his own wealth into women's wealth in the ways described above.

The interchange between yams and women's wealth I describe as the core of the relationships between a woman, her brother, her husband, and in most cases, her father (Weiner 1976, 1978b). If a man does not work hard enough for his wife in accumulating wealth for her, then her brother will not increase his labor in the yam garden. Men evaluate their labor vis-à-vis each other in terms of the production that is being channeled through women. Women receive *yams* in their own names from their brothers, and they receive *women's wealth* in their own names from their husbands. The production in yams and women's wealth is always being evaluated and calculated in terms of effort and energy expended on both kinds of production. The value of a husband is read by a woman's kin as the value of his productive support in securing women's wealth for his wife.

In addition to an annual yam harvest, men also present annual baskets of yams and taro to a range of women whom they call "sisters," by dint of blood relation, an extension of the kin term to women of the same clan, and fictive kinship. These women are obligated to present their "brother's" wife with additional women's wealth when she needs to distribute bundles and skirts in the mortuary distribution (i.e., when one of her kin dies). Therefore, men develop and maintain ego-centered networks of exchange relationships with women. Through these kinds of transactions, men also establish important relationships with other men (e.g., relationships between brothers-in-law). But women, as direct transactors in these exchanges, are never merely the object of relationships between men as Lévi-Strauss (1969:114–16, 481, 496) would have us believe.

If men stopped contributing their wealth to their wives, they in turn would stop receiving annual yam harvests from their wives' brothers. Access to yams is of major concern, for yams serve as a medium of exchange, securing many other important commodities. For example, yams serve as payment for fish, the performance of magic spells, stone ax blades, *kula* shell valuables, pigs, betel nuts, and so on. Yams are also important for distributions at feasts, usually in political contexts, and for distributions at mortuary ceremonies (see Weiner 1976:144). Only if cash ever came to be completely substitutable for the exchange value of yams would the annual harvest presentations lose most of their economic value.

During the early 1970s, when tourism was at its height, villagers often complained to me that men were not working hard in the gardens because they could get cash by selling woodcarvings to the visiting weekend tourists. Cash was being substituted for access to some of the above items, but cash could not replace yams for feasts, mortuary distributions, or for filling a man's yam house. In fact, during the peak years of tourism (1971 and 1972 until the small Trobriand Hotel was destroyed by fire and the charter flights were cancelled), women told me that men who could carve were able to provide their wives with one or two additional baskets of women's wealth. (Each basket would be equivalent to $50-$100.) Thus, even with a decrease in yam production, much of the additional cash circulating was being drained off into women's wealth. At the time, a good correlation existed between "wealthy women"—those women with large amounts of women's wealth—and "strong men"—those men who still received substantial yam presentations.

Such situations provide two additional insights. First, over a period of time, women sustain variations in the amounts of women's wealth available to them, just as men must adjust to variations in the size of any individual annual yam presentation. Throughout the past 70 years, the *Annual Reports* indicate that total annual yam production in Kiriwina has never been constant. Because of drought or local political conflicts, production decreased significantly from time to time. Prior to colonization, warfare caused the diminution of yam production for many men, and full yam houses were set on fire by the victors. Even today, political events and personal feuds often leave some men the recipients of very few or no annual yam presentations (Weiner 1976:211–26). But the constant necessity for men to aid in supplying women with bundles and the fact that the distribution of women's wealth takes place in a public arena may serve to stabilize political, personal, or natural disruptive forces. In other words, the cycle of yam production is firmly connected to women's wealth and therefore, relationships between men continually involve relationships between women and men. The necessity for women's wealth may function to overcome lean years of yam production by eventually forcing a return to more productive harvests.

Second, and from a different perspective, any substantial shift in access to Western cash and/or goods seems to enable some young married men to advance more rapidly into positions of political and economic promise. During 1971 and 1972, I noted that in some cases, younger women were exceeding older women in their accumulations and distributions of women's wealth. Older women sometimes complained that other women's husbands had more cash because they sold carvings. I suspect that what I observed may have been similar to what happened periodically throughout the colonial period. Younger men found jobs more frequently with traders, pearlers, missionaries and in the administrative headquarters. Although they were never paid very much, the payment did provide them with access to Western goods, notably tobacco. In some other parts of New Guinea (see especially Lawrence 1964 and Schwartz 1962 on cargo cults), young men exposed to Western goods and ideology rebelled against their elders by rejecting core traditions such as brideprice and notions concerning ancestors. But in Kiriwina, the relationship between younger and older men seems to have been more supportive and far less traumatic (Weiner 1976:137–67).

At the beginning of the colonial period, chiefs seemed to have had much greater control over a range of resources such as pigs, coconuts, and betel. But throughout this century these controls have lessened considerably, and rank and age differentiations in political and economic domains gradually are becoming more attenuated. A significant aspect of these shifts is that women's wealth has continued to operate as a major economic force. Women's wealth not only absorbs the influx of Western cash and goods, but in the inflation of women's wealth we find embedded a process which has allowed greater egalitarian control over indigenous resources, and has lessened the socioeconomic distance between old and young men and women. All of these changes occurred without causing a major break in traditional ways.

The colonial situation, in comparison with other parts of the world, was rather benign in Kiriwina. Except for pearls and *bêche de mer*, there were few enticing resources for foreigners to exploit. Early government land ordinances prohibited the purchase of major tracts of land by non-natives. Malinowski's extensive publications on Trobriand society may have given Kiriwina a special place in that many government officials were concerned to understand, and not to disturb, important traditions (see especially Austen 1934, 1941, 1945; Rentoul 1931; Julius 1960). Only on the island of Vakuta did copra production ever become more than an occasional occupation. Cooperative stores failed, as did attempts to introduce new kinds of crops such as rice. Except for the periodic arrival of canoes from Fergusson Island selling sacks of betel nuts, a formal market has never developed. Socioeconomic, political, and ecological reasons could be given for each case of failure. But in critically evaluating the rejection of outside influences and the strength of Trobriand traditions, the significance of women's wealth must be given a primary place.

MATRILINY AND REPRODUCTION

In order to expand on the significance of women's wealth, I examine briefly the meaning of human and social reproduction in Kiriwina. So far, I have emphasized that outsiders, including anthropologists, have ignored the role of Kiriwina women, but my discussion has concerned the economic role of women's wealth vis-à-vis men and their wealth. The problem becomes more complex, however, because ignoring Kiriwina women has also contributed to misconceptions regarding cultural and symbolic concerns surrounding birth, death, and the meaning of matrilineality. This perspective has significant implications for understanding stability in banana leaves.

The Trobriand Islands are often cited as a classic example of a matrilineal society—a society in which descent is reckoned through women. Malinowski's definition of the opposition between "father love" and "mother right" still remains the most distinguishing feature in the classification of matriliny. According to this classification, although descent may be traced through women, it is men—the brothers of women—who control property, women, and all things of value. A man may love his own children, but he is forced to give to his sister's son. When feminists turned to anthropological accounts of matriliny, they found anthropologists describing "matriarchy" as nothing but a myth (e.g., Bamberger 1974). Women seemed to fare no better in these systems than in any other. Further, since the time of Morgan and McLennan, matrilineal societies have been analyzed as societies that are less well structured than those with patrilineal systems of descent. This view persists.

For example, Mary Douglas (1969) argued that descent through women may exert too great a strain on the nuclear family; therefore, in some cases such societies cannot withstand changes in economic and political sectors (see also Epstein 1964). The conflict between a man's obligation to give to his sister's son rather than to his own son has led anthropologists to discuss a range of attributes of matriliny resulting in instability (e.g., Schneider and Gough 1961; Richards 1950; Murdock 1949). Therefore, it is not surprising to find sociobiologists using examples of matriliny to show their evolutionarily unstable position because, at base, men are faced with the conflict of having to invest in their sisters' sons rather than in their own sons (see especially van den Berghe and Barash 1977). At the same time, Marshall Sahlins (1976) argues against the tenets of sociobiology, using the specific example of Malinowski's description of matriliny in the Trobriands.

My analysis of matriliny in the Trobriands, however, is opposed to Malinowski's example and his position regarding father love and mother right (see e.g., Weiner 1976; especially 1979). The traditional exchange system seems to be inherently stable, and a large measure of that stability I attribute to the complementary exchange relationships between women and men. Recently, Jill Nash presented another important example from the Nagovisi of South Bougainville Island. Among the Nagovisi, effects of modernization such as access to cash crops and changes from traditional wealth objects to Australian currency served to reinforce, rather than to collapse, matrilineal institutions (1974). The apparent dilemma of father love versus mother right results from the examination of the social system from a male perspective, which accords primacy and full attention to those material objects of wealth that men exchange and focuses on marriage without considering seriously what kinds of exchanges take place at death. The problem is not only that women have been ignored, but the full range of what men do has been ignored.

In traditional Trobriand thought, conception occurs through the combination of a woman's blood and an ancestral substance—the process regenerates matrilineal identity through time. With the believed entrance of an ancestral spirit-child into a woman's body (Malinowski 1916), a child is thought to be conceived as a member of its mother's lineage (*dala*) and clan (*kumila*). Malinowski was told by informants that men make no contribution to conception, and he therefore wrote extensively about the Trobrianders' lack of knowledge of physical paternity (1916, 1927, 1929). His views generated many later arguments (e.g., Leach 1967a, 1967b; Powell 1968; Spiro 1968), but if we take what informants tell us seriously we find that men are thought to contribute directly to the growth and nurturance of the fetus by frequent sexual intercourse (see Weiner 1976; Powell 1968; Austen 1934; Rentoul 1931).

Using a female-male perspective for an analysis of the processes of regenerating *dala* and reproducing human beings, we find that women contribute to the unchanging, internal identity of *dala*, while men (their husbands, who are members of a different *dala*), augment their child's natal *dala* with contributions from another *dala*. Following a birth, men continue this external process of growth and nurturance by providing their children with names and other paraphernalia associated with their own *dala*. In this way, each child is built up by having an internal identity—contributed by its mother (with rights to property contributed by its mother's brother) and additional resources gained through its father (and later augmented by its father's sister) (see Weiner 1976: 121–130). Therefore, a woman and her husband reproduce a human being that at birth is perceived to have input from another *dala*, in addition to its own *dala*.

But in order to understand further the role that women and men play in complement to each other, it is necessary to depart from the perspective of a woman and her husband and to view a woman and her brother as an integral unit, making complementary contributions both to a woman's brother's children and to a woman's own children (see Weiner 1979). In the former instance, a man and his sister (father and father's sister to a child) contribute their own *dala* resources to the man's children, thus building up these children with resources that they may use, but may not subsequently pass on to their own children. At some later time, these *dala* resources must be reclaimed by the members of the original *dala*. A woman and her brother (or her matrilineal descendants) make payments to her brother's children (or their matrilineal descendants) in order to replace those *dala* resources originally given. In the latter case, a woman and her brother (mother and mother's brother) contribute to the regeneration of *dala*—the woman through the process of conception and the man through the control and transmission of *dala* property such as land and palm trees (Weiner 1976, 1979).

The system is one in which use rights to a range of resources are extended to a man's children. In this way, a man and his sister build up long-term relationships with his children that may last even after he dies. Further, as a man's children grow into adulthood, they begin to reciprocate to their father and father's sister for what has been given earlier (see Weiner 1976). Therefore, traditional accounts of matrilinity notwithstanding, a man invests in his own children (as does his sister), securing returns for himself and his sister later in life. Children, in turn, secure access to the use of property in addition to their use of their own natal rights to the control or use of *dala* property. The system, then, allows for the investment of wealth in "others" who are not members of one's own *dala*. Through this system, individuals are built up by "others", but the investment has returns for the original givers. One's self, one's position, and one's potential as a reproductive agent depend upon relations with "others" because the reproductive process depends upon the circulation of possessions received from "others."

In a similar vein, men invest yams in their married sisters with the expectation that their sisters will accumulate large amounts of wealth. The distribution of a woman's wealth at a mortuary ceremony not only makes a woman publicly wealthy, but the distribution also states publicly the status of her brother and her husband. Therefore, throughout an individual's life the process of embedding wealth in others and receiving something back for what has been given is fundamental and may lead to the ability to expand one's resources extensively. In order for the system to continue and to maintain this process, a reclamation from other *dala* of what has been given must occur periodically.

Death is the mechanism that regulates this "reproductive" process (see Weiner 1978b, n.d.a, n.d.b. on a model of reproduction). Death is the moment when what has been given away must be reclaimed. For women and their brothers, members of the *dala* of the deceased, the reclaiming process constitutes an enormous drain on personal resources. These women and men are responsible for payments of wealth to hundreds of individuals who are not members of the deceased's *dala*, but who have been connected to the deceased during her or his life through various kinds of exchanges. In distributions held throughout the mourning period, men—with their wealth (yams and stone valuables)—and women—with their wealth (bundles and skirts)—by their payments reclaim as *dala* all that through time has been given away. In addition, they also make payments to public mourners for the deceased (see Weiner 1976:chs 3, 4). The major recipients of wealth are the father and the spouse of the deceased (and their extended kin), the two most important others in the life of the deceased.

Women, members of the deceased's *dala*, who are the major distributors of women's wealth, will give away the equivalent of between 500 and $1000 on the day of the women's mortuary ceremony. This distribution, occurring about five months after burial, marks the end of the major mourning period. Women distribute bundles and skirts to "others" as noted above. In so doing, women symbolically "untie" the deceased from all these hundreds of relationships.

In this way, women with their wealth reclaim at death what they once regenerated at conception: *dala* identity, an identity free from "other" associations. At some unmarked time, an unnamed spirit of a deceased person will return to Kiriwina and enter a woman's body, regenerating *dala* identity and beginning the reproductive cycle of a new human being.

CONCLUSION

Thus, the economic aspect of women's wealth must be examined as it reflects the ideological aspects of the regeneration of *dala*, circumscribed through the culturally defined processes of human reproduction. The fact of women's control over extremely large quantities of wealth cannot be analyzed as an isolated economic fact without considering the wider implications of the relationship between matriliny and cycles of birth and death. Historically, there is no reason to believe that these connections were either inoperative or less important in the past.

That men may "feed" the system of women's wealth (through yams as brothers and other commodities as husbands) must be assessed as indicative of the strength and primacy of what women do. Without men, women manufacture their own wealth so that men remain unnecessary for the basic production of women's wealth. (In the same way, men are thought to be unnecessary in causing conception to occur.) Men's role vis-a-vis women is to expand the amount of women's wealth available to any one woman, just as men, unable to contribute *dala* identity to their children, expand the availability of external resources for their own children.

From an individual, ego-centered perspective, the interplay between women and men and women's wealth allows for political maneuvering and publicly defined statements of power and status—for both sexes. From a systemic perspective, the domain of women's wealth allows for the process of crossing *dala* boundaries and building up in "others" representations (i.e., material wealth, property, identity) of *dala*. At the same time, the accumulation and distribution of women's wealth reverses the process by reclaiming for an original *dala* such representations that formerly have been placed in circulation. Men's direct economic input into this system enables them to play out the same relationships with "others"—creating and maintaining extensive relationships with "others"—relationships which may be passed on to successors and thus remain operative through succeeding generations. In this way, men are able to establish intergenerational lines of paternal kin at the same time that matrilineal relationships are reconstituted through generations.

The process of the circulation of *dala* property (representations), which builds up "others" to whom it is given, allows for the maintenance of large, ego-centered, intergenerational networks of relationships. Without death momentarily halting the process, however, the circulation would in time deplete the property of *dala*. Death then serves as a regulatory mechanism, securing rights to the reclamation of *dala* property and identity. Women's wealth operates as a major force in this system.

From this perspective, the domain controlled by women and the domain controlled by men must be analyzed as separate, yet interlocking, units which, taken together, constitute the total social system. The vitality and primacy of the women's domain—anchored at death and conception—is verifiable through the dynamics and the central position of women's wealth. As an economic, political, and social force, women's wealth exists as the representation of the most fundamental relationships in the social system. As the verification of women's role in the reproductive cycle, women's wealth stands as a cosmological force, a force holding together the very premises of matriliny and paternal kin. Without this force—without women's wealth—the reification of these relationships in the form of cosmological and social interconnections could not be publicly demonstrated. Without such demonstration, men would be unable to maintain their role in the regeneration of social relations—a role that is primary to the maintenance of men's political domain.

Joshua's message lacked this insight; he was unmarried and had lived away from Kiriwina for many years. But as Kiriwina men continue to spend their wealth on their wives, the insight remains strongly embedded in the very structure of the social system. Women and their bundles have been the key units in the continuity of this system for a very long time.

NOTES

1. The research on which this chapter is based was carried out in Northern Kiriwina, Papua New Guinea, for 14 months during parts of 1971, 1972, and 1976. I am indebted to the following institutions for their support: Bryn Mawr College, National Institute of Mental Health, National Endowment for

the Humanities, American Council of Learned Societies, and the University of Texas Research Institute. I also thank my friends in Kiriwina for their time, concern, and their support of my work, and I am very grateful to the excellent editorial comments on an earlier draft of this essay made by Eleanor Leacock and Mona Etienne.

2. The Kiriwina term *sagali* is a general term for all distributions. The specific term for the women's mortuary distribution is *lisaldabu*. *Lisaldabu* occurs approximately five months after someone has been buried. There are other kinds of mortuary distributions prior to the women's distribution (see Weiner 1976).

3. The extent of the power of chiefs, and whether or not the title given by Seligman, "paramount chief," is appropriate, have been the subjects of long debate (see Weiner 1976:44–50 for a review).

4. Meggitt (1972) gives an account of *tee* exchanges. The *tee* system consists of long-term, delayed exchanges which occur in highly ceremonial contexts and involve relationships with close kin and distant allies. These kinds of exchange cycles can be found in many New Guinea Highlands societies.

5. Bundles are divided into categories called "new," "clean," "dirty," and "old" (Weiner 1976:94-95). For a pig transaction, all bundles returned must be newly made.

6. But even today, for villagers of no rank, there still exist implict sanctions against owning too many pigs and allowing sows to breed too often.

7. The size of a yam house will indicate a man's status and wealth. Not all men own yam houses, however. A man must wait until his wife's relatives make him a large garden and they then come and build his yam house. Some men never achieve this status and store smaller yam presentations in the roofs of their houses or in small yam houses.

REFERENCES

Allen, M. R. 1967. *Male Cults and Secret Initiations in Melanesia.* Melbourne: Melbourne University Press.

Austen, L. 1934. "Procreation Among the Trobriand Islanders." *Oceania* 5: 102-13.

———. 1941. "Applied Anthropology in the Trobriand Islands." *Mankind* 3:67.

———. 1945. "Cultural Changes in Kiriwina." *Oceania* 16:15-60.

Bamberger, Joan. 1974. "The Myth of Matriarchy: Why Men Rule in Primitive Society." In M.Z. Rosaldo and L. Lamphere, eds., *Women, Culture, and Society.* Stanford: Stanford University Press.

Bellamy, R.L. 1913. "Magisterial Report, Trobriand Islands." *Papua Annual Reports.* Port Moresby.

Berde, Stuart. 1974. "Melanesians as Methodists: Economy and Marriage on a Papua and New Guinea Island." Ph.D. diss., University of Pennsylvania.

van den Berghe, Pierre L. and David P. Barash. 1977. "Inclusive Fitness and Human Family Structure." *American Anthropologist* 79, 4:809-23.

Codrington, R.H. 1891. *The Melanesians: Studies in Their Anthropology and Folklore.* Oxford: Oxford University Press.

Damon, F. H. 1978. "Modes of Production and the Circulation of Value on the Other Side of the Kula Ring Woodlark Island, Muyuw." Ph.D. Diss., Princeton University.

Deacon, Arthur B. 1934. *Malekula: A Vanishing People in the New Hebrides.* London: Routledge & Kegan Paul.

Douglas, Mary. 1969. "Is Matriliny Doomed in Africa?" In M. Douglas and P. Kaberry eds., *Man in Africa.* London: Tavistock.

Epstein, T.S. 1964. "Personal Capital Formation Among the Tolai of New Britain." In R. Firth and B.S. Yamey, eds., *Capital, Saving and Credit in Peasant Societies.* London: George Allen & Unwin.

Ernst, T. 1978. "Aspects of Meaning of Exchanges and Exchange Items Among the Onabasulu of the Great Papuan Plateau." *Mankind* 11, 3:187-99.

Faithorn, E. 1976. "Women as Persons: Aspects of Female Life and Male-Female Relations Among the Kafe." In P. Brown and G. Buchbinder, eds., *Man and Woman in the New Guinea Highlands.* Washington: American Anthropological Association.

Feil, D. K. 1978a. "Women and Men in the Enga *Tee.*" *American Ethnologist* 5, 2:263-79.

———. 1978b. "Enga Women in the *Tee* Exchange." *Mankind* 11, 3:220-30.

Gilmour, R.F. 1905. "A Few Notes on the Kiriwina (Trobriand Group) Trading Expeditions." *British New Guinea Annual Report.* Port Moresby.

Heider, K. 1970. *The Dugum Dani: A Papuan Culture in the Highlands of West New Guinea.* Chicago: Aldine.

Julius, Charles. 1960. "Malinowski's Trobriand Islands." *Journal of the Public Service* 2. Papua, New Guinea.

Kelly, R. C. 1976. "Witchcraft and Sexual Relations: An Exploration in the Social and Semantic Implications of the Structure of Belief." In P. Brown and G. Buchbinder, eds., *Man and Woman in the New Guinea Highlands.* Washington: American Anthropological Association.

Langness, L. L. 1967. "Sexual Antagonism in the New Guinea Highlands: A Bena Bena Example." *Oceania* 37:161-77.

———. 1974. "Ritual Power and Male Dominance in the New Guinea Highlands." *Ethos* 2, 3:189-212.

Lawrence, Peter. 1964. *Road Belong Cargo.* Manchester: Manchester University Press.

Leach, E.R. 1967a. "Virgin Birth." *Proceedings of the Royal Anthropological Institute* :39-50.

———. 1967b. "Correspondence." *Man* (n.s.) 3:655-56.

Leach, Jerry W. and Gary Kildea. 1975. *Trobriand Cricket: An Ingenious Response to Colonialism.* A film produced under the sponsorship of the government of Papua New Guinea.

Leacock, E. 1978. "Women's Status in Egalitarian Society: Implications for Social Evolution." *Current Anthropology* 19, 2:247-75.

Lévi-Strauss, C. 1969. (orig. in French, 1949) *The Elementary Structures of Kinship* (2nd ed.). Boston: Beacon Press.

Malinowski, B. K. 1916. "Baloma: The Spirits of the Dead in the Trobriand Islands." *Journal of the Royal Anthropological Institute* 45. Reprinted in B. Malinowski, *Magic, Science, and Religion and Other Essays.* New York: Doubleday.

———. 1920. "Kula: The Circulating Exchanges of Valuables in the Archipelagoes of Eastern New Guinea." *Man* 53:87-92.

———. 1922. *Argonauts of the Western Pacific.* New York: E. P. Dutton.

———. 1927. *Sex and Repression in Savage Society.* New York: Meridian Books.

———. 1929. *The Sexual Life of Savages in North-Western Melanesia.* New York: Harvest Books.

Meggitt, M.J. 1964. "Male-Female Relationships in the Highlands of New Guinea." In P. Brown and G. Buchbinder, eds., *Man and Woman in the New Guinea Highlands.* Washington: American Anthropological Association.

———. 1972. "System and Subsystem: The *Te* Exchange Cycle Among the Mae Enga." *Human Ecology* 1, 2:11-24.

Moreton, M.H. 1905. "Resident Magistrates Report—South-Eastern Division. *British New Guinea: Annual Report.* Port Moresby.

Murdock, G. P. 1949. *Social Structure.* New York: Free Press.

Nash, Jill. 1974. *Matriliny and Modernisation: The Nagovisi of South Bougainville.* New Guinea Research Bulletin, No. 55. Canberra: Australian National University.

Powell, H. A. 1950. *Trobriand Islanders.* A film produced by University College, London.

———. 1956. "An Analysis of Present Day Social Structure in the Trobriand Islands." Ph.D. diss., University of London.

———. 1960. "Competitive Leadership in Trobriand Political Organization." *Journal of the Royal Anthropological Institute* 90:118-48.

———. 1968. "Correspondence." *Man* (n.s.) 3:65-102.

———. 1969a. "Genealogy, Residence, and Kinship in Kiriwina." *Man* (n.s.) 4:177-202.

———. 1969b. "Territory, Hierarchy, and Kinship in Kiriwina." *Man* (n.s.) 4:580-604.

Read, K. E. 1952. "Nama Cult of the Central Highlands, New Guinea." *Oceania* 23:1-25.

Rentoul, A. C. 1931. "Physiological Paternity and the Trobrianders." *Man* 31: 152-54.

Richards, A. I. 1950. "Some Types of Family Structure Among the Bantu." In A. R. Radcliffe-Brown and D. Forde, eds., *African Systems of Kinship and Marriage.* London: Oxford University Press.

Sahlins, M.D. 1976. *The Use and Abuse of Biology.* Ann Arbor: University of Michigan Press.

Schneider, D. M. and K. Gough, eds. 1961. *Matrilineal Kinship.* Berkeley: University of California Press.

Schwartz, T. 1962. "The Paliau Movement in the Admiralty Islands, 1946-1954." *Anthropological Papers of the American Museum of Natural History* 49, 2.

Seligman, C. G. 1910. *The Melanesians of British New Guinea.* Cambridge: Cambridge University Press.

Spiro, M. E. 1968. "Virgin Birth, Parthenogenesis, and Physiological Paternity: An Essay in Cultural Interpretation." *Man* (n.s.) 3:242-61.

Strathern, M. 1972. *Women in Between: Female Roles in a Male World, Mount Hagen, New Guinea.* London: Seminar Press.

Weiner, A. B. 1976. *Women of Value, Men of Renown: New Perspectives in Trobriand Exchange.* Austin: University of Texas Press.

———. 1977. "Trobriand Descent: Female/Male Domains." *Ethos* 5:54-70.

———. 1978a. "Epistemology and Ethnographic Reality: A Trobriand Island Case Study." *American Anthropologist* 80:3.

———. 1978b. "The Reproductive Model in Trobriand Society". *Mankind* 11, 3: 175-86.

———. 1979. "Trobriand Kinship from Another View: The Reproductive Power of Women and Men." *Man* 14, 1.

———. 1980. "A World of Made is Not a World of Born'—Doing Kula in Kiriwina". In E. R. Leach and J. W. Leach, eds., *New Perspectives on the Kula.* Cambridge: University of Cambridge Press (in press).

———. n.d.a. "Sexuality Among the Anthropologists, Reproduction Among the 'Natives.'" In S. Ortner and H. Whitehead, eds., *Sexual Meaning* (forthcoming).

———. n.d.b. "Reproduction: A Replacement for Reciprocity."

Young, Michael W. 1971. *Fighting with Food: Leadership, Values, and Social Control in a Massim Society.* Cambridge: Cambridge University Press.

12 Putting Down Sisters and Wives:
Tongan Women and Colonization

CHRISTINE WARD GAILEY

The British search for advantages over France, for new trade routes to East Asia and for Australia resulted in James Cook's voyages in the late eighteenth century. Sixteenth-century Spanish and Portuguese explorers had not touched most of the Pacific islands east of the Solomons, and Dutch commercial voyagers of the seventeenth century sought new routes to the East Indies, and in the process landed at many South Pacific island groups, including Tonga, but—for reasons ranging from a lack of precious metals or large potential markets to the problem of violating Dutch East India Company prerogatives—Oceania had not been appreciably penetrated commercially before the mid-eighteenth century. After the Seven Years' War (1756-63), both England and France sponsored voyages of discovery and acquisition to the Pacific. Cook, commissioned by the British Admiralty, filled in navigation charts and provided information for the traders, missionaries, whalers, and settlers who followed.

At the same time in England, industrialization—beginning with textile manufacturing—had engendered tremendous misery in the working classes. In the eighteenth century, political turmoil was defused largely through the Methodist evangelical revival movement. In the nineteenth century, Protestant missionary activity in the Pacific and elsewhere was an outgrowth of this movement. Middle-class and politically conservative, the revivalists nevertheless opposed slavery and backed certain social reforms. The discovery by Cook of so many "unsaved" souls led to the organization of London Missionary Society and, later, Methodist Missionary Society expeditions to the South Seas.

The wars of American independence and 1812, in conjunction with the Napoleonic Wars, diverted British and French attention from Pacific colonization. The absence of competition along with English naval command of the Atlantic gave an artificial impetus to U.S. whaling in the Pacific. Britain's loss of settler and debtor colonies in America, the failure of a convict settlement in West Africa, and the increasing threat of French involvement in the Pacific had, however, led the British to establish a convict colony in New South Wales in 1788. And shortly thereafter, settler colonies were founded in Australia and in New Zealand.

With the exception of Australia and New Zealand, there was no British annexation in the South Pacific until the 1870s. The period from 1830 to 1845 was marked in Britain by serious labor unrest, middle-class reform movements, protection of domestic wheat prices at the expense of working class consumers, and a severe depression. From 1850 to 1870 there was a transformation of industrial production from textiles to steel, coal, iron, and steamship and railroad production. Labor conditions in the textile sector improved somewhat, and the Free Trade laws were soon to generate interest in expanding trade.

In addition to the domestic situation, the suspension in Pacific colonization reflected both preoccupation with colonial wars elsewhere in the empire and the administrative time and expense involved in colonizing areas which were not considered particularly lucrative. In any case, annexation was unnecessary for purposes of trade, so long as other European states did not assert sovereignty. The presence of British missionary groups and traders was deemed an adequate safeguard of British interests in the absence of active colonizing by France.

In the course of the nineteenth century, during Victoria's reign, missionary activities received the tacit approval of the state. British government officials served on the boards of missionary societies, while Protestant missionaries often became ministers of state in the Polynesian "native kingdoms" they helped to organize. Missionary belief in the possibilities of political and religious "progress"—the establishment of institutions on the British model—for Polynesians received moral, but rarely military, support from the Colonial Office, which was enmeshed in wars in India, Burma, China, and South Africa.

The second wave of British annexation in the Pacific followed the first organized attempts at commercial plantation agriculture by Euro-Americans in the area. With the British victory in the Opium War—and the "opening" of China—the volume of sea traffic expanded greatly. British planters urged annexation to protect their investments. French Catholic missionary activity, which had begun in the 1830s, was closely allied to the French annexation of several island groups from the 1840s to the 1870s, Australian and New Zealand colonists' demands for British intervention began to be echoed by the Methodist missionary groups, whose fierce anti-Catholicism in this case fit into Great Britain's increasing concern about French expansion. In 1874, Britain annexed Fiji, and the struggle among the remaining industrial powers—Germany, the United States and Great Britain—over unclaimed island groups did not end until 1900, when Britain incorporated Tonga and the Cook Islands into a protectorate.

The capitalist colonization of stratified, but still kinship-organized, societies has frequently catalyzed the formation of state structures. Tonga, a group of islands southwest of Samoa and east of Fiji, is one of the "native kingdoms" which emerged in Polynesia in the course of the nineteenth century as a response to the perceived threat of colonial annexation. The chiefs' efforts to avoid British annexation were not entirely successful; the islands were made a protectorate in 1900 and were not returned to full political independence until the 1950s. How women—both chiefly and nonchiefly—have been involved and affected in this process of Western penetration and indigenous state formation is the concern of this chapter.

The status of Tongan women before significant European presence is matter of considerable debate. The first part of this chapter will address the vagaries of rank and gender. I will contend that 1) there was no fixed gender hierarchy, 2) considerations of rank and gender had political implications for chiefly groups, 3) both chiefly and nonchiefly women had sources of authority and relative autonomy which were not dependent on personal attributes, and 4) Tongan chiefly women were chiefly first—that is, the division of labor by gender and rank associated chiefly men and women more closely than chiefly women and nonchiefly women, or chiefly men with nonchiefly men. The processes of production and social reproduction will be examined, paying particular attention to the conceptual separateness and interdependence of men's and women's labor and products.

The analysis will then shift to changes during the European experience. I will argue that all Tongan women have lost important sources of structural authority and autonomy through a complex interaction of missionary zeal and influence; the institution of production for exchange; changes in industrial production in Europe and the introduction of European commodities; the interests of missionaries, Tongan chiefs, and colonial administrators in revising and codifying customary inheritance and land-use arrangements; and the creation of a civil sphere especially associated with chiefly men.[1]

It is important to remember that missionaries, traders, and colonial advisors were not a united front; their mutual mistrust and hostility are recognized. But all shared certain assumptions about maleness and femaleness, appropriate spheres of activity for women and men, and progress through civilization in the Western sense (cf. Diamond 1964). For Tongan chiefly people, capitalist and patriarchal ideology had fewer deleterious consequences, since the Europeans shared with the chiefly groups a belief in the inferiority of the producing people, in both a moral and "civilized" sense. Chiefly women have lost many prerogatives they had enjoyed as sisters but have retained considerable power as elite people. The nonchiefly people in general, and nonchiefly women in particular, have had the most constraints placed upon them by these transformations. Legally and structurally, nonchiefly women are the most dependent with regard to their access to subsistence resources and their relation to subsistence production.

I have analyzed early travelers' accounts, missionary and colonial officers' journals, written records of Tongan chiefly oral histories, Tongan myths and legends, colonial office records, and twentieth-century ethnographic reports. Each author, each reciter of history, has vested interests, and these are often as significant as the manifest content. Utilizing myths and legends is particularly problematic, since changes over time in myth do not directly mirror societal changes, yet the myths do speak to social contradictions.

This chapter is not intended as a treatise on either Tongan kinship or on state formation[2] and gender; it is intended to present an overview of some of the processes involved in Western colonial penetration and some of the consequences of those processess for women in a ranked, kinship-organized society.

KINSHIP RANKING VERSUS CLASS

Tongan women, like all Tongans, were ranked vis-a-vis all other persons according to three abstract relations of superiority and inferiority: older, whether chronologically or genealogically, was considered superior to younger; "maleness" was superior to "femaleness" (a gender category which did not mean men to women); but sisters were higher-ranking than brothers. No one's status could be determined solely on the basis of gender, since sibling gender and seniority were also considered. In Tonga, as in other ranked, kinship-organized societies, the principles of ranking were inconsistent: personal status was not predicated on any abstract factor taken out of the context of particular relationships. These structural contradictions militated against the formation of permanent hierarchical relations between groups. As in other Polynesian societies (see Sahlins 1972; 205—10), each person was ranked "relatively," that is, with respect to other individuals who were actual and fictive kin. For example, a man was considered "chiefly" to his younger brother, but the man's sister was "chiefly" to both of them.

The ambiguity of such personally based ranking disguised to some extent the existence in Tonga of two overarching, relatively ranked groups, chiefs and nonchiefs. But these groups should not be confused with classes. Classes refer to groups which have structurally differential access to subsistence and other strategic resources (see Fried 1967). Chiefly groups included people directly involved in subsistence production, though most were not. (Chiefly women, it should be noted, were involved in the production of valuables, *koloa*, which was considered honorable and "chiefly.") Access to strategic resources by chiefly groups is best described as "preferential," rather than exclusive (Sahlins 1972:92—94). Chiefly people did not "own" land or other resources necessary for social reproduction; rather they distributed or allocated resources in their capacity as guardians of Tongan fertility and prosperity (Gifford 1929:76, 144, 171). Use rights to land, labor, and other subsistence necessities were allocated according to kinship-determined rank. (This determination could become highly politicized because of the plethora of kinship connections between any two persons.) Access could not be denied any kinsperson, provided they did not violate kinship notions of reciprocity. (Certain chiefly groups, attempts to redefine the mutual responsibilities and expectations that mark kinship relations sparked precolonial struggles for and against the formation of classes, as well as centralized administration.) Chiefly and nonchiefly groups, then, lacked critical differences in control of the means of production and are better conceived as "estates" rather than classes, following Rousseau's (1978) formulation. In other words, the groups were hereditarily ranked, but the ranking entailed differential privileges, a greater call on resources, rather than ownership. Tongan society, then, was not egalitarian, even before European contact, but the relations of production were still kinship-dominated.

SISTERHOOD IS POWERFUL

Tongan kinship has typically been analyzed as a "conical clan" or "pyramidal ramage" system based on patrilineal primogeniture—the inheritance, especially of titles, from father to oldest son. People were ranked according to closeness to a common ancestor, preferably through the direct (oldest son of oldest son) line, with ties through mothers being opportune but "second-best" connections (see Goldman 1970:293). These categorizations inhibit our understanding of inheritance, authority, and rank in Polynesia, and are particularly misleading in Tonga.[3] Ranking principles of seniority and sibling gender were at cross purposes; in operation, even the chiefly groups were openly bilateral. Seniority could take precedence over gender considerations, and closeness to a strategic relative (alive or dead) was more important than who formed the links. Alliances through marriage were crucial for chiefly groups and, over time, a pattern of generalized exchange between chiefly lines emerged. But to conceive of chiefly women as being passively exchanged (see, for example, Levi-Strauss 1969) by their fathers and brothers understates their authority and reduces women's status to that of only one role, wife.

In the conjugal relationship wives were supposed to defer to husbands (Beaglehole 1969:3:945), and chiefly husbands tended to outrank their wives (chiefly men were also polygynous), but chiefly women had authority in their marital lineage in certain contexts (:3:117n; Wilson 1799:104). Moreover, Tongan women—especially chiefly women—exercised social authority throughout life as *sisters.* Nonchiefly women (and nonchiefly men) had no *political* authority, but chiefly women had political authority in their natal lineages, including command over the labor of those women defined as inferior to them. It is likely that sisters and brothers had parallel lines of authority—sisters over lower-ranking women, brothers over lower-ranking men (see Martin 1827:2:212)—which for chiefly people was expressed in their call on lower-ranking people's labor and products.

Because the sister—especially the eldest sister—was ranked superior to her brother, sisters' children outranked brothers' children (Gifford 1929:22). For chiefly people this ranking involved political and material rights vis-à-vis maternal uncles and their children. These rights—often called privileges in the literature—included the sister's call on her brother, his household, and his descendants, and were subsumed under the term *fahu,* meaning "above the law" (:23). The father's sister, the imposing *mehekitanga,* was the focus of avoidance by her brother and his children, especially his sons. The father's sister arranged and vetoed her brother's children's marriages. She could command the labor and products of her brother's spouse(s), including the right to adopt her brother's children. And a curse from the *mehekitanga* threatened the brother's children and brother's wives with sterility or painful childbirth (Burrows 1970:64; Collocott 1923b:130). Women, considered by many researchers to be a simple "medium" of exchange between groups of men (see Levi-Strauss 1969:ch. 19; cf. Leacock 1977), could, in fact, negate the purpose of marriage alliances; a woman could threaten the reproduction of the lineage that had ostensibly "alienated" her.

The *fahu* relationship brought benefits to a woman's sons as well as to herself and her daughters and those benefits were recognized as emanating from the mother, rather than from the mother's brother. Even today, Tongans appreciate that their *fahu* rights—although illegal, they are still locally exercised—derive from their mothers' statuses; any presumption that the mother's brother is the "real authority" seems irrelevant in this context. Among chiefly groups, there were wife-receiving and wife-giving relations between lineages. In the Tongan perception, wife-receiving lineages were superior to wife-giving lineages because sisters were higher ranking than brothers. Benefits accruing to the husband's lineage (e.g. children, co-wives) were the result of the husband's relationship to a woman and her relationship to her brother.

Chiefly people were supposedly more concerned with the political aspects of the *fahu* than with material benefits. But whole lineages were *fahu* to other lineages, entailing a tributary relationship (Gifford 1929:115) as well as political inferiority. Because the *fahu* relationship was not restricted to single households, but included entire kin groups, the analysis of kinship in precontact Tonga should not allow women to "drop out" by arranging the kinship structure to focus solely on married couples and their descendants.[4] The sibling pair was extremely important in inheritance, alliance, and descent, and the sibling-based descent group fills out the one-sided representations of the lineage. There is evidence of specific terms designating lines descending from the sister, and titles of high-ranking chiefs show a similar parallelism (Collocott 1928:134, 153; Martin 1827:2:184). The first attempt to reunite the sacred and administrative chiefly titles (and responsibilities) was made at the end of the eighteenth century by the widow of the sacred chief, who was a sister to the administrative chief (Wilson 1799:104). The attempt failed, but the struggle can hardly be understood from a strictly "widow as regent" viewpoint.

DIVISION OF LABOR

Prior to European intervention, the division of labor was based on factors of rank, gender, and age. Most, but not all, chiefs did not produce their own food, but were dependent on nonchiefly labor for their subsistence. Land was vested in the highest-ranking (paramount) chiefs, who assigned usufruct (use right) estates to lower-ranking chiefs in return for support in warfare, donations of food and durable products, and labor service by the "commoner" or *tua* people living in the area. (Such corvée labor was demanded of both men and women; the workers would be given food for the duration of the project.) In addition, there were several ranks of *matapules*, who were titled, but neither chiefly (*eiki*) nor commoner (*tua*). These were craft specialists, attendants, warriors, supervisers of production, and petty administrators attached to district and paramount chiefly people (Gifford 1929:66). High-ranking chiefly women only rarely held male chiefly titles, but they seem in many cases to have held parallel titles related to their natal lineages (Collocott 1928:134). Chiefly women could order productive activities for lower ranking women. For the primary wife of a paramount (who was a paramount herself), these women were her co-wives, her husband's concubines (her attendants), the wives and daughters of lower-ranking chiefs and *matapules*, and nonchiefly women (Martin 1827:2:212). Those subject to a female paramount's call for labor would include women in both her husband's (her marital) and her brother's (her natal) lineages. Evidence is contradictory as to whether male chiefs could order female labor (excluding sexual services) and whether female chiefs could order male labor (Gifford 1929:98).

The division of labor by rank was complicated by gender. All things made or grown by men were considered *ngaue* ("work"); things produced or gathered by women were considered *koloa* ("valuables"). *Koloa*—woven mats, bark cloth (*tapa* or *ngatu*), baskets, bags, shellfish, coconut oil, and certain "chiefly" prepared foods—were superior to *ngaue* (agricultural products, deep-sea fish, canoes, weapons) (Martin 1827:1:122; West 1865:267; Collocott 1928: 165). Men did the cooking, which had low status (West 1865:267). Tasks such as child care and house building involved both genders. Both women and men went on long-distance voyages (Martin 1827:2:260), but women's activities on those voyages are not clear (Beaglehole 1969:3:939). It is likely that they bartered women's products while men bartered theirs; certainly, women and men took these opportunities to visit relatives and sometimes married in other islands. Women also accompanied war parties; they guarded the canoes, and frequently entered the field of battle to take revenge or to assist the wounded (Martin 1827:2:82, 147).

There were part-time specializations open to both genders, as well as gender-specific ones, though such specializations were generally associated with lower-ranking people. Medical doctors were either female or male, but midwives, since they were connected with childbirth, were female only, the skill being passed from mother to daughter (Thomson 1904:375). (In birth rituals the child was called *koloa*, a creation of the woman (Collocott and Havea 1922:169; Beaglehole and Beaglehole 1941:81).) There were priests and priestesses, but they were not chiefly and not nearly as influential as those in, for instance, Hawaii. Tongan deities were female, male, and androgynous (Gifford 1929:287, 291), but the configuration did not mirror the secular stratification. Certain deities were incarnations of historical personages—especially powerful female chiefs—who were seen as protectors of those oppressed by male paramount chiefs (Williamson 1924:1:148), and whose god houses were sanctuaries (Gifford 1929:324).

Old age entitled all Tongans to additional respect. For chiefly women political maneuvering did not cease with the end of childbearing. A chiefly woman (as much as any powerful individual) had structural means of determining who would receive chiefly titles, including male ones. A man's sister could arrange a marriage of his daughter to one of her sons or marry his son into a lower-ranking lineage. Since older, high-ranking women kept the chiefly genealogies, they had the ability to further the claims of, or discredit, a rising chief by calling attention to less illustrious ancestors or by juggling the ancestors. Chiefly women were not "used" by men as a means to title and power; they were involved in the contention themselves, if not for themselves, for their children or their brothers' children. And since rank followed the mother, the problem of high-ranking women's posing a threat through their children to the brother's lineage titles recurs as a theme in Tongan history.

Tongan men considered women the weaker of the sexes (Martin 1827:2: 95). This was the men's explanation for why women did no "menial" tasks or much physical labor (although reef fishing is hardly a leisurely activity). But there is no indication in early accounts of how women viewed men, or how they viewed their own strengths and weaknesses.

Rank and administrative authority were not necessarily related at the time of contact. The highest-ranking persons were the sister (Tui Tonga Fefine) of the sacred paramount chief of Tonga (Tui Tonga) and her even higher ranking daughter, the Tamaha ("sacred child"). Through time, these highest-ranking women had become somewhat removed from direct contention for administrative authority for two major reasons. At first, their positions in the changing chiefly marriage patterns tended to make them less of an immediate threat. Later, the Tui Tonga's administrative authority was usurped by junior lines.[5] Although eclipsed by the administrative chief, both the Tui Tonga and Tui Tonga Fefine, as well as those who succeeded them, retained administrative control of their respective districts and were owed tribute from lower ranking lines; over time, however, this tribute became increasingly symbolic (Gifford 1929:103). Land remained vested in the Tui Tonga, and the sister of the administrative paramount—always titled in her own right—was in each generation married to the sacred chief. After a considerable period of political turmoil, it became established that the Tui Tonga Fefine from then on would always marry into one of the lines of the honorable "house of Fiji," the "foreign" lineages resident in Tonga, where presumably she would be defused politically. (Her "foreign" children, although high ranking, would not be suitable to preside over Tongans.) Although subsequent Tui Tonga Fefines were certainly implicated in a number of chiefly intrigues (Gifford 1929:48; Goldman 1970:283), the sister of the administrative paramount chief became increasingly disruptive (1970:283). This woman was also the wife of the sacred paramount chief.

It is clear that chiefly women and men sometimes disagreed about women's political involvement. When a male high chief went to war against his father's sister over the control of Vavau island (which she had assumed on the death of another of her brother's sons), one of his wives defected. He requested that his aunt return the woman, saying, "It was a war between men, and not women." She refused his request (Martin 1827:1:185).

SPHERES OF EXCHANGE

The division of labor by gender and rank set up separate spheres of exchange (cf. Sahlins 1972). Nothing *ngaue* (men's products) was acceptable as a return for a gift or presentation of *koloa* ("valuables"), no matter what the relative amounts or quality of the products. The entire ritual structure rested on the exchange of things made by women and, because of the prerogatives of the father's sister through the *fahu*, was controlled by women (Collocott 1923b: 223). Women could give valuables to men (as a gift for sexual favors, for example), but only chiefs could order the production of valuables.

It has been shown that women's role in production was making valuables, including children; as producers of children for the husband's lineage or the local kindred, they symbolized group continuity. "Work" done by men insured the women's well-being. This seems to imply that women accepted food in return for valuables (children) and, like foreigners and strangers, mixed the separate spheres of exchange. Chiefly lineages could be seen as exchanging women for women—balanced in kind, though not in numbers and rank. *If* one thus assumes the lineage to be a masculine sphere, then male-male exchange was formally balanced (women for women), while male-female exchange (food for children) was negative for women as women got less ("work" products) than they gave ("valuables"). But this view of the lineage ignores both sibling and chiefly-nonchiefly ranking.

The father's sister, however, transcended marriage-based affiliation: before, during, and after marriage she had similar rights in her lineage. Through the *fahu*, a woman had access to the valuables she had created and those of her brother's lineage created by other women. The father's sister could adopt the brother's children, thus receiving "valuables" produced by her brother's wife. Were it not for this critical right to adopt, her marriage into another lineage would be the exchange of *productivity* (a valuable maker) in exchange for *products* (valuables given as marriage gifts).

These spheres of exchange had meaning for chiefly people only; marriage alliances were not as politically charged for nonchiefly groups. Lineage affiliation was increasingly tenuous for nonchiefly people as the chiefly groups sought to dissociate themselves from local kin groups. In addition, nonchiefly people did not entirely control the distribution of their labor and products, although they would rebel against an oppressive chief (Gifford 1929:182). Whether women gave children for food is academic for nonchiefly people: everyone gave to the chiefs, rebelled, or faced punishment (Goldman 1970:303). The exercise of *fahu* material rights was risky for nonchiefly people: the transfer of goods might transgress chiefly prerogatives. To limit possible chiefly interference, nonchiefly people tended to marry locally (Beaglehole and Beaglehole 1941:78), so goods transferred through the *fahu* would remain in one chiefly district.

Exchange between chiefs and nonchiefly producers formed a separate sphere as well. The nonproduction of "work" was a mark of rank for men. Chiefly women produced only valuables and had nonchiefly women's valuables and productive capacity at their disposal as well. As an early traveler reported,

> The women employ themselves (particularly nobles) in making a variety of articles, chiefly ornamental; these employments, however, are considered accomplishments, not professions. Some of the higher class of women not only make these...but actually make a sort of trade of it, without prejudice to their rank; which is what the lower class of women could not do, because what they make is not their own property, but is done by order of their superiors (Martin 1827:2:97).

It should be noted that nothing chiefly people did was considered a "profession," because all specialists were *matapules,* who were lower ranking than chiefs. Even if male chiefs could command nonchiefly women's labor at gender-specific tasks (they *could* for undiscriminated tasks like fishing), more would be implied about the importance of emerging classes versus gender than about gender relations per se. Chiefly women controlled the disposition of the goods they produced (subject to the demands of higher ranking female chiefs) and indirectly controlled the valuables (children) of their natal lineage. In addition, chiefly women received the subsistence goods identified as men's "work" in their own right as high ranking people, rather than through their husbands.

Women assured kin-group continuity in return for necessary subsistence goods made by men, but they could demand those goods and services irrespective of their position in marriage-alliance networks or their particular fecundity, because they outranked their brothers. Even among nonchiefly people, women *as sisters* were relatively chiefly and were thus assured flexible structural authority through the *fahu.*

SUMMARY: PRECONTACT TONGA

At the time of European contact in the seventeenth century, then, Tongan chiefly women had means of support independent of their husbands. Chiefly women were also engaged in the production and distribution of valuables, in the arrangement of strategic marriages, and directly and indirectly in contention for chiefly titles. Nonchiefly women produced valuables for their bilaterally integrated kin groups and for the chiefly groups. All women could rely on their brothers and maternal uncles for support regardless of their marital status.

Gender relations were symbolically, materially, and politically ambiguous; certainly, there was no discernible gender hierarchy. All people had complexly balanced roles of authority and deference. For women, the two key roles were those of wife and sister, entailing deference and authority respectively. The content of each role varied with rank, chiefly women's marital and sibling relations being far more charged politically than those of nonchiefly women.

With European contact and gradual colonization, the relative importance of sisterhood for both chiefly and nonchiefly women diminished and, at the same time, women—especially nonchiefly women—became dependent on husbands.

CONTACT AND COLONIZATION

Explorers and Early Travelers

From the earliest explorers' accounts (Beaglehole 1969:3:863), it is notable that Tongans of both sexes bartered foodstuffs and certain valuables for axes (used in canoe building and bark cloth production), iron nails, beads of particular colors (worn by women and men in similar ways), cotton and woolen clothing, red cotton fabric, and linen goods, (Beaglehole 1969:2:245, 3:863). The initial heaping of foods and valuables for European items rapidly settled into hard bargaining. The exasperated James Wilson remarked as early as 1797 that "their demands were so high that but little was purchased" (Wilson 1799: 97). Tongan amusement at the Europeans' lack of discretion in barter is evident.

> it [the sailors' bartering for curiosities] even went so far as to become the ridicule of the Natives by offering pieces of sticks stones and what not to exchange, one waggish Boy took a piece of human excrement on the end of a stick and hild it out to every one of our people (Beaglehole 1969:2:255).

In addition, Tongans were quite light fingered, a practice reserved for foreigners who were not established trading partners.

Such early travelers' reports raise the issue of what Europeans considered "prostitution" among the Tongans (and other Polynesian peoples). Lower-ranking, unmarried women would willingly sleep with Europeans in return for iron items or cloth. Tasman landed at Tongatapu, the largest island, in 1643 and described the women's behavior when many of them first came on board:

> "Other women felt the sailors shamelessly in the trouser-front, and indicated clearly: that they wanted to have intercourse. The [Tongan] men incited the sailors to such a transgression" (quoted in Sharp 1968:45).

One should notice that the Tongan men were urging the foreign men rather than the women in this.

Nonchiefly Tongan women were traditionally free to explore sexually until marriage. Children born before marriage were incorporated into the woman's kin group without difficulty, and this did not prejudice the mother's possibilities of marriage. Sexual trysts between Tongans were typically marked by an exchange of valuables; if the woman were a virgin she would give her first lover a mat as a token (Collocott 1923b:228). With regard to Europeans, a woman, or those male or female relatives speaking on her behalf (*never* independently of her wishes), proposed an appropriate present for the European to give her. When an older woman brought a young woman to James Cook, the younger woman "wanted a shirt or a nail." The older woman explained that he could have her and then present the gift later (which signified a closer relationship between the two parties) but "this not suteing me niether the old Lady began first to argue with me and when that fail'd she abused me" (quoted in Beaglehole 1969:2:444). It is plausible that such a preliminary agreement would have been necessary, since the Europeans might otherwise insult the woman by not presenting a suitable or useful gift. And since women traditionally gave a gift to the man they slept with (Alpers 1970:289), the ignorance of Europeans in such gifting might well have been taken advantage of by the single women.

The eagerness of the young women who did seek out particular sailors perhaps reflects in part an attitude towards sexuality that is difficult for many Westerners to understand. One officer on Cook's first voyage commented about the Tongans:

> Both men and women seem to have little knowledge of what we call delicacy in Amours; they rather seem to think it unnatural to suppress an appetite originally implanted in them perhaps for the same purposes as hunger or thirst, and consequently make it often a topic of public conversation, or what is more indecent in our judgement, have been seen to cool the ardour of their mutual inclinations before the eyes of many spectators (quoted in Beaglehole 1969:3:945).

Rape, in fact, seems to have been rare, being limited to times of warfare (perpetrators are not mentioned) and to the whims of young male chiefs (Martin 1827:2:147). It should be noted that all lower-ranking people were subject to the sexual desires of chiefs—both male and female—and it was quite unwise to refuse chiefly advances. Children of such unions were honored (Collocott 1923b:226). In times of war, female prisoners could be raped, though this was not an inevitability; female captives of high rank were not raped but were used as hostages (Martin 1827:1:216). In any case, the raped women were not considered tainted or dishonored (:2:147).

Women were not coerced into sexual liaisons with Europeans; they were free to refuse: "There are many women who either from their connections [i.e., higher rank], natural timidity, or absolute aversion to such promiscuous engagements are not pregnable on any terms, independent of those who are understood to be married" (Beaglehole 1969:3:945). It is also apparent that women generally chose only one sailor and would not sleep with another until the affair was terminated. Several women chose to accompany their lovers to other Tongan islands before deciding to take their leave. As one rather appreciative seaman wrote, "They [the accompanying women] made shift before they left us of getting most of our Linnen from us, especially from those who were not rich in Hatchets. They are of a very amorous complexion & highly deserving of what they got" (quoted in Beaglehole 1969:3:1044). The sailors were a means for unmarried, nonchiefly women to acquire the highly desirable iron items and exotic cloth that they would doubtless redistribute on returning to their kin, thereby gaining prestige not generally accorded women of their age and marital status.

The period of early contact—sporadic visits between 1643 and 1800—entailed a roughly balanced exchange of foodstuffs and indigenous cloth and mats for European ornaments (e.g., beads) and valuables (iron and cloth). Nonchiefly women sealed their sexual liaisons with Europeans through agreed-upon valuable gifts. This was seen by the Europeans as prostitution—especially since chiefly women (whose connections with the Europeans seem to have been limited to exchange) were rather guarded before marriage—and by the Tongans as premarital adventure with prestige benefits.

All the early travelers were impressed with the high status of Tongan women. Cook noted with surprise that chiefly women "tip of their Cup of the liquor made of the [*kava*] root in their turn with the men without the least ceremony, nay, I have even seen the men so genteel as to help the Ladies first" (:2:268). This latter comment may reveal more about recognition of rank than male Tongans' courtesies, since *kava* drinking at that time was restricted to chiefly people, and since the order of drinking reflected personal rank. All authors commented about the women's eating with the men, not separately as in most of Polynesia, and one added that Tongan women "have even a great sway in the management of [economic and political] affairs" (:3:933). The travelers' accounts reflect an awareness of the differences in behavior, privileges, duties, dress, and diet both between chiefly and nonchiefly groups and within the ranks of chiefly people. All mention the Tongatapu goddess of rains, wind, sky, and thunder, who was considered the most powerful deity of the island and for whom the *inasi* or first fruits offerings may have been destined.[6] The exotic and sometimes strenuous activities in which women were involved at times shocked the visitors, especially women's skills in boxing and reef fishing.

Cook and others were aware that certain women outranked the male sacred high chief, though the accounts disputed whether this was due to sisterhood or seniority. One European falsely attributed the Tamaha's high rank to the rank of her Fijian father: it seems to have been quite difficult for many of the men to accept the explanation of sisters' higher rank. When the Tui Tonga (sacred male paramount) was attempting to explain who the Tamaha and her mother, the Tui Tonga Fefine, were, and why they were so high ranking, he informed one of Cook's officers that "when his father was alive the sister of his father, who is the woman mentioned at Vavaoo [i.e., the *Tui Tonga Fefine*], reign'd jointly with him at Tonga [tapu]" (:3:954).

The dominant European attitude toward the Tongans in this early period seems to have been one of somewhat ambivalent admiration for the "noble savage." They appreciated the orderly way of life and the coupling of industriousness with leisure, of amorousness with marital fidelity. They were shocked by the seemingly capricious power of the chiefs, by the sacrifice of finger joints and, occasionally, of lower-ranking individuals in times of mourning and death. Several expressed concern that contact with Europeans had already had, and would continue to have, deleterious consequences for these Pacific cultures. This attitude contrasts sharply with those of the Europeans who followed, the missionaries and traders: missionaries were proselytizing in favor of progress in the Western mode as well as Christianity; traders' attitudes were variable but were molded by their concern for profit irrespective of Tongan interests.

European Trade: Coconut Oil and Tapa

The exclusivity of men's and women's spheres of exchange did not survive the transformation of Tongan products into commodities through European trade. Symbolically, women's products were demeaned in this transition; materially, one of the most important women's products was replaced by a European commodity. Labor demands on nonchiefly people intensified with the expanding production for trade. This intensification drew workers away from traditional tasks and resulted in changes in the division of labor that might have been temporary. But accompanying this economic change was the imposition of a male-centered ideology—Christianity—which was to make the contingency division of labor permanent and rigid, bringing about a corresponding loss of prestige for women.

Following the period of provisioning explorers' ships in return for iron and novelty items, trade with Europe focused on sandalwood (which soon was exhausted) and, especially, coconut oil. Before the expansion of the Euro-American whaling industries and the subsequent emphasis on whale oil, coconut oil fueled lamps in Europe and was used in cosmetics and soaps. Tongans produced coconut oil before contact, but on a small scale and for domestic consumption. Distribution of the oil was limited to chiefly women and men, who used it daily as a skin salve and ointment (Beaglehole 1969:3:932, 1309). The oil was produced by women and was thus considered a valuable. Although weaponry had been acquired sporadically by chiefly groups through raiding occasional American and European vessels, the trade in sandalwood and, above all, in coconut oil served the chiefly people as a consistent source of firearms. There is little mention of the chiefly-ordered intensification of women's production of the oil, but the work was probably—like mat and bark-cloth production—done in groups under the supervision of the agent of a male or female chief.

As the Pacific whaling industry burgeoned from 1830 to 1850, demand for coconut oil fell off but, by the time the whales were becoming scarcer, a new process had been developed in Europe for mechanically extracting coconut oil. Consequently, a demand was created in Tonga for coconuts, but no longer for coconut oil itself. European weapons and other commodities were assured by the growing interest in copra, the dried coconut kernel. With the invention of nitroglycerine (which used coconut oil) demand for copra further increased. The production of copra, also traditional, was *ngaue*, men's work, and much less labor intensive than coconut-oil extraction, a difference which—because it eased the demand on their labor—must have been appreciated by nonchiefly women. Men usually gathered, split, and hulled the nuts, which were then sun-dried and shipped. While copra was not considered a valuable, it could be exchanged for commodities that had been received for coconut oil, a valuable.

As long as women were engaged in coconut-oil extraction for the chiefs, there was no confusion of spheres of exchange—valuables were received for valuables. With intensified copra production, however, more pressure was placed on households for male labor time, taking men away from "domestic" tasks. Women, then, were apt to assume the men's "work," which was ordinarily demeaning, though not so in such an "emergency" situation. The exigencies of chiefly labor demands were easily incorporated into a temporary division of labor, but Christian missionaries insisted that women do the cooking and other "womanly" work, when men were available. At the same time, increased demands from outside the household—by chiefs for their own needs and for state taxes, by European traders who had lent money or credit, by missionaries for the prestige involved in voluntary mission donations—meant that women were needed to help with the copra at peak periods. Nonchiefly women, then, were disadvantaged in two ways through this change in commodity trade, coupled with missionary penetration. They were forced to do work traditionally done by men, especially cooking and copra production, and this labor was either auxiliary (copra) or of very low status (cooking).

The deterioration of women's economic status, in the interest of chiefly Tongans and European traders and missionaries, was compounded by the undermining of bark-cloth production through the introduction of manufactured cotton fabric. Missionaries, with few exceptions, strongly urged women and men to use the imported fabric as it was more "civilized" than *tapa*. A law specifically concerning *tapa* was issued in 1875 and provided for the eradication of *tapa* manufacture and wearing. The law was suspended in 1880, but it reflected the attitude of the state officials, European traders, and many missionaries.[7]

This artificially stimulated demand for cotton cloth affected women in several ways. Even with *tapa* no longer banned, cotton cloth became more prestigious for everyday wear. This undercut domestic uses of *tapa*, and in many places production for everyday use became obsolete. It continued to be important in ceremonial, including state-associated, functions, but household members no longer relied on women's work groups for clothing. Previously, the production of *tapa* was one result of the Tongan division of labor by gender and rank. *Tapa* had been made by women in formally organized local groups, usually under the direction of an older woman (Gifford 1929:147). They worked in a women's house especially constructed for the work group—the only such communal building in the settlement. With the replacement of *tapa* by cotton cloth, the work groups were called by chiefs less frequently, though production of mats and coconut oil for Tongan consumption continued. Furthermore, the commoditization of cloth made households dependent on European sources for an item necessary for subsistence. Cotton fabric had to be purchased, and men had greater access than women to copra, and later money, which were used to purchase cloth. Thus, not only was the valuable women's product, *tapa*, replaced by a commodity, cotton cloth, for everyday purposes and relegated to ceremonial use, but women's access to the new commodity was mediated through men, rather than established by virtue of their own rank.

As is the case with many products deprived of subsistence functions and restricted to a prestigious but symbolic sphere, *tapa* and the decorated versions, *ngatu*, have become elite goods, considered works of art. More recently, *ngatu* has become "collectable" in the Western, art-as-commodity sense. An integral aspect of Tongan women's social identity—women as valuable makers for their households and communities—has been drastically redefined.

Tapa and *ngatu* had been valuable because they were made by women. The value of a particular piece derived from the rank of the maker(s) more than any quality (such as design) abstracted from the producer (Collocott 1928:141). The social quality of the producer deeply influenced the quality of the fruits of her labor, as a child's rank followed from the rank of the mother. Her labor was socially necessary, socially organized, and socially valued from the household outward. As *ngatu* and *tapa* have acquired a limited "art" market, the source of value has shifted from the creator to the creation, and production itself has become somewhat disembodied. Not all women continue to produce *tapa* and *ngatu;* production has become specialized, and specialists are evaluated by the "beauty" of their products. Tongan and alien buyers exhibit the Tongan "cultural heritage" and "endangered art forms." Creating the product becomes an activity divisible both from the maker and from other activities of the maker, even as the maker becomes a specialist dependent on the qualities of the item and its value as a commodity.

Aboriginally, *tapa* was one expression of a woman, as a *kinswoman* working in a group—for herself if she were chiefly, for chiefs as redistributors and embodiments of *community* prosperity and prestige, if she were nonchiefly. While *tapa* was an expression of the social self, it was a subsistence necessity for all Tongans, chiefly and nonchiefly. *Tapa* was valuable and reflected the status of women in general, just as a piece of *tapa* reflected the status of the women who made it and the female chief who had ordered it (ibid.).

The commoditization of women's products as art objects in the latter half of the twentieth century tiresomely echoes Euro-American categories of differential value—for example, painting versus "decorative" arts. Basketry and woven mats, traditionally considered valuables, have only recently joined painted (not plain or glazed) bark cloth as "art," acceptable to Western collectors. Production is no longer for local consumption and, at the same time, no longer reflects and increases local prestige: production is for exchange. Such commodity production has been energetically organized in certain places by Christian religious personnel, expressly to support church activities and community development along lines acceptable to the church, just as other commodities supported Christian efforts in the past.

Commodity trade, then, has had a double-edged effect on women's production and prestige in Tonga. First, the initial demand for coconut oil put pressure on nonchiefly women for labor time to obtain for the chiefly groups a commodity—firearms—which enabled chiefs to command resources and labor irrespective of kinship expectations of generosity. Changing production processes in Europe, coupled with diminishing alternative resources (whales), shifted European demand to copra, a man's product. The increasing amounts of copra required of the producing people involved women as periodic, auxiliary laborers in a men's sphere. Second, the introduction of European commodities other than weaponry undercut local production of certain subsistence goods, *tapa* and *ngatu*, which were also prestigious. Women's products are still considered prestigious, but their multifaceted functions have been reduced to ceremonial functions. And woman, as the provider of clothing for the household, does not control her own raw material, but sews cloth obtained mostly through men, who have easier access to cash.

Missionary Impact

From the outset, the London Missionary Society and later, Wesleyan Methodist missionaries sought alliances with chiefly people; the strategy of conversion was "from the top down." This meant that, although initial proselytizing was directed toward chiefly people, the more far-reaching changes wrought by the missionaries were focused on the lower-ranking people, lest the chiefly alliance be endangered. Missionaries functioned as advisers to the chiefs and as Tongan state structures began to emerge, as ministers of state. This theocratic and patriarchal influence had particularly severe consequences for women's—and especially nonchiefly women's—sources of authority and autonomy.

The London Missionary Society sent nine men to Tonga in 1797; they became associated with the administrative paramount chief in Tongatapu, and thereby became involved along with him in the struggle for political centralization against other chiefs. Three were killed as a result of the Tongan civil wars, and the others left the islands. More successful missionizing began in

1826 with the arrival of Wesleyan Methodists who again attached themselves to Taufaauhau, an heir of this administrative chief who would later become the first Tongan King, George I. This alliance alienated the Tui Tonga and Tui Tonga Fefine groups. All chiefly groups received munitions through the trade in coconut oil and through plunder, but the Wesleyans' chiefly allies had the additional support of firearms received through the mission trade. Christianity was not widely accepted until its utility in the interchiefly rivalries and in the future king's consolidation effort were demonstrated (Wright and Fry 1936: 251; Gifford 1929:192). Before he converted to Methodism, Taufaauhau had convinced his kin not to give a wife to the Tui Tonga (thus defying the sacred chief's wife-receiving superiority) and abducted for himself the Tui Tonga's primary wife (Collocott 1923a:184). This latter action would not have been condoned by the missionaries, but they were a demonstration of Taufaauhau's successful absorption of major titles in all the Tongan island groups and his willingness to challenge even the symbolic authority of the Tui Tonga. On converting to Methodism in 1828, he adopted the name George, and his followers became Christians en masse.

When French Roman Catholic priests arrived in 1842 and began to compete with the Methodists for both Christian and pagan souls, the Tui Tonga and Tui Tonga Fefine groups, antagonized by both the Methodists and George, became Catholic. The Methodist mission poured arms into the anti-Papal cause. The long, violent struggle ended in 1852 with the starvation surrender of the rebellious Tui Tonga/Catholic faction and the exile of the French priests. A later internecine Methodist war in 1885 reflected both chiefly rivalries and opposition to Wesleyan Methodist trade relations. It led to the establishment of a state church, which still has adherents, long after the rift was mended. Groups associated with the former Tui Tonga and Tui Tonga Fefine remain Catholic.

The Methodist missionaries struggled against Tongan conceptions of sexuality. One married woman explained her situation from the Tongan point of view to a British colonial officer: "She was born into the world, she said, to enjoy herself, and as the capacity for enjoyment wanes when one is old and ugly, pleasures must all be crowded into the fleeting hours of youth" (Thomson 1904:147). The imposition of Victorian middle-class standards of female sexuality was much more difficult for nonchiefly than for chiefly women. A chiefly woman's behavior before marriage had been closely guarded (Gifford 1929:129–30) although her husband's older female relatives—who attended the consummation, and helped arrange the marriage—would usually cover for any lack of virginity (Collocott 1923b:223). After marriage, chiefly women were not supposed to take lovers, but information is quite contradictory on this point. It seems that certain chiefly women—perhaps the *Tamaha* especially, as an extremely sacred symbol of Tongan fertility—were supposed to take numerous lovers and could bear children to them (Collocott 1923b:225). Indeed, chiefly women were admired by their people if they had many lovers.

One account emphasizes the importance of fidelity for chiefly women, but adds, "As to considerable faults, such as a woman's infidelity to her husband, it would remain as much a secret with any of her own sex...as it possibly could with herself" (Martin 1827:140). Adultery by a chiefly woman might be severely punished, but this was not likely if the woman were high ranking. The man involved was liable to be killed or sacrificed at the first opportunity. Lower-ranking co-wives, if caught, brought punishment to all co-wives except the primary wife (Collocott and Havea 1922:120). The missionary campaign against Tongan female sexual mores had, at times, unexpected results. Before the arrival of the missionaries, a nonchiefly woman's hair was cut when she was about 20 years old, and she was then called an "old woman" (*fefine motua*). This recognition of maturity was at the same time an inducement to marry, since a woman feigning youth would be ridiculed by her age-mates. The missionaries thought that short hair was unbecoming a proper woman and insisted that all women wear their hair long. The result?

> By a mockery of fate, a laxer moral tone allows a girl to prolong her independence to the limit set by time to her attractions, and she finds life so amusing that she defers marriage until the last possible bridegroom has left her for a younger generation" (Thomson 1904:373-74).

The observer exaggerates, but the missionaries' rigidity and lack of investigation into Tongan customs are evident. And with the missionaries' concentration on making women conform to patriarchal notions of wifely behavior, one can appreciate why young women wanted to defer marriage. Missionaries insisted that women cover their breasts. So women added a flap of *tapa* to their wraps, but as late as the 1870s a visitor commented: "The women, however, evidently have little idea of shame in the matter, and often the cloth is put on so loosely that it affords no cover at all" (Mosley 1879:287).

Missionary redefinitions of marital responsibilities particularly disfavored wives. As early as the late eighteenth century, when an English missionary wished to marry a Tongan woman, other missionaries were careful to explain Christian marriage to her. When the phrase "Till death do you part" was explained, the woman refused to go through with the marriage (Collocott 1923b: 225). Missionaries did not move to change divorce proceedings, which officially had been the discretion of the husband. But a woman who deserted a cruel husband was not returned by her kin; nor was she forced to return if she had taken up with someone else. Children requiring parental care went with the mother, but the residence of older children, or of younger children when they grew up, is not clear. After divorce, a woman had been free to take lovers, to live with a man without marrying him—which meant she did not concern herself with household arrangements (Martin 1827:2:145)—remarry, or return to her natal household (Somerville 1936:369). Since a woman retained the right to support by her brother throughout life, she had other alternatives than remarriage, but most divorced persons remarried quickly. Divorce proceedings were made a civil concern as early as 1850, but enforcement was impossible before 1875, when the first civil courts were established. Court costs, however, to be paid in cash, were prohibitive to all but the chiefly. Even after the divorce reforms instituted by the British, court costs made it virtually impossible for nonchiefly women to get divorced legally, since their access to money was even more restricted than nonchiefly men's. Thus, extralegal divorces and remarriages had become common by the 1940s (Elkin 1948:359—60). Children of such "illegal" marriages were considered legitimate by the community, but they could not legally inherit property.

Before the missionaries, widows had been expected to remain single if they had children, although they could openly take lovers. If the widow were childless and capable of childbearing, she was expected to remarry. The missionaries sought to enforce widows' chastity through disinheriting any widow who was proven to have "fornicated," or who had remarried.

Infanticide seems to have been rare. Bearing many children was, however, thought to make a woman physically less desirable (Collocott 1928:131), and, although abortion was verbally condemned to outsiders, it seems to have been practiced. The missionaries may have inadvertently encouraged abortion through their virulent condemnation of "illegitimate" children and their mothers, coupled with the introduction of steel blades in the late nineteenth century. A British colonial officer blamed the declining birth rate (not so today) on "the increased skill of women in the forbidden forms of surgery" (Thomson 1904:374). By insisting on sexual availability as a wifely duty, missionaries also put an end to the sexual abstinence of women after childbirth, which had lasted until all the child's teeth were in, and was explicitly intended to prevent pregnancy and premature weaning (:375). This, of course, contributed to the need for abortion.

Missionary pressure on women in general and on nonchiefly women in particular—missionaries were careful not to alienate their chiefly sponsors—focused on the division of labor, on female sexuality, on wifely obedience and other duties, and on kinship relations which were deemed unseemly for women's estate. Women were urged to take up tasks defined as feminine in the English Victorian middle class—that is, sewing, housekeeping, child care, and cooking. Sewing, certain household tasks, and child care were sufficiently related to Tongan practices as to be unobjectionable, especially since the missionaries did not expect that such activities be carried on individually. Older children continued to be associated with the same-sex parent or peers. It is unclear how involved fathers were with infant care, but at contact men did virtually all cooking (West 1865:267)—which was of extremely low status—with the exception of a few "chiefly" dishes prepared by women on special occasions. For women to be required to cook was tantamount to shame.

Missionaries actively discouraged the exercise of authority by sisters as detracting from the husband's authority. *Fahu* rights were one of the "heathen customs" condemned by the missionaries in the early legal codes. It was seen—rightly—as inimical to "proper" inheritance, that is, patrilineal primogeniture.

Jural Changes

The transformation of custom into law has serious consequences for kinship groups generally (Diamond 1974). Codification involves a notorious rigidity which is absent from kinship structures, a lessening of ambiguity which usually affects men and women differentially (Rapp 1978a, 1978b). The *tapa* law and the missionary-influenced codes of the middle and late 1800s were not the sole jural restrictions placed on women and women's activities. After the British Protectorate of 1900, legislation relating to land tenure, voting, wage regulation, and inheritance and kinship practices continued to limit access to resources, occupations, and traditional sources of both authority and personal autonomy for women and especially for nonchiefly women.

The land laws of the past century have adversely affected all nonchiefly people. Land in Tonga—traditionally vested in the sacred high chief—had been claimed by the state and distributed as hereditary holdings to Tongan chiefs who supported the first king in the consolidation struggles. Certain chiefly groups thus either lost their preferential access to land or had their holdings severely reduced. Estates and governorships for the state lands have come to be inherited through patrilineal primogeniture, that is, along the male line and through the eldest son of the former holder. The traditional association of chiefly people with the land as guardians of community welfare, has been transformed into private holding and state ownership. Estate holding implies responsibilities to the state rather than to the people living on the land. The association of the chief—and, I would argue, the chiefly pair (brother/sister) in Tonga as embodying group authority (Clastres 1977:chs. 1–3) has been transmuted into the power of the state vis-à-vis the group, as embodied in the landholder. Indeed, these hereditary estate holders are now called *nobili*, a class separate from other chiefly people and from the nonchiefly.

The first laws relating to land tenure merely codified custom: land was to be allotted to every eligible Tongan under conditions similar to those in force before centralization. In precontact Tonga, eligibility had been determined by residence in a region associated with a particular chiefly group and membership in a household. The nineteenth-century land laws redefined this eligibility by allocating land-use rights to *heads* of households. A later change specified *male* heads of households and widows under certain restrictions. These adult male heads of household became defined in the twentieth century as male taxpayers (Maude 1971), thus making cash necessary for continued use of the land. Cash income was possible either through the cash cropping of copra or bananas, or through wage labor on copra- and banana-growing estates. Today, land is allocated to male taxpayers 16 years and older, whether or not they are heads of households, provided they cultivate the land. A widow can continue to use her dead husband's allotment only as long as she does not remarry. Chastity for widows was an implied condition in the 1929 code (Horne 1929:332) for continued tenure.

Allotment depends on registration of the taxpayer, and registration on nonstate lands is in the hands of the estate holders. These *nobili* receive revenues from the copra and bananas on their lands, and allotment applicants are frequently required to provide additional produce or labor service to the estate holder in return for registration. In this exploitative situation, widows are especially oppressed; they must obtain some cash income for taxes, and to do this they must perform male-associated tasks for less time and at much lower pay than men. Wage scales for men and women are quite unequal, and there are "protective" laws which restrict women's involvement in wage labor. At the same time, they must be very discreet about their sexual activities or risk losing these hard-earned use rights. In other words, a woman's access to subsistence resources is through her husband; if he is dead, she must obtain adequate cash to meet state and/or estate holders' demands.

Laws relating to wage scales discriminate against nonchiefly women. Laws have also restricted the kind of work women may do, the degree of advancement they may reach, and the benefits they may enjoy from state-associated jobs (Horne 1929:87, 327). These legal bounds include agricultural, clerical, and teaching professions. Voting is restricted to adult men paying a poll tax, although nonchiefly men generally have little to say about the elections, since voter registration is at the discretion of the governors and estate holders.

While all land in Tonga is technically state-owned and not alienable to foreigners (though leasing is allowed), access to land has become increasingly restricted for nonchiefly people. Because land is not privately alienable, nonchiefly men have not been made landless in vast numbers as in other parts of Polynesia. But women's access has become associated solely with their marital status (see Ledyard 1956:202), and for widows, even made contingent on their sexual behavior. Land-tenure changes alone, however, did not establish this dependency. Women can no longer call on their brothers and mother's brothers—and their children—for goods and necessary male and female labor.

The legal ban on the *fahu* rights of sisters and their children (Neill 1955: 19; Horne 1929:700) has been perhaps the most serious structural limitation placed on women. The missionaries, with their interest in making women conform to Christian notions of wifely conduct, attempted to suppress the exercise of *fahu* prerogatives. It is significant that British colonial advisers took no action to prevent the illegalization of *fahu* rights. In addition to material benefits accruing to the sister and her children throughout the lifetime of brothers and mother's brothers, the *fahu* gave the sister side benefits after the death of these relatives. The father's sister, among nonchiefly and lower-ranking chiefly people, distributed the dead man's valuables (subject always to chiefly depredations), conserving the larger share for herself. There is also evidence that a woman's children had rights to their mother's brother's land (see Gifford 1929: 175), though this was restricted to chiefly groups. This is especially important, since the lands a chiefly woman brought into marriage were appropriated by her husband's (her children's) lineage upon her death (:171).

With the *fahu* prerogatives made illegal, the autonomy of women vis-à-vis their husbands has been eliminated. The right to the mother's brother's goods during his lifetime survives surreptitiously (N. Blatchley, personal communication), but the father's sister's control over inheritance, over the fertility of the brother's wife, and over her brother's children's marriages has been usurped by church and state prerogatives and restrictions. For chiefly women, the *fahu* ban has additional implications: the possibility has been eliminated for a father's sister or a sister to become regent for minor heirs to title and lands. A *nobili* woman can still inherit the title to hereditary estates, but only if she is the firstborn of a sonless male line (Horne 1929:322). Even then, however, if her father had a brother, she must wait until her paternal uncle's death before she can inherit.

Without the *fahu* as a structured relationship of authority and deference favoring sisters over brothers, the kin group—and especially the lineage—loses the major source of bilateral integration. A bias toward male title holding becomes patrilineality. Women "fall out" of the kinship structure as sisters; they remain as wives only, and traditionally wives had less authority. Certainly, women had far less access to political and material resources as wives than as sisters.

CONCLUSION

State formation in Tonga, complexly related to internal struggles and European intervention, has resulted in a loss of social authority and personal autonomy for Tongan women. In this process, chiefly people have become differentiated into royalty, hereditary estate holders, state-associated landholders, and those who are not state-associated. Chiefly women, while they have advantages related to their now class-based access to resources, have those advantages through accident of birth (when there are no male heirs) or alliance (as chiefly wives), rather than in their own right as sisters. Although they have lost significant sources of authority vis-à-vis chiefly men, chiefly women still consider themselves, and are considered by others, elite people; they retain authority vis-à-vis nonchiefly people.

Nonchiefly (*tua, matapule*) women have lost status as nonchiefly people generally have been increasingly burdened with conditions for land-use rights, taxation, and the need for wage labor. In the face of the chiefs' predominant access to the European technology of coercion and jural structures, nonchiefly people are less able to assert their rights to chiefly reciprocal-exchange relations. Through the impact of male-dominant Christian ideology, women have lost authority even within those kin groups which were not directly weakened by state demands, for example, the extended family.

The imposition of middle-class Victorian standards of wifely behavior on Tongan women—especially on nonchiefly Tongan women—coincided with the replacement of women's products that were necessary for subsistence by commodities to which men had greater access. In addition, there were new legal restrictions on women's access to both old and newly introduced subsistence resources. Directly and indirectly, these processes made nonchiefly women especially dependent on husbands for subsistence needs. (A chiefly woman can still call on the labor and resources of people living in her father's or husband's district.)

The theocratic, patriarchal, and antiegalitarian ideology—promoted, with chiefly sponsorship, by Wesleyan Methodist and, later, Roman Catholic missionaries—has reduced women's authority. The emphasis on Western Christian modes of behavior has directly altered the gender division of labor, restricted the kinship-based sources of flexible authority for women, and weighted traditionally ambiguous gender relations in favor of men. As ministers of state, the missionaries and later colonial administrators helped legitimize predominantly male institutions and realms of authority, while legally banning those kinship relations which prevented the formation of gender hierarchy. Inheritance, land-tenure, and labor laws underscore the erosion of structures which provided authority and autonomy for women in the precolonial era.

Tongans in the past 150 years have experienced interchiefly struggles for political centralization, the imposition of Christian ideology, the creation of a significant sector of production for exchange on the world market, the introduction of certain Western commodities (cloth and firearms), and the adoption of Western state institutions. The interaction of these processes has resulted in the restriction of Tongan women's authority as sisters, and the redefinition of their role as wives in such a way as to transform what was simple deference behavior toward husbands into structural and economic dependency.

NOTES

1. This chapter is dedicated to Jane K. Sallade, my friend and colleague, whose untimely death cut short an already impressive career in archaeology. Her long-term interest, animated discussions and steadfast support have contributed profoundly to my research and to my development as an anthropologist. I would like to thank Rayna Rapp for her consultation, pertinent criticisms, and the title; Stanley Diamond for helping me avoid mechanistic

argumentation; Tim Parrish and Nick Blatchley for their suggestions; and Mona Etienne for her confidence and for clarifying my prose.

2. By "state formation" is meant a process which involves the attenuation or restriction of kinship in the organization of production and in which production comes to include the institutionalized extraction of labor and products from local kin groups, to support a nonproducing elite.

3. Goldman's "status lineage" is a more useful formulation. He recognizes the ambiguities in Tongan ranking, but privatizes sisters' high rank, thereby minimizing the political involvement of chiefly women (Goldman 1970:291). His distinction of ranking by relative seniority and by sibling gender is careful, but he associates each with a different realm, public for the former and domestic for the latter. In light of the prerogatives of chiefly sisters vis-a-vis their natal lineages, this seems unwarranted.

The problem centers on the difficulty of understanding kinship-organized societies in the process of state formation. Kinship is used in different manners by higher- and lower-ranking people. Chiefly kin groups emphasized an ideal of patrilineality for title succession, but structural contradictions necessitated matrilateral ties for all ranks. The lineages (*haa*) in Tonga—never strictly patrilineages—were not a separate system from the local bilateral kindreds (see Korn 1974), although chiefly groups were attempting to distance themselves from local expectations of chiefly and kinship generosity.

4. Recent research into local kin groups in Tonga has been conducted by Kaeppler (1971), Aoyagi (1966) and Korn (1974). Korn's work on the *famili* and *kainga* as overlapping bilateral kin networks beyond the household, involving different degrees of mutual aid, is particularly useful. The possibility that the *famili* (from the English) is a recent form which has assumed functions previously fulfilled by the *kainga*—which has weakened since contact and Westernization (especially the *fahu* aspects)—warrants additional investigation. The invention of such new cultural forms to fulfill traditional functions—and changing functions of older forms to meet new needs (see Diamond 1974)—is well documented for other areas experiencing fundamental socioeconomic change such as state formation and colonization. See, in particular, Diamond (1951), Silverblatt (1978), Muller (1978), Rapp (1978a, 1978b) and Van Allen (1972).

5. This process is typical of ranked descent groups or ramages with patrilineal bias (see Sahlins 1958).

6. Farmer believed the deity for whom the *inasi* offerings were intended was Hikuleo, and that Hikuleo was the deity for whom the *Tui Tonga* was intermediary and priest (Gifford 1929:289). Gifford goes on to say that some of his informants identified Hikuleo as masculine, and others as feminine (:291). He says it is "not improbable" that Hikuleo, like certain other Tongan deities, appeared as a man to women and as a woman to men. If this was the case, then it is equally probable that the Tui Tonga Fefine was a co-intermediary, representing the feminine aspects of Tongan fertility, to appeal to the masculine aspects of Hikuleo. This symbolic unity of male and female aspects is reflected in myths and oral histories relating sacred marriages of the Tui Tonga and his sister (:52). The "sacred child" or Tamaha would be the result

of such a supremely sacred union. It is clear that the Tui Tonga Fefine and the Tamaha received part of the first fruits of any endeavor (:103).

7. Why this law was framed is matter of debate (Latukefu 1974; Rutherford 1971). A British consul considered a missionary responsible and accused him of receiving a commission on sales of cotton sold by the international merchant establishment of Godeffroy and Sons. (Godeffroy and Sons handled Wesleyan Mission copra, extending cash credit to Tongans in exchange for future copra so they would have money to donate at the annual collections.) Other sources claim that King George wanted to demonstrate that Tonga was civilized in the European sense, in order to avoid colonization. Certain missionaries opposed the law because it threatened mission coffers (money would be spent on clothing rather than on collections), but traders certainly encouraged it (see Rutherford 1971:60-61).

REFERENCES

Alpers, Anthony. 1970. *Legends of the South Sea.* London: John Murray.

Aoyagi, M. 1966. "Kinship Organisation and Behavior in a Contemporary Tongan Village." *Journal of the Polynesian Society* 75:141-76.

Beaglehole, Ernest and Pearl Beaglehole. 1941. *Pangai.* Wellington, N.Z.: The Polynesian Society.

Beaglehole, J.C., ed. 1969. *The Journals of Captain James Cook,* 3 vols. Cambridge: Cambridge University Press, Hakluyt Society.

Burrows, Edwin. 1970. *Western Polynesia.* Dunedin: University Book Shop Ltd.

Clastres, Pierre. 1977. *Society Against the State.* New York: Mole Editions, Urizen Books.

Collocott, E. E. V. 1923a. "An Experiment in Tongan History." *Journal of the Polynesian Society* 32:166-84.

———. 1923b. "Marriage in Tonga." *Journal of the Polynesian Society* 32:221-28.

———. 1928. *Tales and Poems of Tonga.* Bulletin no. 46. Honolulu: B. P. Bishop Museum.

———. 1929. *Kava Drinking in Tonga.* Honolulu: B. P. Bishop Museum Occasional Papers.

Collocott, E. E. V. and John Havea. 1922. *Proverbial Sayings of the Tongans.* Honolulu: B.P. Bishop Museum Occasional Papers.

Diamond, Stanley. 1951. *Dahomey: A Protostate in West Africa.* Ann Arbor, Mich.: University Microfilms.

———. 1964. *In Search of the Primitive: A Critique of Civilization.* New Brunswick, N.J.: Transaction Books, E.P. Dutton.

Edwards, E. and G. Hamilton. 1915. *Voyage of the H.M.S. "Pandora."* London: Francis Edwards.

Elkin, A. P. 1948. Review of *Pangai* [Beaglehole and Beaglehole 1941]. *Oceania.* 18, 4:359-60.

Erskine, J.E. 1853. *The Islands of the Western Pacific.* London: John Murray.

Fison, Lorimer. 1907. *Tales from Old Fiji.* London: De La More Press.

Fried, Morton. 1967. *The Evolution of Political Society.* New York: Random House.

Gailey, Christine. 1977. "The Transition from Kinship to Class: The State and Gender Hierarchy." Paper presented at the meeting of the Northeastern Political Science Association, Mt. Airy, Pennsylvania.

———. 1979. "Gender Hierarchy and Class Formation: The Origins of the State in Tonga." *Dialectical Anthropology.* forthcoming.

Gifford, E. W. 1923. *Tongan Place Names.* Bulletin no. 6. Honolulu: B. P. Bishop Museum.

———. 1924a. *Tongan Myths and Tales.* Bulletin no. 8. Honolulu: B. P. Bishop Museum.

———. 1924b. "Euro-American Acculturation in Tonga." *Journal of the Polynesian Society* 33:281-92.

———. 1929. *Tongan Society.* Bulletin no. 61. Honolulu: B. P. Bishop Museum.

Gill, Rev. William W. 1876. *Myths and Songs from the South Pacific.* London: Henry S. King and Co.

Goldman, Irving. 1970. *Ancient Polynesian Society.* Chicago: University of Chicago Press.

Horne, William K. 1929. *Revised Edition of the Law of Tonga.* Nukualofa, Tonga: Government Printing Office.

Kaeppler, Adrienne. 1971. "Rank in Tonga." *Ethnology* 10:174-93.

Kirchoff, Paul. 1959. "The Principles of Clanship in Human Society." In Morton Fried, ed., *Readings in Anthropology*, vol. 2. New York: Crowell.

Korn, S. Dektor. 1974. "Tongan Kin Groups: The Noble and the Common View." *Journal of the Polynesian Society* 83:5-13.

Latukefu, Sione. 1974. *Church and State in Tonga.* Canberra: Australian National University Press.

Leacock, Eleanor. 1977. "The Changing Family and Levi-Strauss, or Whatever Happened to Fathers?" *Social Research* 44, 2:235-59.

Ledyard, Patricia. 1956. *A Tale of the Friendly Islands.* New York: Appleton-Century-Crofts.

Levi-Strauss, Claude. 1969. *The Elementary Structures of Kinship.* Boston: Beacon Press.

Martin, John. 1827. *An Account of the Natives of the Tongan Islands* [Will Mariner's Journal] 2 vols. Edinburgh: Constable and Co.

Maude, Alaric. 1971. "Tonga: Equality Overtaking Privilege." In Ron Crocombe, ed., *Land Tenure in the Pacific.* Melbourne: Oxford University Press.

Moseley, Henry N. 1879. *Notes by a Naturalist on the "Challenger", 1872-1876.* London: John Murray.

Muller, Viana. 1977. "The Formation of the State and the Oppression of Women: A Case Study in England and Wales." *Review of Radical Political Economics* 9, 3:7-21.

Neill, J. S. 1955. *Ten Years in Tonga.* London: Hutchinson.

Oliver, Douglas. 1961. *The Pacific Islands.* New York: Doubleday.

Rapp, Rayna. 1978a. "Gender and Class: An Archaeology of Knowledge Concerning the Origin of the State." *Dialectical Anthropology* 2, 4:309-16.

———. 1978b. "Review Essay: Anthropology." *Signs* 4, 3.

Rousseau, Jerome. 1978. "On Estates and Castes." *Dialectical Anthropology* 3, 1:85-95.

Rutherford, Noel. 1971. *Shirley Baker and the King of Tonga.* Melbourne: Oxford University Press.

Sahlins, Marshall. 1958. *Social Stratification in Polynesia.* Seattle: University of Washington Press.

———. 1972. *Stone Age Economics.* Chicago: Aldine.

Sharp, Andrew. 1968. *The Voyages of Abel Janszoon Tasman.* Oxford: The Clarendon Press.

Silverblatt, Irene. 1978. "Andean Women in the Inca Empire." *Feminist Studies* 4, 3.

Somerville, Adm. H. B. T. 1936. *Will Mariner.* London: Faber and Faber, Ltd.

Strauss, W. P. 1963. *Americans in Polynesia.* East Lansing: Michigan State University Press.

Thomson, Basil. 1904. *The Diversions of a Prime Minister.* Edinburgh: William Blackwood and Sons.

Van Allen, Judith. 1972. "Sitting on a Man." *Canadian Journal of African Studies* 6.

West, Rev. Thomas. 1865. *Ten Years in South-Central Polynesia.* London: James Nisbet and Co.

Williamson, Robert W. 1924. *The Social and Political Systems of Central Polynesia,* 3 vols. Cambridge, England: Cambridge University Press.

Wilson, James. 1799. *A Missionary Voyage to the Southern Pacific Ocean, 1796-1798.* London: S. Gosnell for Chapman.

Wood, A. H. 1932. *History and Geography of Tonga.* Nukualofa, Tonga: Government Printing Office.

Wright, L. B. and M. I. Fry. 1936. *Puritans in the South Seas.* New York: Henry Holt and Co.

Index

Aankaawoo, 95
Abenaki, 50
Aboriginal Councils, 248
Aborigines, 239-267, land tenure, 240, 241, 247, 248; law, 248, 249, 255, 264; marriage patterns, 19, 242-266, 267f; religion, 242, 243, 244, 248, 251, 253, 256, 264, 265; resource distribution, 241; social structure, 244-245; socioeconomic organization, 242, 244, 250; sociopolitical organization, 244-245, 247-250, 266; women's social status, 241-242, 246, 247, 250, 251, 256, 265
Abortion, 314. See also Birth, control
Accomack, 46
Acculturation, 5, 267f; Bari, 111, 117, 124-131; forced, 175; Seneca, 65, 82; Trobriand society, 274, 277, 284
Aclla, 178
Adelaide, Australia, 263
Adelaide Advertiser, 240, 245
Adlum, John, 80
Admiralties, Melanesia, 270
Adultry, 143, 252. See also Sexual freedom
Africa: early exploration, 6, 7, 43
Agbara, 117
Agriculture, 8; African, 6; Aztec, 136, 137, 144; Bari, 110, 111, 113, 114, 129; Baule, 7, 218, 222, 226, 228; cash crops, 19, 20, 129, 196, 197, 218, 226, 228, 230, 234f, 315; children and, 56; commercial, 190, 296; fallow system, 192-193, 222; garden production, 272, 282; Hurons, 26; Inca, 162; insecticides, 226; Luo, 6, 187, 190, 198, 207, 208; removal of women from, 73, 74; Seneca, 68-71, 73-78, 82; slash and burn, 114, 272; Tonga, 301, 315; Trobriand society, 272, 276, 282, 284; women in, 11, 12, 22, 54-56, 68, 74-78, 144, 192, 207, 208, 228, 230. See also Horticulture
Ainswort, John, 198
Akan, 217
Alaska: China, 89; Europe, 88, 89, 91; fur trade, 89, 91, 95-101; Native Land claims, 105, 106f; Russia, 88, 89-92, 98; The United States, 88, 92, 93; Tlingit, 6, 88-108
Albany, N.Y., 57
Albuquerque, Rodriguez de, 140
Alcacer, Antonio, 112, 115, 116, 122, 123

Alcohol, 38, 72, 144; Aborigines and, 242, 245, 248; trade good, 57, 112
Aleuts, 91
Alexander Archipelago, 94
Alfinger, Ambrose, 110, 112
Algeria, 216
Algonkian, 5, 6, 10, 11, 18, 21, 41f, 43-59; agriculture, 55, 56; marriage patterns, 52, 53, 54; religion, 53-54; resource distribution, 46, 48, 55; social structure, 46; socioeconomic organization, 46, 52, 54-59; sociopolitical organization, 46-49, 59; status of women, 48-50, 52, 53. See also *tribes and confederacies by name*
Algonkin, 26, 41f
Alice Springs, Australia, 240, 242, 260
Aljawarra, 242
Allegheny region, 66
Allegheny Reservation, 74
Allegany Seneca, 65, 72
Alliances, 114, 119, 120, 311; between men and women, 52; between "sisters," 253; through marriage, 299, 303
Allinson, William, 69, 77
Amaru, 176
Amaru, Tupac, 164
Amazon societies, 115
America. See North America; South America; Central America; *and countries by name*
American Revolution, 63, 65, 72, 295
Amur Basin, 89
Andean Society. See Inca
Anglican missions, 98
Animal husbandry, 77
Annual Report on British New Guinea, 277
Appalachian Mountains, 46
Arabia, 6
Arawak, 139
Arnum, John Van, 74, 75
Art: Baule, 221, 229; Tonga, 310, 311
Ashanti, 217
Asia, 10, 43, 89
Australia, 6, 10, 11, 239-267, 295, 296; Aborigines, 6, 10, 11, 239-267; colonial power, 270, 271; government policies, 241, 242, 263, 264, 267f; government services, 242; post colonial, 11; racism, 250, 263; sexism, 250, 254, 260, 267f
Authority: Algonkian, 45, 47-50; Bari, 118; Baule, 219; colonially appointed,

29, 47, 124-126, 169, 197; in egalitarian societies, 9, 10, 27, 111, 115; Inca, 153, 154; Luo, 197, missionary appointed, 27, 116, 117; Montagnais-Naskapi, 27, 29, 30; of elders, 14, 49, 57-58, 115, 137, 244, 245, 299; Tlingit, 97; Tonga, 296, 297, 299, 302; Trobriand society, 273, 275; women's economic, 54, 59, 97; women's loss of, 297, 305, 311, 315-318; women's military, 49-51, 53, 69, 80; women's political, 16, 20, 49, 59, 102-104, 170, 296, 299, 301, 302, 306; women's religious, 41, 53, 54, 57-59, 80, 95, 98-101, 136, 137, 156, 157, 162, 171-173, 176-180, 262
Autonomy: Aborigine, 241, 244; Algonkian, 47, Andean, 158; Aztec, 18, 20, 21; Bari, 19, 111, 113, 118, 122; Baule, 219, 232; children's, 123; in egalitarian societies, 10, 111; in stratified societies, 18; Luo, 187, 207; Montagnais-Naskapi, 28, 29, 38; Seneca, 69; Tlingit, 102; Tonga, 296, 297; women's, 6, 10, 11, 15, 18, 19, 20, 21, 102, 111, 244; women's loss of, 297, 305, 311, 315-318
Avila, Francisco, 179
Avunculocal, 273
Awashonks, 51, 52
Ayacucho, Department of, 172
Ayala, Guaman Poma de, 168-169
Ayllu, 152-158, 165, 166, 169, 171, 177, 179, 181f
Aztec, 7, 15, 16, 135-145; agriculture, 136, 137, 144; land tenure, 137, 140; marriage patterns, 139, 140, 141, 145; religion, 136, 137, 141; social structure, 137, 145; socioeconomic organization, 137; sociopolitical organization, 135, 137; status of women, 134-137, 143-145

Bahr-el-Ghazal, Sudan, 190
Banana leaves. See Women, wealth of
Band societies, 6
Baranov, Alekandr, 91
Bari, 11, 17, 19, 109-131, agriculture, 110, 111, 113, 114, 129; land tenure, 111, 112, 124; marriage patterns, 123; religion, 112, 119-120, 125, 130; resource distribution, 110, 111, 112, 117, 124; social structure, 111, 113-118, 120-122, 128, 129; socioeconomic organization, 111, 124, 127-129, 130-131; sociopolitical organization, 118, 124, 125; status of women, 111, 124-131
Bark cloth, 18, 218, 301, 308-311, 313
Barnes, Ruth Carol, 55
Barrow Creek, Australia, 240

Bastides, Micaela, 164
Batuto, Ibn, 7
Baule, 14, 19, 21, 214-233; agriculture, 218, 222, 226, 228; land tenure, 219, 235f; marriage patterns, 219, 220-221, 229, 231, 233f; social structure, 219-221; socioeconomic organization, 217, 218, 220, 224, 226, 227, 228; sociopolitical organization, 232; trade, 217, 234f; women's status, 219, 221, 222
Beaver. See Fur trade
Beckerman, Stephen, 116
Bekri, Al, 6
Bell, Diane, 11, 17, 19, 21
Bellamy, R.L., 277, 280
Beson, 54, 57
Beverly, Robert, 50, 53
Bigamy, 138
Birth, 121; control, 13; houses for, 94; rituals, 138, 301
Bismarck Archipelago, 270
Blacks, 143
Blood money, 48
Bacanegra, Perez, 170
Borah, Woodrow, 144
Boser-Sarivaxevanis, R., 225
Boston, Mass., 50
"Boston men," 91
Bouake, Ivory Coast, 218
Brideprice, 284
Bridewealth, 99, 219, 233f
British colonial law, 187, 189, 284; Crown Lands Ordinance, 187; forced labor, 197; land tenure reform, 196-209; Native Reserve Ordinance 197; pass system, 197; Swynnerton Plan, 201; Tonga, 309, 314-317, 320f
British colonialism, 16, 150, 216; Alaska, 89, 92; Atlantic seaboard, 44, 49-51, 63, 66, 70, 72; East Africa; 186, 196-209; in Canada, 25; Ivory Coast, 214-233; Kenya, 186-202; Melanesia, 270, 271; Oceania; 294-296; Tonga, 297, 305, 308-311; Trobriand Islands, 272, 274-276, 284
British Columbia, 98
British New Guinea, 271
British trading companies. See Trading companies, British
Brother. See Sister
Brown, Judith, 68
Brown, Susan E., 11, 17, 19
Buganda, 186, 197
Buenaventura-Posso, Elisa, 11, 17, 19

Cabot, John, 44
Caciques, 139, 141
Calpullec, 137

Calpulli, 137
Cameroons, 215
Canada, 16, 25-42; early exploration, 25, 26, 44; egalitarianism, 9, 10, 11, 17; missionaires in, 10, 11, 13, 25-42; Montagnais-Naskapi, 25-42,; precolonial, 5, 6; reservations in, 78
Canneries, 98, 101-102
Capitalism, 8, 9, 10, 15, 16, 19, 161, 216, 266; Bari, 124; Baule, 230, 231; development of, 150, 174; Tonga, 296, 297; Trobriand society, 274
Captivity: Baule, 218, 219, 221, 232; Mary Rowlandson, 51; Province of Venezuela, 110; rights of, 219, 224, 233f; Seneca, 67. See also Slavery
Capuchin missionaries, 112, 115, 116
Carhua, Lucia Suyo, 123
Carribean, Arawak, 139; early exploration, 44, 134; slavery, 142
Carthaginians, 214
Cartier, Jacques, 25
Cash crop. See Agriculture, cash crop
Cash economy, 19, 196
Caste laws, 101
Castile, Spain, 150
Castilian dynasty, 150
Castillo, Bernal Diaz de, 140
Castizos, 143
Catalonia, 150
Catholicism: adaptations of, 99, 171-172; and colonialism, 18, 155-158, 216; and the devil, 173-176; conversion to, 31, 32-38, 134, 139; ideology, 20, 26, 30-35, 90; impact on women, 18, 20, 30-35, 173-175, 297, 309, 318; Inca, 166-180; resistance to, 22, 33, 176-180, 200; tithe, 166
Cattaraugus Seneca, 65
Ceremonies. See Ritual/Ceremonial activities
Central America: early exploration, 43, 44, 134. See also countries by name
Champlain, Samuel de, 26, 44
Chapultepec, Mexico, 137
Charles V, King of Spain, 110, 150
Chastity, 36. See also Virgins
Chesapeake Bay, 46, 47, 49-50, 54, 59
Chibcha, 111
Chibcha Empire, 110
Chiefs, 6, 14; Algonkian, 47-50; appointed by colonizer, 29, 47, 124-126, 197; appointed by missionaries, 27, 29, 30, 116, 117; Aztec, 137, 141; Bari, 115, 116, 125-126; Luo, 197; Montagnais-Naskapi, 27, 29, 30; Seneca, 65, 66, 68, 80; Tlingit, 94, 95; Tongan, 296-302, 306, 309-311, 317, 318; Trobriand society, 272, 273, 275, 276, 280, 284, 290f; women as, 11, 46-53, 56, 58, 59, 94, 296-299, 301, 302, 306. See also Authority; Leadership; Sachems; Squa-Sachem; Sunksquaw
Chilcats, 100
Child care and socialization, 17; Aborigine, 242, 251, 263; Bari, 118, 123, 124; Jesuit ideology, 27, 28; men's involvment in, 40, 104, 118, 124, 301; Montagnais-Naskapi, 27; Tlingit, 104; Tonga, 301. See also children
Childbearing. See Reproduction
Children, 123; betrothal of, 219, 250, 263; custody, 313; half-caste, 253, 263; illegitimate, 143, 305, 314; matriliny, 286, 287, 288; patrilineage, 191. See also Child care and socialization
China, 296; fur trade, 89
Christianity: male-centered ideology, 308, 318. See also Missionaries; Missions; and religions by name
Chuschi, Peru, 172
Circumcision, 244, 255, 256, 263, 264
Cisneros, Cardinal, 139
City-state, Aztec, 135, 136; Inca, 7
Clan mothers, 66, 68
Clans: Algonkian, 46; Conical, 298; Seneca, 66, 68; Tlingit, 95; Trobriand, 286
Class, socioeconomic, 15; Aztec, 136-138, 140-145; Inca, 157-160, 162-165; vs. ranking, 298
Classless societies. See Egalitarian societies
Cloth: as art, 221; as wealth, 219, 231, 234f; cotton, 218, 220, 221, 223-233; manufactured, 226, 229, 295, 309, 310. See also Bark cloth
Cockarouse, 47
Coconut Oil, 308, 309, 310, 312
Collectives, 11
Columbia: Bari, 109-131; independence of, 112; precolonial, 6, 111; Spanish Empire, 110-112
Colonial reorganization, 13, 16, 17; Aborigine, 263, 264, 266, 276f; Bari, 117, 124, 125-131; Baule, 218, 225-229; Inca, 160, 161, 165-180; Luo, 196-210; Tonga, 297, 305, 308-318; Trobriand society, 272, 276. See also Colonialism; Colonialism, resistance to; Jural restructuring
Colonialism, 216; accomodation to, 20-22; production relations, 17-19; women and, 17-22, 120, 124, 125-131, 161-180. See also British colonialism; Colonial reorganization; Colonialism, resistance to; Spanish colonialism
Colonialism, resistance to, 17, 19, 20-22; Aborigine, 240, 241, 245; Andean, 160, 164, 173, 176; Bari, 111, 114-115, 117-

118, 131; Baule, 218, Luo, 189, 200, 201; Tlingit, 96-97; Tonga, 296; Trobriand society, 274-276, 285
Complementarity: Aborigine, 11, 244; Bari, 11, 118-119; egalitarian society, 6, 10; Inca, 145, 160, 166; Luo, 193; Seneca, 12, 82; Trobriand, 286
Concubines, 139, 169, 170, 300
Condemayta, Tomasa Tito, 164
Confederacy: Esopus, 52; Massachusett, 50; Powhatan, 49; Wampanoag, 50; women in, 49
Conference of Berlin, 216
Conical clan, 298
"Coniston Massacres," 241, 245
Coniston Station, 241
Conjugal relations. See Marriage patterns
Conjuration, 53
Connecticut, 46, 50
Conoy, 46
Conquistadores, 155. See also Spanish conquest
Contraception. See Birth, control
Cook, James, 91, 294, 296, 306-308
Cooperative societies, 13, Algonkian, 46; Baule, 223; Luo, 191; Montagnais-Naskapi, 38, 40
Cooperatives, 199, 284
Copper. See Trade goods
Cpora, 309, 310, 315, 316
Cordoba, Vicar Pedro de, 141
Corn mother, 157
Cornplanter, 72, 75, 76, 80
Corregidores, 141-142
Corregimiento, 141-142
Cortes, Hernando, 7
Cortes, Pedro, 139
Cotton, 196-197, 198
Councils, tribal, 12; Aboriginal, 248; Algonkian, 48-52
Co-wifeship, 190, 250-251, 253, 259, 262, 300, 313
Coya, 155, 157, 158
Coyotes, 143
Creoles, 143
Crimean War, 89
Cuba, 109
Culhuacan, 138
"Cultural persistence," 76, 82
Culture as female, 180
Culture vs. nature, 3, 4
Curacas, 153, 154, 158, 166, 169-170, 176, 181f
Curanderos, 126. See also Medicine
Cutting Packing Company, 101
Cuzco, Peru, 151, 154, 155, 159, 162, 164
Cuzco, Department of, 162

Dala, 273, 282, 286-289

"Dear Abby," 252
Death, 53, houses, 94; mourning, 252, 258-260, 288; penalty, 138; Taboos, 258-260; Tonga, 317; Trobriand society, 273, 286, 287, 289
Decision making, 1, 4, 9, 10; Aborigine, 243, 244; Algonkin, 46-48; Bari, 114-118; Inca, 153; Montagnais-Naskapi, 29-30; Seneca, 12, 22, 66, 68; Tlingit, 97, 104
Deities, 158, androgynous, 301, 319f; female, 53, 137, 154, 157, 159, 177, 301; male, 301
Delawarans, 47, 49, 52, 53, 54, 57
Delaware, 44, 46
Delmarva Peninsula, Delaware, 46
Demographic pressure. See Population
Depression, economic: 1830-1845, 295; 1873-1895, 216; 1930's, 199
Descent: cognatic, 219; matrilineal, 14, 46-48, 66, 69, 73, 95, 99, 100, 105, 139, 167, 170, 219, 233f, 243, 272, 273, 285, 288-289; parallel, 152, 153, 157, 166, 167, 300; patrilineal, 14, 15, 137, 156, 167, 243, 244, 298, 315, 317. See also Lineage; Matrilineal, Patrilineal
Devil, the, 173, 174
Disease: Black Death, 44; bubonic plague, 50; cattle epidemic, 192, 193; epidemic, 38, 45, 135, 142, 239; smallpox, 50, 113. See also Medicine
Divale, William T., 3
Divorce, rights of: Aztec, 145; Luo, 191; Montagnais-Naskapi, 28, 30; Seneca, 69; Tlingit, 95; Tonga, 313, 314
Dixon, Captain, 96
Doba, 274, 279
Doctors. See Medicine
Doggers, 263
Domestic labor. See Labor
van der Donck, Adriaen, 55
"Double standard," 17, 22, 143
Douglas, Mary, 285
Dreaming, Aboriginal, 119, 243, 248, 249, 251, 253
Drought, 190
Duashina, 117
Duncan, Reverend William, 98
Dutch Colonialism, 44, 150; Canada, 26; Melanesia, 270, 294; New Guinea, 271; New Netherland, 50, 52. See also Traders
Dutch East India Company, 294
Dutch New Guinea, 271

"Earth Mother", 154-155
East Africa Protectorate, 6, 186, 187, 196
Ecuador, 172
Education: and westernization, 27, 28,

36, 105, 126; Australian services, 242; bilingual, 248; mission schools, 98; Tlingit, 98; Trobriand, 276; women excluded from, 138, 144, 164; women in, 20, 103, 104
Egalitarian relations, 6, 7, 8, 9, 10, 12, 111, 118; Algonkian 59; Amazon, 115, Aztec, 137, Bari, 111, 114, 115, 118, 122, 131; Montagnais-Naskapi, 28-30, 39-41; Trobriand, 284
El Canto de las Flechas, 130
El Dorado, 110
Elders: as leaders, 14, 49, 244-245; authority of, 57-58, 115, 137, 299; autonomous, 219; rank by seniority, 297, 301, 307; status of, 156; work of, 54, 56-59
Eliot, Charles, 187
Eliot, John, 53
Elopement, 259
Empire. See Aztec; Hapsburg; Holy Roman; Inca; Spanish
Encomienda, 112, 140, 141, 167
Endogamy, 69, 70
Engels, Frederick, 14, 16
England; industrialization, 295. See also British Colonialism
Ernabella Mission, 263
Esopus Confederation, 52
Esopus wars, 52
Ethnocentricity, 4, 266. See also Male bias, anthropological
Etienne, Mona, 14, 19, 21
European: expansion, 43, 44, 45; colonization, 10, in Alaska, 89, 91. See also countries by name.
Evans-Pritchard, E. E., 1, 2, 11
Everette Commission, 74
Exogamy, 48, 191, 193, 245
Explorers, early contact, 43, 44; Africa, 214-215; Alaska, 96; Australia, 240; Canada, 25, 26; Pacific, 270, 271, 294, 305-308. See also Traders

Fahu, 15, 18, 299, 300, 303, 304, 316, 317
Family structure: Aborigine, 267f; Luo, 191, Montagnais-Naskapi, 13; nuclear, 9, 11, 16, 18, 19, 28, 40, 124, 128, 129, 130, 285; patriarchal, 11, 19, 28; Seneca, 80; westernization, 28, 30, 73, 124, 125, 128-130
Famine, 190
Farming. See Horticulture; Agriculture
"Father love," 285, 286
Fearn, Hugh, 198
Female deities. See Deities, female
Female priests, 41, 53-54, 95, 136, 137, 156, 157, 177-180. See also Authority, women's religious

Female religious cults, 155, 156, 157, 172, 176-180
"Feminine" - "Culture," 180
Feminism, 1, 22, 285
Ferdinand, King of Spain, 139, 149
Festivals. See Ritual-ceremonial activities
Feudalism, 15; Spanish, 150, 161
Fiji, 270, 296
Filial relations. See Child care and socialization
Fishing, 6; Alaskan waters, 89; Algonkian, 45, 46; Bari, 118, 128; cooperative, 56, 118, 128; Tonga women, 304, 307; Trobriand, 272
Florida, 44
Fornezinos, 143
Fort Archangel, 91
Fort Chimo, 40
Fox, George, 50
France. See French colonialism
Franco-Prussian War, 216
French colonialism, 16, 44, 150, 216; Africa, 214, 216, 218; Atlantic seaboard, 66; Canada, 25, 26, 29, 35, 36-39; Pacific, 270, 294, 295. See also Trading companies, French
Freilich, Morris, 76
Frew River Station, 245
Fried, Morton H., 9, 14
Fur trade, 12, 13, 16; Alaska, 89, 91, 96-101; Algonkian, 44; Montagnais-Naskapi, 25, 38, 39, 40; Seneca, 67, 70, 71, 75

Gailey, Christine Ward, 20
Gama, Vasco da, 7
Gant, Pedro de, 144
Garden production. See Agriculture
Gas, Alaskan, 105
Gathering and hunting societies, 3, 4, 6, 8, 10, 11, 13; Algonkian, 45-46, 56; Montagnais-Naskapi, 29. See also Hunting and gathering societies
Gem, Kenya, 202
Genessee Seneca, 66, 67
Genocide, 65
George I, King of Tonga, 312
German colonialism, 110, 186, 270, 296
Gerontocracy, 244-45, 253, 261, 265, 266
Ghana, 6
Gilmour, R.F., 277
Gold, 16, African, 7, 198, 215, 218, 219, 221, 232; Australian, 240; Massim, 271; South American, 110; Spanish, 150
Gold Coast, 215, 217
Gonfreville textiles, 226-232
Goodale, Jane C., 254
Gookin, Daniel, 53, 56

Great Britain. *See* British colonialism; England
Granites, Australia, 240
Grumet, Robert Steven, 10, 11
Guarmi Paso, 157
Guillen, Sabastian Joseph, 115, 116, 118, 121, 122
Gunther, Erna, 97
Guro, 221

Handsome Lake, 80, 81
Hapsburg Empire, 110, 150
Harris, Marvin, 3
Hatches Creek, Australia, 240
Hawaii, 301
Health, *See* Medicine
Heckewelder, John, 49, 53, 54, 57
Herbalists. *See* Medicine
Hermana mayor, 172
Heyer, Judith, 199
Hidalgos, 141
Hierarchical relations, 6, 7, 8, 10, 13, 14; Aztec, 135-144; Bari, 111; Inca, 156-158, 170, 171; Montagnais-Naskapi, 28; parallel, 170; Tonga, 296, 298
Hijos naturales, 143
Hilliard, Winifred, 263
Hitsati, 95
Hobbism, 3
Holland. *See* Dutch colonialism; Trading Companies, Dutch
Holy Roman Empire, 150
Hooker Creek people, Australia, 248, 260
Horticulture, 6, 8, 13; Algonkian, 45, 46; Amazon, 115; Bari, 111, 113, 118; egalitarianism and, 10, 118; Luo, 15. *See also* Agriculture
Household as unit of production, 16, 222
Household structure, 11, 16; Algonkian, 45; Bari, 113, 116, 117, 122, 128-130; Luo, 191; Montagnais-Naskapi, 29; Seneca, 66, 69, 80; Tlingit, 94, 95, 99, 100. *See also* Family structure
Huacas, 156, 157, 177
Hudson, Henry, 44, 57
Hudson Valley, 44, 47, 52
Hudson's Bay Company, 26, 92, 96
Huitzilopochtli, 137
Hunt, George, 67
Hunting: Algonkian, 45, 46; Aztec, 136; Montagnais-Naskapi, 29; Seneca, 81; Tlingit, 93. *See also* Gathering and hunting societies; Hunting and gathering societies
Hunting and gathering societies, 3, 4, 6, 8, 10, 11, 13; Aborigine, 244; Algonkian, 45-46, 56. *See also* Gathering and hunting societies; Hunting
Huron, 26

Idolatry, 174
Illegitimacy. *See* Children
Inca, 7, 15, 16, 18, 20, 21, 109, 149-180; agriculture, 162; land tenure, 150, 152-155, 161, 162, 163, 166, 180; marriage, 152, 153; social structure, 153, socioeconomic organization, 151, 152, 154, 165-169; sociopolitical organization, 151, 153, 154, 157-159, 169, 170, 173; religion, 156-160, 170-180; women's status, 153, 155, 156, 171-173; resource distribution, 151-153, 170
Incest, 3
India, 6, 186, 187
Indians. *See* Native Americans; *tribes by name*
Indonesia, 271
Industrialization, 8, 88, 295
Infant betrothal, 219, 250, 263
Infanticide, 13, 179, 314
Inheritance patterns: Algonkian, 58; Aztec. 140, 141, 145; Bari, 121; Baule, 219; Inca, 152, 162-165, 167, 170, 181f; Luo, 191, 195, 196, 201, 207, 208, Seneca, 73; Spanish Empire, 140, 141, 145, 150; Tlingit, 105; Tongan, 297-299, 315, 317, 318; Trobriand, 273, 287
Inuit, 93
Iroquois, 6, 11. *See also* Seneca
Isabella, Queen of Spain, 109, 139, 149
Isdora, 116
Islam, 217, 221
Isodoashina, 117
Italy, 186
Itzcoatl, King, 138
Ivory Coast, 7, 214-233

Jackson Halliday, 76
Jackson, Sheldon, 98
Jamestown, Va., 44, 49
Japan, 89
Jaulin, Robert, 116, 118, 122, 129, 131f
Jemison, Mary, 71, 78
Jesuit. *See* Catholicism; Missionaries
Jesuit Relations, 29, 35, 36, 37
Jilimi, 11, 244, 251, 252, 253, 259, 261, 262, 265, 266
Jivaro, 115
Jokakwaro, 202
Joluo, 189, 190. *See also* Luo
Juet, John, 57
Jukurpa, 243
Jural restructuring, 166, 171, 173, 187, 189, 196-209, 284, 309, 314, 315-317, 318, 320f

Index   329

Kaberry, Phyllis M., 254
Kaileuna, Trobriand Islands, 271
Kaititj, 242
Kakamega, Kenya, 198
Kalenjin, 199
Kenya, 7, 186-210
King Philip War, 51, 52
Kings, 6. See also Chiefs; *individual names*
Kinietz, W. Vernon, 49
Kinship systems, Aborigine, 245, 257, 264; Algonkian, 46, 48; Aztec, 16, 135, 137; Bari, 120-121, 129-130; bilateral, 299, 300, 303, 319f; conical clan, 298; Inca, 152-158, 165-167; Luo, 191; pyramidal ramage, 298; Tlingit, 94, 106f; Tonga, 296-300, 303-304, 315, 317-318, 319f; Trobriand, 272, 282, 286, 298. See also Descent; Lineage
Kirda, 243, 252, 256
Kiriwina, Trobriand Islands, 271-289
Kisumu, Kenya, 189, 190, 191, 198, 205
Kitava, Trobriand Islands, 271
Klawock, Alaska, 101
Klein, Laura F., 15, 20
Knox, Henry, 64
Kokwaro, 202
Koloa, 298, 301, 303
Kolosh. See Tlingit
Kostlivstov, State Councillor, 91
Krause, Aurel, 98
Kula, 276, 277, 283
Kurdungurla, 243, 252, 256

La Perouse, Jean Francois de Galaup, 96
Labor: corvee, 154, 165, 300; domestic, 168; encomienda system, 112, 140, 141, 167; exploitation of, 187, 189, 198, 216-217; exploitation of female, 127, 141-142, 167, 168, 170, 176; forced, 19, 110, 112, 167-168, 197, 198; Inca tribute system, 151-153, 155, 158, 165-166; mita service, 154, 165, 168; Spanish tribute system, 151, 165-166, 168; Tonga tribute system, 300, 302; unrest, 295. See also Labor, division of; Labor force; Labor laws; Labor, sexual division of; Work, women's
Labor, division of: by age, 300; by rank, 12, 300, 301, 302; in stratified society, 15. See also Labor; Labor force; Labor laws; Labor, sexual division of; Work, women's
Labor force: Colonial demand for, 141, 150, 308; "coolies," 187; men in, 128, 129, 228, 315; Native Americans in, 12, 21, 40, 65, 76, 141; women in, 20, 21, 101-104, 230, 232, 259. See also Labor; Labor, division of; Labor laws; Labor,
sexual division of; Work, women's
Labor laws, 141-142, 316. See also Labor; Labor, division of; Labor, sexual division of; Work, women's
Labor, sexual division of, 9, 12-14; Aboriginal, 244; Algonkian, 54-59; Bari, 114, 118-119; Baule, 219, 222-223; Montagnais-Naskapi, 39; Seneca, 67-68, 70, 77, 78, 79; Tonga, 296, 299, 300-302, 308, 310, 314, 318; Trobriand, 272. See also Labor; Labor, division of; Labor laws; Work, women's
Labrador, Canada, 25-42
Lake Champlain, 26
Lake Maracaibo, 111, 112
Lake St. John, 40
Lake Victoria, 189, 192
Land and Freedom Army movement, 200
Land companies, 73, 79, 84f
Land tenure/use rights: Aborigine, 240, 241, 247, 248; alienation from, 15, 111; Aztec, 137, 140; Bari, 111, 112, 124; Baule, 219, 235f; collective, 19, 20, 21, 80, 113, 167; colonial demands for, 16, 45, 50, 63-64, 72, 79, 150; corporate, 188, 194, 195; dispossession from, 240, 241, 242, 247, 263, 264; expropriated, 19, 111, 162; fragmentation of, 193, 201; Inca, 150, 152-155, 161-163, 166, 180; individualized tenure, 15, 19, 21, 73, 79, 155, 161, 162, 188, 189, 201, 209; Luo, 187-190, 192-210; Native American claims, 105, 106f; ranking society, 12; reforms, 196, 199-208; Tonga, 297, 300, 302, 315-318; Trobriand, 273, 284-287; usufructory rights, 15, 20, 152, 154, 167, 188, 195, 203, 208, 228, 300; women's rights to, 11, 21, 50, 52, 68, 137, 140, 162-163, 166-167, 170, 188, 204-208. See also Inheritance patterns
Law. See Aborigines, law; British colonial law; Jural restructuring; Spanish colonial law
Le Jeune, Paul, 26, 27, 29, 30, 32, 33, 36-38
Leacock, Eleanor Burke, 17-19
Leadership, Aborigine, 244; Algonkian, 47, 48-53; Aztec, 135, 139, 141; Bari, 114-118; by women, 11, 49-53, 170; colonial appointment, 29, 47, 124-126, 169, 197; Inca, 153, 154, 169, 170; military, 14. See also Authority; Chiefs; Sachems; Squa-Sachem; Sunksquaw
League of the Iroquois, 66, 67, 75
Leakey, L.S.B., 201
Legal status of women, 16, 18; Aztec, 137, Inca, 162-164, 167; Spanish Empire, 137
Levi-Strauss, C., 3, 4, 283, 299

Lineage: Luo, 15, 191, 193-196, 197, 204, 207, 208-209; matrilineage, 286; maximal, 194, 197; patrilineage, 191, 194, 195, 197, 204, 319f; segmentary, 193, 194; Tlingit, 94; Tonga, 299, 300, 301, 303, 317-318, 319f. See also Descent
London Missionary Society, 295, 311
Long Island, (New York), 46
Long, Jeremy, 246
Los Cantos, 119, 130
Love, doctors, 53, 54; rituals, 259, 260; romantic, 19, 246, 263, 265
Lumbering, 74, 75, 81, 98
Luo, 6, 7, 15, 19, 186-210; agriculture, 6, 187, 190, 198, 207, 208; land tenure, 187-190, 192-210; marriage patterns, 193-195, 207; resource distribution, 187, 197, 209; social structure, 190, 191, 193, 194, 200; socioeconomic organization, 187-188, 191, 193, 196, 198-200, 207; sociopolitical organization, 197; status of women, 189, 191, 203-210
Luoland, 190-210
Lutheran Reform, 110

Macehuales, 136
Magnus, 50
Mahican, 52
Maine, 50
Male absenteeism, 198, 203, See also Male mobility
Male bias, 176; anthropological, 1, 2, 4, 11, 12, 243, 247, 253, 262, 266, 286; sociobiology, 10
Male chauvinism, 249
Male courtship, 36
Male dominance, Aborigine, 11, 253; Aztec, 137, 143; Bari, 111, 124; universality of, 1, 2, 3, 10; Western society, 243, 265
Male head of household, 28, 128, 315. See also Family structure, nuclear
Male mobility, 67, 70, 71, 72, 75, 81, 83f
Malekula, 278
Malinache, 139-140
Malinalxoch, 137
Malinowski, Bronislaw, 4, 14, 272, 275, 276, 282, 285, 286
Malthusianism, 3
Mamanuchqua, 52
Mamaprocht, 52
Mamaareoktwe, 52
Mamaroch, 52
Mamasaras, 157
Mande-Duula, 217
Manicheanism, 173, 175
Manifest destiny, 92

Maracaibo, Venezuala, 110
Market economy, 19, 70, 71, 127, 130-131, 160-169, 198, 199, 215-216, 228, 229, 231, 309, 311, 318
Marriage patterns: Aborigine, 19, 240, 249-266, 267f; Aborigine with European, 245-246, 261; Algonkian, 52-54; Aztec, 139, 140, 141, 143, 145; Bari, 123, Baule, 219-221, 229, 231, 233f; European model, 18, 252; endogamy, 69, 70; exogamy, 48, 191, 193, 245; fidelity, 2, 28, 36; Inca, 152, 153; Luo, 193-195, 207; restructuring of, 30-35; Montagnais-Naskapi, 18, 30-35, 36, 39; Seneca, 69, 70, 81; Tlingit, 95, 100, 101; Tonga, 299, 300-305, 312, 314; Trobriand, 273, 278-279, 284, 286. See also Residence Patterns
Maryland, 50
"Masculine as Civilization," 23f, 180
Massachusett, 46, 50; Squaw-sachem of, 50, 56
Massachusetts Bay, 44, 46, 47, 50
"Massachusetts Queen," 50
Massim, the, 270, 271, 272
"Mat money," 277
Matantuck, 50
Mataoka, 49
Matapules, 300, 301, 304
Matriarchy, 285
Matriclan, 46
Matrilineage, See Lineage
Matrilineal, 285-286; Aborigine, 243; Algonkian, 46, 47, 48; Arawak, 139; Baule, 219, 233f; Inca, 167, 170, Seneca, 66, 69, 73; Tlingit, 95, 99, 100, 105; Trobriand, 272, 273, 285, 286, 287; undermining of, 14. See also Descent
Matrilocality: Algonkian, 46; Bari, 129-130; Inca, 167; Montagnais-Naskapi, 46; Seneca, 66, 69, 83f
Matrimoieties, 245
Mau Mau rebellion, 189, 200, 201
Maya, 139
McFarland, Amanda, 98, 100
Media, 105, 263
Medicine: beson, 54, 57, 144, 301; women in, 53, 54, 95, 126-127, 136, 137, 144, 301. See also Midwifery; Shaman
Mediterranean, 6
Meggitt, M.J., 243, 245, 246, 248, 266, 267f
Meillassoux, Claude, 3, 234f
Melanesia, 270, 277, 278
Melpa, 279
Men's wealth, 275, 277, 281, 288
Menstrual lodges, 94
Menzeros, 143
Mestizo, 135, 136, 139-140, 143, 145
Methodist church, the, 18, 295. See also Missionaries, Methodist

Index   331

Methodist Missionary Society, 295
Methodist Wesleyan Church, 275
Mexanno, 50
Mexico, 7; precolonial, 18; revolution, 140; Spanish conquest, 135. See *also* Aztec
Mexico City, 7, 136
Michelet, Jules, 173
Midwifery, 301
Millet, Kate, 265
Mining, 98, 241
Missionaries, 50, 241, 295; Anglican, 98; Baptist, 242; Bari Westernization plan, 125-131; British government and, 295, 296; Capuchin, 112, 115, 116; French Catholic, 296, 312; Franciscan, 144; in Alaska, 90, 95-101; in Australia, 239, 241, 242; Jesuit, 10, 11, 18, 25-42, 170; Lutheran, 242, 263; Methodist, 311, 312-318; Presbyterians, 98-100; Protestant, 295, Quakers, 64-83; Russian Orthodox, 91; women as, 99, 100. See *also* Missions; Religion
Missions, 18; Anglican, 98; in Australia, 239, 242, 247, 250, 263; in Trobriand Islands, 275; Methodist, 275; Quaker, 72; Russian Orthodox, 91. See *also* Missionaries; Religion
Mita, 154, 165, 177
Mitakata, 275, 280
Mohawk, 52, 66
Mohegan, 46, 50
Moieties, 95, 106f, 245
Mombasa, 186
Monogamy, 36; Aborigine, 248, 264; Aztec, 135, 138; serial, 81, 247, 250, 266. See *also* Marriage patterns
Montagnais-Naskapi: marriage patterns, 30-35, 36; religion, 39, 40, 41; resource distribution, 40; social structure, 40, 44; socioeconomic organization, 27, 29, 30, 38, 39, 40; sociopolitical organization, 27, 28, 40; status of women, 26, 27, 38, 39, 40, 41
Montauk, 46
Moors, 150
Morner, Magnus, 139
Mortuary distribution, 274, 279, 281, 287, 288, 290f
Mother right, 285, 286
Motherhood, authority of, 53, 69, 81, 153, 256; status of, 298, 299, 300; working, 104
Motilon Development Plan, 125, 126-131
Mulatto, 140, 143
Mundurucu, 115
Munn, Nancy, 243, 246, 248
Murra, John, 154

Nagovisi, 286

Nanepashemet, 50
Nanticoke, 46
Napoleonic Wars, 216, 295
Narragansett, 46, 49, 50, 51, 53
Nash, Jill, 286
Nash, June, 16, 18, 20
National Times, 254
Native Americans; as laborers, 16, 65, 76; enslaved, 111, 112; land claims, 105, 106f; Pan-Indianism, 140; vs. the United States, 63, 64, 101-103. See *also* tribes by name
Native Authority Ordinances, the, 197
Native Land Tenure Rules, 201
Native Registration Ordinance, 197
Native Reserve Ordinance, 197
Nature as feminine, 23f, 174
New Caledonia, 270
New England: colonization, 50; early exploration, 44; precolonial, 6, 11, 54
New France, 26-41
New Guinea, 6, 270, 284
New Guinea Highlands, 279
New Hebrides, 270, 277
New Ireland, 270
New Jersey, 46
New Netherland, 44, 50, 52, 55
New South Wales, 295
New York: colonial, 52, 57; precolonial, 6, 11, 46; Seneca, 65, 74
New Zealand, 295, 296
Newfoundland, 44
Ngatu. See Bark cloth
Ngaue, 301-303, 309
Niantic, 46, 51
Nile Valley, 190
Ninigret, 51
Nipmuck, 51
"Noble savage," 308
Nobility: Inca, 161-165, 170
North America: early exploration, 43, 44; precolonial, 5
North Pacific Trading and Packing Company, 101
Norton, John, 75
Notos, 143
Nuclear family. See Family structure
Nununiga, 279
Nyakach, Kenya, 202
Nyanza Egg Service, 199
Nyatobay, 116, 117

Oceania, 6, 43, 294. See *also* Tonga; Trobriand Islands
Ohio, 64, 66
Oil: Alaska 105; Columbian-Venezualen, 113, 131
Ojibara, 120, 121, 129
Okeyo, Pala, 15, 19
Okoth-Ogendo, H.W.O., 199, 201

Ominde, S.H., 200
Onondaga, 66, 67
Oneida, 66
Ooldea, 263
Opium War, 296
Ortner, Sherry, B., 4

Pachamama, 154-155
Pacific coast, 8
Pan-Indianism, 140
Papua (British New Guinea), 271
Parallel cousins, 29, 41f, 253
Parallel descent. See Descent, parallel
Pasteral societies: African, 6, 7, 8; communal grazing rights, 200; Luo, 15, 187, 189, 190, 199, 208
Patriarchy, 16, 18, 19; Aztec, 135-136, 145; Tonga, 297, 313
Patrilineage. See Lineage
Patrilineal, 14, 285; Aborigine, 243, 244; Aztec, 137; Inca, 156, 167; Luo, 15; Tonga, 298, 315, 317. See also Descent
Patrilocality, 41, 167
Patrilodge, 244, 251
Patrimoieties, 245
Patrimony, 150
Peasantry and "commoners:" Inca, 151, 152, 154, 158, 165-169
Penn, William, 64
Pennsylvania, 46; Seneca, 64, 65, 72
Pequot, 46, 50
Peru, 7; early exploration, 150-151
Peterson, Nicolas, Stephen Wild, Patrick McConvell, and Rod Hagan, 246, 248, 254
Petroleum. See Oil
Philadelphia, 64
Phillip Creek Baptist mission, 242, 250
Pigs, 272, 277, 280, 283, 290f
Pinton, Solange, 116, 121, 122, 123, 129, 131f
Pipiltzim, 136, 138
Pit jant jarra, 263
Pittsburgh, 75
Plymouth, Mass., 44, 50, 51
Pnieses, 59
Pocahontas, 49
Polo de Ondegardo, Juan, 176
Polygamy: Algonkian, 48; Montagnais-Naskapi, 30; Tlingit, 95; Trobriand, 273, 275
Polygyny: Aborigine, 244, 248, 253, 258, 261, 263, 265, 266; Aztec, 135, 138; Baule, 222; Luo, 194; Montagnais-Naskapi, 30; Tonga, 299
Polynesia, 298, 299
Poma, Guaman, 170, 179
Population: Aboriginal Mexican, 142, 143; and land shortages, 189; and migrations, 191; controls of, 13; demographic pressures, 191, 208, 209, 258; sedentarization, 189
Port Augusta, Australia, 240
Portuguese colonialism, 16, 43, 214
Potencias, 126
"Potlatch," 94, 96, 99
Powell, Harry A., 276
Powhatan, 46, 50
Powwow, 53. See also Shamans
Pregnancy, 221. See also Birth
Presbyterian missions, 98
Priesthood, women in, 53-54, 95, 136, 137, 301. See also Missionaries
Primogeniture, 48, 298, 315
Principe, Hernandez, 156
Production relations, 8; Algonkian, 48; alienation from, 230-233, 309, 310, 311; Aztec, 135; Baule, 218-233; cooperative, 57, 58; in capitalism, 15, 16, 19; in colonial society, 17, 18, 218; in egalitarian society, 9, 10, 59; in ranking society, 12-16; in stratified societies, 15, 16, 159-160; Inca, 151; Montagnais-Naskapi, 27, 40; Seneca, 68; the Massim, 271; Tonga, 296, 298, 300, 303, 309, 310, 311; women's control of, 3, 57, 58, 68, 300
Property: private, 15, 19, 21, 73, 79, 155, 161, 162, 188, 189, 201, 209; rights of women, 21, 68, 137, 140, 162, 163, 188, 189, 203, 204-208, 221, 228. See also Land
Prostitution, 11, 21; Aborigine, 250, 253; Aztec, 136; Baule, 231-232; Inca, 169; Tonga, 305-307. See also Concubines
Protestant. See Missionaries; Missions
Puberty, 94, 99
"Public vs. private spheres," 4, 7, 9, 14
Puna, 22, 176, 177-180, 181f
Punishment: corporal, 33-41; Tlingit, 95
Pyramidal ramage, 298

Quaiapan, 51
Quaker, 18, 22, 50; and the Seneca, 63-83; Roger Williams, 49, 53, 55, 56
Quebec, 25, 26, 28, 37, 38
"Queene of Appamatuck," 49
Queensland, 271
Quinnapin, 51
Quiquijana, 172

Racism, 5, 38, 40, 140, 142-143, 187; Australia, 250, 253; "separate development", 187
Railroad, 76, 81; Australia, 240, 245, 263; East Africa, 186-187, 198; Ivory coast, 218
Ramirez, Codex, 137

Randle, Martha, 70
Ranking Societies, 8, 12-16; Inca, 153, 158; Tlingit, 6, 93, 99; Tonga, 6, 296-300, 303, 304, 306, 307, 310, 319f; Trobriand Islanders, 6, 272, 277, 278, 280, 290f
Rape, 38, 115, 255, 306
de Rasieres, Isaack, 55
Ration depots, 247
Read Poter and Engineer Jack Japaljarri, 240
Reay, Marie, 253
Reciprocity, Aborigine, 243; Algonkian, 48; Bari, 118, 119; Baule, 223; egalitarian societies, 6, 9; Inca, 151, 152, 158-160, 170; Montagnais-Naskapi, 36, 38; Seneca, 12. See also complimentarity
Red Jacket, 68
Reformation, The, 44
Religion: Aborigine, 242, 243-244, 248, 251, 253, 256, 264, 265; authority of women, 41, 53, 54, 57-59, 80, 95, 98-101, 136, 137, 156, 157, 162, 171-173, 176-180, 262; Aztec, 136, 137, 141; Bari, 112, 119-120, 125, 130; Female cults, 155-157, 172, 176-180; Inca, 156-160, 170-180; Montagnais-Naskapi, 39, 40, 41; Seneca, 73, 80; Tlingit, 95, 98-101; Tonga, 301, 303, 307, 312, 319f. See also Missionaries; Missions; *religions by name*; Ritual-ceremonial activities
Repartimientio, 141
Reproduction, 188; biological, 135, 138, 139-141; of the labor force, 135, 138, 141-143; of the social production, 135, 138, 144-145, 296; women's status and, 3, 4, 303. See also Women, as reproducers
Reservation, 78; East Africa, 187, 188, 199, 200; Seneca, 69, 72, 74
Residence patterns. See Matrilocality
Resistance: to the church, 22, 33, 176-180, 200; Mau Mau, 189, 200-201; women's, 17, 21, 22, 33, 79, 164, 173, 176, 232, 236f. See also Colonialism, resistance to; Revolution
Resource distribution: Aborigine, 241; Algonkian, 46, 48; Bari, 110, 111, 112, 117, 124; Inca, 151-153, 170; Luo, 187, 197, 209; Montagnais-Naskapi, 40; Seneca, 68, 79; Tonga, 297, 315, 318; Trobriand, 273, 276 284, 287; United States, 105
Revolution: Amaru (Andean), 176; American, 63, 65, 72, 295; in third world, 22; Mau Mau, 189, 200, 201; Mexican, 140. See also Colonialism resistance
Rhode Island, 46, 51

Richards, Cara, 68
Ritual-ceremonial activities: birth, 138, love, 259, 260; male initiation, 11, 243-244, 247-248, 255-257; women's, 155-157, 172, 176-180, 243-244, 248; women's participation in, 11, 80, 130, 253, 256, 257, 263, 264. See also Death; Religion
Roman Empire, 214
Romantic love, 19, 246, 263, 265
Rowe, John, 168
Rowlandson, Mary, 51
Rupert's House, 26
Russia: and Alaska, 88, 89, 92, 98. See also Fur trade, Russian; Trading companies, Russian
Russian-American Company, 91
Russian Orthodox Church, 91

Sachems: Algonkian, 47-53, 56, 58, 59; Seneca, 66, 68, 80; women as, 49, 50-53, See also Squa-Sachem
Sacks, Karen, 4
Sadodi, 120-121, 129. See also Kinship systems
Sagali, 274, 282
Sagamores, 47
Sahlins, Marshall, 285
St. Lawrence River, 44
St. Lawrence Valley, 25, 29, 41f
Sakonnet, 51
Sakwa, 196
Santa Cruz, 270
Santo Domingo, 109
Saraguro, Ecuador, 172
Sardinia, 89
Saunksquuaog. See Sunksquaw
Secret societies, 277
Sedentarization, 197
Seligman, C.G., 272
Seme, 196
Seneca: Agriculture, 68, 69-71, 73-78, 82; female work groups, 69, 70, 78; land tenure, 68, 73, 79, 80, 82; marriage patterns, 69, 70, 81; religion, 73, 80; resource distribution, 68, 79; social structure, 66-69; socioeconomic organization, 67, 68, 70, 73, 81, 82; sociopolitical organization, 65, 66, 68, 81; status of women, 68, 69, 70, 78, 80
Serrano, 151
Seven Years War, 294
Sex roles, Tlingit, 90, 97, 100, 101, 105
Sexes, relations between: Aborigine, 245, 265; Baule, 219; in egalitarian societies, 6, 7, 9, 20, 119, 123; Inca, 159; Luo, 191, 208; Montagnais-Naskapi, 36, 38; post colonial, 17, 19, 20, 22, 36, 115, 125, 130-131, 169, 245. See also Reciprocity

334 Index

Sexual asymmetry: universality of, 1-3
Sexual division of labor. See Labor, sexual division of
Sexual freedom, 11, 21; Aborigine, 246, 260; Bari, 123; Montagnais-Naskapi, 30, 33; Tonga, 305, 306-308, 312, 313, 314
Sexual hierarchy, 8, 296
Sexual parallelism: Inca, 152, 155, 156, 157, 159
Sexual politics, 265
Sexual stereotypes, 4; of men, 10; of women, 1, 2, 22
Sexual symmetry. See Egalitarian relations
"Shaking-tent rite", 39
Shamans, 41, 95
Shatterick, 100
Shimony, Annemarie, 78
Siaya, Kenya, 189, 191
Sibling. See Sister
Silver, 150
Silverblatt, Irene, 16, 18, 20, 21
Simmons, William, 53
Siskind, Janet, 220
Sisters: alliances, 253, 262; fahu rights, 15, 18, 299, 300, 303, 304, 316, 317; in kinship ranking, 297, 299, 300, 302, 307, 308, 314, 315, 318; sister-brother dyad, 14, 275, 282, 283, 286-288
Sitka, 91, 96, 101
Six Nations Reserve, 78
Skinner, Dorothy, 74
Slavery, 44; African, 6, 215, 216-217; Aztec, 136; missionary opposition to, 295; Negro, 142; of Native Americans, 52, stratified societies, 15; Tlingit, 95; United States, 17; Venezuela, 109. See also Captives
Smallpox. See Disease
Smith, John, 49, 54-55
"Snake Woman," 137
Social structure: Aborigine, 244-245; Algonkian, 46; Aztec, 137, 145; Bari, 111, 113-118, 120-121, 128, 129; Baule, 219, 220-221; Inca, 153; Luo, 190, 191, 193, 194, 200; Montagnais-Naskapi, 29, 40, 41; Seneca, 66, 67, 68, 69; Tlingit, 94; Tonga, 296, 297, 302; Trobriand, 272-273, 275, 286, 289
Sociobiology, 3, 10, 285
Socioeconomic organization: Aborigine, 242, 244, 250; Algonkian, 46; Aztec, 137, Bari, 111, 124, 127-129, 130, 131; Baule, 217, 218, 220, 224, 226-228; Inca, 151, 152, 154, 165-170; Luo, 187, 188, 191, 193, 196, 198-200, 207; Montagnais-Naskapi, 29-30; Seneca, 12, 67, 68, 70, 73, 81, 82; Tlingit, 93, 96, 97, 101, 102-104; Tonga, 296, 297, 303,
309, 310, 311; Trobriand, 272, 275, 277, 279, 280, 281, 284
Sociopolitical organization: Aborigine, 244-245, 247-250, 266; Algonkian, 46-48; Aztec, 135, 137; Bari, 118, 124, 125; Baule, 232; Inca, 151, 153-154, 157-159, 169, 170, 173; Luo, 197; Montagnais-Naskapi, 27, 28, 40; Seneca, 12, 65, 66, 68, 81; Tlingit, 95-104; Tonga, 296-297, 299-300, 302, 311, 312, 319f; Trobriand, 272, 274-276, 289
Solomon Islands, 270
Sorcery. See Witchcraft
South America: precolonial, 6; early exploration, 44. See also countries by name
South Bougainville Island, 286
South Nyanza, Kenya, 189-191, 193, 196-198, 205
Spanish Civil War, 113
Spanish colonial law, 166, 171, 173; tribute system, 141, 151, 164-166, 168
Spanish colonialism, 43, 44; and the church, 18, 144, 145-158; and the oppression of women, 7, 17; Aztec, 21, 134-145; Inca, 160-180; resistance to, 96, 97, 160, 164; women's status and, 134, 135, 162, 163
Specialization, 310; Baule, 224; by gender, 301; by rank, 301, 304; trade and, 13; warfare, 137, 138
spheres of exchange, 302-304, 308, 309
Spuri, 143
Squa-Sachem, 50-53, 56
Squaunit, 53
State bias, 4
State societies, 217
Stereotypes of women. See sexual stereotypes
Stratified society, 15, 16; Algonkian, 16; Aztec, 136-145; Bari, 114-118; Baule, 217; Inca, 151, 158, 165; precolonial, 18; Tonga, 296
Subincision, 263, 264
Subordination of women. See Women, subordination of
Sudan, 6, 189, 190, 193
Suez Canal, 186
Sumeria, 16
Sunksquaws, 46-53
Swynnerton Plan, 189, 201
Symbolic systems, 3, 4. See also Religion; Ritual-ceremonial activities

Taboo: incest, 3, 259; Jilimi, 244; death, 258, 259, 260
Tadoussac, 25
Tapa cloth, 18, 218, 301, 308, 309, 310, 311, 313
Tanami, 240

Tanni, 220, 221, 229
Tantaquidgeon, Gladys, 53
Tanzania, 190
Taufaauhau, 312
Taussig, Michael, 173, 175
Tea industry, 198
Tee exchanges, 278, 290f
Telegraph depots, 240, 245, 247
Tennant Creek (Australia), 242, 253
Tenochtitlan, 7, 137
Tepanec, 138
Theft, 95
Three Rivers (Canada), 26
Tiassale, 218, 221
Tlacutlo, 137
Tlingit, 6, 8, 15, 20, 88-108; land tenure, 105; marriage patterns, 95, 100, 101; religion, 95, 98-101; resource distribution, 105; social structure, 94; socioeconomic organization, 93, 96, 97, 101-104; sociopolitical organization, 95, 104; status of women, 94, 96-97, 99-102, 105; trade, 93, 94, 96-101
Tobasco, 139
Takamona, 51
Toledean laws, 170
Toltec, 137
Tonawanda Seneca, 65
Tonga, 20, 294-320; agriculture, 301, 315; land tenure, 297, 300, 302, 315-318; marriage, 299-305, 312, 314; religion, 301, 303, 307, 312, 319f; resource distribution, 297, 315, 318; social structure, 6, 15, 296, 297, 302; socioeconomic organization, 296, 297, 303, 309-311; sociopolitical organization, 296-297, 299-300, 302, 311, 312, 319f; status of women, 296, 297, 299, 301, 304, 305, 307-310, 317-318; trade, 302, 308
Tongatapu, 307, 311
Totem poles, 94
Touluwa, 275
Trade, 6, 13, 15; Algonkian, 48, 54-59; Baule, 217, 234f; Luo, 198, 199; routes, 186, 214, 294; Seneca, 67-68, 70-71; Tlingit, 93, 94, 96-101; Tonga, 302, 308; women in, 11, 14, 21, 54-59, 81, 93, 97, 199, 231, 281, 302
Trade goods, African, 6, 215; Algonkian, 45, 56, 57; Baule, 218, 221; European, 13, 67; Seneca, 67, 70, 71; Tlingit, 96; Tonga, 308; Trobriand, 278-281. See also Gold; Silver; Slavery
Traders, European, 26, 44, 52, 89, 91
Trading companies: Dutch, 294; English, 16, 26; French, 16, 25, 26; German, 271; in Africa, 214, 218; Quaker, 72; Russian, 91

Treaty of Paris, 89
Tribute systems: Inca, 151-153, 155, 158, 165-166; Spanish, 151, 165-166, 168; Tonga, 300, 302
Trobriand Cricket, 276
Trobriand Islands, 271-290; tourism, 276, 283; World War II, 276
Trobriand society, 6; agriculture, 272, 276, 282, 284; land tenure, 273, 284-287; marriage, 273, 278-279, 284, 286; resource distribution, 273, 276, 284, 287; social structure, 272, 273, 275, 286, 289; socioeconomic organization, 272, 275, 277, 279, 280, 281, 284; sociopolitical organization, 272, 274-276, 289; women's status, 14, 20, 274, 275, 277, 278, 281, 288; women's wealth, 274-277, 279-285, 288, 289
Tsimahians, 98
Tuck, James A., 67
Tui Tonga, Tui Tonga Fefine, 302, 308, 312
Tula, 137
Turkey, 89
Turner, Lucien, 39
Tuscarora, 66

Unemployment, 242, 250
Ungava, 40
United Aboriginal Mission, 263
United States: Alaska, 88-90; Civil War, 89, 92; colonialism, 216; Everett Commission, 74; in the Pacific, 295, 296; Indian policy, 63, 64, 72, 74, 75, 90; slavery in, 17
Upper Guinea Coast, 214
Urban centers, 6, 7, 8, 15
Uyoma, 196

Vakuta, Trobriand Islands, 271, 284
Varaoq, 156, 172, 173, 180
Venezuela, 6, 109, 111
Village Headman Ordinance, 197
Viracocha, 160
Virilocality, 15
Virginia, 44, 49, 50, 53
Vitus, Bering, 91
Virgins, Andean, 173, 178, 179; Aborigine, 250; Tonga, 306, 312

Wage labor. *See* Labor
Wahunsunacock, 49
Walkill Valley, 52
Wallace, Anthony F.C., 67, 74, 77, 80
Wampanoag Confederation, 46, 50, 51, 53
Wankili, 256
Warburton, P.E., 240
Warfare: Algonkian, 12, 47, 48, 50, 51, 52;

Bari, 112; Baule, 218; female military authority, 49, 50-53, 69, 80, 302; Seneca, 67, 69, 80; Specialization, 137, 138; Tonga, 300, 301, 311; Trobriand, 276, 283. See also wars by name
Warlpiri, 10, 17, 21, 242-266
Warrabi, 242-247, 254
Warramunga, 242, 248
War of 1812, 295
Wars. See by name
Washington D.C., 90
Weetamoo, 51
Weiskel, Timothy, 218
Welfare, 242, 263, 264; ration depots, 247
Welser Banking house, 110
Wesleyan Methodist Missionaries, 311, 312, 318
West Indies, 52, 109
Whaling industry, 98, 271, 295, 308, 309
Widows, 250, 267f; care for, 58, 99; marriagability, 254, 258, 259, 262; of chiefs, 50, 300; rights of, 140, 314-316
Wife-husband dyad, 14
Williams, Roger, 49, 53, 55, 56
Wilson, James, 305
Witchcraft, 53, 54, 81; Inca, 157, 174, 175-180, 181f; Tlingit, 95, 100
Witch hunts, 175
Wizards, 53. See also Witchcraft
Wrangell (Alaska), 98, 99
Women: anthropology of, 1, 17-22, 22f, 285; as commodities, 21, 138, 139, 248, 278, 299; as dependent, 19, 20, 127, 136, 264, 305, 318; as mediators, 81; as public officers, 16, 20, 102, 103, 104, 170; as reproducer, 3-5, 15, 16, 18, 135-137, 139-145, 188, 191, 288-289, 303; as sexual objects, 16, 18, 21, 169, 250; as weaker sex, 302; autonomous, 6, 10, 11, 15, 19, 20, 102, 111, 244; boxers, 307; chiefs, 11, 46-53, 56, 58, 59, 94, 137, 296-299, 301, 302, 306; concubines, 139; conservative, 22, 70, 78-80, 82; disenfranchised, 81; economic power of, 19, 54, 55-59, 68, 69, 81, 97, 102, 103, 188, 288, 309; economic roles of, 15, 20, 27, 54-59, 69, 78, 102, 103, 277, 288; in agriculture, 11, 12, 22, 54-56, 68, 74-78, 144, 192, 207, 208, 228, 230; exchange of, 3, 299, 303; exploitation of, 18, 21, 127, 142, 167-169; fahu rights of, 15, 18, 299, 300, 303, 304, 316, 317; in the media, 105; in Medicine, 11, 53-54, 126, 127, 136, 137, 144; legal status of, 16, 18, 134, 137, 140, 162-164, 167, 174, 175; menstrual lodges of, 4; merchants, 136, 137, 199; oppressed, 7, 16, 18, 173-174; passive, 3, 4, 10, 17, 21, 22; political power of, 80, 153, 170, 232, 301, 302; priests, 41, 53, 54, 95, 136, 137, 156, 157, 177-180; producers, 3, 5, 15, 16, 18, 21, 78, 81, 136, 144, 188, 191, 208, 219, 279, 288, 298, 303, 304, 309, 310; property rights of, 21, 68, 137, 140, 162, 163, 188, 189, 203, 204, 205-208, 221, 228; resistance, 17, 21, 22, 23, 33, 79, 164, 173, 176, 232, 236f; sexual abuse of, 38, 115, 138, 169, 255, 306; sedentary, 67-70, 81, 129; subordination of, 1, 2, 3, 17, 229; traders, 11, 14, 21, 54-59, 81, 93, 97, 199, 231, 281, 301; violence toward, 115, 253, 265, wealth of, 4, 20, 93, 102, 274-277, 279-285, 288, 289; work groups of, 69, 308, 310
Women's groups, 172, 177; as separate sphere. See Jilimi; Puna
Women's social status: Aborigine, 241, 242, 246, 247, 250, 251, 256, 265; Africa, 7; Algonkian, 48, 49, 54; Aztec, 134-136, 137, 143-145; Bari, 111, 124, 125-131; Baule, 219, 221, 222; Inca, 16, 153, 155-156, 171-173, Luo, 189, 191, 203-210; Montagnais-Naskapi, 26, 27, 41; Seneca, 68-70, 78-80; Spanish, 7; Tlingit, 94, 96-97, 99-102, 105; Tonga, 296, 297, 299, 301, 304, 305, 307, 308-310, 317, 318; Trobriand, 14, 20, 274, 275, 277, 278, 281, 288
Work, women's, 9, 16, 27; Algonkian, 54-59; Bari, 126-131; Baule, 221, 222, 230; cooperative, 56, 69; groups, 69, 70, 78; Inca, 168; Luo, 199, 208; Seneca, 69, 71, 78; Tlingit, 93, 102-103, Tonga, 298, 301, 303
World War I, 198, 271
World War II, 198, 199, 226, 271, 276

Xicalango Indians, 139

Yuendumu, 248
Yalata Aboriginal Reserve, 242, 263-264, 266
Yams, 220, 221, 228, 271, 272, 275, 276, 277, 279, 281-283, 287, 290f
Yanomamo, 115
Yaqalyu, 256

Zaire, 190
Zanzibar, 186
Zeisberger, David, 49, 54, 56, 57

About the Authors

DIANE BELL is a post graduate scholar in the Department of Prehistory and Anthropology, School of General Studies, Australian National University, Canberra, and a trained teacher. Her doctoral research and fieldwork beginning in 1976 have concerned Aboriginal women's rituals in Central Australia. Women's studies, hunter gatherer society and ethnohistory are fields of study on which she has published several articles. Other activities and commitments include land rights, women and the law, and the care of her two children.

SUSAN E. BROWN received a Ph.D. in Cultural Anthropology from the University of Michigan in 1972, conducting dissertation research on lower economic sector female survival strategies in the Dominican Republic. Her post-doctoral work includes advocacy research with Spanish speaking populations both in the U.S. and Colombia, as well as ongoing research and teaching on a feminist critique of traditional anthropology. On a trip to Columbia in 1975-76 she carried out research on self-help low-income housing as well as research on the Bari indigenous population. Currently she and Elisa Buenaventura are writing a text on anthropology for women's studies.

ELISA BUENAVENTURA-POSSO received an M.A. in Biophysics from Brandeis University in 1966 and remained in the Boston area to become a long-term participant in the Women's Movement. She was a founding member of the National Women's Studies Association and in 1977 served on the National Coordinating Committee of that association. On a trip to Colombia in 1975-76 she conducted ethnohistorical and ethnographic research on the Bari. Presently she and Susan Brown are compiling a feminist critique of anthropology for women's studies.

MONA ETIENNE, after studying literature and philosophy in the United States and France, received training in anthropology at the University of Paris. She has taught anthropology and sociology in France, Ivory Coast and the United States. In addition to research among the Baule, she has done fieldwork among other Ivory Coast peoples, as a UNESCO expert and as a development consultant. She has published articles in several French and American scholarly journals. She presently lives in New York and is a doctoral candidate at the Ecole des hautes études en sciences sociales, Paris. Her dissertation is on structural and historical factors in the urban migration of Baule women.

About the Authors

CHRISTINE WARD GAILEY is a doctoral candidate in critical anthropology at the New School for Social Research. She teaches anthropology in the Politics, Economics and Society Program at the State University of New York/College at Old Westbury, and is Assistant Editor of the journal *Dialectical Anthropology*. Her dissertation concerns Tongan state origins and changing gender relations during the colonial era. The integration of political and economic anthropology characterizes her other ethnohistorical and contemporary research involving kinship and gender structures during processes of class formation and capital penetration.

ROBERT STEVEN GRUMET. Born in the Bronx, New York on September 19, 1949, Robert graduated from the High School of Music and Art in 1967 and obtained his bachelor's degree from the City College of New York in 1972. He was awarded his doctorate in Anthropology by Rutgers University in 1979. Robert has been engaged in the study of North American Indian archeology, ethnohistory, and ethnography for over fifteen years and has conducted extensive research in the Northeastern Woodlands and the Northwest Coast culture areas. He has taught in the departments of Anthropology and History at Rutgers University and at the College of Staten Island. The author of a number of publications on North American Indian ethnohistory, he is currently preparing his doctoral dissertation for publication.

LAURA F. KLEIN is an assistant professor of anthropology at Gettysburg College. She earned her doctorate at New York University in 1975. She has done fieldwork on the "big" Navajo Reservation, with urban ecology groups in the Northeast and, most recently, a 22 month study with the Tlingit of Southeastern Alaska in a traditional town. Her research interests include local-level politics, social change, sex roles, and seasonality. Her 1975 dissertation is entitled *Tlingit Women and Town Politics* and it has been followed by a number of articles and papers based upon her Tlingit fieldwork.

ELEANOR LEACOCK, Professor of Anthropology at the City College, C.U.N.Y., has written introductions to *Ancient Society* by Lewis Henry Morgan, and *The Origin of the Family* by Frederick Engels, and has lectured and published widely on the cross-cultural status of women. Her research also includes educational anthropology, and North American Indians. She has written *Teaching and Learning in City Schools* and has edited *The Culture of Poverty: A Critique*, and *North American Indians in Historical Perspective* (with Nancy Lourie). She is presently editing (with Richard Lee) *Politics and Processes in Foraging Societies*. She has served on the executive bodies of the American Anthropological Association and the Society for Applied Anthropology, and has been invited to serve on the Commission on women of the International Congress of the Anthropological and Ethnological Sciences.

JUNE NASH is a Professor of Anthropology at City College of the City University of New York. She has done fieldwork with contemporary Maya and Bolivians. Her books include *In the Eyes of the Ancestors; Belief and Behavior in a Maya Community; We Eat the Mines and the Mines Eat Us: Dependency and Exploitation in Bolivian Mines*, as well as coauthored and coedited autobiographies and anthologies. She has recently produced and directed a film on the Bolivian miners in English and Spanish, *I Have Spent My Life in the Mines.*

ACHOLA PALA OKEYO is a Kenyan social anthropologist. She holds a Ph.D. from Harvard University. She is currently a Visiting Staff Associate at the Population Council, Center for Policy Studies in New York and on leave from the Institute for Development Studies, University of Nairobi, Kenya, where, as a Research Fellow, she has been conducting research on rural development in Kenya. Her specific research emphasis has been on socioeconomic processes that have contributed to the social transformation of African societies over time. She is also interested in the history of ideas and the conceptual biases in the study of social change. She has published a number of papers on the status and roles of African women in development.

DIANE BRODATZ ROTHENBERG (Ph.D. Anthropology, The Graduate School and University Center, City University of New York, 1976) has taught at Queens College (CUNY) and The University of Wisconsin-Milwaukee. Her fieldwork (1972-1974) was carried out on the Allegany Seneca Reservation. Her publications and addresses have considered Seneca history, inheritance patterns, missionary activities and theoretical evaluations of ethnohistorical problems. Her current research continues an exploration of Seneca material, as well as research in shamanism and contemporary performance, shamanism and western science, and nutritional anthropology.

IRENE SILVERBLATT is currently a doctoral candidate in Anthropology at the University of Michigan, and has conducted ethnohistorical and ethnographic research in Peru on the position of women in Andean society. She has published articles in Spanish and in English on the role of women under the Inca Empire, and has coauthored several papers on Andean cosmology and the relation between myth and history.

ANNETTE B. WEINER is an Assistant Professor of Anthropology at The University of Texas at Austin. Dr. Weiner has conducted ethnographic field research in Kiriwina, Trobriand Islands, Papua New Guinea during parts of 1971, 1972, and 1976. She is the author of *Women of Value, Men of Renown, New Perspectives in Trobriand Exchange.* Her research interests include kinship, exchange theory, women in society, and ethnographic film theory. She has been awarded a Guggenheim fellowship to pursue a comparative study of female/male relationships in Melanesia. She is also co-director of an ethnographic research project in central Texas, and is editing a book on ethnographic film theory and criticism.

www.ingramcontent.com/pod-product-compliance
Lightning Source LLC
Chambersburg PA
CBHW050836230426
43667CB00012B/2015